EYEWITNE

BACK ROADS
GREAT
BRITAIN

WITHDRAWN

CONTRIBUTORS

Pat Aithie, Robert Andrews, Donna Dailey,

Rebecca Ford, John Harrison, Nick Rider,

Rose Shepherd, Gillian Thomas, Roger Williams

DK

CONTENTS

PUBLISHER Douglas Amrine
LIST MANAGER Vivien Antwi
MANAGING ART EDITOR Jane Ewart
EDITORIAL Michelle Crane, Alastair Laing, Georgina Palffy, Hugh Thompson, Vicki Allen, Nichole Morford
ART EDITORS Shahid Mahmood, Kate Leonard
PRODUCTION CONTROLLER Linda Dare
PICTURE RESEARCH Ellen Root, Rhiannon Furbear
DTP Jason Little, Jamie McNeill
CARTOGRAPHY MANAGER Uma Bhattacharya
SENIOR CARTOGRAPHIC EDITOR Casper Morris
CARTOGRAPHY Stuart James, Schchida Nand Pradhan, Zafar-ul-Islam Khan, Hassan Mohammad
JACKET DESIGN Tessa Bindloss, Meredith Smith
ILLUSTRATIONS Arun Pottirayil, Pallavi Thakur, Dev Datta

Printed and bound in China

First published in the UK in 2010 by
Dorling Kindersley Publishing, Inc.,
345 Hudson Street, New York 10014

First American Edition 2010

15 16 17 18 10 9 8 7 6 5 4 3 2 1

Reprinted with revisions 2013, 2016

Copyright 2010, 2016 © Dorling Kindersley Limited, London

A Penguin Random House Company

A CIP catalogue record is available from the Library of Congress.

ISBN 978 1 4654 4025 9

Jacket Cottages at Lower Slaughter in the Cotswolds, Gloucestershire

Above Sandy Porthmeor Beach with St Nicholas chapel beyond it on the Island, St Ives, Cornwall

Above The Circus, an elegant 18th-century terrace designed by John Wood, Bath

Above Silbury Hill, Europe's largest man-made ancient monument, Avebury

Above King's College Chapel from The Backs, Cambridge

Below left Crescent Gardens in bloom, Harrogate, North Yorkshire **Below center** Road sign near Aysgarth, Wensleydale, in the rolling green Yorkshire Dales **Below right** Fishing port of Whitby with St Mary's Church on the hill behind, North Yorkshire Coast

Title page: Ardnamurchan Forest on the West Coast of Scotland **Half-title page:** Track across fields near St Abb's Head in the Scottish Borders

About this Book

Away from the fast-track motorways and uniform city centres, these drives along the back roads take you to some of the less-visited towns and villages of Britain. Taken at a gentle pace, they allow the driver time to appreciate what makes Great Britain unique – the landscapes, villages, grand country houses, castles and gardens. This book goes beyond the must-see tourist sights to lesser-known places that will reveal a more intimate experience of Britain's people and architecture. This island nation encompasses three countries – England, Wales and Scotland – each with a distinct history and different traditions. The landscape ranges from hillside pastures to mountain peaks, wild coastlines and open moorland. Glimpses of past cultures can be seen in the prehistoric standing stones and Roman ruins. And the castles and villages document the emergence, over many hundreds of years, of a single nation. Expect delightful surprises round every bend, and the reward will be the timeless culture of Great Britain.

Getting Started

The front section of this guide gives all the practical information necessary to plan and enjoy a driving holiday in Great Britain. It includes an overview of when and how to get there, advice on renting vehicles or bringing one into the country. The motoring advice ranges from driving rules to road conditions, to buying petrol and breakdown/accident procedures – the kind of background knowledge that will help make a driving trip stress free. Tips on money, opening hours and other practical matters will save time and confusion. There is also advice on accommodation and dining options from luxury hotels to farmhouse bed-and-breakfasts and gourmet meals to pub food to allow visitors to sample the range of British hospitality.

The Drives

The main section of the guide is divided into 25 drives, which range from two to five days in duration, leading from the tip of Cornwall to the north of Scotland. All tours can be driven in a standard car or other vehicle. No special driving skills are required.

The drives cover every region of the country. Each begins with an overview of the highlights and a clear map of the itinerary to help plan the trip. There is useful advice on the best time of year to make the drive, road conditions, local markets and festivals.

The tours contain descriptions of each sight, including opening times and contact details, where applicable, linked by clear driving instructions. Side panels offer information on authentic places to stay and eat. Tinted boxes provide background information and anecdotes.

Each drive features at least one mapped walking tour, designed to take a maximum of three hours at a gentle pace with stops along the way. Some walks cover the highlights of towns or cities, while others explore glorious countryside walks on safe, clearly marked paths.

The tours are flexible and can be linked to create a longer holiday; alternatively, they can be used to plan day trips within a region.

Using the Sheet Map

A pull-out road map of the entire country is attached at the back. This map contains all the information necessary to drive around the country and to navigate between the tours. All motorways, major roads, airports – both domestic and international – plus all the ferry ports are easily identified. This makes the pull-out map an excellent addition to the drive itinerary maps within the book. The pull-out map has a comprehensive index to help find the sights, and is further supplemented by a clear distance chart so drivers can gauge the distances between the major cities.

Above Driving through Langstrothdale Chase near Oughtershaw, North Yorkshire

Top left The Church of St Peter and St Paul, Northleach **Top right** Cove at St Abb's Head, Berwickshire, Scotland **Centre left** Fishing boats at Whitby **Centre right** Edinburgh – a famous festival venue **Below left** Traditional sweetshop, Rye **Below right** Field of sunflowers, Cornwall

Introducing Great Britain

The back roads of Great Britain are a refreshing antidote to the bustle of its world-famous cities. Though it is possible to zoom along motorways from London to Manchester, Cardiff, Glasgow or Edinburgh in a few hours, it's the smaller roads away from these urban centres that lead into the true heart of the country. Here, through castles and ruined abbeys, and mining, farming and fishing villages, the rich history of Britain's regions is waiting to be discovered. Take time to appreciate the landscapes, from the Scottish Highlands to the Yorkshire Dales and the watery Fens. Britain's rural hills and fields, lined with stone walls and hedgerows, are quietly beautiful. The rest is stunning, from the Kent coast to the Welsh mountains. Follow the back roads to find the farmers' markets, pubs, festivals, gardens and wildlife that form the heart of the country.

When to Go

The itinerary for each of the drives offers suggestions on the best times to visit. Some regions are known for their gardens or their seasonal produce, others for outdoor activities from surfing to climbing. Festivals and events can make for an unforgettable experience, so check with local tourist boards and consider these when planning your trip. The weather varies by region. July and August generally guarantee the hottest, sunniest weather but, for fewer crowds, April to June and September to October are a better bet. Summer's other advantage is the long hours of daylight, especially in Scotland where darkness doesn't fall until 10 or 11pm. Scenery is another factor – spring can be magical with bluebells, daffodils, colourful blossom and the brightest greens. Autumn brings red and gold to the trees and purple heather on the moors. Winter may be wetter and colder, but off-season rates are cheaper and most attractions are open year-round.

Times to Avoid

As mentioned already, July and August are the busiest times to visit – when British schools are on summer holiday and when the majority of foreign tourists arrive. Prices are also highest and traffic is heaviest, especially around popular coastal resorts. Throughout summer, biting insects known as midges are common in the western Highlands of Scotland. November–March has the rainiest, coldest weather and days are shorter,

especially the further north you go, with dusk falling as early as 4pm.

Climate

Thanks to the Gulf Stream, Britain's climate is moderate year-round and seldom drops below freezing. Snow is rare, except in mountainous areas. Average winter temperatures are 5–10°C (40–50°F), while summers average 18–25°C (65–77°F), although they can rise to over 90°F (32°C). In general, temperatures in the north are a few degrees lower than the south. Spring comes first to the southwest, with gardens in Devon and Cornwall budding out in February and March. The western coast is usually rainier and warmer than the east.

Festivals

Many festivals and events, in villages and market towns, centre around regional produce from apples to oysters to cheeses to wines. There are also craft fairs, music and the arts.

Some traditional celebrations date back centuries and involve clog dancing, inter-village football and other fun pastimes. Notable events include the Hay Festival of Literature (May), Cambridge Folk Festival (Jul), and Highland Games, held in Scottish towns Jun–Aug. Across the country, bonfires blaze and noisy fireworks flare into the sky on Guy Fawkes' Night (5 Nov).

Public Holidays

New Year's Day (1 Jan)
Good Friday (Fri before Easter)
Easter Monday
May Day Holiday (1st Mon in May)
Spring Bank Holiday (last Mon in May)
Summer Bank Holiday (last Mon in Aug)
Christmas Day (25 Dec)
Boxing Day (26 Dec)

Left A quiet back road through the ancient and pristine forests of Argyll, Scotland

Above The pretty market town of Ashbourne in the Derbyshire Dales

Getting to Great Britain

Great Britain is an international travel hub. As the gateway to Europe and beyond for North American travellers, Britain's major airports enjoy direct transatlantic flights as well as a direct service from most of the rest of the world. London is the western terminus of Eurostar, the high-speed rail line from Paris, Lille and Brussels, while other rail services connect with ferries across the English Channel and Irish Sea. Ferry services link Britain to Europe and Ireland, and the Channel Tunnel provides road access from Europe via Calais, France. There is also a low-cost coach service from Europe with Eurolines.

Above Colourful flower displays at Dovedale, in the Derbyshire Peak District

DIRECTORY

ARRIVING BY AIR

British Airways
0844 493 0 787 (UK);
www.britishairways.com

EasyJet
0330 365 5000 (calls cost 65p per minute; calls from mobiles and other networks may cost more); www.easyjet.com

Gatwick Airport
www.gatwickairport.com

Glasgow Airport
www.glasgowairport.com

Heathrow Airport
www.heathrowairport.com

London City Airport
www.londoncityairport.com

Luton Airport
www.london-luton.co.uk

Manchester Airport
www.manchesterairport.co.uk

Ryanair
0871 246 0000 (UK: calls cost 10p per minute); 0818 30 30 30 (Ireland: calls cost national rate); www.ryanair.com

Stansted Airport
www.stanstedairport.com

Virgin Atlantic
0344 209 7777; www.virgin-atlantic.com

Arriving by Air

Great Britain is served by most international airlines. Its own major carriers, **British Airways** and **Virgin Atlantic**, have direct flights from cities worldwide. In addition to the full service airlines, budget carriers such as **EasyJet** and **Ryanair** fly from Ireland and continental Europe to London, Glasgow and regional airports throughout the country, often with several flights a day in peak season. From the United States and Canada, there are direct flights to London, Glasgow and Manchester from major cities on international carriers, with internal connections to regional airports. From Australia and New Zealand there are connecting flights via Bangkok and Singapore.

London is served by five airports. Most long-haul international flights arrive at **Heathrow**, 24 km (15 miles) west of the city centre, or **Gatwick**, 43 km (27 miles) to the south. Heathrow is Britain's largest airport, serving around 90 airlines. It has five terminals. The newest, Terminal 5, is dedicated to British Airways. Most other long-haul and many European flights arrive at Terminals 3 and 4. Terminal 2 deals with mainly European flights, while all

domestic as well as some European and long-haul flights go through Terminal 1. London Underground trains and the Heathrow Express train connect the airport to the city centre.

Gatwick has two terminals. The North Terminal serves British Airways and charter flights, while the South Terminal is home to around 50 airlines. The Gatwick Express to Victoria Station is the fastest way into the city centre.

Luton Airport, 48 km (30 miles) north of London, and **Stansted Airport**, 56 km (35 miles) northeast, have many flights to/from Ireland, Europe and beyond, on full service and budget airlines. Both have good connections to central London. **London City Airport** in East London serves domestic and European destinations.

Glasgow International Airport, is 13 km (8 miles) from the city centre, and **Manchester International Airport**, 16 km (10 miles) south of its city, also handle international flights. Bristol, Cardiff, Birmingham, Liverpool, Newcastle and Edinburgh are among Britain's many regional airports.

Flight times to London are: Paris 1 hour, Dublin 1¼ hours, Montreal 7 hours, New York 6½ hours, Los Angeles 10 hours, Sydney 21½ hours.

Arriving by Sea

The easiest way to compare the many services, routes and prices for ferry services is online at *www. directferries.co.uk*.

From France: **P&O Ferries** has frequent crossings between Calais and Dover (travel time 1½ hours). **DFDS Seaways/LD Lines** also has daily sailings linking Calais and Dunkerque with Dover; it also operates a service between Dieppe and Newhaven. LD Lines also runs between Dover and Boulogne. **Condor Ferries** has fast ferry services (4½–5½ hours) from St Malo and Cherbourg to Weymouth, Poole and Portsmouth, and **Brittany Ferries** plies similar routes to Britain's south coast with overnight and fast crossings.

From the rest of Europe: P&O Ferries serves Great Britain from Belgium, Netherlands, Spain and Ireland, as does DFDS Seaways from Germany, Poland, Netherlands, Denmark, Norway and Sweden. **Stena Line** has daily crossings from the Hook of Holland to Harwich (6¼ hours). P&O North Sea Ferries sails overnight from Zeebrugge in Belgium (13½ hours), and also from Rotterdam, Netherlands (11 hours) to Hull.

Brittany Ferries has overnight crossings from Santander in Spain to Plymouth (18 hours) or Portsmouth (24 hours), while P&O has a Bilbao to Portsmouth route (29 hours).

From Ireland: Stena Line crosses between Belfast and Liverpool (8 hours). There are also services from Belfast to Cairnryan in southwest Scotland (2¼ hours), and from Larne to Cairnryan (1 hour) or Troon (2 hours) in southwest Scotland with P&O Irish Sea. Dublin to Liverpool routes (7 hours) are operated by P&O Irish Sea and DFDS Seaways. **Irish Ferries**

runs 2-hour crossings from Dublin to Holyhead in North Wales, as does Stena Line from Dublin and Dun Laoghaire. Irish Ferries crosses from Rosslare to Pembroke in South Wales (4 hours), while Stena Line has daily 2-hour crossings from Rosslare to Fishguard.

Arriving by Rail

Eurostar is the fastest and easiest way into Great Britain from Europe by rail. This high-speed train travels through the 52-km (31-mile) Channel Tunnel. Passengers board at Brussels, Paris, Lille or Calais and travel -to Ashford in Kent, Ebbsfleet International or London's St Pancras Station. The journey from Paris to London can be as little as 2¼ hours. Direct trains also run from Marseille, Avignon and Lyon to London. From London, there are train connections to all parts of the country through the British Rail network.

If travelling by rail from Ireland, there are combined train and ferry tickets direct to most destinations in Britain. For information contact **Irish Rail**.

Arriving by Road

Cars can also be taken through the Channel Tunnel on the **Eurotunnel** rail shuttle, which runs between Sangatte near Calais and Folkestone in Kent. Travel time is 35 minutes. Passengers remain with their car. LPG-powered vehicles are not permitted. The terminals link to the A16 motorway in France and the M20 in England.

Eurolines provides long-distance coach (bus) service to Britain from cities across Ireland and Europe. Journey times can be long, but the fares are relatively inexpensive.

Below left Departure lounge at Gatwick airport
Below centre Ferry terminal, Dover Harbour
Below right Boeing 747, Heathrow Airport

DIRECTORY

ARRIVING BY SEA

Brittany Ferries
0871 244 0744 (UK); 08 25 82 88 28 (France); www.brittany-ferries.com

Condor Ferries
0845 609 1024 (UK); 08 25 13 51 35 (France); www.condorferries.co.uk

Direct Ferries
www.directferries.co.uk

DFDS Seaways
0871 574 7235; +44 (0)20 8127 8303 (from outside the UK); www.dfdsseaways.co.uk

Irish Ferries
0818 300 400; www.irishferries.com

LD Lines
0844 576 8836; www.ldlines.co.uk

P&O Ferries
0800 130 0030 (UK); 08 25 12 01 56 (France); www.poferries.com

Stena Line
08447 70 70 70; www.stenaline.co.uk

ARRIVING BY RAIL

Eurostar (railway)
03432 186 186 (UK); +44 (0)1233 617 575 (from outside the UK); www.eurostar.com

Irish Rail (Iarnród Éireann)
1850 366 222 (Ireland); 353 (0)1 836 6222 (from outside Ireland); www.irishrail.ie

ARRIVING BY ROAD

Eurolines
08717 818 178 (UK); www.eurolines.com

Eurotunnel
08443 35 35 35 (UK); 0810 63 03 04 (France); www.eurotunnel.com

Practical Information

Travelling in Great Britain is easy, thanks to its generally up-to-date infrastructure. Public services usually operate smoothly and its health care system is among the best in the world. Police and security services may appear low-key, but they are highly trained to deal effectively with any emergency. Communication networks from broadband and Wi-Fi to mobile phone services are usually good, and most banks have ATM machines for out-of-hours use. In smaller towns and villages, shops are often closed on Sundays.

Above Easily identifiable green pharmacy sign displayed outside a chemist's shop

Passports and Visas

Nationals of European Union countries and Switzerland, Iceland, Norway and Liechtenstein may enter Great Britain with a passport or national identity card. Irish citizens do not need a passport or visa if they are entering from Ireland.

However, it is generally advisable to always have a valid form of photo identification handy, as most airlines and ferry companies will require either a passport or driving licence. If you don't have a passport, check with the carrier to see if an alternative form of ID is acceptable. All other visitors must have a passport, ideally with at least six months validity remaining to avoid problems at entry.

Travellers from the United States, Canada, Australia, New Zealand and South Africa do not need a visa if they are staying for less than six months. For longer stays, or for student or working visas, apply well in advance of departure.

Other nationalities may require a visa, and visitors should contact the British Embassy, Consulate or High Commission in their home country prior to travelling. Check on the website of the Foreign and Commonwealth Office for details.

Travel Insurance

All travellers are strongly advised to take out comprehensive travel insurance. In addition to medical insurance *(see below)*, a full policy will normally cover travellers for loss or theft of luggage and belongings, personal accident, damage to a third party, delayed or cancelled flights, and in some cases the cancellation of your trip due to personal illness or that of a family member. Most policies also cover some legal costs. A standard travel policy will not cover hazardous sports, so anyone planning to go surfing, skiing or rock-climbing must check their cover; it can usually be added for a small premium.

Read the terms to see what the excess is, and what cover is on valuable items such as cameras and jewellery.

Check to see what cover, if any, is offered under a home insurance policy. Some credit card companies offer limited travel insurance if the card is used to book the trip or rental car. But these are often not as good as specialist travel policies.

Health

Currently no vaccinations or immunization documents are required to enter Great Britain unless travelling from a country where infectious diseases such as yellow fever are present.

There are no undue health hazards in Great Britain. Tap water is safe to drink and bottled water is available everywhere. In summer, the Highlands of Scotland are plagued with tiny biting flies called midges, so buy some strong insect repellent if planning to hike or camp.

Standard over-the-counter remedies can be bought in local pharmacies or chemists, but make sure to bring enough prescription medication from home to last throughout the trip, otherwise it will take a visit to a doctor to obtain a prescription. Pack them in carry-on luggage with their original labels to avoid problems at airport security.

In the unlikely event of an illness while travelling, the hotel staff should be able to locate a doctor or dentist. In the event of a genuine medical emergency, dial 999. **NHS 111** provides round-the-clock medical advice by phone and has walk-in centres in many cities and larger towns. Most pharmacies – look for a green cross – are open Mon–Sat during regular business hours. If they are closed there is often a sign in the

LOOK RIGHT →

Above left European Union passports **Above centre** ATM or cashpoint machine **Above right** British community support officers, on patrol at a train station

window advising of the nearest all-night chemist. Pharmacists are highly trained, too, and can usually advise on minor medical matters.

Visitors from Ireland and other EU countries are covered for medical treatment in Great Britain under the EU's social security regulations, but they must see an NHS (National Health Service) doctor. To be eligible, they will need identification and a European Health Insurance Card (**EHIC**), which has replaced the old E111 form. Otherwise visitors will be liable for NHS charges. Obtain the card at home before travelling to the UK.

Visitors from all other countries are strongly advised to have private medical insurance, as they will only be eligible for free emergency treatment. Without insurance, they will have to pay for follow-up care, doctor's visits, medication, etc. Check home health insurance plans for cover when abroad. But travel insurance with medical coverage is a simple option and will give peace of mind.

Personal Security

Great Britain is a relatively safe country. Although most serious crime takes place in inner-city areas where visitors are unlikely to go, they should take the same precautions against petty crime as they would in any large town.

Areas where there is a high volume of tourists are frequently targeted by petty thieves. Leave passports, jewellery and valuables in the hotel safe, if possible. Keep an eye on handbags and wallets, particularly in crowds and on public transport, and don't carry large amounts of cash around. Never leave bags, cameras or luggage unattended, or visible in cars, even if locked. If it's not possible to take them with you, it's best to put items in the car boot before arriving at an attraction, as car parks are sometimes watched by thieves.

British police and community support officers are generally helpful. Street officers wear dark blue uniforms (and often the famous domed hat), but do not usually carry firearms. If you are a victim of crime, contact the police who can also provide victim support. To telephone the **Emergency Services** –police, fire, or ambulance – dial 999.

Below far left Pedestrian road crossing, known as a zebra crossing **Below left** Emergency ambulance **Below centre** Police officers helping two visitors with directions **Below right** Busy scene at Barnstaple's Pannier Market

DIRECTORY

PASSPORTS AND VISAS
American Embassy
24 Grosvenor Square, London W1;
020 7499 9000; www.usembassy.gov

Australian High Commission
Australia House, The Strand,
London WC2; 020 7379 4334;
www.uk.embassy.gov.au

British Foreign and
Commonwealth Office
020 7008 1500; www.fco.gov.uk

Canadian High Commission
Canada House, Trafalgar Square,
London, SW1; 020 7004 6000;
www.canadainternational.gc.ca

Irish Embassy
17 Grosvenor Place, London SW1;
020 7235 2171;
www.ireland.embassyhomepage.com

HEALTH SERVICES
NHS 111
111; www.nhs.uk

EHIC
www.nhs.uk/ehic

PERSONAL SECURITY
Emergency Services
For Police, Fire or Ambulance, dial 999

Telephone System

Telephone service is provided by British Telecom (BT). Phone numbers in Great Britain have an area code of four or five digits beginning with "0", followed by a local number. When dialling within the country, use the full area code. When dialling from abroad, drop the initial 0. When calling within the same area code on a landline, you only need to dial the local number.

To call Great Britain from abroad: first dial your country's international access code, followed by the country code for Britain (44), and the local area code (minus the initial 0), and number.

Public pay phones take either coins or phonecards. These are the cheapest way to make calls and you can buy cards at newsagents and post offices in various amounts. International phonecards can be an even cheaper way to call abroad. Making calls from your hotel room is generally expensive, as most hotels add a surcharge. Check the charges at reception before using the telephone.

Peak period is Mon–Fri 7am–7pm. Both local and international calls are cheaper after 7pm and at weekends. There is a charge for using Directory Enquiries, but you can look numbers up for free on the Internet. Calls to mobile phones are more expensive. Numbers beginning with 0845 are charged at a local rate and 0870 at national rate. 0800 and 0808 numbers are toll-free. Avoid numbers beginning with an 09 prefix – these cost up to £1.50 per minute.

Mobile phones are convenient but it's worth finding out what the roaming charges will be. Great Britain is part of the GSM system – US phones need to be tri-band or quad-band and have international roaming activated to operate here. Check with your supplier before leaving. If you plan to make a lot of calls, consider buying a cheap "pay-as-you-go" mobile in the UK.

Internet and Mail Services

You'll find Internet cafés in all the large towns and cities. Many hotels and guesthouses have Internet access and there are Wi-Fi hotspots at coffee shops and around the country.

The national postal system is **Royal Mail**. In addition to main post offices, there are sub-post offices in shops and newsagents throughout the country, where you can send packages as well as letters and cards. You can also buy stamps at many newsagents. First-class mail within the country takes 1–2 days. Allow 3–10 days for international air mail, depending on the final destination. Post boxes are painted red.

Symbol for a Tourist Information Point

Banks and Money

Sterling is the currency in Great Britain. One pound is divided into 100 pence. There are £5, £10, £20, £50 and £100 notes, and 1p, 2p, 5p, 10p, 20p, 50p, £1 and £2 coins. Scotland issues its own bank notes, which are usable in England. But some shops south of the border won't accept them, so it's best to ask for change in English notes if you're nearing the end of your stay.

Traveller's cheques are a safe way to carry money abroad, but they have been largely replaced by Cash Passports – a prepaid currency card.

Above Foreign newspapers for sale on a newspaper stand

These can be loaded with money before travelling and used in various shops and ATMs abroad. They are available from **Thomas Cook**, **Travelex** and various banks. Most airports have foreign exchange counters, but it is easier to use a debit or credit card to withdraw cash from one of the many ATMs or "cashpoints" around. Check with your bank or card provider what they will charge you for using your card abroad. Symbols on the ATM will tell you which cards it accepts. Cirrus and PLUS are widely used in Britain.

Major credit cards including Visa, Mastercard and American Express are accepted at most hotels, restaurants, shops and petrol stations, but you will need cash at pubs, small shops, guesthouses and B&Bs. Credit card companies are increasingly vigilant against fraud, so it is wise to let them know you will be using the card abroad, so that they don't put a block on its use. It is also a good idea to carry a different card for back-up.

Great Britain has largely converted to the chip-and-pin system, which requires the purchaser to enter the card's pin number rather than a signature. If your card does not have a chip and uses the magnetic strip and signature system, then it may not be accepted.

Above left Logo of the Scottish Tourist Board **Above centre** An ATM or cashpoint showing the different cards accepted **Above right** Old clock face, Cambridge

Tourist Information

Visit Britain is the national tourism authority and its website has a wealth of information including destination guides, maps, and an accommodation booking service. The websites **Visit England**, **Visit Scotland** and **Visit Wales** offer similar visitor information. There are also local tourist information centres (TIC) in most towns and tourist areas that serve drop-in visitors; hours vary and some are only open seasonally– look out for the tourist information symbol. You'll also find links and contact details on the main websites. For castles, stately homes and gardens, contact **English Heritage**, **The National Trust** and the **National Trust for Scotland**.

Opening Hours

Normal business hours are Mon–Fri 9 or 9.30am to 5.30 or 6pm. Shops open on Saturdays too and some have late-night shopping until 8 or 9pm on Thursdays. Supermarkets stay open later, and some are open 24 hours. Sunday trading hours, limited by law, are generally 11am or noon to 4 or 5pm; in smaller places shops do not open on Sundays.

Banks are open Mon–Fri 9.30am– 4.30pm. Larger branches have longer hours and may open on Saturdays. Post offices are open weekdays from 9am to 5.30pm and Saturdays from 9am to 12.30pm or later. Small sub-post offices may close for lunch or on Wednesday afternoons.

Disabled Facilities

Many visitor attractions are accessible to wheelchair users, and a growing number of hotels and restaurants also provide facilities for guests with disabilities. The **Holiday Care Service** helps disabled and older travellers and can offer advice and information.

Time and Electricty

Great Britain is on Greenwich Mean Time (GMT). The clocks are put forward one hour during Summer (Daylight Saving) Time, from mid-March to the end of October.

Britain's electric current is 220-240 volts AC (50 cycles). Plugs have 3 pins. Many visitors will need a transformer and a plug adaptor to operate appliances from abroad. You can buy them at airports and electrical shops.

Below far left Old-fashioned telephone boxes
Below left Shopping street reflected in a shop window selling tourist souvenirs **Below centre** A traditional wall-mounted postbox **Below right** One of York's narrow shopping streets

DIRECTORY

TELEPHONE SYSTEM

International Access Codes
Australia: 0011; New Zealand 0170; Ireland: 00; US and Canada: 011

Country Codes
Australia: 61; New Zealand 64; Ireland 353; US and Canada: 1

Directory Enquiries
118 500 (BT), www.bt.com; for business numbers, www.yell.com

International Directory Assistance
118 505 (BT)

INTERNET AND MAIL SERVICES

Royal Mail
www.royalmail.com

BANKS AND MONEY

Thomas Cook
www.thomascook.com

Travelex
www.travelex.co.uk

TOURIST INFORMATION

Visit Britain
www.visitbritain.com

Visit England
020 8846 9000;
www.visitengland.com

Visit Scotland
0845 859 1006;
www.visitscotland.com

Visit Wales
08708 300 306; www.visitwales.com

English Heritage
0370 333 1181;
www.english-heritage.org.uk

The National Trust
0844 800 1895;
www.nationaltrust.org.uk

The National Trust for Scotland
0131 458 0200; www.nts.org.uk

DISABLED FACILITIES

Holiday Care Service
0845 124 9971; www.holidaycare.org.uk

Driving in Great Britain

It's easy to travel the length and breadth of the country on Great Britain's major roads. Although many of these are scenic, running through beautiful countryside, the most memorable views are to be found off the beaten track. Driving along single-track roads in the Scottish Highlands, down the winding lanes of rural England and across the mountains of Wales, reveals many more facets of this diverse country. To make the most of your trip, it's best to learn the basics of driving in Great Britain before setting off.

Above Typical B-road sign, pointing to villages and indicating the distance

Insurance and Breakdown Cover

Third-party motor insurance is compulsory in Great Britain, with a minimum cover level of £1,000,000. If you bring your own car to Britain, you must have an insurance certificate that is valid in this country. You do not need a green card if you are an EU national, but you should check with your insurer before travelling to make sure you are covered on the trip. Most companies give you automatic coverage in EU countries for up to 90 days. Citizens of other countries will need green card insurance. If your policy has breakdown cover, check if it applies abroad. If not, it is worth purchasing additional breakdown and accident cover. Motoring organizations such as the AA and RAC *(see p18)* may also provide assistance.

What to Take

In order to drive in Great Britain, you must have a valid driving licence issued in your home country, or an International Driving Permit. Drivers whose documents are not in English should bring an official translation from their embassy or internationally recognised motoring association. If your licence does not have a photograph, do carry your passport or other form of official photo ID. If you are bringing your own vehicle, or caravan or motorcycle, bring the vehicle registration. If it is not registered in your name, bring a letter of authorization from the owner.

Great Britain does not yet require that you carry the visibility vests that are compulsory in many EU countries, though this may soon change. While it's not compulsory to carry a first aid kit, it is a good idea. A warning triangle, torch (flashlight) and petrol container are also recommended.

Road Systems

Main roads in Great Britain are classified in three categories. Motorways have the prefix "M". In theory they are the fastest way of driving long distances, but traffic jams are common around large cities such as London and Birmingham and you may experience long delays. Primary roads are indicated by the prefix "A" and may be either single- or dual-carriageway. "B" roads, or secondary roads, are usually single-carriageway (one lane in each direction). These, along with the smaller, unclassified roads in rural areas, may offer some of the most rewarding and enjoyable driving.

There is currently only one toll road in Britain, the M6 Bypass at Birmingham. Tolls are charged at several river crossings, including the Dartford Tunnel, Humber Bridge and the Severn Suspension Bridge. If you have to drive into central London, you will have to pay the **Congestion Charge** (currently £11.50 per day). Information on how to pay is posted on the Transport for London website. Similar schemes are being considered in other cities and on busy roadways to help reduce the volume of traffic.

Speed Limits and Fines

Speed limits are given in miles per hour throughout the country. Unless otherwise posted, the speed limits are 70 mph (112 kph) on motorways and dual carriageways, 60 mph (96 kph) on single carriageways, and 30 mph (48 kph) in towns and built-up areas.

Police cannot make on-the-spot fines for speeding violations in Great Britain. Speed cameras, however, are widely used; fines are automatic and tickets are sent to the address of the vehicle's registration. You won't escape the penalty by driving a rental car. The car hire company will bill you for the ticket, along with an administration

Above left Narrow Cornish street during the busy summer period **Above right** The only toll motorway in Great Britain, the M6 bypass at Birmingham

fee. Speed camera detectors are illegal and will be confiscated.

Do not drink and drive. The laws are very strict and penalties are high. The legal limit is 80mg per 100ml of blood (50mg per 100ml in Scotland) – about equal to a pint of strong beer. Police are authorized to administer a breathalyser test or a blood test at any time, and you can be prosecuted if you don't agree to take one or the other.

Rules of the Road

Driving is on the left in Great Britain. Most visitors get used to it quickly, but pay extra attention at crossroads and roundabouts, where it is easy (and dangerous) to forget or get confused. Always turn left into a roundabout, and give way (yield) to traffic already on the roundabout and approaching from the right. Drive clockwise, staying in the right hand lane until you are approaching your left-hand exit.

Overtake on the right. Do not overtake if there is a continuous white line in the centre of the road. At a junction where no road has priority, yield to traffic coming from your right.

Seat belts must be worn at all times, by the driver and all passengers, front seat and back. Using a hand-held mobile phone while driving is illegal and carries a fine and penalties.

Pedestrian crossings, often called zebra crossings, are marked by white striped lines across the road. Many have orange lights at either end to make them more visible at night. Drivers must yield to pedestrians if they step out into a zebra crossing and also at crossings when the "green man" is flashing, signalling it is safe to cross. Buy a copy of the *British Highway Code* from newsagents and petrol stations.

Please note that some signs in Wales may be in Welsh *(see right)*.

Buying Petrol

There are petrol stations all over Great Britain, and unleaded petrol as well as diesel is widely available – if hiring a car, find out which type of fuel it uses. Most petrol stations are self service and nearly all take major credit cards. Many stations on motorways are open 24 hours. In remote areas, opening hours are shorter and some may be closed on Sunday.

Petrol is sold by the litre and is expensive because it is highly taxed. Supermarket petrol stations, on the outskirts of larger towns, are among the cheapest places to fill up your tank, motorways the most expensive.

DIRECTORY

ROAD SYSTEM

London Congestion Charge
www.cclondon.com

SOME WELSH ROAD SIGNS

Araf *Slow*
Arafwch Nawr *Reduce Speed Now*
Bwsiau yn unig *Buses only*
Canol y dref *City centre*
Cerddwyr ymlaen *Pedestrians ahead*
Dim Mynediad *No Entry*
Dim o gwbl *At any time*
Gyrrwch yn ofalus *Please drive carefully*
Ildiwch *Give Way*
Un Ffordd *One Way*
Ramp o'ch blaen *Ramp ahead*
Rhybudd *Warning*

Below far left Multiple signage entering a popular Cotswolds town **Below left** Prices advertised outside a petrol station at night **Below centre** Self service at a petrol station **Below centre right** Road winding through the dramatic Cheddar Gorge **Below right** Single-lane road over a small bridge in the countryside

Above left A warning road sign **Above centre** A pay-and-display parking ticket machine **Above right** Parking along the roadside in a Cotswolds village

Road Conditions

Most roads in Great Britain are well surfaced and maintained. Distances are given in miles, and roads are usually well marked. Many parts of the country suffer from traffic congestion, not only in and around the major cities but also in parts of the country popular for holidays and weekend breaks. Traffic to the West Country (Dorset, Devon and Cornwall) in summer can be maddeningly slow. Many people make an early getaway on Bank Holiday weekends, resulting in busy roads from Thursday evening through to Monday night. Rainy weather can also slow things down. Get up-to-date reports on traffic conditions online or by phone from the **Met Office**, **Highways Agency** or **AA Roadwatch**.

In the Highlands of Scotland and in some other rural areas, the roads are single-track. Slow down for sheep, cattle and other animals who may run out in front of your car. These roads are often so narrow that one car will have to pull over to the side to let an oncoming car pass. Courtesy dictates that the car closest to a wide spot waits. There are designated passing places along these roads. When you meet oncoming vehicles, always pull in to the closest one on your left. You may need to reverse to find a space. It is easier for a car to reverse than farm machinery or large vehicles. Always give drivers who make way for you a friendly wave.

Taking a Break

If you are feeling tired or lost, it's a good idea to pull over and take a break. Many roads have signposted areas where you can pull off and stretch your legs, have a snack and consult your map. The scenery can be a distraction, so if you find it hard to keep your eyes on the road, it's best to stop and admire the view. Parks and areas with nature trails also make good picnic stops. Motorway service stations are generally well signposted along the route. They have coffee bars, sit-down restaurants, fast food, snacks, toilets, shops and other public facilities as well as petrol stations. On the A and B roads, services are smaller and public toilets are often found in petrol stations or restaurants.

Breakdown and Accident Procedures

If you have car trouble, try to park safely and turn on your hazard lights or put out a warning triangle to alert other drivers. There are SOS telephones at regular intervals along the hard shoulder (spare lane on the far left) of a motorway. It is dangerous to walk along any motorway, so take care when getting out of your car.

Car rental companies will normally give you a number to call in case of breakdown or problems with the vehicle. They will advise or arrange for assistance, and can usually provide a replacement vehicle. You should not undertake any repairs to a hire car without the company's permission. If you belong to a motoring association in your country, the UK motoring services – **Automobile Association** (AA) and **Royal Automobile Club** (RAC) – may have a reciprocal arrangement of co-operation – check before leaving.

If you have an accident you must stop and exchange name, address and car registration details with the other parties involved. Police must be notified within 24 hours if anyone is injured, and a report will be filed. Call the emergency services (see p13) if there are serious injuries. Be sure to get the insurance details of the other driver, and give them yours. You must also notify your car rental company as soon as possible.

Circumstances can be confusing at the time of an accident, so don't admit fault for the accident, accept liability or give money to any party. If possible, take down any details from

Above left Traditional signpost and brown tourist sign in the Avon Valley **Above right** Old stone cottages in West Witton, Yorkshire Dales

independent witnesses. It's also a good idea to take photographs of the vehicles and the accident scene.

Parking

Finding a place to park is one of the most frustrating aspects of driving in Great Britain. Parking is prohibited at all times on a double yellow line. A single yellow line means no parking during business hours – these will be displayed on a sign nearby. Signs with a red "P" in a circle crossed by a diagonal line also indicate a no-parking zone. A red line is a clearway and you cannot stop at all. Don't be tempted to flout the rules and park illegally, even for a few minutes. Traffic wardens are eager to write expensive tickets. Wheel-clamping and towing companies are even more predatory and expensive.

Park in designated car parks, which will be indicated by a blue sign with a white "P". These are often pay-and-display – obtain a ticket from a nearby machine and display it on your windscreen (windshield). Disc parking is another system used in many towns, whereby you must buy a scratch card from nearby shops and scratch off the date and time before displaying it in your car. In larger cities there are parking

garages such as NCP; these may be more expensive, but you don't have to worry about the time as you pay for your stay when you leave.

It is often possible to park on the street, but read the signs along the pavement carefully. Many streets have residents' parking only, with visitors restricted to particular hours and/or parking vouchers – if you are visiting someone who lives there, they may have a voucher for you. Others are pay-and-display, with the meter somewhere along the pavement.

In many rural towns and villages, there is little room for parking in the centre, but there are car parks, usually free, at the edge of town. In the countryside, be sure not to block farmers' gates or private roads if you are walking or exploring. On single-lane roads, never park in passing places as this is a traffic hazard.

Maps

Free tourist maps are widely available, but they are seldom useful for back-roads driving. It's well worth buying an up-to-date road atlas for more detailed coverage. There are several good ones published by Michelin, the AA, and A–Z. Buy them at petrol stations, bookshops, newsagents and tourist information centres.

DIRECTORY

ROAD CONDITIONS
Met Office
0370 900 0100; www.metoffice.gov.uk

Highways Agency
0300 123 5000;
www.highways.gov.uk/traffic

AA Roadwatch
84322 ("The AA") (from mobile phones);
0906 888 4322 (from landlines);
www.theaa.com/traffic-news

BREAKDOWN AND ACCIDENT PROCEDURE
Automobile Association (AA)
08457 887 766; www.theaa.com

Royal Automobile Club (RAC)
0800 197 7815; www.rac.co.uk

Below far left Farmer's sign reminding drivers to close the gate through grazing land near Oban, Scotland **Below left** Prices outside a petrol station **Below centre** Narrow country road between Cirencester and Chedworth in Gloucestershire **Below right** Horse riders on a quiet lane flanked by hedgerows near Lower Slaughter in the Cotswolds

Caravans and Motorhomes

Caravans and motorhomes (RVs) are subject to the same rules of the road as other vehicles. However, camper vans or cars towing caravans are restricted to speeds of 50 mph (80 kph) on regular roads and 60 mph (96 kph) on motorways. Many of Britain's back-country roads, particularly in remote parts of Scotland, are narrow and winding and not suitable for caravans, motorhomes or towed vehicles. Signs are often posted, but they are easy to miss. Ask locally about the conditions before setting out on these roads. Narrow bridges, sharp bends, and steep gradients can be dangerous for large vehicles, so pay attention to road warning signs.

Above An estate car driving into a camp site just outside Brecon in Powys, Wales, towing a caravan

If you are bringing your own caravan to Britain, you must be sure that your LPG gas has been turned off correctly for the ferry crossing. With Eurotunnel, the valves must be sealed and your roof vents opened for safety.

You can also hire motorhomes and touring caravans. Some, such as those available from **Just Go**, come with XBox 360, DVD/CD players and other creature comforts. **Motorhomes Direct** has a huge selection of luxury models for hire nationwide, while **Freedom Campers** caters for travellers on a budget. There is a wide network of camping and caravan parks. For online directories try **Camping and Caravanning UK** and **UK Caravan Parks and Campsites Directory**.

Motorbikes

All motorcyclists and passengers must wear protective helmets. Drivers must have a valid driving licence to cover a motorcycle or moped and an insurance policy. You may not carry a passenger if you hold a provisional licence; you must have a full licence and an insurance policy that allows you to do so. Motorcycles must have rear number plate lighting. Dipped headlights during the day are not required, but they are recommended to make you more visible.

The rules of the road are the same for motorcyclists as for other drivers, though you should take additional safety precautions. Go slow when filtering or driving between traffic lanes. Give other vehicles a wide berth when overtaking them, and be aware they might not always see you.

Driving with Children

Drivers must ensure that all children under the age of 14 wear seat-belts or sit in an approved child restraint, if required. Older teenagers must wear adult seat-belts. If a child is under 1.35 m (approximately 4 ft 5 in) tall, a baby seat, child seat, booster seat or booster cushion suitable for the child's height and weight must be used. The correct child restraint must be used in both the front and back seats. Babies must never be placed in a rear-facing child seat in the passenger seat if there is an active airbag fitted, as it can cause serious injury or death to the child in a crash. Children must not sit behind the rear seats in an estate car or other vehicle unless a special child seat has been fitted. Remember to request any necessary child seats in advance when making your car hire booking.

Disabled Drivers

Drivers with disabilities should contact **Disabled Motoring UK**, a charity that promotes mobility and represents the interests of disabled drivers, for advice on obtaining a UK blue badge for disabled parking spaces or using their Disabled Parking cards in the UK. If you are bringing your own car through Ireland first, you may be able to get a discount from the ferry company on some sailings. Contact your motoring association (or the **Disabled Drivers' Association** in Ireland) for a form.

Car Hire

Most of the big international car hire companies, such as **Budget**, **Avis** and **Hertz**, have locations at airports and ferry ports and in all the larger cities, and offer a wide range of vehicles. A good local firm with offices in Scotland and Northern England is **Arnold Clark Car and Van Rental**. To rent a car you will need a valid driving licence and a credit card. Normally, drivers must be between the ages of 21 or 23 and 75, but check before

Above left Sign for a guesthouse in Bude, Cornwall **Above right** Camp site in a field in Dorset, tucked away behind the trees

you make your reservation regarding their age restrictions. It's highly recommended that you book in advance, especially during peak season – you will often get a better rate. Rental rates usually include unlimited mileage, but double check. Most rental cars in Great Britain are standard (manual) shift. Automatic cars are available but they cost more and must be booked in advance. Consider renting a smaller car than you may be used to at home, as they are much easier to handle on narrow country roads than big SUVs. If you need a child seat, these should be booked in advance as well.

Third-party insurance is compulsory and is included in the rate. Some rental agreements also include Collision Damage Waiver (CDW) which limits your liability for damages to the rental car, theft loss cover and personal injury insurance; others charge additional fees for these items. Be sure to read your agreement carefully so that you fully understand what your coverage and liabilities are. Some drivers may be able to use insurance from a personal credit card to claim CDW, but check carefully with your card company to make sure they cover your trip abroad and be prepared to show proof of cover.

Driving in Bad Weather

When conditions reduce light levels, dipped headlights should be used. Turn on fog lights whenever visibility is less than 100 m (328 ft). If you bring a left-hand drive vehicle with you, adjust the headlights. Buy beam adjusters at ferry terminals, or check with your motoring organization.

Always reduce speed in adverse conditions, as you will need a greater braking distance, and poor visibility gives less time to react. In Scotland and other mountainous areas, you may encounter ice and snow in winter. Slow down, especially for curves and turns, and make your actions steady and deliberate to avoid sliding out of control. If you find the car skidding, take your foot off the accelerator – do not brake – and turn the wheel into the skid until the car corrects itself. Watch out for "black ice", especially on bridges and overpasses which freeze up first. If you hit a patch, do not brake or turn the wheel, but keep as straight as possible and coast over it.

Below far left Signs on the Kennet and Avon Canal **Below left** Pay-and-display ticket machine, Penwith, Cornwall **Below centre** Old-fashioned road sign at Lacock in the Cotswolds **Below right** Sheep by the roadside in Ashdown Forest, the home of Winnie the Pooh, Sussex

DIRECTORY

CARAVAN AND MOTORHOMES

Camping and Caravanning UK
http://camping.uk-directory.com

Freedom Campers
0121 778 3720;
www.freedom-campers.biz

Just Go
01525 878 000; www.justgo.uk.com

Motorhomes Direct
0800 612 8719;
www.motorhomefreedom.com

UK Caravan Parks and Campsites Directory
www.uk-sites.com

DISABLED DRIVERS

Disabled Drivers' Association
+353 (0) 94 936 4054; www.ddai.ie

Disabled Motoring UK
01508 489 449;
www.disabledmotoring.org

CAR HIRE

Arnold Clark Car and Van Rental
0141 237 4374; www.arnoldclarkrental.com

Avis
0808 284 0014; www.avis.co.uk

Budget
0808 284 4444; www.budget.co.uk

Hertz
08708 44 88 44; www.hertz.co.uk

Where to Stay

The picturesque views seen while driving the back roads of Great Britain will perhaps raise the question: what would it be like to live here? The accommodation in each of the driving tours has been selected to give a taste of life in this varied country, whether it be a cosy bed and breakfast in the Scottish Highlands, a boutique hotel on the Cornish coast or even an ancient castle. There is also a range of luxury golf and spa resorts, and camp sites with heavenly views from forests to mountains to seaside.

Above Doorway to cottage accommodation with plaque displaying its grading

Hotels and Inns

Great Britain is known for its traditional hotels, many of which have been operating for over a century. Historic inns offer some of the most characterful accommodation, often in village pubs, converted mills or old coaching inns, which served travellers as far back as the 17th century. Because of the age of the buildings, some rooms may be small compared to modern hotels. Many inns have excellent restaurants or pub menus.

Country-house hotels usually have beautiful grounds and bigger rooms. Food is often a highlight here, with more formal dining rooms, creative set menus and top chefs in the kitchen. Be aware that some may not cater for young children.

Boutique hotels are not just for cities anymore. Chic, high-concept hotels dot the smaller towns and resort areas, with everything from the reception area to the bathroom sinks (basins) featuring the best in modern design. These establishments usually have lively bars and restaurants, too.

National and international chain hotels offer accommodation in all price ranges, and these can be found in the larger towns and cities or along the motorways throughout Britain. Depending on their quality rating,

hotels will normally have at least one restaurant and a bar. Most include breakfast in the room rate, but some do not. Most hotel rooms have en suite bathroom facilities, and some also offer family rooms and suites.

Guesthouses

Guesthouses are smaller and usually less expensive than hotels. Many were formerly large family homes, with all or several rooms converted for guests, often with simple but charming decor. Those with higher ratings will have en-suite bathrooms. Breakfast is usually included in the rate, but most guesthouses do not have restaurants or bars, though they may have snacks and drinks available for guests. In the countryside, pubs and, increasingly, restaurants have guest rooms available and this can be an good way to enjoy the local nightlife without worrying about driving afterwards.

Bed-and-Breakfasts (B&Bs)

Bed-and-breakfast accommodation is offered in private homes around the country, from town centres to country farmhouses. They usually have several guest rooms – often en suite, but sometimes with shared bathrooms. Facilities and decor vary, but they are usually clean and comfortable. Some

hosts will offer an evening meal for an additional charge, but this must be arranged in advance. B&Bs are often cheaper than hotels and guesthouses, and are a great way to meet local people and pick up local tips.

Castles and Historic Homes

Stunning accommodation can be found in the castles and historic homes that have opened some of their rooms to overnight visitors. You will certainly pay for the privilege, but a night or two in one of these glorious landmark buildings can be the most memorable of your trip – book early.

Luxury Resorts

Golf resorts have long been popular, especially in Scotland, and now most luxury resorts feature spa facilities, too. These establishments have a range of activities on offer, as well as fine dining and casual restaurants – an attractive option when you want a relaxing break from the road.

Booking a Hotel

It's essential to book ahead for July and August, and during festivals, events and busy holiday periods, to ensure you get your choice of accommodation. Book by phone or (in most cases) online directly with

Above left Traditional inn, Chipping Campden, made out of the local stone **Above right** Smart interior of a Chipping Campden hotel

the establishment, using a credit card. Or take advantage of the service offered by tourist boards *(see p15)*. Some local tourist offices in Scotland will book accommodation ahead at your next night's destination for a deposit and small service charge. You can also find properties of character and luxury through organizations such as **Great Inns of Britain**, **Welsh Rarebits** and **Scotland's Hotels of Distinction**.

Be sure to check if the rate quoted is per person or per room – B&Bs and guesthouses are almost always per person, as are many hotels. Rates in Britain generally include VAT (tax), but double-check in the pricier city hotels.

Facilities and Prices

British hotel rooms usually have a double or twin beds; if you need a cot or child's bed, request it when booking. Coffee- and tea-making facilities are a welcome standard. Most places serve a full "English" breakfast with eggs, bacon, sausage and all the trimmings, although "Continental" breakfasts are usually also available.

All types of accommodation, from camping parks to luxury hotels, are rated from one to five stars in their respective categories. The rating system has finally been standardized across the various tourist boards and

other rating agencies, such as the AA. Properties are visited and assessed every year. Be aware that many establishments with lower star ratings still offer excellent quality, but simply have fewer facilities and services.

Generally, the higher the star rating, the more expensive the room, but prices also vary seasonally. Check for special offers, and remember that some of the lowest rates are offered online through the hotel website.

Camping

Camping and caravanning are popular activities in Great Britain, and there is a broad network of sites throughout the country. These are graded for their quality and facilities, similar to other types of accommodation. The **Camping and Caravanning Club** is a good source of information. Wild camping (outside of designated camp sites and caravan parks) is not legal in England and Wales. It is permitted in Scotland, but you should always obtain permission from the landowner before parking your caravan or pitching your tent.

Below far left Cosy room at the Abbotsbury Hotel, Dorset **Below left** Four-poster bed in the hotel at Amberley Castle, Sussex **Below centre** Ees Wyke Country House hotel in the Lakes **Below right** Camp site by Glencoe, Scotland

Where to Eat

Britain's love affair with food has bloomed in recent years, inspired by TV chefs and innovative restaurateurs, and there is an enticing array of top-notch eating places at all prices. At the top end, British chefs are racking up Michelin stars in village restaurants, and there are countless fun, fashionable eateries with international themes as well as impressive gastro-pubs that won't break the bank. Menus increasingly feature local, seasonal produce, and there are shops and markets where you can stock up on gourmet goodies. But never fear – traditional favourites such as cream teas and fish and chips are as popular as ever, too.

Above Sign listing the food and facilities of the Castle Coffee House, Dunster

Practical Information

A full cooked breakfast at your guesthouse or hotel can set you up for the day – and don't be afraid to try local specialities such as black pudding (blood sausage), kippers (split, smoked herring) or Welsh laverbread (minced seaweed). Lunch is usually served from noon until 2 or 3pm; in smaller towns, restaurants and cafes may stop serving at 2.30pm. Dinner is the main meal of the day in Great Britain. Restaurant opening times vary widely; however, most open at 6 or 7pm. In larger towns and tourist areas they may serve until 10 or 11pm, but in smaller towns and villages they often close at 9pm, with last orders half an hour earlier. Many pubs serve bar food from lunchtime until 9pm. High-end restaurants often close one or two days per week (usually Mondays and Sunday evenings), but many smaller establishments in busy areas stay open seven days. Off the beaten track, they may close out of season. It's wise to phone ahead.

Credit cards are widely accepted, but pubs, tea shops and take-away establishments may take cash only. Tax is always included in the bill, but the service charge varies. If it is added,

it will be listed separately on the bill; if it isn't, leave 10–15 per cent for the waiting staff. You can also leave an extra tip for excellent service.

Casual dress is acceptable in most restaurants, though you may want to dress smartly for more expensive establishments. Most places are wheelchair accessible, but check in advance for older buildings. Some upmarket restaurants may not welcome children under a certain age. Children are allowed in pubs with their parents until 9pm; look for those which are family friendly with gardens and play areas. Smoking is banned inside all restaurants and bars.

Menus are generally displayed outside near the door or window and fine-dining establishments usually offer a set-price (prix fixe) menu as well as à la carte. These can be great value, especially at lunchtime, and allow you to enjoy a top restaurant at an affordable price.

Restaurants

Restaurants in Great Britain run the gamut from cosy, casual eateries to impressive dining rooms with beautifully laid tables and crystal

chandeliers. Famous chefs run top restaurants specializing in seafood, game or local produce all around the country, and you'll need to book well ahead to get a table. Look for quality symbols such as the **Taste of Scotland** restaurants, which feature creative menus based on regional produce.

Nearly all restaurants feature at least one vegetarian option, usually more. Fine-dining establishments have full wine lists, and often feature a wide selection of whiskies and other spirits.

Ethnic restaurants and those specializing in European cuisine are popular around the country. Along with a multitude of Indian and Chinese restaurants, you'll find Italian, French, Greek, Turkish, Polish, Spanish, and many other offerings.

Pubs and Bars

Many pubs offer simple, inexpensive meals at lunchtime and usually in the evenings, too. Shepherd's pie, lasagne, fish and chips and ploughman's lunch (cheese, bread and pickles) are standard offerings. Sunday lunch is popular at many pubs, often with a carvery serving roast meats, Yorkshire pudding (batter) and vegetables.

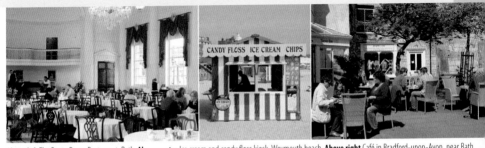

Above left The Pump Room Restaurant, Bath **Above centre** Ice cream and candy floss kiosk, Weymouth beach **Above right** Café in Bradford-upon-Avon, near Bath

In a class of their own are gastro-pubs (short for gastronomic pubs). These are traditional pubs that have upgraded their menus with a range of exciting dishes featuring innovative and often local cuisine. You can enjoy restaurant-quality meals in a relaxed atmosphere – often at lower prices.

Bars and wine bars sometimes have sandwiches or light meals on offer at various times of the day.

Cafés and Take-aways

The weather is not conducive to a café culture in Britain similar to that in other parts of Europe. But whenever it's warm and sunny, you'll find restaurant, pub and café tables spilling out onto every available pavement space.

Cafés are generally open for breakfast and lunch, but most close by 6pm. Most museums and visitor attractions have cafés where you can get light refreshments. The coffee craze has taken Britain by storm, and coffee-shop chains are ubiquitous in larger cities. Many sell sandwiches, muffins and pastries as well. Not to be missed are traditional tea shops, where you can have a pot of tea or coffee along with home-made cakes, breads and local specialities – often in delightful surroundings. Be sure to try a traditional cream tea with scones, clotted cream and jam, especially if

you're touring Devon and Cornwall. Fast-food chains are plentiful, but far more satisfying are the local versions. Look for small shops selling fish and chips, Cornish pasties, or even shish kebabs, which make quick, filling and usually inexpensive take-away meals.

Picnics

Nearly every high street in every town will have at least one sandwich shop, where you can grab ready-made picnic supplies. Supermarkets also sell sandwiches and snacks. More fun are the independent food shops and delis, which sell a great range of meats, cheeses and tasty local delicacies.

Best of all are the local markets, which are a showcase for regional producers. Look for picnic supplies of artisan breads, locally made cheeses, honey and preserves, or apple varieties that you can't buy in a supermarket. Each driving tour in this book notes the location and days of the week for markets around the region; tourist information centres can provide details of local farmers' markets.

Below far left Retro-style tea-shop window **Below left** Colourful fresh fruit and veg stall, selling good-value produce **Below centre** The pretty Rising Sun Hotel, Lynmouth **Below centre right** Café in the heart of Hay-on-Wye **Below right** Rick Stein's Seafood Restaurant, Padstow

DIRECTORY

PRICE BANDS IN THE BOOK

Restaurants
Three-course meal for one with half a bottle of wine and including VAT (tax)

Inexpensive – under £25

Moderate – £25–50

Expensive – over £50

RESTAURANTS

Taste of Scotland
www.taste-of-scotland.com

ROCHESTER

the Welles

Upchurch   Ivade   Chap. and Isle   Har

Isle

Woldham   Capston   Milton Chu.   Milton   Murston   Tong

Boxley   More Str: Bobbing   Newington

Wood   Lyding   Rainham   Hartlip   Tenham   Buckland

Chap.   Bredherst   Borden   Tuddingham

Boreham

Guilsted Str.   Siltingbourn   Bapchild

Hill Green   Stockbury   Rodmersham   Norton

Aylesford   Boxley   Stockly Valley   Bredgate   Tunstall

Sandling   Delling   Hucking   Bickvor   Linsted

Allington   Thornham   Wormoell   Hogshare   Kingsdown   Ospringe

Ditton   Hollingborne   Frinsted   Newnham

Maidstone   Barsled   Wichling   Eastling   Sheld

the Bower   Otham   Leeds   Bromfield   Otterden   Throwley

ingbury   E. Farley   Lenham   Stallsfield

Dane Str.   Langley   Kings Wood   Heslewood Str.   Charing

W. Farley   Loose   Ulcomb   Broughton   Pote

Linton   Chart juxta Sutton   Egerton   Challock

Hunston   Boughton   Sutton Valence   Westwell

the Twist   Munchelsea   Frigin Fostle   Eastwell

Muttenden   Lit: Chart   Wilmerton

Crossa hand   Hedcorne   Paveington

Beula R.   Pluckley   Hothfield

Marden   Smarden

Downe   Dowle Str.   Goddenton

Staplehurst   Rounden   Runsill   Great Chart

Hamden   Willesbor

Goudhurst   Frittenden   Surrenden   Shingleton

New Street   Mers

Camdens   Biddenden   W E A L D   King

Hill   Biddenden   High Halden   Shadoxherst   Bilsing

Cranbrook   Green   Bromley Green

linwell   Goford   O F K E N T   Orleston

High Street   Green   Woodchurch   Warhorn   Ror kin

Benenden   Rolvenden   Tenderden

Sand urst   Broad Tenterden   Kenarton

Newenden   Smallhythe   Horn Pla.   Snave

THE DRIVES

Lizard Point and the South Cornwall Coast

St Ives to Tavistock

Highlights

- **Artists' haven**
  Picturesque St Ives, home to national museums and brimming with galleries

- **Cape Cornwall and the Lizard**
  Wild, rugged and beautiful coastal scenery at England's extremities

- **Porthcurno**
  Perfect Cornish cove below the Minack Theatre, cut into the cliffside

- **Gardens galore**
  The South West has some of the UK's best gardens, thanks to its mild climate

- **Roseland Peninsula**
  Beautiful and unspoiled peninsula with the picturesque St Justus Church

Classic Cornish cove at Porthcurno, a gem of a beach in an area of outstanding natural beauty

Lizard Point and South Cornwall Coast

The coastline around the most southerly part of the British mainland is outstandingly beautiful – dramatically rugged with tiny coves punctuating the shore below granite and imposing cliffs. Seabirds such as fulmars, gannets, cormorants and shags wheel and cry overhead while basking sharks, seals and dolphins can often be seen in the water when the sea is calm. Ancient standing stones and redundant mine workings are evidence that the area has been well used by man for millennia, but never more so than today. Visitors pour in to enjoy holidays in and around the beaches and quaint old fishing villages, which previously thrived on huge catches of pilchards. The area's mild climate has also contributed to its rich legacy of exotic gardens, some planted in previous centuries by keen local horticulturalists.

ACTIVITIES

Enjoy Cornish clotted cream on scones with jam or in ice cream

Take on the Atlantic surfing in St Ives or kite-surfing at Marazion

Admire great art in St Ives and invest in an artwork from one of the small galleries there

Go underground at the Geevor tin mine in Pendeen

Enjoy a clifftop drama at the Minack Theatre, Porthcurno

Explore an exotic garden at Trebah, the Lost Gardens of Heligan or the Eden Project

Take a boat trip from Fowey for the scenery, wildlife and seabirds

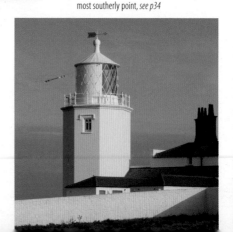

Below The Lizard Point Lighthouse at England's most southerly point, see p34

KEY

━━ Drive route

Above View across the beautiful estuary from Polruan to Fowey, a popular yachting destination, *see p36*

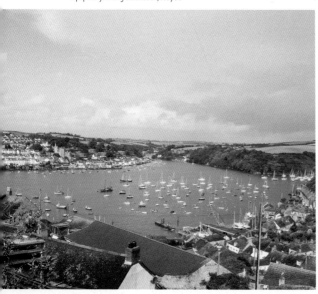

PLAN YOUR DRIVE

Start/finish: St Ives to Tavistock.

Number of days: 4–5, allowing half a day to visit the galleries in St Ives. Visits to a garden, especially Heligan or the Eden Project, will take up to half a day at least, as will a trip to Dartmoor.

Distance: 275 km (171 miles).

Road conditions: Although well-paved and signed, many of the country roads are narrow. Those leading down to old fishing harbours are often steep and tend to be congested in high season.

When to go: Cornwall is a popular tourist region so the whole area gets very crowded in July and August. In winter, when the weather is usually still comparatively mild, towns return to "normal" but villages can be very quiet. Because of the number of tourists, most places have well-signed car parks, usually pay-and-display. In peak time, look for park-and-ride schemes.

Opening times: Museums and attractions are generally open 10am– 5pm, but close earlier (or are closed altogether) Nov–Easter. Shops are often open longer. Churches are usually open until dusk.

Market days: St Ives: Thu; Tavistock: Pannier Market, Tue–Sat.

Shopping: Local crafts, paintings, Cornish pasties and clotted cream.

Major festivals: St Ives: September Festival; **Porthcurno:** Minack Theatre season, May–Sep; **Helston:** Furry Dance Festival, early May; **Widecombe:** Widecombe Fair, 2nd Tue in Sep; Fowey Words and Music Festival, May.

DAY TRIP OPTIONS

Enjoy the **sandy beaches** and **art galleries** of St Ives, then head down the coast to explore old **tin mines, cliff-tops** and the spectacular **Porthcurno theatre**. On the Lizard, swim in the **Atlantic surf** or visit a **seal sanctuary**. From St Austell or Fowey, see the **Lost Gardens of Heligan**, learn about **shipwrecks** at Charlestown or visit the amazing Eden Project with its **space-age biomes**. For full details, *see p37*.

Parking
The steep streets get very congested. Park at the top of the town and walk down to the harbour. Upper Trenwith Car Park provides a shuttle bus down.

Tourist Information
The Guildhall, Street an Pol, TR26 2DS; 0905 252 2250 (charges apply); www. stivestic.co.uk; closed Sat pm, Sun

WHERE TO STAY

ST IVES

Rivendell *inexpensive*
Award-winning family-run guesthouse near sea and town centre; offers sea views, packed lunches and car park.
7 Porthminster Terrace, TR26 2DQ; 01736 794 923; www.rivendell-stives.co.uk

Boskerris Hotel *moderate–expensive*
Smart but friendly hotel above Carbis Bay with 15 stylish rooms (most have sea views), decked terrace and a garden.
Boskerris Road, TR26 2NQ; 01736 795 295; www.boskerrishotel.co.uk

AROUND ZENNOR

Gurnard's Head *moderate*
Small and cosy inn in an imposing building near the sea, amidst a wild Cornish landscape. Excellent restaurant.
Treen, TR26 3DE (3 km/2 miles west of Zennor); 01736 796 928; www.gurnardshead.co.uk

ⓘ St Ives

Cornwall; TR26 2DS

Once Cornwall's busiest pilchard-fishing port, St Ives suffered as fish stocks declined at the start of the 20th century. Help had arrived with the advent of the railway in 1877, as the trains brought holidaymakers to the town. Artists, including Turner, were also drawn by the clear light there, and many of the harbourside net lofts were now converted to artists' studios. The fishing never recovered, but the visitors kept coming, attracted by the fine sandy beaches and many art galleries.

A two-hour walking tour

Walk downhill from the **Tourist Information Centre (TIC)** ①. Turn left along St Andrew's Street to Market Place, which is overlooked by the 15th-century **St Ia's** ②, built in the local textured granite, with a 24-m (80-ft) tower. It has carved sandstone pillars, choir stalls, a gilded roof and a Madonna sculpture by Barbara Hepworth.

Turn right to join **Wharf Road** ③ which leads around the harbour to a tiny 16th-century chapel on **Smeaton's Pier** ④ where, nowadays, just a few fishermen still land their catch.

A warren of cobbled streets climbs steeply up into Downalong, the oldest part of town, once home to the fishing community. Go along Sea View Place to **St Ives Museum** ⑤ *(open Easter–Oct, closed Sun)* in Wheal Dream which tells the town's history – one gallery has paintings from the 1880s when the celebrated St Ives School of Artists was formed. Continue down a narrow walkway to steps above the sea and around the car park above the tiny Porthgwidden Beach and its excellent café. With the sea on your right, continue onto the grassy headland of the Island, which has the tiny **St Nicholas Chapel** ⑥ at the top. Drop down again to the car park. Carry on along Porthmeor Road and right on Back Road West and right again onto the seafront for the **Tate St Ives Gallery** ⑦ *(Mar–Oct, open daily; Nov–Feb, closed Mon)*, a striking white building with a large convex window. It features artists who painted in Cornwall in the mid-20th century.

Walk back along the seafront, bearing right into The Digey and right again into Fore Street, the main street. Fork right uphill, following signs to the **Barbara Hepworth Museum and Sculpture Garden** ⑧ *(open daily)* on Barnoon Hill. The sculptor, a key figure in the development of abstract art in Europe, worked in the house for 26 years, and her sculptures are spread around house and garden.

Head downhill from the museum, turn right and go steeply uphill at the next junction signed Trewyn Gardens. Cross these to the far exit leading to a T-junction. Turn left towards the High Street. Return to the TIC via Tregenna Place, past the Library which, like many of the galleries in town, displays work by local artists or which has been created locally.

🚗 *Exit on the B3306 towards St Just and Land's End. Zennor is just off the road on the right after 8 km (5 miles).*

St Ives Museum sign

② Zennor

Cornwall; TR26 3DA

Did the mermaid depicted on a pew in the 12th-century church of **St Senara** really lure a chorister to his death by her singing? Or did the story serve to discourage outsiders from venturing down to the cove, a local smugglers' haunt? Whatever the truth of the tale, the factual side of Zennor's history since the Bronze Age is shown in the **Wayside Museum** (open daily, Apr–Oct) housed in a 16th-century miller's cottage. The great Methodist evangelist John Wesley preached in Zennor in the mid-18th century and another notable visitor was the writer D H Lawrence during World War I. He stayed with his German wife, Frieda, at the Tinners Arms pub, while writing Women in Love. The **Zennor Quoit** burial chamber, just southeast of the village on Amalveor Downs, is one of the area's many prehistoric remains.

🚗 Carry on along the B3306 to Pendeen. Geevor Tin Mine car park is on the right.

③ Pendeen

Cornwall; TR19 7EW

The ruined stacks and engine houses dotted along the coast, a UNESCO World Heritage site for Cornish mining, are reminders of the area's boom time in the 19th century. At Pendeen, **Geevor Tin Mine** (closed Sat) shows how tin was mined and processed. Carry on along the B3306, past granite outcrops, where remains of prehistoric habitation, such as standing stones and burial mounds, can often be seen among the bracken. Turn right at St Just to **Cape Cornwall**, a windswept headland topped by a slender chimney stack which evokes a true end-of-the-world feeling. In fact, **Land's End** lies

slightly further west but much of the majesty of the site has been lost due to the development of the area.

🚗 Take the B3306 to St Just and then take the A3071, then turn right onto B3306 (signed Land's End). Turn right onto A30. After Sennen, turn left onto B3315, then right to Porthcurno. Follow signs and park at the Minack Theatre.

④ Porthcurno

Cornwall; TR19 6JX

The unique feature of this small sandy cove is the **Minack Theatre**, hewn out of the cliffs above it. With the sea as a backdrop, the Greek-style theatre, created in the 1930s, has an incomparable setting. The visitor centre tells its story (open daily; performances May–Sep; www.minack. com). A small white pyramid on the cliff marks the spot where the first transatlantic telephone cable was laid in 1880. The history of telegraphy is told in the **Porthcurno Telegraph Museum** (Apr–Oct, daily; Nov–Mar, Sat–Mon).

🚗 Return to B3315; after 8 km (5 miles), turn right for Mousehole car park.

Above left Shop selling traditional beach toys, St Ives **Above centre** The Tate St Ives building overlooking Porthmeor Beach **Above** The stage and beautiful setting of the Minack Theatre, Porthcurno

EAT AND DRINK

ST IVES

Sloop Inn inexpensive
Overlooking the harbour and noted for its seafood, this is one of Cornwall's oldest inns. It dates back to 1312 with wood beams, slate floors and cobbles. The Wharf, TR26 1LP; 01736 796 584; www.sloop-inn.co.uk

Porthgwidden Café moderate
Small white stone building with terrace at Porthgwidden Beach. Noted for its steak, fresh fish and seafood. Porthgwidden Beach, TR26 1PL; 01736 796 791

AROUND PORTHCURNO

Logan Rock Inn inexpensive–moderate
Pub known for its real ales and home-cooked food – pasties, steaks and crab. Open fire in winter, beer garden and pre-Minack theatre dinners available. Treen, TR19 6LG (1.5 km/1 mile east of Porthcurno); 01736 810 495

Below Smeaton's Pier and the harbour at low tide, St Ives, Cornwall

Above The Castle, dominating St Michael's Mount, off Marazion **Top right** Picturesque harbour and granite houses at Mousehole **Right** Sign at Lizard Point, mainland England's most southerly point

Cornish Wreckers

As any Cornishman will tell you, "wreckers" were really bounty-seekers, not heartless criminals who deliberately lured ships onto the rocks by placing a decoy light on the shore. The Cornish coast, with its jagged rocks and fierce currents, scarcely needed any help to cause shipwrecks as hundreds of boats floundered on it over the years. On stormy nights, wreckers would be ready and waiting to plunder any cargo, though responsible ones would rescue the sailors first. Often wrecking led to battles with local "preventive men" – customs officers.

WHERE TO STAY

AROUND THE LIZARD PENINSULA

Mullion Cove Hotel
moderate–expensive
Originally built for wealthy Victorians, this gleaming white clifftop hotel enjoys extensive sea views.
Mullion Cove, TR12 7EP; 01326 240 328; www.mullion-cove.co.uk

AROUND TREBAH

Budock Vean *expensive*
Large hotel in vast parklands beside the Helford River. Award-winning restaurant, sports activities and natural health spa.
Helford Passage, Mawnan Smith, TR11 5LG (1 km/0.5 mile from Trebah); 01326 250 288; www.budockvean.co.uk

ST JUST-IN-ROSELAND

Round House Barns *moderate*
A Cornish cream tea greets guests at this award-winning B&B in a tastefully converted 17th-century barn.
St Just-in-Roseland, TR2 5JJ; 01872 580 038; www.roundhousebarnholidays.co.uk

ST MAWES

Tresanton *expensive*
Award-winning hotel stylishly created in a cluster of old houses. Rooms and restaurant have sea views.
27 Lower Castle Road, TR2 5DR; 01326 270 055; www.tresanton.com

⑤ Mousehole
Cornwall; TR19 6SD
This quintessential Cornish fishing village – pronounced "mouzel" – with a granite sea-walled harbour held over 400 pilchard fishing boats in the 19th century. A tangle of steep narrow lanes lead down past pretty cottages to waterside pubs, cafés and shops. **Mousehole Bird Sanctuary** on Raginnis Hill cares for injured sea birds *(open daily)*.

🚗 *Return to the B3315 to Newlyn and join A30 (towards Truro). Turn right to Marazion at the junction with A394. Follow signs to St Michael's Mount.*

⑥ St Michael's Mount
near Penzance, Cornwall; TR17 0EF
This islet, looming out of the sea near Marazion, is dramatically topped by a 12th-century **castle** *(open Sun–Fri Apr–Oct)* – in turn a church, priory, fortress and now private home. At low tide it can be reached on foot across a causeway first used by pilgrims in the Middle Ages; a small ferry runs from Marazion at other times. A cobbled path leads up to the castle past terraced gardens. Home of the St Aubyn family since 1660, it has a mix of architectural styles.

🚗 *Return to the A394 to Helston, then turn right onto the A3083 to the Lizard Peninsula. Turn right at signs for Kynance Cove after Mullion.*

⑦ The Lizard Peninsula
The tip of this windswept peninsula is England's most southerly point. Paths trace around the cliffs of this jagged coastline, dropping to secluded coves and harbours. Rare wildflowers grow on the heathland where ponies graze.

At much-photographed **Kynance Cove**, tilted pinnacles of rock stand like giants paddling in the sea off the sandy beach surrounded by cliffs.

At the end of the A3083, the **Lizard Point Lighthouse** is the most powerful in England, visible for 34 km (21 miles) in one of the world's busiest shipping lanes. In summer, basking sharks can often be seen just offshore.

Back up the A3083, to the right, tucked below the cliffs, lies **Cadgwith**. Here, pretty whitewashed thatched cottages surround a tiny harbour whose fishermen entered the record books in the 19th century by landing 1.3 million pilchards in one day. Now they mainly catch lobster and crab, which can be sampled with a glass of real ale at the Cadgwith Cove Inn.

Drive through Ruan Minor and Kuggar, turning left onto the B3293 to go past the **Goonhilly Earth Station**. On the open heathland stands a cluster of huge, futuristic satellite dishes – the largest is 46 m (151 ft) high. Formerly British Telecom's satellite centre, the site is now to be used for radio astronomy and deep space communications. A visitor centre focusing on space science is also being planned.

Carrying on the B3293, turn off right to Gweek. Children of all ages will love the **Gweek Seal Sanctuary** *(open daily)*. Above Helford estuary, the sanctuary cares for sick or injured seals. There are also otters, ponies, goats and a children's play area.

🚗 *From Gweek carry on towards Falmouth; at Constantine turn right at sign to Mawnan Smith where Trebah Gardens (and car park) are signed.*

Above Winged cherub statue in the leafy, green Lost Gardens of Heligan

⑧ Trebah Gardens
Mawnan Smith, Cornwall; TR11 5JZ
In the 1830s, prosperous shipping agent and enthusiastic horticulturalist Charles Fox collected a wealth of sub-tropical plants and trees from around the world to create **Trebah Gardens** *(open daily)*. This lush paradise, set in a wooded ravine which descends 61 m (200 ft) to a private beach on Helford River has tumbling waterfalls, a pool of giant koi carp and great banks of blue and white hydrangeas. Paths lead under the shaded canopy of giant gunnera leaves and through a bamboo maze and flower borders.

🚗 *Return to Mawnan Smith, follow signs to Penryn. Turn left onto A39. Next take B3289 right to the King Harry Ferry (toll) across the Fal and back on B3289 to St Just-in-Roseland.*

⑨ St Just-in-Roseland
Cornwall; TR2 5HY
Designated an Area of Outstanding Natural Beauty for its leafy lanes and seascapes, the Roseland peninsula includes **St Just-in-Roseland** whose 13th-century St Justus Church with its squat crenellated tower nestles beside a wooded tidal creek, framed by trees – a truly picture-postcard scene. The churchyard, entered either

through a 17th-century lych (roofed) gateway or via the beach, is notable for its subtropical plants and borders of granite stones inscribed with Biblical texts and hymns.

🚗 *Head south on A3078 to St Mawes. Fork right for castle; park in car park.*

⑩ St Mawes
Cornwall; TR2 5DE
Terraces of old cob cottages and smart modern houses command glorious seaviews from their position above the harbour. The views and two sandy beaches make St Mawes a popular spot for holidays and retirement, as well as for sailing and walking. The **castle**, the best preserved of Henry VIII's coastal fortresses, has gun ports on the three huge circular bastions overlooking the busy Carrick Roads waterway, a large natural harbour created during the Ice Age.

🚗 *Head north on A3078. After Ruan High Lanes, turn right (signed Portloe) and follow signs to Mevagissey through Tippetts Shop and Tubbs Mill. The gardens (with car park) are to the right.*

⑪ Lost Gardens of Heligan
Pentewan, Cornwall; PL26 6EN
The "lost" gardens of Heligan *(open daily)* were restored in the 1990s after 75 years of neglect. Their original designs, laid out between 1766 and World War I, included Italian and New Zealand gardens, summer houses, a rocky ravine, crystal grotto and wishing well. Just as remarkable is the story of Tim Smit, the force behind this restoration (and the Eden Project, *see p36*), who took it on after a successful career in pop music.

🚗 *Turn right out of the gardens then left onto B3273 towards St Austell. Turn right to Charlestown.*

Above Futuristic satellite dish at Goonhilly Earth Station on the Lizard Peninsula

Above The beautiful and luxuriant gardens at Trebah, near Mawnan Smith

EAT AND DRINK

MOUSEHOLE

2 Fore Street *moderate*
French-style bistro noted for its fresh fish, interesting puddings and home-made bread; courtyard in summer.
2 Fore Street, TR19 6QU; 01736 731 164; www.2forestreet.co.uk

THE LIZARD PENINSULA

Gweek Inn *inexpensive*
Friendly Cornish pub offering a large selection of real ales. Menu includes traditional English puddings served with custard, ice cream or clotted cream.
Gweek, TR12 6TU; 01326 221 502; www.gweekinn.demon.co.uk

AROUND TREBAH

Red Lion *inexpensive*
Picturesque thatched pub (1545) with three atmospheric bars offers bar lunches and restaurant in the evening.
Goldmartin Square, Mawnan Smith, TR11 5EP (1 km/0.5 mile from Trebah); 01326 250 026; www.redlioncornwall. com

ST MAWES

The Victory *inexpensive*
Traditional pub with bar meals and first-floor restaurant with terrace.
St Mawes, TR2 5DQ; 01326 270 324; www.victory-inn.co.uk

HELIGAN

Lobbs Farm Shop *moderate*
This shop by the Gardens' entrance sells fresh Cornish produce and picnic fare.
Pentewan, PL26 6EN; 01726 844 411; www.lobbsfarmshop.com; closed Sun Jan–Feb

Eat and Drink: inexpensive, under £25; moderate, £25–£50; expensive, over £50

Above left Close up of one of the biome domes, the Eden Project **Above centre** Inside the "Temperate" biome at the Eden Project **Above right** View of Fowey across the estuary, seen from Polruan

VISITING FOWEY

Tourist Information
5 South Street, PL23 1AR; 01726 833 616; www.fowey.co.uk

Ferry Services
Take the Bodinnick car ferry, and then follow signs to Polruan Ferry (car park). The passenger ferry crosses to Fowey every 15 minutes. The last ferry back is at 11pm (7pm Oct–Apr). www.looe. org/ferries.html

WHERE TO STAY

AROUND THE EDEN PROJECT

Boscundle Manor *expensive*
Comfortable 18th-century country house with gardens and indoor pool.
Boscundle, PL25 3RL (1.5 km/1 mile south of the Eden Project); 01726 813 557; www.boscundlemanor.co.uk

FOWEY

Old Quay House *expensive*
Elegant modern interiors and an award-winning restaurant overlooking the estuary grace this 150-year-old hotel.
28 Fore Street, PL23 1AQ; 01726 833 302; www.theoldquayhouse.com; no under-12s

POLPERRO

Claremont Hotel *inexpensive*
Traditional small family-run hotel, partly dating back to the 17th century, in the heart of the village.
The Coombes, PL13 2RG; 01503 272 241; www.theclaremonthotel.co.uk

TAVISTOCK

Bedford Hotel *inexpensve*
This stately building, on the site of a Benedictine abbey, was once the residence of the Dukes of Bedford.
1 Plymouth Road, PL19 8BB; 01822 613 221; www.bedford-hotel.co.uk

⑫ Charlestown
Charlestown, St Austell; PL25 3NJ
Soon after china clay was discovered 250 years ago in the downs north of St Austell, a major industry evolved. The "white gold" was exported around the world from Charlestown dock, formerly just a small fishing harbour. The **Shipwreck Museum** *(Mar–Oct, open daily)* on the quayside evokes local history through tableaux, models and photographs; visitors can also enter dark tunnels through which clay was conveyed in trucks to the dock-side. Today, the dock is quiet once more, home to three full-size replicas of historic sailing ships, used on film locations. Tours of ships available when in dock *(Easter–Oct, open daily)*.
🚗 *Turn right and take A390 through St Austell. Follow signs to Eden Project.*

⑬ The Eden Project
Bodelva, St Austell, Cornwall; PL24 2SG
Moving on from Heligan, Tim Smit's next visionary idea was the **Eden Project** *(open daily)* which has turned a huge disused china clay quarry into

Above Historic Square Sail Rigger at Charlestown harbour, near St Austell

a "living theatre of plants and people". The result is a series of incredible geodesic "biomes", the largest greenhouses in the world, in which different environments have been created – rainforest, temperate and arid, all surrounded by gardens. There is also a programme of seasonal events and exhibitions.
🚗 *Rejoin the A390, turning right onto the A3082 to Fowey. Parking can be found near the Tourist Information Centre on Albert Quay. For a car-free visit, see left.*

⑭ Fowey
Cornwall; PL23 1AR
Two ruined blockhouses, one in Fowey (pronounced "foy"), the other across the estuary in Polruan, are a reminder of medieval times when a defensive chain stretched between them to demast any undesirable ships trying to enter the deep anchorage. Today the river is busy with pleasure craft, and neat Edwardian terraces linked by narrow streets climb up from the busy water's edge. The

Walking on Dartmoor
Much of Dartmoor National Park can only be explored on foot by fairly experienced walkers. However, the going is easier around the edges, where gentle woodland footpaths run beside small rivers, for example, along Lydford Gorge and by the East Dart at Bellever. The **High Moorland Visitor Centre** *(Tavistock Road, Princetown)* is a good starting point for circular walks, detailed in a free leaflet; other walks start from visitor centres at **Haytor**, **Postbridge** and **Newbridge**. In addition, there is a year-round programme of guided walks graded by length and difficulty, see **www.dartmoor-npa.gov.uk**.

Where to Stay: inexpensive, under £80; moderate, £80–£150; expensive, over £150

town's focal point is the 15th-century **St Fimbarrus Church** with a Norman font. The nearby **Daphne du Maurier Literary Centre** *(5 South St; open daily)* reveals local literary connections and houses the Tourist Information Centre. Look for the original Elizabethan panelling and ceiling in the **Ship Inn** *(Trafalgar Square)*. Take a boat trip aboard **Moogie** *(Town Quay; 07792 625 908)* to see the many cliff-nesting sea birds and, perhaps dolphins, seals or even basking sharks.

🚗 *Take the Bodinnick car ferry and follow signs to Polperro. The village is car free, so park at the top, then either walk down to the harbour or ride in one of the "trams".*

Above The small ferry town of Polruan, looking across the estuary towards Fowey

🔵15 Polperro

Cornwall; PL13 2QR
A single main street of whitewashed cottages, old mill houses, inns and boathouses, with the little River Pol beside them, runs down a wooded valley to the fishing harbour and tiny stone Roman bridge. With seagulls

wheeling and crying overhead, this 13th-century former pilchard-fishing village is almost too pretty for its own good – it gets very busy in summer.

🚗 *Leave Polperro on A387 (signed Looe), turning left onto B3359. At the junction with A390, turn right to Tavistock (40 km/25 miles). Park in Bedford Square.*

Plaque outside the Town Hall, Tavistock

🔵16 Tavistock

Devon; PL19 OAE
Gateway to Dartmoor National Park, Tavistock became a prosperous market town during the 19th century, thanks to the discovery of copper in mines owned by the 7th Duke of Bedford. As a result, he paid for the remodelling of the town hall in grand Gothic style and built other buildings around Bedford Square in the local grey-green Hurdwick stone, including the Bedford Hotel and the Pannier Market. A small local history **museum** *(Easter–Oct, open daily)* is housed in the monastery gatehouse on the square.

To the east lies the wild moorland of **Dartmoor**, populated by ponies and sheep and dominated by granite tors. In the centre, Princetown, famous for its prison built in Napoleonic times, is the highest town in England. Near the edges lie interesting old market towns such as **Moretonhampstead** and Chagford as well as atmospheric villages like **Buckland-in-the-Moor** and **Drewsteignton**, both with pretty thatched stone cottages and small granite churches. The 36-m (120-ft) tower of St Pancras Church at **Widecombe-in-the-Moor**, a village immortalized by the folk song about its fair, is a landmark for miles around.

Above left View over the Tamar Valley, seen from Kit Hill near Tavistock

VISITING TAVISTOCK

Tourist Information
Bedford Square, PL19 OHE; 01822 612 938; www.tavistockonline.co.uk

EAT AND DRINK

FOWEY

Sams *moderate*
Popular small restaurant specializing in seafood and American diner-style dishes.
20 Fore Street, PL23 1AQ; 01726 832 273; www.samsfowey.co.uk

POLPERRO

Three Pilchards *inexpensive*
Traditional old pub with a small roof garden; renowned for its ales and food.
The Quay, PL13 2QZ; 01503 272 233

Couch's *moderate*
Smart restaurant that mixes old-world charm with modern influences.
Big Green, PL13 2QT; 01503 272 554; www.couchspolperro.com; open evenings only

AROUND TAVISTOCK

Copper Penny Inn *inexpensive*
18th-century village pub with real ales and meals based on local produce.
Gulworthy, PL19 8NT (4 km/2.5 miles west of Tavistock on the A390); 01822 833 288

DAY TRIP OPTIONS

As well as the beauty of its coastline, Cornwall has a wealth of superb gardens thanks to its mild climate.

Culture and Coast
Explore St Ives 1 and its galleries in the morning, then grab a pasty and head along the coast to pretty Zennor 2, Pendeen 3 and Cape Cornwall – for a clifftop picnic. Finish the day watching the sun sink into the sea at the Minack Theatre, Porthcurno 4.

Follow the B3306 from St Ives on to St Just and then take the B3315.

The Lizard
The Lizard Peninsula 7 offers plenty of attractions for both kids and adults. Take a dip at Kynance Cove, visit the Lizard Lighthouse and have lunch at Cadgwith. Drive past the futuristic Goonhilly Earth Station to see the seals at Gweek. Then, if there's still time, explore the gardens at Trebah 8.

Use the A3083; then take the B3293 to Goonhilly and Gweek and drive on to Trebah.

Harbours and Gardens
Find the Lost Gardens of Heligan 11 and then learn about shipwrecks in Charlestown 12. Tour the Eden Project 13 before returning to Fowey to end the day by the water's edge 14.

The B3273, A390 and A3082 connect Fowey to Heligan with Charlestown and the Eden Project well signed on the way.

Headlands and Coves

Bideford to Bodmin Moor

Highlights

- **Magnificent coastal scenery**
  Walk along grassy clifftops where Atlantic surf breaks onto rocks below and headlands frame distant beaches

- **Legendary King Arthur in Tintagel**
  On a windswept promontory, explore the ruins of the medieval castle that inspired tales of royal chivalry

- **Gourmet cuisine**
  Eat out in Padstow, home of chef Rick Stein, who has turned this small fishing port into a gastro heaven

- **Literary connections**
  Visit locations immortalized by writers Charles Kingsley, Daphne du Maurier and Henry Williamson

Fishing trawlers and yachts moored side by side in Padstow's picturesque harbour

Headlands and Coves

The coast that runs south-west from north Devon into Cornwall is extremely dramatic. Grassy clifftops fringed by rocks are pounded by Atlantic waves. In places the cliffs drop down to stunning sandy beaches and coves, while jutting headlands stretch into the distance on either side. Find a place to leave the car and walk along a section of the South West Coast Path to enjoy the best views or, for a contrasting moorland panorama, head inland to Bodmin Moor and climb up one of its windswept tors. The area's rich scenery is complemented by fine historic houses and beautiful gardens as well as plenty of opportunities to sample some of England's freshest and best-cooked seafood.

ACTIVITIES

Cycle along the Tarka Trail between Bideford and Great Torrington or by the Camel Estuary from Padstow to Bodmin

Laze on the beach at Bude or surf the waves as they roll onto the sand

Discover the ruined castle at Tintagel, the legendary gathering place of King Arthur's knights

Take a ferry ride to Rock from Padstow or enjoy a day trip by boat to Lundy Island from Bideford

Savour a plate of fresh fish and chips at a waterside fish restaurant in Appledore, Bude or Padstow

Walk a stretch of the South West Coast Path or climb to the top of Brown Willy on Bodmin Moor

Left Cliffs plunge to the bay below the medieval castle of Tintagel, see p45

0 kilometres 8

0 miles 8

Hartlan
Poi
**HARTLAND
PENINSULA**
Ste
Hartland Quay

Docton M.

Morwenstow

*Bude
Bay*

Stibb

Stratto

BUDE 6

Marhamchurch

Widemouth Bay

Widemouth

St Gennys
Week St Ma

Crackington
Haven
Wainhouse
Corner
A39

Boscastle
B3263
Canworthy
Water

Tresmee

TINTAGEL 7
B3263
B3266
Davidstow
A35

**DELABOLE
SLATE** 8
Camelford
Laneast

*Port Isaac
Bay*
B3314
West Downs
B3267
Rough Tor
400m
Altarnun

Port Isaac
St Teath
Michaelstow
Brown Willy
419m

*Trevose
Head*
St Endellion
A39

St Minver
St Kew
B3266
Bolventor

PADSTOW 9
Rock
B3314
C O R N W A L L
13

St Merryn
A389
Blisland
A30
**BODMIN
MOOR**

B3276
St Issey
Wadebridge

St Breock
A389
10 **PENCARROW**

St Eval
Washaway
Cardinham
St Neot

B3274
A39

Withiel
11 **BODMIN**
Fowey
A38

St Wenn
A391
12
A30
Lanivet
LANHYDROCK
B3268

Lostwithiel

Below The seaside town of Bude, framed by hills covered with a patchwork of fields, *see pp44–5*

PLAN YOUR DRIVE

Start/finish: Bideford to Bodmin Moor.

Number of days: 3–4, allowing half a day for a coastal walk in Bude.

Distance: 205 km (128 miles).

Road conditions: Well-paved and signposted throughout, including some busier roads as well as winding country lanes that sometimes have steep gradients.

When to go: The area is busy from June to September, particularly along the coast, which is very popular for family holidays. Spring and autumn benefit from mild weather, but winter can be stormy. Many attractions and some places to stay and eat are closed from November to Easter.

Opening times: Museums and attractions are generally open 10am–5pm, but close earlier (or are closed altogether) Nov–Easter. Shops are often open later. Churches are usually open until dusk.

Market days: Bideford: Tue, Fri and Sat; **Great Torrington:** Pannier Market, daily; **Bude:** Fri.

Shopping: Pasties and clotted cream; surf and beach equipment.

Major festivals: Bideford: Regatta, late Aug; **Appledore:** Visual Arts Festival, Jun; Book Festival, late Sep; **Bude:** re-enactment at Stratton of Battle of Stamford Hill in 1643, May; Jazz Festival, last week in Aug; **Padstow:** "Obby Oss" spring festival, with procession and dancing through the streets, 1 May.

DAY TRIP OPTIONS

Spend a day visiting the tranquil **Hartland Peninsula** or, a favourite with children, **exploring Tintagel** with its castle situated on a dramatic headland. Indulge in some **gourmet eating** in Padstow, then work it off **cycling** along the **Camel Estuary** towards Bodmin, or **walking** the **South West Coast Path**. For full details, *see p47*.

VISITING BIDEFORD

Parking
Park in the Victoria Park car park next to the Tourist Information Centre.

Tourist Information
Burton Art Gallery, Kingsley Road, EX39 2QQ; 01237 471 455; www.torridge. gov.uk

Bideford Cycle, Surf and Kayak Hire
Torrington Street, EX39 4DR; 01237 424 123; www.bidefordbicyclehire.co.uk

Boat Trips to Lundy Island
Up to five 2-hour sailings a week from April to October. *Bideford Quay, 01271 863 636; www.lundyisland.co.uk*

WHERE TO STAY

BIDEFORD

Orchard Hill *moderate*
A smart yet friendly hotel on the hillside, with a south-facing veranda. *Orchard Hill, EX39 2QY; 01237 472 872; www.bidefordhotel.com*

Yeoldon House *moderate*
A former Victorian residence, this riverside hotel has a a fine restaurant. *Durrant Lane, EX39 2RL; 01237 474 400; www.yeoldonhousehotel.co.uk*

HARTLAND PENINSULA

Hartland Quay Hotel *moderate*
This remote hotel is dramatically sited under the cliffs by the sea. *Hartland, EX39 6DU; 01237 441 218; www.hartlandquayhotel.com; closed 20 Dec–2 Jan*

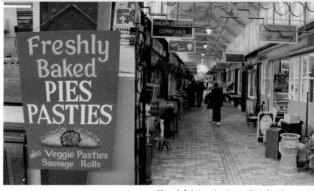

Above left A sign advertises traditional pasties
Above right Bideford's Pannier Market hall

① Bideford
Devon; EX39 2QQ

Described 150 years ago by local writer Charles Kingsley as "the little white town which slopes upward from its broad river tide", Bideford is still much the same, busy with fishing vessels, pleasure craft and the MS *Oldenburg*, which ferries visitors to the National Trust's **Lundy Island** bird sanctuary, 17 km (11 miles) away. The promenade beside the Taw Estuary has been set off since the 13th century by the 24-arch **Long Bridge**, originally built from wood but encased in stone since 1535. Narrow old streets crowded with small shops and pubs lead up from the water to the **Victorian Pannier Market hall**, named for the baskets in which farmers' wives used to bring produce for sale. **Burton Art Gallery** *(open daily)* in Victoria Park on the riverside has sections on the town's history. It's possible to hire a bike nearby and cycle along the **Tarka Trail** to Great Torrington.

🚗 *From the Victoria Park car park, turn right on to Kingsley Road (B3235) and cross A39 on to A386, signposted to Appledore. Park in car park on quay.*

② Appledore
Devon; EX39 1QS

Along tiny streets and alleyways, colour-washed Georgian cottages with bow windows line the Taw and Torridge estuaries; no wonder Appledore has become a favourite with local artists – several galleries show their work. Fishing and ship-building were the town's life blood for centuries, as explained in the small **North Devon Maritime Museum** in Odun Road *(open Apr–Oct: daily)*. Fishing trips are available from the quay.

🚗 *Follow signs to Westward Ho!*

③ Westward Ho!
Devon; EX39 1QS

The neighbouring seaside resort, named after Charles Kingsley's novel of Elizabethan seafarers, is notable mainly for having England's oldest golf links, a long sandy beach and a pebble ridge.

🚗 *Take B3236 and A39 to Bideford, take A386 to Great Torrington, follow signs to Dartington Crystal. Park in the car park.*

Far left Fishing boats moored at the quay at Appledore **Above left** Wall sculptures created by one of Appledore's artists **Below left** A statue of local author Charles Kingsley in Bideford

④ Great Torrington
Devon; EX38 8AA

It's a scenic drive beside the River Torridge to Great Torrington, home of **Dartington Crystal**, where visitors can see glass being hand blown *(tours Mon–Fri; visitor centre and shop daily)*. At the **RHS Rosemoor Gardens**, there are areas devoted to roses, fruit and vegetables, a lake and an arboretum *(open daily)*. The Battle of Torrington – a Royalist rout in the English Civil War in 1646 – features strongly in the small, volunteer-run **Great Torrington Heritage Museum** *(open daily)*.

🚗 *From Great Torrington, take B3227 to Stibb Cross; turn right on minor road to go through Woolfardisworthy to A39*

Lundy Island
This car-free island 17 km (11 miles) off the coast is a sanctuary for puffins with a resident human population of 30 – joined in summer by hordes of day-trippers who come to go seal watching, visit its 13th-century castle and have a drink at Marisco Tavern.

(signed Bude). At Higher Clovelly, turn right onto B3248 to Hartland, then follow signs on minor road through Stoke to Hartland Quay; park in car park. Return to Stoke and turn right down tiny lane to Docton Mill at Milford.

⑤ Hartland Peninsula
North Devon; EX39 6DU

This blissfully quiet rural pocket is criss-crossed by narrow country lanes leading to windswept **Hartland Quay**, where dramatic cliffs give way to a tiny 16th-century harbour with a small shipwreck museum *(open Easter–Oct, daily)*. In **Stoke**, St Nectan's 14th-century church is known as the cathedral for its 350-m (128-ft) high tower. Nearby are 16th-century stately **Hartland Abbey** *(open Apr–Sep, Sun–Thu)* and pretty **Docton Mill Gardens & Tea Rooms** *(open Mar–Sep daily)*, where tea is served in a beautiful room or by the mill pond.

🚗 *From Docton Mill, take minor road via Edistone and Tosberry to rejoin A39 to Bude. Park in canalside Tourist Information Centre car park.*

Above left Windswept headlands of Hartland Peninsula **Above right** Docton Mill Gardens **Below** Mill pond at Docton Mill Gardens

EAT AND DRINK

AROUND BIDEFORD

Boathouse *moderate*
Lively waterside restaurant and bar looking across the Torridge Estuary to Appledore.
Marine Parade, Instow, EX39 4JJ (take B3233 out of Bideford along the estuary towards Barnstaple); 01271 861 292; www.instow.net/boathouse; no reservations

Instow Arms *moderate*
Upmarket pub fare is served in the first-floor restaurant, and there is also a cosy downstairs bar.
Marine Parade, Instow, EX39 4JJ; 01271 860 608; www.instowarms.com

APPLEDORE

The Royal George *inexpensive*
An old beamed pub with a dining area overlooking the estuary.
Irsha Street, EX39 1RY; 01237 474 335; www.theroyalgeorgeappledore.co.uk

Beaver Inn *moderate*
Atmospheric old pub beside the Torridge Estuary, with panoramic views from its terrace. Noted for its fresh fish dishes.
Irsha Street, EX39 1RY; 01237 474 822; www.beaverinn.co.uk

HARTLAND PENINSULA

Docton Mill Gardens Tea Room *inexpensive*
Small café in the delightful gardens serving snacks and award-winning Devonshire clotted cream teas.
Lymebridge, EX39 6EA; 01237 441 369; www.doctonmill.co.uk; open Mar–Sep

Eat and Drink: inexpensive, under £25; moderate, £25–£50; expensive, over £50

Above Dinghies lined up against the wall on Bude's quayside

VISITING BUDE

Parking
Park in Crescent car park beside the canal, signposted to the right in town.

Tourist Information
Crescent car park, EX23 8LE; 01288 354 240; www.visitbude.info

Raven Surf School
Lessons on Bude's beaches.
01288 353 693; www.ravensurf.co.uk; from £35 for a 2-hour lesson.

WHERE TO STAY

BUDE

Falcon Hotel *moderate*
Originally a lodging house for sea captains, this hotel has sea and canal views and a walled garden.
Breakwater Road, EX23 8SD ; 01288 352 005; www.falconhotel.com

Stratton Gardens Guesthouse *moderate*
A five-bedroom guesthouse in a 16th-century house with a bar and garden.
Cot Hill, Stratton, EX23 9DN; 01288 352 500; www.stratton-gardens.co.uk

TINTAGEL

Lewis's Tea Rooms *inexpensive*
Comfortable B&B in a stone house built in 1586. Noted for its cream teas.
Bossiney Road, TL34 0AH; 01840 770 427

Below Stone mile-post marks path on clifftops above Bude

❻ Bude
Crescent car park, Bude; EX23 8LE

Bude is more than just a popular seaside resort. As well as two large sandy beaches, it has some of Britain's best coastal walks along its grassy clifftops. There are reminders too of its past, when it was a battlefield, a busy port and home of Cornwall's "forgotten inventor".

A two-hour circular walk
The walk starts from the car park at the **Tourist Information Centre** ① in Bude, where a good selection of local guidebooks is on sale *(open daily, except Sun in winter)*. The restored stretch of canal beside it is the remains of a 56-km (35-mile)-long canal built in the early 19th century to transport lime-rich beach sand inland as fertilizer.

Heading towards the sea, cross the canal bridge – originally a swing bridge to let ships through – and continue past the impressive white **Falcon Hotel** ②. Opposite it, the canal-side castle now houses the excellent **Castle Heritage Centre** ③ *(open daily)*, where the town's varied story is imaginatively told, alongside working models of Sir Goldsworthy Gurney's pioneering Victorian inventions; these included a steam

Buckets and spades for sale at Bude

engine, sewer ventilation system and revolving lights for lighthouses.

Heading along the path towards the sea you come to a restored **sea lock** ④, which enabled boats to "lock in" to unload their cargoes at a quay rather than on the beach. Turning left, the path climbs sharply to the coast path, signposted to Widemouth, 5km (3 miles) away. From the clifftop there are views over Bude Haven beach, where the small River Neet flows into the sea. Before it silted up, this was a thriving harbour. Because of its trade, the village of Stratton, inland, was granted a royal charter by King John in 1207.

A long breakwater stretches out to Chapel Rock, lit in medieval times by a light to guide ships into port. The curious octagonal **tower** ⑤, known as the "pepper pot", was a Victorian

0 metres 500
0 yards 500

Tower ⑤
Sea Lock ④
Castle Heritage Centre ③
Tourist Information Centre ①
Falcon Hotel ②
P
⑨
Bude Marshes Nature Reserve
⑥ Efford Down
LYNSTONE ROAD
LYNSTONE
BREAKWATER RD
VICARAGE RD
A3073
A3073
BAGBOR ROAD
⑧ Mile-post
⑦ Rodd's Bridge
UPTON

coastguard's hut, erected in Grecian style as a symbol of Bude's ambitions.

Look back past the Haven over twin sandy beaches Summerleaze and Crooklets; in Victorian times Crooklets was for women's use only.

The path along the clifftop crosses **Efford Down** ⑥. Here in 1643 Cornishmen in the Royalist Army camped on the eve of the English Civil War battle of Stamford Hill, where they defeated the Parliamentarians.

At Upton, turn left inland and follow the lane down to the canal at **Rodd's Bridge** ⑦. Turn left along the towpath, noting the stone **mile-post** ⑧ beside it, dating from 1820, and carry on along the towpath that flanks **Bude Marshes Nature Reserve** ⑨, where a variety of birds and flowers flourish, back at the start.

🚗 *Turn left out of car park and leave Bude on small clifftop road signposted to Widemouth Bay to rejoin A39 in direction of Camelford. Turn right onto B3263 to Boscastle and then Tintagel, where several car parks are signposted in village and near castle.*

⑦ Tintagel
Cornwall; PL34 0HE

Was this clifftop castle the birthplace of the legendary King Arthur? Did the medieval kings of Cornwall live there? Mystery surrounds the ruins perched on a rocky headland beyond the village's single main street. The **castle's** ruined battlements *(open daily)* date back to the 13th century and are well worth the steep climb for exhilarating views of the dramatic coastline. In the village

itself are the 14th-century **Old Post Office** *(open Mar–Oct daily)* and **King Arthur's Great Halls** *(open daily)*, telling the legend of the king. On the rugged clifftop you can see the 12th-century church of St Materiana.

🚗 *Return to B3263 in direction of Camelford, turning right at sign to Delabole on B3314. Delabole Slate quarry is signed to the left in the village. Park in the quarry car park.*

⑧ Delabole Slate
Cornwall; PL33 9AZ

The largest man-made hole in Britain, at Delabole Slate, has been quarried for more than 600 years. Over 1 km (half a mile) across and nearly 1,500 m (500 ft) deep, the hole is Europe's oldest continuously worked quarry, producing 120 tons of slate a day. *(tours of surface works May–Aug, Mon–Fri).*

🚗 *Leaving Delabole Slate, turn left onto B3314 and left at Westdowns onto B3267 to join A39 towards Wadebridge. After Wadebridge, turn right at St Breock onto A389 to Padstow. Prideaux Place is on the edge of Padstow, off B3276 towards Newquay. Park on the quay or in Prideaux Place car park.*

Above left Bude's grassy clifftops **Above right** Life's a Beach café at Summerleaze

EAT AND DRINK

BUDE

Pengenna Pasties *inexpensive*
Beef, lamb, cheese & onion, vegetable or vegan is the choice of traditional Cornish pasties at this small bakery. *Arundell House, Belle Vue, EX23 8JL; 01288 355 169; www.pengenna pasties.co.uk*

Cafe Limelight *moderate*
Smart café with sea-facing terrace in the Castle Heritage Centre; strong emphasis on local produce. *The Wharf, EX23 8LG; 01288 357 300; www.thecastlebude.org.uk*

AROUND BUDE

Life's A Beach *daytime: inexpensive; evening: expensive*
By day this is a popular beachside café; at 7pm it turns into a sophisticated restaurant, specializing in fish. *Follow signs from Bude to Summerleaze Beach (1 mile), EX23 8HN; 01288 355 222; www.lifesabeach.info*

TINTAGEL

Cornishman Inn *inexpensive*
Atmospheric, beamed pub with a restaurant noted for its steaks; 11 rooms. *Fore Street, PL34 0DB; 01840 770 238; www.cornishmaninn.com*

Below left The rocky headlands of Tintagel **Below right** Medieval battlements at Tintagel Castle

Eat and Drink: inexpensive, under £25; moderate, £25–£50; expensive, over £50

Above The still waters of Padstow's harbour reflect yachts and wharf buildings

VISITING PADSTOW

Parking
Park on the quay, or at The Lawns.

Tourist Information
*Red Brick Building, North Quay,
PL28 8AF; 01841 533 449;
www.padstowlive.com*

Padstow Cycle Hire
*South Quay, PL28 8BL; 01841 533 533;
www.padstowcyclehire.com*

WHERE TO STAY

PADSTOW

Old Ship Hotel *moderate*
Centrally located hotel with estuary views whose bar has live music. Restaurant noted for its fresh fish.
*Mill Square, PL28 8AE; 01841 532 357;
www.oldshiphotel-padstow.co.uk*

St Petroc's Hotel *expensive*
A short walk uphill from the harbour, this 10-room hotel in a white wisteria-clad Georgian building is one of Rick Stein's properties.
*4 New Street, PL28 8BY; 01841 532 700;
www.rickstein.com*

Below The imposing façade of Bodmin Gaol, which now houses a pub and brasserie

9 Padstow
Cornwall; PL28 8AF
Fame has been bestowed on this small port on the Camel Estuary thanks to a fish restaurant opened in a Victorian drill hall in 1975 by a local chef, Rick Stein. Now famous for his TV appearances, he has four restaurants in the town, plus gourmet shops and a cookery school, making it a gastro heaven. Alternatives to eating include clifftop walks, a ferry trip across to Rock, a stop at the intriguing fishery *(open daily)*, where lobsters are hatched, or a visit to **Prideaux Place** *(open May–Oct, Sun–Thu)*. This sumptuously furnished family-owned Elizabethan manor has often been used as the location for period films, among them *Oscar and Lucinda*, Trevor Nunn's *Twelfth Night* and several Rosamund Pilcher novels. From Padstow bikes can be hired to cycle along the River Camel to Bodmin.

🚗 *From Padstow, return to the A389 past Wadebridge towards Bodmin. Pencarrow is signposted off to the left 6 km (4 miles) after Wadebridge. Park in the car park.*

10 Pencarrow
Washaway, Cornwall; PL30 3AG
Tall conifers from around the world soar above the long drive leading to this Georgian mansion, owned by the same family since it was built in the 1770s. In spring, rhododendrons, camellias and azaleas create patches of vivid colour in the gardens. The house is notable for its Adam furniture, upholstered in rose silk damask that matches the curtains – "treasure" captured from a Spanish ship in 1762. Joshua Reynolds painted many of the portraits on show *(house open Apr–Sep, Sun–Thu; gardens open Mar–Oct, daily)*.

🚗 *From Pencarrow, continue to Bodmin on A389. Several car parks signposted, one on left as you enter town, at end of Camel Trail.*

Literary Connections
Westward Ho! is the only town in England to be named after a book – and to have an exclamation mark! Charles Kingsley wrote his historical romance while living in Bideford; after its publication entrepreneurs developed the resort. Daphne du Maurier found inspiration for her novel *Jamaica Inn* while staying at the coaching inn on Bodmin Moor, a notorious smugglers' haunt, in 1930. Henry Williamson's 1927 story *Tarka the Otter* is set in North Devon. The places he describes in it are now linked by a 290-km (180-mile) long trail, including a section between Bideford and Great Torrington.

11 Bodmin
Cornwall; PL31 2DQ
Guilty or not guilty? Visitors to Courtroom One in **Shire Hall** *(tours Mon–Sat)*, the old county court, can decide the verdict in a realistic re-enactment of a famous murder trial held here in 1844, and then visit the cells. The life of an 18th-century prisoner is depicted in the former **Bodmin Gaol**, a forbidding building that now houses various eateries. The 500-year-old **St Petroc's Church**, which has a 12th-century font and the saint's ivory casket, is the largest medieval church in Cornwall.

🚗 *Take B3268, signed Lostwithiel, out past the station. Lanhydrock is signed to the left after 3 km (2 miles). Park in the car park.*

Where to Stay: inexpensive, under £80; moderate, £80–£150; expensive, over £150

⑫ Lanhydrock

near Bodmin, Cornwall; PL30 5AD

After this stately 17th-century house was gutted by fire in 1881 it was rebuilt, battlements and all, to match the surviving north wing and gatehouse. The interior was replanned to include the latest amenities – central heating, bathrooms and "modern" servants' quarters, all in typical Victorian style. The gardens, laid out at the time of rebuilding, feature rhododendrons, magnolias and camellias, with woods and parkland leading down to the banks of the River Fowey *(open Mar–Nov, Tue–Sun)*.

🚗 **Return towards Bodmin and follow signs to join A30 towards Launceston. Blisland is signed off to the left, from where minor roads take you to the tors. The A30 continues across the moor, passing Jamaica Inn at Bolventor. Turn right there towards Liskeard and after 8 km (5 miles) turn left to Minions.**

⑬ Bodmin Moor

Blisland: PL30 4JE; Jamaica Inn: PL15 7TS; Minions: PL14 5LA

With its small 11th-century church, St Protus and St Hyacinth, **Blisland** is typical of the quiet villages that nestle in leafy valleys on the western slopes of the moor. In complete contrast, the wild and often desolate uplands are strewn with huge boulders, dotted with ancient standing stones and topped by brooding tors like **Rough Tor**, an Iron Age fort, and **Brown Willy**, which at 420 m (1,377 ft) is the moor's highest point. Around **Minions**, on the south side of the moor, darkly picturesque relics of the mining industry can be seen – chimneys, engine houses and spoil dumps. **Jamaica Inn** at Bolventor, an 18th-century slate-hung inn which inspired Daphne du Maurier's novel of the same name, is mainly notable for its bleak evocative setting – and gets very crowded in high season.

Above left Passenger ferry departs Padstow for Rock *Above right* A signpost in Blisland indicates its old-fashioned charms

EAT AND DRINK

PADSTOW

The Basement Café
moderate–expensive
A quayside restaurant specializing in local fish and seafood, The Basement Café also prepares hearty breakfasts. *11 Broad Street, PL28 8BS; 01841 532 846; www.thebasement.co.uk; closed Sun evening*

Seafood Restaurant *expensive*
This is the Rick Stein place that started Padstow's rise to culinary fame in the 1970s. Bright and airy, it's just across the quay from where the lobster boats and trawlers tie up. A less exalted option (eat-in or take-away), but just as special, is **Stein's Fish & Chips Café** on *South Quay, PL28 8BL*. Another option is to hone your own talents by signing up for the famous chef's cookery course of 1, 2, 4 or 6 days. *Riverside, PL28 8BY; 01841 532 700; www.rickstein.com*

DAY TRIP OPTIONS

A great range of day trips is possible along this route, taking in bike rides, beautiful coastline and historic sites.

Tarka Country
Hire a bike at Bideford ❶ and spend a leisurely day cycling along the Tarka Trail up the Torridge Valley to Great Torrington ❹, looking out for otters on the river banks. Visit Dartington Crystal and RHS Rosemoor Gardens before cycling back to Bideford. Drive to the head of the Taw and Torridge estuaries at Appledore ❷ and then relax over a well-earned drink and a fish supper at the atmospheric old Beaver Inn or Royal George.

Park in the Victoria Park car park at Bideford and hire a bike at Bideford Cycle, Surf and Kayak Hire. Follow driving instructions from Bideford to Appledore and park on the quay.

Castles and Cliffs
Whatever the weather, the castle at Tintagel ❼ on its dramatic headland is an exciting place to explore, and the clifftop coast path provides magnificent sea views. Discover the legend of King Arthur, then drive to Bude ❻ to build sandcastles inspired by the medieval ruins, surf or simply laze on one of its twin sandy beaches. Pick up traditional pasties for a picnic from Pengenna Pasties, or lunch at Life's A Beach café.

Park in the car park nearest Tintagel Castle, if you can, to visit the ruins. Take B3263 to Boscastle, then join A39 to Bude, turning left off it at Widemouth.

Gourmet Padstow
Take a boat trip across the Camel Estuary to Rock, see how the lobsters are hatched, and work up an appetite for a fish lunch at Rick Stein's Seafood Restaurant or fish and chips on the quayside. Energetic types can hire a bike and cycle beside the River Camel to Bodmin with its weighty judicial past; alternatively visit the Elizabethan manor at Prideaux Place.

Park on the quay at Padstow.

North Devon Coast and Exmoor

Taunton to Barnstaple

Highlights

- **Historic steam-train ride**
  Take a trip back in time through the lovely, rolling countryside on the preserved West Somerset Railway

- **Exmoor and its outlaws**
  Explore exhilarating moorland scenery and learn the legend of the 17th-century outlaws, the Doone family

- **Coastal pleasures**
  Relax on swathes of golden sand or be awed by cliffs and crashing waves along the South West Coast Path

- **Market bound**
  Discover the rich heritage of historic market towns such as Taunton, Dunster and Barnstaple

The South West Coast Path and spectacular coastline on the way to Morte Point, Devon

North Devon Coast and Exmoor

The countryside of Somerset and North Devon is as varied as any in Europe. Secluded coves, sand dunes and wide sandy beaches, washed by powerful Atlantic waves, make the area a top choice for beach lovers – families and surfers alike. The windswept moorlands of Exmoor National Park are bordered by grassy clifftops that run along the dramatic coastline. Here and there a patchwork of fields covers gently rolling hillsides dotted with thick woods and crossed by clean and swift-flowing streams. The interior has plenty of small towns and pretty villages. All of this route lies in prime walking country, with spectacular coastal paths and a network of trails inland.

KEY

ACTIVITIES

Catch a vintage steam train through the Somerset countryside from Washford

Indulge in a Devon cream tea – soft scones topped with thick clotted cream and fruity strawberry jam

Explore Exmoor on foot and enjoy outstanding views from Dunkery Beacon, its highest point

Cycle along the scenic Tarka Trail, part of Cycle Route 27 which runs from Ilfracombe to Barnstaple

Ride the wild Atlantic rollers at Woolacombe Bay by hiring a wet suit and body board

Go bargain-hunting for crafts and antiques in Barnstaple's airy and atmospheric Pannier Market

Below The Museum of Barnstaple and North Devon, Barnstaple, *see p55*

Above Beautiful Woolacombe Bay – a wide, sandy beach with great surf, *see p55*

Below Pretty Periwinkle Tearoom, Selworthy, *see p53*

PLAN YOUR DRIVE

Start/finish: Taunton to Barnstaple.

Number of days: 2–3 days.

Distance: 134 km (84 miles).

Road conditions: Well-paved and signposted, country roads are often narrow and winding. Be prepared to stop in a passing place if there is oncoming traffic. On Exmoor, watch out for ponies or sheep on the road. Most places have well-signed car parks, usually pay-and-display.

When to go: In April–May, wild flowers border the roadsides; autumn sees the leaves turn rich brown and the moors are splashed with purple heather. During July and August, families crowd into the area for seaside holidays. It can get very busy. In winter, the weather is often relatively mild and towns return to "normal", but villages can be quiet.

Opening times: Museums and attractions are generally open 10am–5pm, but close earlier (or are closed altogether) Nov–Easter. Shops are often open longer. Churches are usually open until dusk.

Market days: Taunton: Farmer's Market, Thu; Barnstaple: Pannier Market: local produce, Tue, Fri, Sat; antiques and books, Wed; also crafts, Apr–Dec Mon & Thu.

Shopping: Look out for Devonshire clotted cream, local cider, surfing gear and beachwear.

Major festivals: Taunton: Carnival, Oct; Exmoor: Walking Festival, May; Mortehoe: Scarecrow Festival, Aug; Barnstaple: North Devon Food Festival, Oct.

DAY TRIP OPTIONS

Beach lovers can enjoy the **golden sands** and **surging surf** at Woolacombe Bay before tucking into a **Devon cream tea**. Walkers can explore the **windswept expanses** and **hidden valleys** of **Exmoor**, home of the legendary outlaws, **the Doones**. From Taunton and Washford, step back in time by visiting **ancient churches**, an **abbey** and a **restored steam train**. For full details, *see p55*.

VISITING TAUNTON

Parking
Park in the car park near the bus station.

Tourist Information
Paul Street, TA1 3XZ; 01823 336 344;
www.visitsomerset.com

VISITING EXMOOR

Exmoor National Park Centre
For more information about Exmoor
National Park including walks, events
and activities: open Mar–Oct.
Dunster Steep, Minehead, TA24
6SE; 01643 821 835; www.exmoor-
nationalpark.gov.uk

WHERE TO STAY

TAUNTON

The Castle *expensive*
This wisteria-covered family-run hotel
in the town centre provides historic
accommodation. It also has a brasserie
and a restaurant.
Castle Green, TA1 1NF; 01823 272 671;
www.the-castle-hotel.com

DUNSTER

Luttrell Arms *expensive*
Small 15th-century hotel facing the Yarn
Market. Used in medieval times as a
guesthouse by the Abbots of Cleeve, it
has several rooms with four-poster beds.
32–6 High Street, TA24 6SG; 01643
821 555; www.luttrellarms.co.uk

LYNMOUTH

Rock House Hotel *moderate*
Family-run small hotel in 18th-century
building at the harbour entrance. It
has a cosy restaurant with sea views.
Manor Green, EX35 6EN; 01598 753
508; www.rock-house.co.uk

Below left The 15th-century Luttrell Arms
Hotel, Dunster **Below right** One of the
pristine, tidily thatched cottages of Selworthy

1 Taunton
Somerset; TA1 3XZ
This county town, in
the heart of apple and
cider country is centred
around its triangular
former market place,
Fore Street. The cattle
market moved to the
outskirts in 1929, but
the 200-year-old red
brick **Market House**
still dominates. Parts
of 12th-century
Taunton Castle survive,
now home to the
Museum of Somerset *(open Tue–Sat).*
Nearby in Hammet Street, the richly
sculptured tower of **St Mary**
Magdelene Church, founded 1308,
soars up 50 m (163 ft) and is a
landmark visible for miles.

🚗 *Turn left out of the car park along*
Corporation Street, left at roundabout
on to North Street (A3207) and left on
to A358 out of town; take B3224 left
just after Bishop's Lydeard, then B3188
right to Washford. Park at Cleeve Abbey
car park, on left as you enter village.

2 Washford
Somerset; TA23 0PS
Cleeve Abbey *(open daily Apr–Oct),*
founded by Cistercian monks in 1188,
is the most complete set of monastic
cloister buildings in England, including
a gatehouse, small chapel, dormitory
and large 15th-century refectory with
an arched wooden ceiling known as a
waggon roof. Washford is also on the
West Somerset Railway *(daily mid-*
Mar–Oct; www.west-somerset-railway.
co.uk), a 32-km (20-mile) stretch of

Right One of the gatehouses of the impressive
Dunster Castle, Dunster

track offering trips in veteran carriages
often hauled by steam locomotives.

🚗 *Turn left out of car park onto B3188,*
then left onto A39 towards Minehead,
turning left into Dunster. Car parks just
off the A39 and in the castle grounds.

3 Dunster
Somerset; TA24 6SL
The quaint 400-year-old open-sided
octagonal **Yarn Market** is a reminder
of the village's once-thriving wool
industry. The nearby **Doll Collection**
(open daily Apr–Sep), displays ancient
and modern dolls. Turreted Norman-
style **Dunster Castle** *(open daily Mar–*
Oct), was home of the Luttrell family
for 600 years until 1976. Perched on a
hilltop and surrounded by terraced
gardens, it was extensively remodelled
in Victorian times. Dunster is a good
base for visiting Exmoor.

🚗 *Continue on A39 past Minehead*
until Selworthy is signposted off to the
right. Park opposite the church.

❹ Selworthy

Somerset; TA24 8TJ

This is a picture-postcard hamlet of thatched cottages with a splendid view over the Vale of Porlock and a white 14th-century Perpendicular church framed by woods. It is part of the Holnicote Estate which extends from Porlock Bay to Dunkery Hill on Exmoor, its spectacular moorland dotted with woods and medieval villages. Home to wild ponies and horned sheep, the moor is criss-crossed by footpaths. On the way to Oare, **Dunkery Beacon** is the highest point on Exmoor (519 m/1,260 ft), with extensive views in all directions.

🚗 *From Selworthy, take A39 towards Porlock, turning left at sign for West Luccombe, then right at sign for Dunkery Beacon. Return to A39, forking right at Porlock onto New Road (toll) to avoid very steep Porlock Hill. Rejoin A39. Turn left at sign for Doone Valley after 1 km (half a mile). Follow road to Oare.*

❺ Oare

Somerset; EX35 6NU

Oare's diminutive grey stone church, in a quiet valley overlooking Oare Water, was the setting in R D Blackmore's famous story, *Lorna Doone*, for the heroine's wedding to John Ridd; 18th-century box pews lead to the altar where the ceremony was interrupted by a gun shot. A plaque by the oak door commemorates the author who brought the area fame.

🚗 *Go through Malmsmead and Brendon to rejoin A39 towards Lynmouth. Follow signs to town car parks.*

❻ Lynmouth

Devon; EX35 6EQ

Picturesquely set at the foot of the wooded valleys of the East and West Lyn rivers, this former herring fishing village is best known for the terrible flood in August 1952. After torrential rain, flash floods washed away the harbour and nearby houses, killing 34 people. The **Flood Memorial Hall** commemorates the disaster with a scale model of the village as it was. From the seafront, an ingenious water-powered cliff railway, opened in 1888, glides 263 m (862 ft) up a steep track to **Lynton** – an exciting two-minute ride with fabulous coastal views *(open*

The Story of Lorna Doone

Stories of an outlaw family, the Doones, who terrorized Exmoor in the 17th century fired the fertile imagination of local author RD Blackmore. In his 1869 novel *Lorna Doone*, he tells the story of John Ridd, an Oare farmer who falls in love with the Doones' adopted daughter, Lorna. He vividly describes the countryside, disguising many of the real locations. Today, leafy footpaths run from Oare and Malmsmead to the so-called Doone Valley. Beyond Blackmore Memorial by Badgworthy Water, look out for Lank Combe Water – was this the secret waterfall that John Ridd climbed?

daily mid-Feb–Oct). Lynton is a small town looking out to sea with a pretty **church**, which has a Norman font and a 13th-century tower.

🚗 *Take B3234 to Lynton, then A39 (signed Barnstaple). Turn left on a minor road (signed) for Arlington Court 1.5 km (1 mile) after Kentisbury Ford.*

❼ Arlington Court and the National Trust Carriage Museum

Arlington, Parracombe; Devon; EX31 4LP

This Regency house *(open daily Mar–Oct; 01271 850 296; www.nationaltrust.org.uk)* is packed with treasures. The stables in the Deer Park house over 50 horse-drawn carriages; rides are available most days.

🚗 *Return to Kentisbury Ford on A39, turn left on B3229 and follow signs to Ilfracombe on A399. Take A361 out of town, turn right onto B3343 and follow signs to Mortehoe on minor road to right. Park in the village.*

Above Pretty harbour town of Lynmouth, rebuilt after the flood of 1952

EAT AND DRINK

TAUNTON

Willow Tree *moderate*
Housed in a 300-year-old gabled building, and noted for its imaginative dishes. *3 Tower Lane, TA1 4AR; 01823 352 835; www.thewillowtree restaurant.com; open eves Tue, Wed, Fri & Sat; booking essential*

SELWORTHY

Periwinkle Tearoom *moderate*
This 17th-century thatched cottage is perfect for a cream tea or snack. *Selworthy Green, TA24 8TP; 01643 862 452; open in daytime Easter–Oct: Tue–Sun; Aug: also Mon*

AROUND SELWORTHY

Piggy in the Middle *moderate*
Small family-run restaurant specializing in fish and chips, and pies. *2 High Street, TA24 8PS (4 km/ 2.5 miles on A39 from Selworthy); 01643 862 647; open Tue–Sat; also Jul–Aug: Sun–Mon*

Below A carriage ride at Arlington Court and the National Trust Carriage Museum

Eat and Drink: inexpensive, under £25; moderate, £25–£50; expensive, over £50

Above St Mary's Church, Mortehoe, with graves of shipwrecked sailors

VISITING BARNSTAPLE

Parking
Green Lanes Shopping Centre,
Boutport Street, EX31 1UL.

Tourist Information
*The Square, EX32 8LN; 01271 375 000;
www.staynorthdevon.co.uk*

WHERE TO STAY

MORTEHOE

Town Farmhouse *inexpensive*
Former farm B&B opposite the church.
*EX34 7DT; 01271 870 204; www.
townfarmhouse.co.uk; open Feb–Nov*

WOOLACOMBE

Woolacombe Bay *expensive*
Large seafront hotel overlooking the
beach with plenty of sporting facilities.
*EX34 7BN; 01271 870 388; www.
woolacombe-bay-hotel.co.uk*

BARNSTAPLE

Royal & Fortescue Hotel *moderate*
Former coaching inn, centrally situated,
with restaurant, bistro and cafe-bar.
*Boutport Street, EX31 1HG; 01271 342
289; www.brend-hotels.co.uk*

❽ Mortehoe
Devon; EX34 7DT

This is one of the most spectacular stretches of the South West Coast Path, England's longest National Trail. A footpath leads along the clifftops from Mortehoe over grassy slopes to Morte Point. In the ancient village of Mortehoe, mentioned in the Domesday Book, a handful of pubs and tearooms cluster around the picturesque 13th-century St Mary's Church, and just around a headland is the golden sandy beach of Woolacombe.

A two-hour clifftop walk

Start at the pay-and-display car park at the end of Station Road and visit the **Heritage Centre** ① *(open Easter–Oct: Tue–Thu, Sat–Sun; also Jul–Aug: Mon)* to learn about the history of the area.

Exit the car park, turn left towards the church passing the Post Office and Village Store – good for provisions. Go through the Victorian lych gate for a look inside **St Mary's Church** ②. Though the entrance porch dates from around 1500, the barrel-roofed nave and chancel were built during the 13th century. The square belfry, which houses six bells, dates from 1275. Much of the decoration is Victorian; the pretty stained-glass windows were re-glazed at this time.

To the right of the church a sign points to the coastal path. Walk to the left of the village cemetery along the path fringed with bracken and gorse. Over a sheep-dotted hillside, the path drops sharply down to a stream where it meets the 1,000-km (630-mile) South West Coast Path running along the clifftop.

There are views past Woolacombe south across Morte Bay to the next headland, Baggy Point, and beyond. Lundy Island is visible out to sea 27 km (17 miles) away and the South Wales coast is just discernible. Walk along the clifftop towards Morte Point, watching the waves crash onto jagged slate rocks. Just past the aptly named **Windy Cove** ③, sticking out of the sea, is Morte Stone (Death Stone), a reminder of the dangers of the rocky reef. In the winter of 1852, five ships were sadly lost off this most treacherous coast. Continue to **Morte Point** ④ itself, and rest on one of the white boulders to admire the seascape – look out for seals on the rocks below. Follow the path around the point to go eastwards.

Turn inland at the sign to Mortehoe and return via a wide grassy path. For a short detour, walk up to the 137-m (450-ft) viewpoint (signed on left) and the megalithic tomb, known as the Cromlech, nearby. Finally, retrace your steps back to the village for a cream tea or a glass of heady local scrumpy cider.

🚗 *Follow signs along a narrow seaside road to Woolacombe and park in the beach car park.*

Below The road down to lovely Woolacombe Bay, North Devon

9 Woolacombe
Devon; EX34 7DL

Woolacombe's beach, which stretches for nearly 5 km (3 miles), is regularly voted one of the world's best. Backed by dunes and washed by Atlantic waves, the beach attracts surfers year round. **Nick Thorn Surf School** (www.nickthorn.com) offers lessons. Clamber over rocks at the north end to Barricane Beach to hunt for shells washed here from the Caribbean. Above the beach is a memorial to American forces who trained there for the D-Day landings in 1944.

🚗 *Follow signs along minor roads to Croyde. Then take B3231 towards Braunton, turning right (opposite sign to Lobb) onto a narrow road to Braunton Burrows car park.*

10 Braunton Burrows
Braunton; EX33 2NU

Behind Saunton Sands, Braunton Burrows is the largest area of sand dunes in England, stretching 6.5 km (4 miles). With 500 species of wild flowers and 33 of butterflies, the area is a SSSI (Site of Special Scientific Interest) and part of North Devon's UNESCO Biosphere Reserve. Kestrels,

skylarks and curlews can often be seen flying overhead. The site of practice beach landings during World War II, the dunes are still used by the army for 10 days a year.

🚗 *Return on the same road, but take first right (unmarked narrow road) to join A361 to Barnstaple. Park in Green Lanes Shopping Centre (signposted).*

11 Barnstaple
Devon; EX32 8LN

The town's fortunes as a sea port have declined but Barnstaple's market still bustles with life in the 150-year-old timber-framed **Pannier Market** (open Mon–Sat). On the Strand riverside promenade, the town's 18th-century maritime heyday is depicted in the **Heritage Centre** (open Tue–Sat). At the end of the Strand is the **Museum of Barnstaple and North Devon** (closed Sun) with an eccentric collection of local archaeology, natural history and crafts. The best views of the scenic Taw Estuary can be enjoyed by cycling the **Tarka Trail**, along a stretch of old railway track. Hire bikes from **Tarka Trail Cycle Hire** (The Railway Station; 01271 324 202; www.tarkatrail.co.uk).

Above The wooden-framed Pannier Market (1855), Barnstaple **Right** South West Coast Path on the way to Mortehoe, Devon

EAT AND DRINK

MORTEHOE

Chichester Arms inexpensive
Next to the church, this 16th-century pub was once the vicarage. It serves good ales and food with a beer garden. *EX34 7DU; 01271 870 411*

AROUND MORTEHOE

The Quay expensive
Artist Damien Hirst's fish restaurant has dining rooms facing harbour and sea. *Take B3343 and turn left on A361 to Ilfracombe; 11 The Quay, Ilfracombe, EX34 9EQ; 01271 868 090; www.11thequay.com*

WOOLACOMBE

Red Barn inexpensive
Lively bar-restaurant near the beach, popular with surfers and families. *The Esplanade, EX34 7DF; 01271 870 264; www.redbarnwoolacombe.co.uk*

AROUND BRAUNTON BURROWS

Squire's Fish Restaurant moderate
Renowned as the best place in the area for traditional fish and chips – large portions and top quality. *Exeter Road, Braunton, EX33 1JR; 01271 815 533*

DAY TRIP OPTIONS

There is a variety of great days out based all around Exmoor.

West Somerset Railway
Start at Taunton ❶ to see St Mary's Church; then it's on to Washford ❷ to visit Cleeve Abbey, before taking a trip on this preserved railway line through the Somerset countryside.

Take the A358 north from Taunton and then left on the A39 to Washford.

Beaches and Coastal Trails
Work up an appetite building sandcastles at Woolacombe ❾, hike the South West Coast Path at Mortehoe ❽ and then indulge in a cream tea.

Follow the B3343 to Woolacombe's car

parks, off the A361, then follow signs to Mortehoe and park in the village.

Lorna Doone Country
Visit the castle at Dunster ❸, then climb Dunkery Beacon for views of Exmoor and follow the Lorna Doone Trail from Oare ❺.

Dunster and Oare are both off the A39.

Hardy Country and the Jurassic Coast

Swanage to Sherborne

Highlights

- **Rolling Dorset hills**
  Meander through Dorset's inland hills and valleys, adorned with giant chalk figures and medieval castles

- **Dinosaur coast**
  Admire the striking formations of Durdle Door, Chesil Beach and fossil-rich Purbeck and Portland

- **Thomas Hardy's home town**
  Explore Thomas Hardy's Dorchester and the remnants of its Roman and prehistoric past

- **Ancient abbeys and churches**
  Marvel at the medieval craftsmanship of tiny churches and the inspiring fan-vaulting of Sherborne Abbey

Spectacular Durdle Door and Bay with the chalk cliffs of the Jurassic Coast

Hardy Country and the Jurassic Coast

Dorset is one of England's comeliest counties, renowned for its soft, undulating hills and cliff-backed coastline. There are few conurbations to blot the landscape, instead gentle sheep-speckled slopes and mellow green prospects soothe the traveller's eye. The past looms large here, from the fossil-rich Jurassic Coast to Ancient British sites, and from Roman remains to medieval monuments. Literary types know the region for its associations with Thomas Hardy and his works, in which it appears as "Wessex", while Hardy's own town of Dorchester ("Casterbridge") offers plenty of entertainment for children and adults alike.

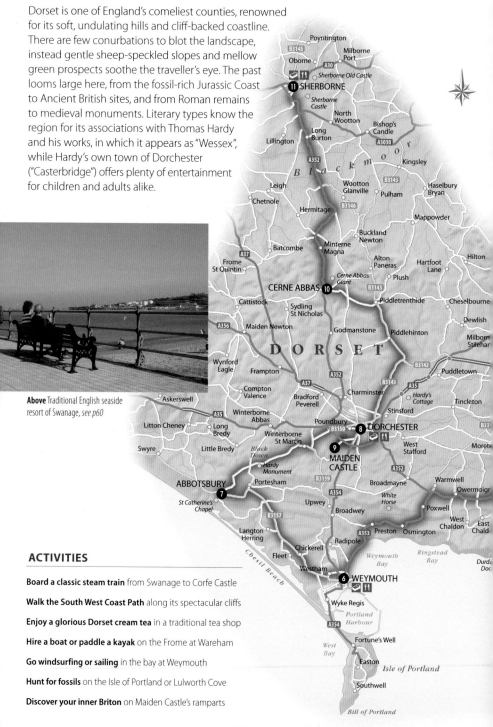

Above Traditional English seaside resort of Swanage, *see p60*

ACTIVITIES

Board a classic steam train from Swanage to Corfe Castle

Walk the South West Coast Path along its spectacular cliffs

Enjoy a glorious Dorset cream tea in a traditional tea shop

Hire a boat or paddle a kayak on the Frome at Wareham

Go windsurfing or sailing in the bay at Weymouth

Hunt for fossils on the Isle of Portland or Lulworth Cove

Discover your inner Briton on Maiden Castle's ramparts

Above The peaceful country village of Abbotsbury, *see p61*

KEY

━━━ Drive route

PLAN YOUR DRIVE

Start/finish: Swanage to Sherborne.

Number of days: 3 days allowing a half-day's tour of Dorchester.

Distance: Around 129 km (80 miles).

Road conditions: Good roads, but sometimes narrow and steep.

When to go: It is possible to tour the area any time of year, but best to try and avoid public holidays and summer weekends, when traffic is heaviest around the coast.

Opening times: Museums and attractions are generally open 10am–5pm, but close earlier (or are closed altogether) Nov–Easter. Shop opening hours are longer. Churches are usually open until dusk.

Main market days: Swanage: Fri; Wareham: Thu & Sat; **Weymouth**: Thu; Dorchester: 4th Sat of month; Sherborne: Thu & Sat, also Farmer's Market on 3rd Fri of month.

Shopping: Dorset is famed for its creamy Blue Vinny cheese; sweet cinnamon-rich Dorset apple cake, and delicious locally produced chutneys and jams.

Major festivals: Swanage: Jazz Festival, Jul; Wareham: Music Festival, Aug; Weymouth: Seafood Festival, Jul; Weymouth Regatta, Jul.

DAY TRIP OPTIONS

Dorchester's many **museums** and **ancient sights** have something for everyone – but especially **dinosaur hunters**; follow the theory with some practical **fossil hunting** on Chesil Beach and Portland. From Swanage enjoy a ride on a **steam train**, visit a **crumbling Norman castle** and then head to the coast to explore the **beach** and awesome **rock formations** near Lulworth. For full details, *see p63*.

Above The pretty stone-quarrying town of Worth Matravers

VISITING SWANAGE

Parking
There's a short-stay car park behind the tourist office, on Horsecliffe Lane, off Victoria Avenue. There's also a longer stay car park on Victoria Ave (A351).

Tourist Information
The White House, Shore Road, BH19 1LB; 01929 422 885; www.swanage.gov.uk

WHERE TO STAY

SWANAGE

Grand Hotel Swanage *moderate*
This old-fashioned Victorian palace has terrific views over the Bay, a splendid lawn and a cocktail lounge.
Burlington Road, BH19 1LU; 01929 423 353; www.grandhotelswanage.co.uk

AROUND WAREHAM

Kemps Country House *expensive*
West of Wareham, off the A352, this former Victorian rectory offers clean, modern and well-equipped rooms.
East Stoke, BH20 6AL (5 km/3 miles on A352 and B3070 from Wareham); 01929 462 563; www.kempscountry house.co.uk

WEYMOUTH

Hotel Rembrandt *moderate*
A 78-room hotel with restaurant, bar, spa and indoor pool.
Doncaster Road, DT4 7JU; 01305 764 000; www.hotelrembrandt.co.uk

Roundhouse Hotel *moderate*
B&B with six rooms in a Georgian townhouse facing the sea, with the 17th-century harbour just behind it.
1 The Esplanade, DT4 8EA; 01305 761 010; www.roundhouse-weymouth.com

① Swanage
Dorset; BH19 1LB
This is a quintessential Victorian resort with a seafront promenade, Punch and Judy shows and a fine sandy beach that curves around Swanage Bay. For something wilder, head 7 km (4 miles) north to **Studland Bay** – the tourist office by the beach has maps for walkers, or take bus no. 50 from Shore Road. The town is not without interest either. The stone façade of the **Town Hall**, built 1833, was taken from the Mercers' Hall in London (designed by Christopher Wren) when it was being remodelled – notice the cherubs holding cloths for the Virgin Mary. Board a **Swanage Railway** *(Apr–Oct)* steam train for a visit to Corfe Castle.

🚗 *Leave on A351, left on B3069 and left to Worth Matravers. Park behind pub.*

② Worth Matravers
Dorset; BH19 3LF
This tiny village's attractions include **The Square and Compass** pub *(see right)*, inspiring views (can be enjoyed from the pub's outdoor tables), and a graceful Norman church, **St Nicholas**. Dating from the late 12th century, the church has a wood-beamed roof and a jagged chancel arch. This is a great place to enjoy a walk along the **South West Coast Path**, starting on one of the footpaths that radiate from the village to the coast on either side.

🚗 *Turn left out of the car park, then left onto the B3069 to A351, then left to Corfe village, castle and car park.*

Below The historic restored railway line at Swanage

Lawrence of Arabia, Wareham

Lawrence of Arabia in Dorset
T E Lawrence – dubbed "Lawrence of Arabia" for his World War I exploits – spent his post-war life in quiet Dorset. See his effigy in Wareham and cottage at **Clouds Hill** *(late Mar–late Oct: open Thu–Sun)*. From here, it's possible to walk to the site of his fatal motorbike crash, to his grave in **Moreton** and to **Bovington Camp** where he briefly served – now a **tank museum** *(open daily)*.

③ Corfe Castle
Dorset; BH20 5EZ
The silhouette of the crumbling castle ruins *(open daily)* that dominate this village presents a truly romantic vista. This once mighty Norman bastion owes its present decrepit state to the English Civil War (1641–51), when Lady Bankes defended it against Parliamentarian troops, who finally blew the castle up after a six-week siege.

🚗 *Carry on along the A351, then take B3075, signposted Stoborough, for Wareham. Car park is on right over river.*

④ Wareham
Dorset; BH20 4LU
Located on the River Frome close to the sea, Wareham was an important port in Saxon times. Now a pretty backwater, it preserves the layout of its old town walls. **St Martin's Church** also has much of its Saxon structure, medieval frescoes and a romantic effigy of T E Lawrence *(see box above)*. Hire a rowing boat or kayak at the bridge and enjoy a river trip from

Far left Corfe Castle's dramatic Norman hilltop ruins **Left** The peaceful town of Wareham, located on the River Frome

Wareham Boat Hire *(01929 550 688; www.warehamboathire.co.uk; Mar–Oct)*.

🚗 *Leave town on A352, turn left on B3070, signed Lulworth Cove, through West Lulworth to the cove and car park.*

⑤ Lulworth Cove
Dorset; BH20 5RQ

Below the Purbeck Hills with dramatic chalk cliffs lie a series of enticing shingle and shale beaches, reached by the coastal path. One of these, the nearly circular **Lulworth Cove** fills with small vessels in summer and offers sheltered swimming. A 15-minute walk west stands spectacular **Durdle Door**, a natural limestone archway in the sea at the popular beach, Durdle Bay. Purbeck's seaboard forms part of the **Jurassic Coast**, a World Heritage Site whose geological makeup has yielded a rich trove of fossil finds.

🚗 *From West Lulworth, follow signs for Dorchester, passing the turn for Durdle Door. Turn left on A352 and left again on the A353 to Weymouth and the town centre – park at ferry terminal.*

⑥ Weymouth
Dorset; DT8 4ED

With its sandy beach, promenade, Punch & Judy and donkey rides, Weymouth is a typical traditional English resort. Sailing, kitesurfing and windsurfing are popular activities, especially since the town hosted

sailing events in the 2012 Olympics. To the south, the **Isle of Portland**, connected to the mainland by a causeway, has a wild coastline worth exploring – dinosaur footprints have been found here. Northwest stretches the 29-km (18-mile) pebble strand of **Chesil Beach**, a bleak, unearthly expanse backed by the Fleet Lagoon, a nature reserve.

🚗 *Take the B3157 northwest, following signs to Abbotsbury.*

⑦ Abbotsbury
Dorset; DT3 4JT

The only remaining building of a Benedictine Abbey, a15th-century tithe barn now houses a **Children's Farm** *(mid-Mar–early Sep & half-term: open daily; early Sep–Oct: open weekends)*, where kids can get close to a range of animals. There is also a garden filled with exotic plants, and the **Swannery** *(mid-Mar–Oct: open daily)*, home to a colony of mute swans, best visited in June, when the swans nest and the young hatch. Climb up to the hilltop **St Catherine's Chapel** for stupendous views (and the path to the Swannery).

🚗 *Turn right at Strangeways Hall and leave via Back St on a steep, narrow ascent with great coastal views. Cross over the junction, following signs to the Hardy Monument. Turn right onto B3159 and left to Dorchester. Park in town centre off Acland Road.*

EAT AND DRINK

SWANAGE

Bull and Boat *moderate*
Enjoy fabulous beach views from this modern eatery with a strong seafood menu. Try the lobster served with steak and giant prawns or the sea bass cooked with leeks and mushrooms. *2 Ulwell Road, BH19 1LH; 01929 422 222; www.bullandboat.co.uk*

WORTH MATRAVERS

The Square and Compass *inexpensive*
Great pasties and real ales are served at this excellent flagstoned pub with great views and a small museum of fossils and other local finds. *Worth Matravers, BH19 3LF; 01929 439 229; www.squareandcompasspub.co.uk*

CORFE CASTLE

Morton's House *inexpensive–moderate*
This 16th-century manor house has been tastefully converted into a smart hotel-restaurant. Lunch on soups, salads and snacks in the bar, or guinea fowl or halibut in the more formal restaurant. *East St, BH20 5EE; 01929 480 988; www.mortonshouse.co.uk*

WEYMOUTH

Old Rooms Inn *inexpensive*
Right by the fishing harbour, with tables outside, this pub offers a range of snacks from salads to burgers and grills, as well as real ales. *Cove Row, DT4 8TT; 01305 771 130*

Crab House Café *moderate*
On Fleet Lagoon, this simple shack with a few wooden tables serves superb fresh seafood such as Portland crab and huge prawns in tarragon butter. *The Oyster Farm, Ferryman's Way, DT4 9YU; 01305 788 867; open Wed–Sun; booking essential; www.crabhousecafe.co.uk*

Below left Traditional seaside facilities at Weymouth's sandy beach **Below right** Sheltered, horseshoe-shaped bay of Lulworth Cove

VISITING DORCHESTER

Tourist Information
11 Antelope Walk, DT1 1BE; 01305 267 992; www.visit-dorset.com

Parking
Park in the town centre, off Acland Road. There is an additional car park nearby on Durngate Street.

WHERE TO STAY

DORCHESTER

Westwood House *inexpensive*
This centrally located B&B in a smart Georgian town house offers six well-equipped rooms. Lavish breakfasts are served in an airy conservatory.
29 High West Street, DT1 1UP; 01305 268 018; www.westwoodhouse.co.uk

The Casterbridge *moderate*
A range of six cosy rooms are available at this family-run hotel on the main street, including one with a four-poster and one with its own patio.
49 High East Street, DT1 1HU; 01305 264 043; www.casterbridgehotel.co.uk

SHERBORNE

The Bakehouse *inexpensive*
Dating from the 18th century, this friendly B&B with flagstone floors has plenty of period character. The rooms are comfortable and of a good size.
1 Acreman Street, DT9 3NU; 01935 817 969; www.bakehouse.me.uk

The Eastbury Hotel *moderate*
Close to the Abbey, this Georgian hotel has a one-acre (4,000-sq metre) walled garden. Public rooms are welcoming, bedrooms are spacious and the staff are friendly. The award-winning restaurant is worth trying, too.
Long Street, DT9 3BY; 01935 813 131, www.theeastburyhotel.co.uk

❽ Dorchester
Dorset; DT1 1BE

With Georgian architecture, tree-lined avenues and quirky museums, Dorchester is also associated with Thomas Hardy as the "Casterbridge" of his novels. Look, too, for reminders of the infamous Judge Jeffreys (1645–89), the Tolpuddle Martyrs, and the town's early Roman inhabitants.

A two-hour walking tour
From the car park, head south, then left onto tree-lined South Walks Rd and on to the **Dorset Martyrs** ① – three bronze figures carved in 1986 by modernist sculptor Elisabeth Frink. Cross Icen Way, then go left on a path across Salisbury Fields to Salisbury St. The **Teddy Bear Museum** ② is at the end of this street, in the same building as the **Terracotta Warriors Museum** *(both open daily)*, dedicated to the red clay army of China's first emperor. Exit left into High East St, and left again into Icen Way to find the entertaining **Dinosaur Museum** ③ *(open daily)*. From here, turn right and follow Durngate St and left on South St to

Barclays Bank ④, said to have been the Mayor of Casterbridge's house in Thomas Hardy's novel. Retrace your steps up South St, which becomes Corn Hill. On the left, the entrance to the **Antelope Walk Shopping Arcade** ⑤ was once the Antelope Hotel, mentioned in *The Mayor of Caster-bridge* and where Judge Jeffreys held his "Bloody Assizes" condemning 74 of those rebelling against James II to death in 1685.

At the top of Corn Hill, turn left into High West St. **St Peter's Church** ⑥, on the right, is mainly 15th century (Thomas Hardy helped to restore it as an apprentice in the 1850s). To the left of the church is the **Dorset County Museum** ⑦ *(closed Sun, except Jul–Sep)*, detailing the cultural and geological history of the region. Past the museum is the **Old Crown Court** ⑧ *(open Mon–Fri)*, where the Tolpuddle Martyrs were sent to Australia for trying to form an agricultural union in 1834. Over the road the **Tutankhamun Exhibition** ⑨ *(open daily)* gives an insight into the life and burial of this Egyptian boy-king.

Cross back over High West St and turn into Glyde Path Rd,

0 metres 250
0 yards 250

following it to the **Roman Town House** ⑩ *(open daily)*. The ruins reveal the elaborate heating system and mosaic floors. At the end of Northernhay, turn left into The Grove, and on to a statue of Thomas Hardy. Cross The Grove and walk up Bridport Rd to the fascinating **Keep Military Museum** ⑪ *(Apr–Sep: open Mon–Sat; Oct–Mar: open Tue–Fri)*, revealing the history of local army regiments. From here, return to High West St to see a fragment of **Roman Wall** ⑫ by Princes St. Cross here and follow West Walks, turning right at the end then left into Cornwall Rd; cross Gt Western Rd into Maumbury Rd, and head to the **Maumbury Rings** ⑬, a Neolithic henge, then a Roman amphitheatre and later a place of public execution. Return on Weymouth Ave to South Walks Rd, back to the car park.

🚗 *Head south on Weymouth Ave, turning off right on Maiden Castle Rd.*

⑨ Maiden Castle
Dorset; DT2 9PP
Prehistoric **Maiden Castle** *(open daily)* is the largest Iron-Age hillfort in Europe. The vast and complex structure of 6-m (20-ft) ramparts and trenches

Above The chalk carving of the Cerne Giant, possibly a fertility symbol

is now all grassed over but the undulating banks vividly evoke the ancient fortification (450–300 BC), overcome by the Romans in AD 43.

🚗 *Return to A35, heading east around Dorchester, turn left on B3150 and right on B3143. At Piddletrenthide, turn left, following signs for Cerne Abbas, up a narrow, steep lane.*

⑩ Cerne Abbas
Dorset; DT2 7JF
Amid the timbered, golden houses of Cerne Abbas stands **St Mary's Church**, dating from the 13th century and boasting a rare stone chancel screen. However, the village is most famous for the **Cerne Giant**, a chalk carving on a hillside north of the village. Little is known about the origins of the 55-m (180-ft) figure, wielding a club and proudly displaying his manhood. It was first recorded in 1694, though some historians believe it dates from around 190 AD, possibly depicting Hercules – it has long been the site of fertility rituals. To view it, turn up Duck St from Long St, following signs for the Giant and a parking area.

🚗 *Turn right out of the viewing area, on the A352, signed Sherborne. Follow signs to Abbey and park opposite.*

⑪ Sherborne
Dorset; DT9 3NL
The chief glory of this charming stone town is **Sherborne Abbey**, a fine example of Perpendicular architecture whose fan-vaulted ceiling is studded with colourful bosses depicting such images as a mermaid, an owl and a dog with a bone. To the east of town stand the ruined **Old Castle** *(Apr–Oct: open daily)*, dating from the 12th century, and the **New Castle** *(Apr–Oct: open Tue–Thu, Sat & Sun)*, built for Sir Walter Raleigh in 1594, with grand state rooms, a Tudor kitchen and now with parkland by "Capability" Brown.

Above Sherborne Abbey, featuring Saxon, Norman and Perpendicular architecture

EAT AND DRINK

DORCHESTER
The Fridge *inexpensive*
Blue Vinny cheese, Dorset Apple Cake and other local specialities are stocked in this award-winning delicatessen.
17 Tudor Arcade, DT1 1BN; 01305 269 088; www.thefridge.biz

Judge Jeffreys *inexpensive*
Great Italian cuisine is served in this former residence of the infamous Judge Jeffreys, with panelled dining areas.
6 High West Street, DT1 1UJ; 01305 259 678; www.prezzoplc.co.uk

Potters *inexpensive*
This casual but smart café offers a healthy selection of home-cooked food, from snack lunches to cakes.
19 Durngate St, DT1 1JP; 01305 260 312

SHERBORNE
The Green *moderate*
Sophisticated modern European cuisine in a semi-formal restaurant using fresh, locally sourced produce.
3 The Green, DT9 3HY; 01935 813 821 www.greenrestaurant.co.uk

The Dining Room *expensive*
Smart restaurant serving British cuisine in an 18th-century building that was originally a school for poor girls.
Westbury, DT9 3EH; 01935 815 154; www.thediningroomsherborne.com

---

DAY TRIP OPTIONS
Dorchester and Swanage are both good bases for exploring the coastline, beaches and museums.

Jurassic Adventure
Spend a morning at Dorchester's ⑧ Dinosaur Museum and Dorset County Museum, pack a picnic and head to

Weymouth ❻ for some fossil-hunting on Chesil Beach or Portland – but keep away from the cliffs. If there's time make a trip to Abbotsbury ❼ with its children's farm and swannery.

Weymouth is on the A354 from Dorchester, then use the B3157 for Chesil Beach; return as per the drive.

Coast and Castles
From Swanage ❶, ride a steam train before lunching at Worth Matravers ❷. Then head on to Corfe Castle ❸ and Wareham ❹, and finish off the day at Lulworth Cove ❺ or Durdle Door.

Take the A351, B3069, A351 and B3070; skip Wareham, if short of time.

Eat and Drink: inexpensive, under £25; moderate, £25–£50; expensive, over £50

A Spiritual Journey

Salisbury to Glastonbury

Highlights

- **Medieval Salisbury**
  Unearth the medieval wonders of Salisbury, crowned by its venerable cathedral and the tallest spire in the UK

- **Neolithic stone circles**
  Experience the different character of England's prehistoric stone circles, from the majesty of Stonehenge to the solemnity of Avebury

- **Inland waterways**
  Soak up the tranquillity of the Kennet and Avon Canal on foot, by bike or on a gentle boat cruise

- **Georgian Bath**
  Follow in the footsteps of Jane Austen in this panoply of Georgian architecture, and tour the ancient, naturally heated baths

The elegant and stately architecture of Bath, by the River Avon

A Spiritual Journey

From the lovely city of Salisbury, dominated by its iconic cathedral spire, to the graceful Georgian terraces of Bath, and west to medieval Wells, this drive takes in some of England's most compelling historic centres. En route, there are appealing stretches of countryside: the grand swathes of Salisbury Plain and the rolling pastures of Somerset, studded by the Mendip Hills, an Area of Outstanding Natural Beauty. And along the way are many reminders of the distant past, in which ancient religions have left their mark: Stonehenge is the most famous of Britain's prehistoric stone circles, but lesser-visited circles exist at Avebury and Stanton Drew. The final stop is Glastonbury, where religion, history and myth are all magically mixed together.

Below Elaborate pinnacles of Bath Abbey, seen across the River Avon, Bath *see pp71–2*

ACTIVITIES

Stroll through Salisbury's water meadows to find the spot from which Constable painted his Salisbury Cathedral picture

Take a tour of the Wadworth Brewery, Devizes

Hire a skiff or narrowboat from Devizes or Bradford-on-Avon to tour the Kennet and Avon Canal

Rejuvenate at Thermae Bath Spa, the modern bathing complex at the heart of Bath

Hike in the Mendip Hills around the beautiful Ebbor Gorge

Rent a bike in Glastonbury and experience the tranquillity of the Somerset Levels, west of town

0 kilometres 5

0 miles 5

KEY

🚋 Drive route

Below Narrowboats on the Kennet and Avon Canal, near Bradford-on-Avon, *see p70*

PLAN YOUR DRIVE

Start/finish: Salisbury to Glastonbury.

Number of days: 4, allowing for a half-day each in Salisbury and Bath.

Distance: 180 km (112 miles).

Road conditions: Good, but allow for congestion in and around Bath.

When to go: Weekdays are best for Salisbury, Stonehenge and Bath, to miss the crowds. Glastonbury is very busy either side of the last weekend of June, when the festival takes place.

Opening times: Attractions are generally open 10am–5pm, but close earlier (or close completely) Nov–Easter. Shops stay open longer. Churches are usually open until dusk.

Market days: Salisbury: Charter Market, Tue & Sat; Farmers' Market, Wed; Devizes: 1st Sat of month; Bath: Farmers' Market, Sat (Green Park Station); Indoor Market, Mon–Sat (Guildhall).

Shopping: Look out for authentic Cheddar cheese in the Mendip Hills – especially in the Cheddar Gorge and discounted Clarks shoes in Street, south of Glastonbury. Anyone interested in New Age trinkets will enjoy Glastonbury.

Major festivals: Salisbury: International Arts Festival (2 wks May–Jun); Food and Drink Festival (mid-Sep); Bath: International Music Festival (12 days May–Jun); Jane Austen Festival (9 days late Sep); Glastonbury: Music Festival (around last weekend Jun).

DAY TRIP OPTIONS

From Salisbury, take in the **prehistoric stone rings, ancient monuments** and **ditches** of Old Sarum, Stonehenge and Avebury. Fans of **architecture** and **shopping** can happily spend several hours exploring Bath followed by a trip to Bradford-on-Avon for **Anglo-Saxon buildings** and then to **medieval** Lacock Abbey. A morning spent touring Wells and Glastonbury will appeal to lovers of **medieval churches**, while cavers and nature-lovers will appreciate the **walks, gorges and wildlife** found among the Mendip Hills. For full details, *see p73*.

Above Salisbury Cathedral, with the tallest spire in the UK **Top right** Narrowboat on the Kennet and Avon Canal, Devizes **Bottom right** Ruins of the Bishop's Palace, Old Sarum

VISITING SALISBURY

Parking
The best car park in Salisbury is Central Car Park (signed) by the Playhouse.

Tourist Information
Fish Row, SP1 1EJ; 01722 342 860; www.visitsalisbury.com

WHERE TO STAY

SALISBURY

Cathedral View *moderate*
Welcoming B&B behind the Cathedral and with views of it from the front rooms; all four rooms are en suite.
83 Exeter Street, SP1 2SE; 01722 502 254; www.cathedral-viewbandb.co.uk

Red Lion Hotel *moderate–expensive*
This characterful coaching inn dates back to the 17th century and is filled with curios and period pieces.
Milford Street, SP1 2AN; 01722 323 334; www.the-redlion.co.uk

DEVIZES

The Bear Hotel *moderate*
This hotel has included royalty among its guests. Comfortable rooms, and live jazz or blues in the cellar at weekends.
Market Place, SN10 1HS; 01380 722 444; www.thebearhotel.net

AVEBURY

The Lodge *expensive*
Wake amid the stones in this lovely 18th-century vegetarian B&B. Only two rooms so book ahead.
High Street, SN8 1RF; 01672 539 023; www.aveburylodge.co.uk

① Salisbury
Wiltshire; SP1 1EJ
One of Britain's great cathedral cities, Salisbury has a compact centre that is ideal for a leisurely stroll. **Salisbury Cathedral** *(open daily)*, built over a period of just 38 years in the 13th century, is an unusually fine example of Early English Gothic. The soaring 123-m (404-ft) tower can be explored on a guided tour and the library holds an original copy of Magna Carta. Learn more about the city's history, as well as that of Old Sarum and Stonehenge in the **Salisbury and South Wiltshire Museum** *(open Mon–Sat; daily Jun–Sep)*, behind the cathedral. Finally, take a short stroll west of the cathedral to the water meadows, to enjoy the classic city views painted by John Constable.
🚗 *From the centre, head north on Castle St onto the A345; park on site.*

Below The huge, impressive Neolithic stone complex at Stonehenge

② Old Sarum
Wiltshire; SP1 3SD
On a windswept hilltop, formidable earthworks and scanty Norman remains mark the site of Old Sarum *(open daily)*, an important settlement that flourished from around 500 BC. Occupied later by the Romans and Saxons, it was then fortified by the Normans who also built a cathedral here in the 12th century. The site was abandoned in the next century, when Salisbury became the regional centre.
🚗 *Turn left out of Old Sarum onto the A345, then left to Upper Woodford. Follow the road until it joins the A303, turn right for Stonehenge. Bear right on the A344 past the stones to the car park.*

The riddle of the stones
Composed of a ring of upright stones topped with lintels, a horseshoe of trilithons (two uprights and a lintel), and a ring of bluestones, Stonehenge remains a mystery. Why was it built? How were the stones moved here, some from as far away as the Preseli Hills in Wales? The most extraordinary fact is that the whole complex was built without any more sophisticated tools than picks made from antlers and shovels made from bone.

③ Stonehenge
Wiltshire; SP4 7DE
England's grandest and best preserved stone circle appears dwarfed by the expanse of Salisbury Plain. Built in stages between 3,000 BC and 1,600 BC, the huge stones and earthworks originally formed part of a much larger complex. The exact function of Stonehenge *(open daily)* is obscure but, given the alignment of the stones relative to the rising and setting sun, it is likely to have had an astronomical and religious function. Its location at

the heart of a dense area of Neolithic and Bronze Age monuments and burial mounds adds to its aura of spirituality. There is no direct access to the stones (visitors must follow a path around them) but free audioguides provide an informative commentary.

Turn right out of the car park and continue northwest along the A344 and A360 to Devizes.

Above Elegant façade of Bowood House, one of the finest stately homes in England

④ Devizes
Wiltshire; SN10 1JG

This historic market town has one of the region's finest main streets, graced by elegant buildings from all eras. On Long St, the **Wiltshire Heritage Museum** *(closed Jan–Mar: Mon)* traces the history of the county from earliest times and has an excellent prehistoric collection. Take an enlightening tour of the Victorian **Wadworth Brewery** *(open Mon–Sat; 01380 723 361; www. wadworth.co.uk)*, on New Park St, with tastings on most days. A brief walk west of town along the **Kennet and Avon Canal** leads to Caen Hill Locks, an extraordinary flight of 29 locks. The canal, which stretches for nearly 96 km (60 miles) between Newbury and Bath, dates from 1810. Explore the outstanding beauty of this great waterway on a narrowboat rented from **Devizes Marina**, north off the A361 *(01380 725 300; www.devizesmarina.co.uk)*.

Head northeast along A361, turn right at a roundabout, through Horton and past a white horse on the chalk hills. Turn left towards Marlborough, then left for East Kennett. Turn left on the A4, then right onto the A4361 for Avebury. Pass West Kennet Avenue, a procession of stones leading to Avebury. Park on site.

⑤ Avebury
Wiltshire; SN8 1RE

Sticking out of the earth like broken teeth, the three concentric stone circles of Avebury *(open daily)* are less famous than Stonehenge but far more accessible. Erected between 2,850 BC and 2,200 BC, the rough-hewn stones extend through the village and beyond and are ringed by a huge ditch and earth mound. The site has suffered much over the years, and the stones largely owe their present appearance to Alexander Keiller, an amateur archaeologist who excavated and re-erected many of them in the 1930s. Other sites within walking distance include **Silbury Hill**, Europe's largest man-made ancient monument, and **West Kennet Long Barrow**, a 100-m (330-ft) chambered tomb mound.

Take the A4361 west, then take the A4 through Calne, follow signs on to Bowood House on the left.

⑥ Bowood House
Calne, Wiltshire; SN11 0LZ

"Capability" Brown and Robert and James Adam were among the garden designers and architects who worked on Bowood House *(open Apr–Oct)*, a superb stately home dating mainly from the 18th century. Inside are displays of costumes, porcelain and Indian artistry, and the laboratory where Joseph Priestley discovered oxygen in 1774. There are spectacular rhododendron walks in the grounds – at their best April to June – as well as grottoes and an adventure playground.

Take the exit to the A4 west, then south on the A342, then right at Sandy Lane for Lacock. Car park is on the left.

Above Silbury Hill, one of several major Neolithic sites close to Avebury

Above Caen Hill Locks on the Kennet and Avon Canal, Devizes

EAT AND DRINK

SALISBURY

Pheasant Inn *moderate*
One of Salisbury's most historic pubs, the Pheasant Inn specializes in locally sourced steaks and real ale, as well as offering varied snack meals.
19 Salt Lane, SP1 1DT; 01722 322 866; www.restaurant-salisbury.com

AROUND DEVIZES

The George & Dragon *moderate*
Inventive modern dishes are served in this welcoming gastro pub on the A342 3.4 km (2 miles) north of Devizes. Spicy crab risotto and game dishes are among the specialities. It also has three stylish rooms for an overnight stop.
High Street, Rowde, SN10 2PN; 01380 723 053; www.thegeorgeanddragonrowde.co.uk

AROUND AVEBURY

The Waggon and Horses *inexpensive*
This large thatched inn lies 2 km (1 mile) from Avebury's monuments on the A4. Tuck into steaks, pies and traditional English dishes, as well as curries and lasagne. There's also a pleasant garden.
Beckhampton, SN8 1QJ; 01672 539 418

Eat and Drink: inexpensive, under £25; moderate, £25–£50; expensive, over £50

Above Half-timbered houses lend charm to the picturesque village of Lacock

VISITING BATH

Parking
There are car parks off Charlotte Street and Avon Street. Or use the "Park and Ride" and leave your car on the outskirts and catch a bus into the centre.

Tourist information
Abbey Churchyard, BA1 1LY; 0906 711 2000 (charges apply); www.visitbath. co.uk

Thermae Bath Spa
Hot Bath Street, BA1 1SJ; 01225 331 234; www.thermaebathspa.com; 9am–9:30pm (last entry 7pm) daily

WHERE TO STAY

BRADFORD-ON-AVON

The Swan Hotel *moderate*
Stylishly refurbished rooms offset the traditional exterior of this cosy hotel, which has broadband and flatscreen TVs. There's a good restaurant, too.
1 Church Street, BA15 1LN; 01225 868 686; www.theswan-hotel.co.uk

BATH

Apsley House Hotel *moderate*
Antiques adorn this stately home built in 1830. Some rooms have four-poster beds, and there is a garden suite. The hotel is located just over 2 km (1 mile) west of the city centre.
Newbridge Hill, BA1 3PT; 01225 336 966; www.apsley-house.co.uk

One Three Nine *moderate–expensive*
Four of the ten rooms in this luxurious B&B near the city centre have four-poster beds. Book in advance.
139 Wells Road, BA2 3AL; 01225 314 769; www.139bath.co.uk

Royal Crescent Hotel *expensive*
Stay in the best address in Bath – the Royal Crescent. Rates are high, but a luxurious stay is assured, and the facilities and restaurant are rightly acclaimed.
16 Royal Crescent, BA1 2LS; 01225 823 333; www.royalcrescent.co.uk

---

⑦ Lacock
Wiltshire; SN15 2LG
Meticulously preserved by its owners, the National Trust, this village has half-timbered houses and a predominantly sleepy flavour. Its unspoiled air has led to many appearances in TV and film productions, including *The Other Boleyn Girl* and the Harry Potter films. At one end of the main street is the cloistered **Lacock Abbey** *(open daily)*, founded in 1232 and gracefully converted into a home after the 16th-century Dissolution of the Monasteries. It includes a **museum** *(open daily)* featuring the work of photography pioneer William Fox Talbot (1800–77).
🚗 *From Lacock turn left onto A350 to Melksham. Take B3107 to Bradford-on-Avon. Cross the bridge, bear right, and park by the tithe barn on the right.*

⑧ Bradford-on-Avon
Wiltshire; BA15 1LF
Rising up from the river, this engaging town deserves a visit. The wealth earned from the cloth trade is evident in the historic buildings, such as the Anglo-Saxon **Church of St Laurence**, possibly founded in AD 705, and the early 14th-century **Tithe Barn**, used to store food owed to the church. See the Norman bridge – with two original pointed arches but rebuilt in the 17th century, and enjoy a stroll along the River Avon and the Kennet and Avon Canal or go for a trip on the narrowboat **MV Barbara McLellan** *(Apr–Oct: Wed, Sat & Sun; Wharf Cottage, BA15 1LE; 07503 445 393; www.katrust.org).*
🚗 *Exit west on B3108, turn right on A36 and left to Claverton Down. Turn left, then right down Widcombe Hill into town. Cross the river and go left to park.*

---

⑨ Bath
Somerset; BA1 1SU
With its golden-hued terraces around a vast natural amphitheatre, Bath is one of England's most congenial cities. At its heart, the Roman Baths and the Abbey are the most compelling of the many attractions to be appreciated on a stroll. Its maze of lanes lined with smart boutiques will tempt shoppers; gastronomes will savour the range of great restaurants, and culture addicts will enjoy the year-round programme of festivals.

A two-hour walking tour
From Avon Street Car Park, walk along Broad Quay and Dorchester St, past the railway station and up Manvers St to reach Orange Grove. Turn left here down York St for Abbey Churchyard. The small piazza is grandly overlooked by the tall façade of **Bath Abbey** ① *(open Mon–Sat & Sun pm)*, mainly 16th-century with a magnificent fan-vaulted ceiling. To one side are the **Roman Baths** ② *(open daily)*, built on natural hot springs between the first and fifth centuries AD and displaying

Below Pulteney Bridge, designed by Robert Adam, spanning the River Avon

---

Where to Stay: inexpensive, under £80; moderate, £80–£150; expensive, over £150

EAT AND DRINK

LACOCK

At the Sign of the Angel *moderate*
Open fires set the tone of this ancient
hostelry with five rooms. The restaurant
serves traditional British cuisine.
*6 Church Street, SN15 2LB; 01249 730
230; www.lacock.co.uk*

BRADFORD-ON-AVON

Mr Salvats Coffee Room *inexpensive*
A unique, fun coffee house (c.1700) that
offers hot and cold snacks and more
substantial dishes in "olde worlde" style.
*Town House, 44 St Margarets St, BA15
1DE; 01225 867 474; open Thu–Sun*

The Tollgate Inn *moderate*
First-class gastro-pub in a village east
of Bradford, with a cosy ambience. The
menu features British dishes with a
Mediterranean slant. It also has rooms.
*Ham Green, Holt, BA14 6PX; 01225 782
326; www.tollgateholt.co.uk*

BATH

Sally Lunn's *inexpensive*
The city's oldest house and home of
the Bath bun brioche, this popular
eatery serves salmon and duck breast.
*4 North Parade Passage, BA1 1NX;
01225 461 634; www.sallylunns.co.uk*

Acorn Vegetarian Kitchen *moderate*
Classy vegetarian restaurant close to
the Abbey. The menu is based on
seasonal ingredients, especially locally-
grown vegetables. *2 North Passage
Parade, BA1 1NX; 01225 446 059;
www.acornvegetariankitchen.co.uk*

Below top left Nave and fan vaulting at Bath
Abbey **Bottom** Grand, impressive sweep of
the Royal Crescent, Bath

finds from the Temple of Minerva.
The adjacent 18th-century Pump
Room was the venue of an elegant
salon during Bath's fashionable
heyday, and now offers a range of
refreshments, as well as samples of
the famous spa waters.

Turn left and then right out of Abbey
Churchyard into Bath Street. At the
end of this on the left is **Thermae Bath
Spa** ③, a stunning bath complex
opened in 2006, sporting a rooftop
pool. Turn right, past the Little
Theatre, into St Michael's Place, then
left and right to pass the 19th-century
Theatre Royal ④. Continue up Barton
St into Queen Square. Just past the
square, on the right, explore the world
of Jane Austen at the **Jane Austen
Centre** ⑤ *(open daily)*. Austen lived at
various addresses in Bath and set
some of her fiction here.

At the top of Gay Street stands **The
Circus** ⑥, an elegant terrace designed
by John Wood and his son (also John
Wood) in the 18th century. Note the
528 individual carvings on the frieze
running along the buildings, including
serpents, theatrical masks and possibly
druidic and masonic symbols. From
here, Brock Street leads to the
grandest of Bath's terraces, Royal
Crescent, the work of John Wood the
Younger, and fronted by a graceful
sweep of lawn. Have a look inside
one of the houses at **No. 1 Royal
Crescent** ⑦ *(open Feb–mid-Dec)*.

Retrace the route to The Circus and walk
up Bennett Street for the Georgian
Assembly Rooms ⑧ *(open daily)*, built
in 1769 with a plain exterior but
sumptuous within. In the same
building, the Fashion Museum *(open
daily)* gives an entertaining overview of
costumes and clothing through the
ages. From here, head down Bartlett
Street, turning right and then left at
George Street for Milsom Street, one of
Bath's main shopping areas. Bear left
into New Bond Street, turn right at
Northgate Street and then left at Bridge
Street to **Pulteney Bridge** ⑨, the
elegant shop-lined crossing over the
pretty River Avon, designed by Robert
Adam in the 1770s. To get the best view,
walk down Grand Parade, past ornamental gardens and back to Orange
Grove, then return to the car park.

🚗 *Follow signs for A4 towards Bristol,
turn off onto A39. Fork right to Compton
Dando, turn left then right. Turn right to
Woollard. Right onto A37, left onto B3130
and left at a thatched toll house. Follow
signs to the stone circles.*

Above Stanton Drew Stone Circle in its delightful rural setting

VISITING THE MENDIPS

The B3135 runs through the **Cheddar Gorge** which offers rock climbing, caving and nature walks *(01934 742 343; www.cheddargorge.co.uk)*. Look out also for authentic Cheddar cheese – the production process can be viewed at **Cheddar Gorge Cheese Company** *(01934 742 810; www.cheddargorge cheeseco.co.uk)*. **Ebbor Gorge** (with car park) has several nature-filled walks –the area is famous for bats, butterflies and mosses and lichens; carry on east to **Wookey Hole** *(01749 672 243; www. wookey.co.uk)*. This has many indoor attractions that will appeal to kids.

WHERE TO STAY

THE MENDIP HILLS

Wookey Hole Inn *moderate*
This Inn provides funky accommodation with a young Bohemian ambience. It also offers a great selection of zesty Belgian beers.
Wookey Hole, BA5 1BP; 01749 676 677; www.wookeyholeinn.com

WELLS

Ancient Gatehouse *moderate*
Quirky old hotel with nine rooms (three with four-posters), some facing the cathedral, and a popular Italian restaurant, Rugantino's.
20 Sadler Street; 01749 672 029; www.rossibrothers.co.uk/ ancientgatehouse

GLASTONBURY

The George and Pilgrim *moderate*
Reputedly haunted and full of character and history, this inn has been in business for 600 years. Some rooms have four-posters and there is a pleasant bar for relaxing and eating.
1 High Street, BA6 9DP; 01458 831 146; www.georgeandpilgrimhotel.com

Right The winding B3135 through the Cheddar Gorge **Far right** The sublime symmetry of Wells Cathedral nave

⑩ Stanton Drew Stone Circle
Stanton Drew, Somerset

After Avebury, this is the second largest of England's Neolithic stone circle complexes and, like Avebury – and unlike Stonehenge – it's an unfenced site, the irregular-shaped rocks sprouting out of meadows where cattle quietly graze. There are three circles here, the largest at 112 m (367 ft) contains 27 stones and is aligned with a burial chamber known as the Cove 500 m (1,640 ft) away, in what is now a pub garden. Originally, avenues of standing stones led up to the circles. Many of the stones have been damaged over the years, so the structure of the complex is not easy to see. However, it remains a calming and mesmerizing site. A local myth tells that the stones are a wedding party whose musicians were tricked by the devil into playing on into the Sabbath, at which point they were turned to stone.

🚗 *Return to B3130 west and fork left on B3114. Turn right on A368 and turn left at Compton Martin on B3371 and then right onto B3135, to the Cheddar Gorge. Carry on to A371 east and fork*

left at Draycott, back to B3135 and on to Priddy. Fork right here for Ebbor Gorge and Wookey Hole. Park on site.

⑪ The Mendip Hills
Somerset

Running for some 40 km (25 miles) and not rising above 325 m (1,067 ft), the Mendip Hills are a comparatively low-key range, but they present a stark contrast to Somerset's gentle, rolling landscape. They are characterized by bare heathland over the higher areas, and deep limestone gorges riddled with cave systems which invite further exploration *(see left)*. **Cheddar Gorge** and **Wookey Hole** *(both open daily)* can get busy and are both somewhat overdeveloped, but there's lots to do here, especially for children, and the caves are spectacular. Unspoiled **Ebbor Gorge**, west of Wookey Hole, is an important National Nature Reserve and has some inviting marked walking trails. The grassland areas are criss-crossed by dry-stone

Mystic Glastonbury

Nowhere else in England has quite the same mix of history and New Age romance, religion and superstition, magic and myth, as Glastonbury. Jesus' uncle, Joseph of Arimathea, is said to have visited here; the Chalice Well on Chilkwell St (and Glastonbury Tor) is supposed to have been the hiding place of the Holy Grail. In the grounds of the Abbey, it is claimed that King Arthur is buried alongside Guinevere. Above the town, ley lines are said to cross on Glastonbury Tor. Believe it or not, there's something special about Glastonbury.

walls and are a vital habitat for wildflowers, insects and wildlife such as dormice and the peregrine falcon.

🚗 *From Wookey Hole carry on down the High St onto Wells Rd, following signs into the centre of Wells.*

⑫ Wells

Somerset; BA5 2RP
England's smallest city, Wells has a **cathedral** that is one of the crowning glories of early English Gothic architecture. Fronted by a swathe of lawn, its stately west façade is a marvel of medieval statuary, and the interior houses an incredible 600-year-old astronomical clock. Close to the cathedral, admire the medieval **Vicars' Close,** said to be the oldest planned street in Europe, and the beautiful walled and moated 13th-century **Bishop's Palace**, from whose springs the city took its name.

🚗 *Follow the A39 southwest, turning right at roundabout. Carry on past Glastonbury Abbey to car park on left.*

⑬ Glastonbury

Somerset; BA6 9EL
A magnet for "New Agers" and those seeking "alternative" lifestyles, medieval Glastonbury is awash with legend and religious symbolism. Close to its heart near the Market Cross, lie the majestic ruins of **Glastonbury Abbey** *(open daily)*, once one of the most powerful abbeys in the land, but razed during the Dissolution of the Monasteries. The abbey dates mostly from the 12th and 13th centuries but a stone church was built here as early as AD 705. To the east, topped by the ruins of St Michael's church, stands the cone of **Glastonbury Tor** – variously said to be a portal to the fairy kingdom, King Arthur's stronghold, or where the Holy Grail was kept. Climb up here for fabulous views over the Somerset Levels – reclaimed marshes. The 5-day **Glastonbury Festival** of contemporary music and arts is staged at Worthy Farm, 13 km (8 miles) east of the town, in late June.

Carving on the Market Cross, Glastonbury

Above left West façade of Wells Cathedral, built between 1209–50 **Above centre** The ruins of St Michael's Church on top of Glastonbury Tor **Above right** The romantic ruins of Glastonbury Abbey, set in picturesque parkland

SHOPPING IN GLASTONBURY

For genuine Clarks shoes often at a discount, visit *Clarks Factory Shop (Clarks Village, Farm Rd, Street, BA16 0BB; 01458 840 064; www.clarks.co.uk)* in Street, south of Glastonbury.

EAT AND DRINK

WELLS

The Good Earth *inexpensive*
This is the ideal place for a coffee or snack, serving wholesome, simple fare such as soups, quiches, pizzas and jacket potatoes, and takeaway items. *4 Priory Road, BA5 1SY; 01749 678 600; open daytime only; closed Sun*

GLASTONBURY

Hundred Monkeys *moderate*
In a town renowned for its hippy cafés, this has a refreshing, down-to-earth feel and serves various main meals as well as great cakes. *52 High Street, BA6 9DY; 01458 833 386; closed Sun evening.*

DAY TRIP OPTIONS

Salisbury and Bath are both good bases for day trips; staying at Glastonbury enables visits to Wells and a trip into the Mendips, with the opportunity for some walking or outdoors activity.

Salisbury and the stones

Learn about the prehistory of the area in Salisbury museum ❶, then see it for real at Old Sarum ❷, Stonehenge ❸ and Avebury ❺. Active families will have most fun in the outdoor sites and might want to consider stopping off in Devizes ❹ for an exursion along the Kennet and Avon Canal.

From Salisbury, follow the directions to visit Old Sarum, Stonehenge, Devizes and Avebury – return via A361 and A342 for speed and convenience.

Beautiful buildings

Explore the amazing architecture of Bath ❾, with its inspiring mix of elegant houses and buildings, its museums and impressive range of shops and restaurants. The Roman Baths are an essential sight. See too, Bradford-on-Avon ❽ for some Anglo-Saxon and medieval treats and Lacock Abbey ❼ for its intriguing blend of medieval and 16th-century design.

From Bath, take the A36/B3108 to Bradford and the B3107/A350 to Lacock.

Glastonbury and the gorges

Staying at Glastonbury ⑬, enjoy the romantic abbey ruins and a scramble up Glastonbury Tor for the views. On to wonderful Wells ⑫ for a tour of the cathedral and adjacent sights, and then a drive through the Mendip Hills ⑪ via Cheddar, Ebbor and Wookey Gorges, stopping off at will.

The A39 connects Wells to Glastonbury; follow the drive's instructions in reverse for the gorges. Return via A371 and A39.

Eat and Drink: inexpensive, under £25; moderate, £25–£50; expensive, over £50

The Villages of the Cotswolds

Cirencester to Broadway

Highlights

- **Picture-perfect scenery**
  Enter a world of thatched cottages, flower gardens and streams, framed by the gentle Cotswold landscape

- **A miscellany of museums**
  Explore a range of nostalgic museums displaying everything from old musical instruments to cars and bikes

- **Cotswold "wool churches"**
  Admire the late-Gothic architecture of the area's magnificent churches, built from the wealth of the wool trade

- **Art and antiques**
  Discover the designs of the Arts and Crafts movement that flourished here a century ago, and browse the many antique shops which grace the villages

Sezincote House and Garden, built in the Moghul Indian style

The Villages of the Cotswolds

From the heart of Gloucestershire to the edge of Worcestershire, this drive takes in some of the most enchanting villages and hamlets of the Cotswold Hills – mellow, dreamy vistas dotted with sheep grazing amid drystone walls. A journey through the Cotswolds will reveal honey-hued cottages, thickly thatched pubs, and great mansions built by farmers and merchants trading in what was once the finest wool in Europe. Many local wool merchants showed off their wealth by erecting or improving rural churches and filling them with grand memorials – those at Cirencester, Northleach and Chipping Campden are among the most exquisite. There's an abundance of quality food and accommodation on offer, and also an array of independent outlets, galleries and workshops selling antiques and handicrafts.

Above Thatched cottage in the village of Chipping Campden, *see p80*

0 kilometres 5

0 miles 5

KEY

 Drive route

ACTIVITIES

Browse among the alluring antiques shops for which the Cotswolds are famous

Take an aromatic tour around the perfume factory in Bourton-on-the-Water

Saddle up for a bike ride in the beautiful country around Chipping Campden

Take a hike on the 160-km (100-mile) Cotswold Way between Chipping Campden and Bath

Fill your plate and support the Great British Pud at Mickleton near Hidcote Manor Garden

Climb up the hilltop folly of lofty Broadway Tower

Drive off the first tee of Broadway Golf club

Peb

Chur
Honeybour

Bretforton

B4035

Wickhamford

Willersey

A44

Childswickham

BROADWAY 9

Broadway Tower

Wormington B4632

Snowshill Manor

Snows

Stanway

Didbrook

Taddington

Hailes

Temple Guiting

Winchcombe

Barton

Charlton Abbot

Hawling B4068

Brockhampton

GLOUCESTERSHI

Whittington

Notgr

Andoversford

Shipton

Hazleton

A436 Foxcote

Compton Abdale A40

Withington

Hampnett

NORTHLEACH

Colesborne

Yanworth

Easti

Elkstone

2

CHEDWORTH ROMAN VILLA Chedworth

Fossbridge

Syde

Rendcomb

Calmsden

Winson Abli

A435

A417 North Cerney

A429 Arlington B

Daglingworth Baunton

Barnsley

Sapperton Stratton

Ampney Crucis

Ampney St Mary

A419 **CIRENCESTER** 1

Coates

A429 Preston

Ampney St Peter

Metse Hampton

A433 Siddington

Driffield

A419 Down Ampney

South Cerney

Mars Me

Shorncote

Cerney Wick

Above Hidcote Manor Garden, an Arts and Crafts masterpiece, *see p81*

Below Early morning view of St James' Church, Chipping Campden, *see p80*

PLAN YOUR DRIVE

Start/finish: Cirencester to Broadway.

Number of days: 2–3 days.

Distance: Around 90 km (55 miles).

Road conditions: Mainly straight A- and minor roads, sometimes narrow – watch out for tractors and people on horseback around unsighted bends.

When to go: In summer, some Cotswold villages can be overrun at the weekends by tourists, day trippers and coach parties – it is best to try and visit during the week.

Opening times: Museums and attractions are generally open 10am– 5pm, but close earlier (or are closed altogether) Nov–Easter. Shops are often open longer. Churches are usually open until dusk.

Market days: Cirencester: Charter Market, Market Place, Mon & Fri; Craft Market, Corn Hall, 2nd & 4th Sat of month; **Stow-on-the-Wold**: Farmers' Market, 2nd Thu of month; **Moreton-in-Marsh**: Tue.

Shopping: Look out for antiques and handicrafts throughout the area – including hand-blown glass and hand-thrown pottery, jewellery and ceramics. Foodwise, expect fine local beers, meats – especially lamb – and cheeses such as the famous Stinking Bishop.

Major festivals: Cirencester: Beer Festival, late Aug; **Chipping Campden**: Music Festival, mid-May; Olympick Games, late May.

DAY TRIP OPTIONS

A few day trips can take in the very best of the Cotswolds region. Families with children will appreciate the combination of the **Roman museum** at Cirencester, Chedworth **Roman villa** and the **instruments**, **toy collections** and **model railway displays** of Northleach and Bourton-on-the-Water. Arts and Crafts devotees can take in the **antiques shops**, **galleries**, **museums** and **workshops** at Stow-on-the-Wold, Chipping Campden and Broadway. For full details, *see p81*.

WHERE TO STAY

CIRENCESTER

The Fleece Hotel *moderate*
This rambling old inn at the heart of town is an atmospheric place to stay. Some rooms are on the small side, but all are functional and pleasant. There is a bar, a restaurant and a patio for drinks. *Market Place, GL7 2NZ; 01285 658 507; www.fleecehotel.co.uk*

BOURTON-ON-THE-WATER

Chester House Hotel *moderate*
This small, traditional-looking hotel has a relaxed atmosphere with modern decor and genial staff. Rooms are all fresh and airy, some with a four-poster bed. Family rooms are also available. *Victoria Street, GL54 2BS; 01451 820 286; www.chesterhousehotel.com*

STOW-ON-THE-WOLD

The Limes *inexpensive*
Simple Victorian B&B run by a friendly young couple on the northern outskirts of Stow, on the A424 (a 5-minute walk from the centre). There are six guest rooms and a lovely garden. *Evesham Road, GL54 1EJ; 01451 830 034; www.thelimes.cotswolds.co.uk*

Stow Lodge Hotel *moderate*
Country-style accommodation in the heart of Stow, with a perfectly groomed garden overlooking the main square, good food, and a comfortable lounge with a log fire. *The Square, GL54 1AB; 01451 830 485; www.stowlodgehotel.co.uk*

MORETON-IN-MARSH

Redesdale Arms *inexpensive*
This old coaching inn has cosy log fires and well-equipped rooms with clean, modern bathrooms. Breakfasts are excellent and tasty meals are served in the bar or restaurant. *High Street, GL56 0AW; 01608 650 308; www.redesdalearms.com*

Manor House Hotel *expensive*
Old but charming and well-maintained, this hotel on the main street has period furniture and modern fixtures. Staff are courteous and attentive, and Mulberry's Restaurant rustles up first-class meals. *High Street, GL56 0LJ; 01608 650 501; www.cotswold-inns-hotels.co.uk*

Near right St John the Baptist Church at the heart of Cirencester **Far right** Chedworth Roman Villa: dining room mosaics

Above The village of Northleach, built of traditional Cotswold stone

① Cirencester
Gloucestershire; GL7 2BX

This relaxed market town's importance in Roman Britain – it was the second largest town – is revealed in the superb **Corinium Museum** *(open daily; Sun closed am)*. The town kept its wealth in the medieval era, as can be seen in the huge church of **St John the Baptist** – the south porch with fan vaulting dates from 1490. The church dominates **Market Square**, home to one of the biggest markets in the Cotswolds. Visit **New Brewery Arts** *(Jan–Mar: closed Sun)* for shops, events and workshops.

Stone relief, Corinium Museum

🚗 *Follow the A429 (Stow Road) north to Stow-in-the-Wold for about 8 km (5 miles). Turn left at the signpost for Chedworth Roman Villa, then continue to follow the signs to the villa and the on-site car park.*

② Chedworth Roman Villa
Yanworth, Gloucestershire; GL54 3LJ

Nestled amid woods, this absorbing site, discovered in 1864, displays part of the bath houses and dining areas of a substantial Romano-British villa *(closed Mon)* inhabited from the 2nd to 4th centuries AD. Vivid mosaics, underfloor heating systems, plunge pools and the latrine, can be seen while audioguides fill in the history. The grounds make a nice picnic area.

🚗 *Follow signs for Yanworth, then for Northleach. Park in the centre of town.*

③ Northleach
Gloucestershire; GL54 3ET

This unassuming village has one of the finest Cotswold "wool churches". The oldest parts of **St Peter and St Paul** date from around 1300, and on the floor, brasses show merchants, with sheep, woolpacks and many children. Look out for the carved corbels (stone brackets) in the porch, depicting such images as angels and a cat playing a fiddle. On the High St, **Keith Harding's World of Mechanical Music** *(open daily)* is well worth a visit, displaying an array of period pieces, ably explained and demonstrated on a guided tour.

🚗 *Take the A429 following signs for Stow-on-the-Wold and Bourton-on-the-Water. Park off Rissington Road.*

④ Bourton-on-the-Water
Gloucestershire; GL54 2AN

This classic, relaxing Cotswold village nestles around a village green and the gentle River Windrush, and has something for everyone to enjoy. The **Cotswold Motoring Museum and Toy Collection** *(mid-Feb–mid-Dec: open daily)* is a nostalgic wallow in the style and technology of yesteryear; the **Model Railway Exhibition**, has an elaborate layout with more than 40 trains *(Jun–Aug: open daily; Sep–Dec & Feb–May: open Sat & Sun; Jan: limited opening)*; the **Model Village** *(open daily)*, is a detailed 1:9 replica of Bourton; and the **Cotswold Perfumery** *(open daily; 01451 820 698; www.cotswold-perfumery.co.uk)* is a fascinating factory-museum-shop that makes its scents by hand; tours are available.

🚗 *Rejoin A429, following signs for Stow-on-the-Wold. Park in the town square or on A429 north of the centre.*

Cotswold Antiques

The Cotswolds are one of the most rewarding areas for shopping for antiques, though don't expect to find many bargains. The main centres are Stow-on-the-Wold, Moreton-in-Marsh, Chipping Campden and Broadway, but it's always worth looking in smaller places, and look out for antiques fairs – local tourist offices should have a list.

⑤ Stow-on-the-Wold
Gloucestershire; GL54 1BN

Eight roads – one of them the Roman Fosse Way – meet at this Cotswold market town, crammed with antiques shops, delicatessens and smart hotels. Stop here for some window-shopping and a bite to eat, with pubs and cafés surrounding the huge main square – once a busy market at the heart of the

Cotswold wool trade. Look out for the stocks here, and the **King's Arms**, where Charles I spent a night in 1645 during the Civil War; the following year, nearby **St Edward's Church** was used as a prison for defeated Royalist troops after the Battle of Stow.

🚗 *Continue north along the A429 for Moreton-in-Marsh; park on the High St.*

⑥ Moreton-in-Marsh
Gloucestershire; GL56 0AF

This lively Cotswold centre is known for its Tuesday Market – the county's largest outdoor market. A short way on the A44 towards Evesham there's a collection of interesting places to visit. **Sezincote** is an onion-domed stately home built in the Mughal Indian style in 1810 *(House: May–Sep: open Thu & Fri pm, no children; Garden: Jan–Nov: open Thu & Fri pm)*. Opposite is the **Batsford Arboretum**, a fabulous collection of exotic trees and shrubs *(open daily)*. And just next door, families will enjoy watching the gripping live demonstrations at the excellent **Cotswold Falconry Centre** *(mid-Feb–mid-Nov: open daily)*.

🚗 *Take A429 north out of town, left towards Batsford. Follow the signs to Draycott, passing through the village, then pass through Broad Campden. In Chipping Campden, park on High St.*

Above left Picturesque bridge at the centre of Bourton-on-the-Water **Above right** Typical Cotswold tearoom in Moreton-in-Marsh

SHOPPING FOR LOCAL CHEESE

Cotswold cheeses are rightly renowned. In **Stow-on-the-Wold** pack a picnic from the cheeses, breads, pâtés and pies at **Maby's** *(Digbeth Street, GL54 1BN; 01451 870 071; www.mabys.co.uk)*. For more than 50 cheeses (including Stinking Bishop) and other local specialities in **Moreton-in-Marsh**, try the **Cotswold Cheese Company** *(High Street, GL56 0AH; 01608 652 862; www.cotswoldcheesecompany.co.uk)*.

EAT AND DRINK

CIRENCESTER

Le Beaujolais *moderate*
Hearty, traditional French cuisine, from onion soup to baked Camembert.
37 Castle Street, GL7 1QD; 01285 644 440; www.restaurantlebeaujolais.co.uk

BOURTON-ON-THE-WATER

Mousetrap Inn *moderate*
Locally-sourced food is the speciality of this 18th-century family-run inn.
Lansdown, GL54 2AR; 01451 820 579; www.mousetrap-inn.com

STOW-ON-THE-WOLD

Old Bakery Tavern *inexpensive*
Delicious cakes and scones, also light lunches, all home-made.
Digbeth Street, GL54 1BN; 01451 832 172; www.theoldbakerytearoom.co.uk

The Old Butcher's *moderate*
This highly rated brasserie serves quality British fare, both traditional and modern.
7 Park Street, GL54 1AQ; 01451 831 700; www.theoldbutchers.com

MORETON-IN-MARSH

Tilly's Teahouse *inexpensive*
Breakfasts and sweet and savoury snacks are served in this friendly tearoom with a courtyard for fair weather.
18–19 High Street, GL56 0AF; 01608 650 000; open daytime only

Left View of the countryside around Stow-on-the-Wold

Above Campden House with St James' Church, Chipping Campden **Below** Flower baskets outside the Eight Bells, Chipping Campden

VISITING CHIPPING CAMPDEN

Tourist Information
The Old Police Station, High Street, GL55 6HB; 01386 841 206; www.chippingcampdenonline.org

Cotswold Country Cycles
Longlands Farm Cottage, GL55 6LJ; 01386 438 706; www.cotswoldcountrycycles.com

WHERE TO STAY

CHIPPING CAMPDEN

Eight Bells *moderate*
Originally built in the 14th century for the stonemasons at work on St James Church, this inn has comfortable rooms and an excellent restaurant.
Church Street, GL55 6JG; 01386 840 371; www.eightbellsinn.co.uk

BROADWAY

The Broadway Hotel *expensive*
Timber beams and creaking floors add character to this traditional hotel. Enjoy the friendly staff and big breakfasts.
The Green, WR12 7AA; 01386 852 401; www.cotswold-inns-hotels.co.uk

The Lygon Arms *expensive*
Stay here to enjoy luxury and old-world charm. Try the first-class leisure facilities and then dine in the Great Hall.
High Street, WR12 7DU; 01386 852 255; www.lygonarms.co.uk

⑦ Chipping Campden
Gloucestershire; GL55 6JE

This uncommercialized Cotswold village was one of the centres for the Arts and Crafts movement that flourished in the Cotswolds at the turn of the 20th century. It still has a vibrant craft movement as well as the Court Barn Museum, devoted to art and design. The village is also the start of the Cotswold Way, a 160-km (100-mile) walking trail to Bath, and ideal for cyclists, who can explore the countryside on rented bikes.

A three-hour walking tour

Start your walk from the High Street at the car park next to the old **Market Hall** ①, dating from 1627. Walk through the archway to the left of the Noel Arms Hotel, and on to George Lane, turning left into Badgers Field. Pass through a kissing gate (designed to contain livestock) into a field. The path cuts across the field and over a stream with views of 17th-century **Campden House** ②, burnt down in the Civil War.

The path ends at Station Rd, turn left for a good look at **St James' Church** ③. Dating from the 16th century, it is one of the finest Cotswold "wool churches". Note the sumptuous memorials and Jacobean pulpit and lectern. Nearby is the **Court Barn Museum** ④ *(closed Mon)*, dedicated to local art, design and crafts. Walk down Church St, past a pretty row of **Almshouses** ⑤ on the right, built in 1612. Turn left into the High St, and back to the Market Hall.

Continue along the High St, taking a detour down Sheep St on the left, to visit the **Old Silk Mill** ⑥, once home to C R Ashbee's Guild of Handicrafts and still dedicated to craft products. Browse the items on display and maybe even buy a little souvenir.

Return to the High St and turn right at the Catholic **St Catherine's Church** ⑦, a Gothic Revival building with early 20th-century stained-glass windows, designed in the Arts and Crafts style by local artist Paul Woodroffe. Follow signs for the Cotswold Way down West End Terrace and Hoo Lane, which soon becomes a footpath to Kingcombe Lane. Turn left here then after about 100 paces, right onto another path, also signed Cotswold Way. This leads to The Common, an area of parkland with a path to **Dover's Hill** ⑧, where there are benches for just soaking up the views. The hill is the venue of the "Olympick Games" – originating in the 17th century, and involving sports such as wrestling and shin-kicking. Brass bands, Morris dancers and a torchlight procession add to the fun, on the Friday after Spring Bank Holiday.

From Dover's Hill, turn left onto the road, cross Kingcombe Lane and head down Dyers Lane. Follow Dyers Lane, then bear left onto Park Road, which leads back to Chipping Campden's High Street.

Dover's Hill lies on the waymarked Cotswold Way and is a great place for a walk, so pick up route maps from the tourist office. Cyclists can hire bikes from **Cotswold Country Cycles** *(see left).*
🚗 *Take the B4035 towards Shipston-on-Stour and turn left to Ebrington. After the level crossing, turn left and follow signs for Hidcote Manor Gardens.*

Where to Stay: inexpensive, under £80; moderate, £80–£150; expensive, over £150

Above High Street shops in the well-preserved village of Broadway

Arts and Crafts

Britain's Arts and Crafts movement flourished in the years around 1900, especially in the Cotswolds. Inspired by the writing of John Ruskin and reacting against industrialization, its followers relied on traditional skills. Its most famous exponents included artist and designer William Morris, furniture maker Gordon Russell and C R Ashbee, who designed jewellery and printed books. Examples of their works can be viewed in museums in Broadway and Chipping Campden.

🔞 Hidcote Manor Garden
Gloucestershire; GL55 6LR

There is no shortage of gardens in the Cotswolds, but Hidcote *(closed Nov–Dec; Mon–Fri)* is one of the finest in the country. It was created in 1907 by an American, Major Lawrence Johnston, who designed a series of "outdoor rooms", each one following a specific style, separated by tall hedges and walls, and often with exquisite topiary. Highlights include the White Garden, the Bathing Pool and the informal Old Garden. Think about having lunch – and a traditional pudding – at

Three Ways House in Mickleton.
🚗 *Turn left out of Hidcote, then next right to Mickleton. Turn right, then left at the mini-roundabout onto B4632. Park off Broadway High St and Church St.*

🄷 Broadway
Worcestershire; WR12 7DT

The elegant main street of this well-preserved Cotswold village is lined with immaculate stone houses, smart shops and a handful of cosy pubs and hotels. The **Gordon Russell Museum** *(closed Mon)* displays examples of the graceful furniture designed by the famous local artisan, along with metalwork and glassware.

Take the High St east to the A44, turn right and first right to **Broadway Tower** *(open daily)*. This castle-like folly was built in 1799 and offers stunning panoramas, displays of local history and a deer park – it's a good area for walking, too.

Go south on Church St to **Snowshill Manor** *(Apr–Oct: Wed–Sun pm; Nov: Sat & Sun)*, built of Cotswold honey-yellow stone with an Arts and Crafts garden. The house is full of curiosities from around the world, from clocks to cow bells, and from toys and bicycles to musical instruments and Samurai armour. Close by is the very scenic **Broadway Golf Club** *(Willersey Hill, WR12 7LG; 01386 853 683; www.broadwaygolfclub. co.uk)*.

Above Looking north towards Birmingham from Broadway Tower

EAT AND DRINK

AROUND CHIPPING CAMPDEN

Ebrington Arms *moderate*
This Cotswold stone inn serves great home-made and locally sourced food. *Ebrington, GL55 6NH (3 km/2 miles from Chipping Camden on the B4035); 01386 593 223; www.theebringtonarms.co.uk*

AROUND HIDCOTE MANOR

Three Ways House *moderate*
Award-winning restaurant (with rooms) serving fabulous traditional and modern British food. It also houses the Pudding Club, dedicated to saving and raising the profile of the Great British Pudding. *Mickleton, GL55 6SB (turn left out of Hidcote and right to Mickleton); 01386 438 429; www.threewayshouse.com*

BROADWAY

Tisanes *inexpensive*
This tearoom provides cream teas as well as breakfasts and light lunches. *21 The Green, WR12 7AA; 01386 853 296; www.tisanes-tearooms.co.uk*

Russell's *moderate–expensive*
Modern restaurant (with rooms) with excellent food – try fried sweetbreads, Dover sole, and sticky toffee pudding. *20 High Street, WR12 7DT; 01386 853 555; www.russellsofbroadway.co.uk*

Left The seemingly haphazard planting in the Old Garden at Hidcote Manor Garden

---

DAY TRIP OPTIONS
Cirencester and Stow-on-the-Wold are good bases for exploring the area.

Romans and Toys
Families with children will love the Roman Museum at Cirencester ❶, Chedworth Roman Villa ❷, the exhibition of mechanical music at

Northleach ❸ and the engaging toy displays at Bourton-on-the-Water ❹.

Cirencester, Northleach and Bourton-on-the-Water are all linked by the A429.

Antiques and design
In the morning, browse the antique shops at Stow-on-the-Wold ❺. Next,

tour a mansion with a difference – Sezincote in Moreton-in-Marsh ❻. In the afternoon, visit Chipping Campden ❼ and Broadway ❾ to explore local arts, crafts, and design.

Stow-on-the-Wold is extremely well-connected – the A424 goes to Broadway and the B4081 to Chipping Campden.

Through the Chilterns

Chalfont St Giles to Henley-on-Thames

Highlights

- **Paradise found**
  Peek inside the sweet 15th-century cottage where John Milton wrote his masterwork, *Paradise Lost*

- **History at large**
  Roam among sheep-dotted open parkland and woods among the many historic buildings at the Chilterns Open Air Museum

- **Phizz-whizzing inspiration**
  Fire up the imagination of adults and children alike at the fascinating Roald Dahl Museum and Story Centre

- **Perfect English villages**
  Enjoy the sturdy flint churches, half-timbered houses and welcoming pubs of these picturesque gems, nestling among gentle hills and ancient woods

Springtime in the gently rolling countryside of the Chiltern Hills

Through the Chilterns

This drive begins just 40 km (25 miles) – but a whole world away – from the turmoil of central London, in the pretty village of Chalfont St Giles. It takes a route through the Chiltern Hills, a designated Area of Outstanding Natural Beauty. Through necessity, some stretches run along main roads, but there are also lovely country lanes with no significant traffic. The proposed stops along the way are varied – grand, quaint and beautiful – while the destination town of Henley offers plenty to absorb the visitor for a day.

Above Cobstone windmill, Turville, *see p86*

Above The Red Lion Hotel, Henley-on-Thames, dating back to the 14th century, *see p87*

PLAN YOUR DRIVE

Start/finish: Chalfont St Giles to Henley-on-Thames.

Number of days: 2 days.

Distances: 56 km (35 miles).

Road conditions: Very good; some lanes can be narrow; good signage with brown tourist signs.

When to go: From late May through to autumn.

Main market days: Amersham: Amersham Country Market, Fri am; Henley-on-Thames: Market Day, Thu; Farmers' Market, last Thu of month, am.

Major Festivals: Amersham: Charter Fair (and market), Sep 19–20; Henley-on-Thames: Henley Royal Regatta, beginning of Jul; Henley Festival of Music and Arts, Jul.

❶ Chalfont St Giles

Bucks; HP8 4JH

With a village green, duck pond, old inns and beamed cottages, this has been hailed as "Britain's most perfect village". Follow a sign just outside the village to **Milton's Cottage** *(open Mar–Oct, closed Mon; www.miltonscottage.org)*, the 16th-century home of poet John Milton. After fleeing London in 1665 to escape the plague, he wrote his masterwork, *Paradise Lost*, here. The cottage contains, among other treasures, first editions of *Areopagitica*, Milton's essay on free speech, and *Eikonoklastes*, his riposte to Charles II's defence of the Divine Right of Kings.

Drive on towards Seer Green and turn left at the sign for the Quaker Meeting House. Enter the village of Jordan's but bypass the right turn to the centre marked "Jordan's village". On the left is a sign for **Jordan's Quaker Meeting House**, one of England's first and dating back to 1688. William Penn, the founder of Pennyslvania, who died in 1718, is buried in the graveyard.

Back in Chalfont St Giles, gourmets can buy top-quality oils, vinegars, spirits and liqueurs from **Vom Fass** *(closed Sun)*, on the High Street.

🚗 *Head up High St and Pheasant Hill; go over double roundabout onto Vache Lane, then right down narrow Gorelands Lane. Follow signs to museum.*

❷ Chiltern Open Air Museum

Newland Park, Gorelands Lane, Chalfont St Giles, Bucks; HP8 4AB

In an ambitious initiative, 30 vernacular buildings of past generations, typical of this region, have been rescued and rebuilt here in a natural setting *(open Apr–Oct; 01494 871 117; www.coam.org.uk)*. Explore a 19th-century farm with animals; wander through a village with a green, cottages, forge and chapel; find out what a 16th-century wood-framed hall house is really like inside, and peer into the tiny Henton Mission Room, a "tin tabernacle" made after the invention of corrugated, galvanized iron in 1882. And, of course, pet the resident shire horse. Other buildings include a 1940s prefabricated bungalow and cast-iron public convenience from1906.

🚗 *Return to A413, turn right at roundabout and drive on to Amersham. Follow signs for old town. Park on street.*

❸ Amersham

Bucks; HP6 5AH

There's no stand-out attraction in Old Amersham *(www.amersham.org.uk)*, the heart of the town, it's just very pretty. See its almshouses, coaching inns, half-timbered cottages and **Market Hall**, topped off with a clocktower and holding the original town jail, and maybe enjoy a nice lunch. Dominating Broadway (the main street) is the flint **Church of St Mary**, built in the12th century with 14th- and 15th-century additions. The Memorial Gardens and tiny River Misbourne are just nearby.

🚗 *Continue up High St to A413. Go right, then left at roundabouts, following signs to Great Missenden. Use main car park on right in Link Rd.*

❹ Great Missenden

Bucks; HP16 0AL

Another appealing small town, at the head of the Misbourne Valley, its main street is lined with lovely half-timbered and Georgian buildings. For 36 years, the children's author Roald Dahl (1916–90) lived and worked in Gt Missenden and the "flushbunkingly gloriumptious" **Roald Dahl Museum and Story Centre** is a major attraction *(closed Mon; www.roalddahlmuseum.org)*. Here, visitors learn about Dahl, man and boy, see where he wrote and admire artwork, photographs, correspondence and manuscripts in progress. With plenty to fire everyone's imagination, a truly whizzpopping time is guaranteed.

🚗 *Follow A4128 towards Prestwood. Continue on this road towards High Wycombe, then take a right, following signs to Hughenden Manor (last one is after a blind bend and easy to miss).*

Above Fountain in the Memorial Gardens, beside the Church of St Mary, Amersham

Above Milton's Cottage, the poet's 16th-century home, Chalfont St Giles

VISITING CHALFONT ST GILES

Parking
From A413, head down Pheasant Hill into Deanway. Free parking at Milton's Cottage and at Quaker Meeting House.

WHERE TO STAY

CHALFONT ST GILES

The White Hart Inn *inexpensive*
This inn has 11 comfortable rooms with en-suite bathrooms in a purpose-built block. It has a good restaurant, too.
Three Households, HP8 4LP; 01494 872 441; www.oldenglishinns.co.uk

AMERSHAM

The Crown Inn *moderate*
This Elizabethan coaching inn has a cool yet traditional style and featured in the film *Four Weddings and a Funeral*.
16 High Street, HP7 0DH; 01494 721 541; www.thecrownamersham.com

EAT AND DRINK

CHALFONT ST GILES

Milton's Head *inexpensive*
Opposite Milton's Cottage, this homely place offers an all-Italian menu.
Deanway, HP8 4JL; 01494 872 962; www.miltonshead.co.uk

AMERSHAM

Gilbey's *moderate*
This bar and restaurant with a garden serves modern British food such as shoulder of Cornish lamb, and Kentish tart with coffee crème fraîche. A three-course set menu is served Mon–Thu.
1 Market Square, HP7 0DF; 01494 727 242; www.gilbeygroup.com

GREAT MISSENDEN

Nags Head *moderate*
A 15th-century pub (with rooms) aiming high and sourcing tip-top organic produce. Try the rib of beef with an ale jus; there's not much for vegetarians.
London Rd, HP16 0DG; 01494 862 200; www.nagsheadbucks.com

Eat and Drink: inexpensive, under £25; moderate, £25–£50; expensive, over £50

Above The gardens and rear of Hughenden Manor, once Disraeli's country home

VISITING HENLEY-ON-THAMES

Parking
On the way in, follow signs to short-stay parking (maximum three hours) on Market Street or Gray's Road.

Tourist Information
King's Arms Barn, Kings Road, RG9 2DG; 01491 578 034

Thames Cruise
To hire self-drive (or even chauffered) motor launches for relaxing trips along the river; or for a scheduled cruise, try **Hobbs of Henley** on Station Rd *(01491 572 035; www.hobbsofhenley.com*

WHERE TO STAY

AROUND WEST WYCOMBE

Frog Inn *moderate*
Pretty family-run inn with attractive en-suite rooms and rural views. The inn is situated directly south of Fingest, close to Turville. Also serves good food. *Skirmett, RG9 6TG (8 km/5 miles west of West Wycombe); 01491 638 996; www.thefrogatskirmett.co.uk*

HENLEY-ON-THAMES

Milsoms Hotel *moderate*
In a listed, red brick former bakery above the Loch Fyne Bar and Grill *(see right)*. Seven smallish, tasteful en-suite rooms. Kippers for breakfast! *20 Market Place, RG9 2AH; 01491 845 789; www.milsomshotel.co.uk*

Hotel du Vin *moderate–expensive*
This boutique hotel, part of a small chain, has 43 luxurious rooms offering style, attention to detail and bistro cooking. *New Street, RG92BP; 0844 736 4258; www.hotelduvin.com*

Red Lion Hotel *expensive*
This red brick 16th-century inn by the bridge has 39 substantial, well-furnished rooms, some with river views. *Hart Street, RG9 2AR; 01491 572 161; www.redlionhenley.co.uk*

⑤ Hughenden Manor
High Wycombe, Bucks; HP14 4LA
Time has not stood still at Hughenden Manor, despite access up a steep, unpaved and rutted track *(house, gardens and park open daily all year, except Christmas; 01494 755 565; www. nationaltrust.org.uk)*. The country home of Queen Victoria's trusted Prime Minister Benjamin Disraeli (1804–81) has seen some alterations, but a few rooms are as they would have been in "Dizzy's" day. The gardens recreate an original design by his wife, Mary Anne. Mementoes, books and paintings bring the interior alive but low lighting, while kind to furnishings, can be less kind to eyes. There are some beautiful walks in the surrounding parkland with glorious views of the countryside.

🚗 *Rejoin the A4128 towards High Wycombe. In town, follow signs to A40 west. Turn left at Pedestal round-about to West Wycombe. After village, turn right, past caves entrance, for free parking.*

Below The "Royal River" running through the heart of Henley-on-Thames

⑥ West Wycombe
Bucks; HP14 3AH
West Wycombe's main attractions are found at **West Wycombe Park** *(Apr–Aug: open Sun–Thu; house open Jun–Aug; 01494 755 571; www.nationaltrust.org.uk)*. The Italianate house is set in landscaped gardens dotted with follies, statues and ornamental lakes. The estate is also home to the **Hellfire Caves** *(Apr–Oct: open daily; Nov–Mar: open Sat & Sun; www. hellfirecaves.co.uk)*, excavated in the 1740s on the orders of Sir Francis Dashwood and running nearly 1 km (over half a mile) underground. See the Gothic "church" entrance and descend dank passages past chambers with portrayals of members of Dashwood's infamous Hellfire Club (1749–60). The final destination is the "Inner Temple". Here were held the bacchanals of the club, whose members included such luminaries as the then Prince of Wales, the Marquis of Granby, and artist William Hogarth. Despite tales of devil worship, the main activities were probably drinking and pornography. Not suitable for anyone with claustrophobia, the caves are reputed to be haunted by the spectre of a steward of the Hellfire Club who kept a tally of drinks consumed. On the hilltop above the caves stand the imposing **Dashwood Mausoleum** and the distinctive **Church of St Lawrence**, its tower topped by a golden sphere that is said to have served as a venue for covert meetings.

🚗 *Take A40 through Piddington and turn left, signed Bolter End. Take B482 to Fingest. It is possible to fork right here for the pretty village and pub at Turville. Otherwise turn right, then right again onto A4155 to Henley-on-Thames.*

Where to Stay: inexpensive, under £80; moderate, £80–£150; expensive, over £150

⑦ Henley-on-Thames

Oxfordshire RG9 2EB

In its leafy setting on the Thames, this Georgian market town, famous for its July Royal Regatta, offers a mix of the historical and fashionable. A graceful 18th-century, five-arched bridge spans the river – a dynamic and defining presence; beautiful, recreational and a haven for wildlife.

A one-hour walking tour

From the car park, walk down Market Street and cross Bell Street to Hart Street, dominated by the red brick **Victorian Town Hall** ①, built in 1901. Walk down Hart Street to the **Church of St Mary** ② with its 16th-century stone and flint tower. The stucco almshouses to the west date from 1830 and the red brick ones on the east were originally built in the 1660s and rebuilt in 1884. Beside them is the Grade I listed 16th-century Chantry House, overlooking the churchyard (with Dusty Springfield's grave) and the river. At the bottom of Hart Street look across the bridge (built in 1786) to the headquarters of the Henley Royal Regatta to the left and the Leander Club – the world's oldest rowing club – to the right. Turn right for a saunter down Thames Side, passing the half-timbered **Old Granary** ③, located on the corner of Friday Street. Next, go past the **Hobbs of Henley Boatyard** ④, a good place to start a motor launch trip or a cruise along the river. Head down Meadow Rd to the **River and Rowing Museum** ⑤ (open daily; www.rrm.co.uk) with its fun Wind in

the Willows Gallery. Children will be enchanted by the models of Mr Toad, Ratty, and Mole, faithful to the illustrations of Ernest Shepard. Retrace the route to turn left onto Friday Street and right onto Duke Street, noticing **Tudor House** ⑥, a venerable-looking antiques' shop – actually a pastiche built in 1934. Cross Hart Street and go down Bell Street, where, on the left, is the **Bull Inn** ⑦, one of the oldest inns in Henley, with walls up to a metre (3 ft) thick. It is rumoured to be haunted by the ghost of a young woman. Turn right onto New Street to pass the **Kenton Theatre** ⑧ (www.kenton theatre.co.uk), opened in 1805, and the former Brakspear's Brewery, opened in 1779 and now the Hotel du Vin. Turn right again onto Riverside and once more, onto Hart Street to return to the car park.

To extend the walk, follow the Thames Path from Thames Side south for 3 km (2 miles), crossing the river at Marsh Lock to Shiplake. Or cross the bridge and walk 3 km (2 miles) north to Hambleden Lock. For more walks and information, visit www.thames-path.org.uk.

Above The 16th-century Church Loft with original clock, West Wycombe **Below** Old Granary, Henley-on-Thames

EAT AND DRINK

AROUND WEST WYCOMBE

Bull and Butcher moderate
This 16th-century real-ale pub, in Turville near Fingest on the route to Henley-on-Thames, serves dishes such as rib-eye steak, cod in batter and hearty puddings. Turville, RG9 6QU (9 km/5 miles from West Wycombe); 01491 638 283; www.thebullandbutcher.com

HENLEY-ON-THAMES

The Three Tuns inexpensive
Warm town centre pub with well done English classics (bubble and squeak, fish and chips) and excellent beer. 5 Market Place, RG9 2AA; 01491 4100 138; www.thretunshenley.co.uk

Loch Fyne Bar and Grill moderate
This popular restaurant and oyster bar, part of a small chain, serves fresh and smoked fish, shellfish and meat options. 20 Market Place, RG9 2AP; 01491 845 780; www.lochfyne.com

AROUND HENLEY-ON-THAMES

St George & Dragon moderate
Cross the river and go south on A321 for 5 km (3 miles) to this riverside pub offering plain or more ambitious fare. High Street, Wargrave, RG10 8HY; 01189 404 474; www.stgeorgeanddragon.co.uk

Eat and Drink: inexpensive, under £25; moderate, £25–£50; expensive, over £50

Exploring the South Downs

Beachy Head to Chichester

Highlights

- **Seaside Fun**
  Explore the shops, cafés and museums of vibrant Brighton

- **Enjoying the ups of the Downs**
  Walk along the South Downs Way – a superb walking path with great views

- **Antiques paradise**
  Hunt for antiques in the shops and galleries of Petworth, Arundel and Lewes

- **A treasury of modern art**
  Country retreats, gardens, cathedrals, sculpture parks and galleries – see a wealth of novel modern art venues

- **Wildlife wonderland**
  Spot flowers, birds and butterflies in Cuckmere Valley, and waterbirds in the Arundel Wildfowl and Wetlands Centre

Market hall and other historic buildings, Weald and Downland Museum

Exploring the South Downs

The great grassy humped back of the chalk Downs, kept trim by sheep and topped with the remnants of Iron-Age forts, forms part of the South Downs National Park and is a beautiful area to explore at leisure. Along its ridge runs the glorious 160-km (100-mile) South Downs Way, and around its base lie scattered flint-stone farms, pretty thatched cottages and friendly pubs. Although the main roads through the area can get busy, there is a surprisingly remote country feel to the back roads, and the life of bygone days conjured in its open-air museums doesn't seem far away.

Below The open road running along the base of the South Downs near Beachy Head, *see p92*

ACTIVITIES

Go on a nature ramble in the Cuckmere Valley near Alfriston

Cool off in the sea at Brighton or the Witterings

Breach the defences of Iron-Age hill forts at Steyning

Take a boat on the River Arun or Chichester Harbour

Go birdwatching in the wetlands of Arundel

Watch a dashing game of polo in Midhurst

Enjoy a day at the races at Glorious Goodwood

Above Sheep grazing on the upper slopes of the South Downs, near Steyning, *see p94*

KEY

Drive route

Below Beachy Head Lighthouse at the foot of the spectacular white cliffs, *see p92*

PLAN YOUR DRIVE

Start/finish: Beachy Head to Chichester.

Number of days: 3–4, allowing for half a day in Brighton.

Distance: Around 160 km (100 miles).

Road conditions: The roads are mostly in good repair. Prepare for the steep hills of the Downs, and be ready to squeeze by other cars on the narrow roads.

When to go: The drive can be enjoyed at any time: spring brings perky lambs; in summer the larks are rising, the sea tempting and the roads at their busiest; autumn delivers golden harvest days and winter bracing temperatures, when pub fires burn bright.

Opening times: Museums and attractions are generally open 10am–5pm, but close earlier (or are closed altogether) Nov–Easter. Shops are often open longer. Churches are usually open until dusk.

Market days: Lewes: Farmers' Market, 1st and 3rd Sat of the month; Brighton: Big Sunday Market, Brighton Marina, Sun; Arundel: Farmers' Market, 3rd Sat of the month; Chichester: 1st and 3rd Fri of the month.

Shopping: Arts and crafts (Lewes), antiques (Lewes, Arundel, and Petworth) and pottery (Amberley).

Major festivals: Charleston: Literary Festival, May; Lewes: Bonfire Night, 5 Nov; Brighton: Brighton Festival, May; Arundel: Arts Festival, Aug; Chichester Arts Festival, Jun/Jul.

DAY TRIP OPTIONS

Brighton has plenty to enjoy: from **shopping**, **restaurants** and **museums** to its **beach** and famous **pier**. Then head to the countryside – visiting Ditchling for the **Beacon's views**. For those interested in art history, visit Lewes, Charleston, Berwick and Ditchling village for **arts and crafts,** the work of the **Bloomsbury set** and **tea in the garden**. Explore Arundel with its **antiques shops** and **castle, river** and **wetlands centre**. Head to Chichester for the **cathedral** and **a Roman palace, boat trips** or a **visit to the beach**. For full details, *see p97*.

Above Skyhouse Sussex, an eco B&B with fantastic views over Lewes

VISITING BRIGHTON

Parking
Park in one of the North Laine car parks, on Church Street or North Road, or in Trafalgar Street, near the train station.

Tourist Information
Royal Pavilion, BN1 1EE; 0906 711 2255; www.visitbrighton.com

WHERE TO STAY

BEACHY HEAD

Tiger Inn Pub *moderate*
A quintessential English pub with six bedrooms.
Gilberts Drive, East Dean, BN20 0BY (take the East Dean turning off the A259 and continue through the village; the pub is on the right); 01323 423 878; www.beachyhead.org.uk

BRIGHTON

brightonwave *moderate*
This small and friendly boutique hotel by the sea epitomizes Brighton's style.
10 Madeira Place, BN2 1TN; 01273 676 794; www.brightonwave.com; minimum two-night stay at weekends

LEWES

Skyhouse Sussex *moderate–expensive*
Luxury eco B&B with fabulous views over Lewes and the South Downs.
Cuilfail, BN7 2BE; 07468 691 860; www. skyhousesussex.com; minimum two-night stay at weekends

Below The ancient George Inn, Alfriston, first licensed in 1397 **Below right** Straw bales on a farm near Lewes, East Sussex

① Beachy Head
Eastbourne, East Sussex; BN20

The white chalk cliffs of Beachy Head, set against the deep blue sea, are an awesome sight, as though the South Downs have just been snapped off to let the English Channel through. At the cliff's giddy edge, look down to the lighthouse 162 m (530 ft) below. The **Beachy Head Countryside Centre** *(www.beachyhead.org)* and car park has displays about the history and nature of the area. A little way along the loop road, past Birling Gap (more excellent views) and close to the A259, is the **Seven Sisters Sheep Centre** *(open daily, Mar–May: lambing, Jul & Aug: shearing)* where children can feed and pet the sheep. West along the A259 is the **Seven Sisters Country Park** *(www.sevensisters.org.uk)*; from the car park you can follow the footpaths along the tidal Cuckmere River as it meanders to the sea, supporting a variety of birds, butterflies and plants.
🚗 *Head to the A259 and turn left. At the Seven Sisters Country Park, turn right (on a sharp left bend) past the small chalk white horse on the left and through Litlington. Turn left down Lullington Road, signed to Alfriston, then left and left again. Park in car park on left on way into village.*

② Alfriston
East Sussex; BN26 5TA

The most attractive village in Sussex has a High Street of handsome old inns, shops and teahouses, and a large green with the medieval thatched **Clergy House** *(closed Tue, Fri)* by the river. Pack a picnic from the excellent deli in the old Post Office and Village Store for a stroll along the river.
🚗 *Backtrack north out of village, but carry straight on to A27. Turn left, then first left for Berwick, and fourth left for Charleston, signposted after Selmeston.*

③ Berwick
East Sussex; BN26 6SZ

The ancient **St Michael and All Angels Church** was decorated in 1943 with paintings by Bloomsbury Group artists, Duncan Grant and Vanessa Bell, and their son Quentin Bell. The Bloomsbury Group were avant-garde intellectuals, writers and artists who first met in Bloomsbury, London in 1905 to share and promote their philosophical and artistic ideas. Other notable members included writers Virginia Woolf and Lytton Strachey, critic Roger Fry and economist John Maynard Keynes.

In 1916 Vanessa and Duncan moved to **Charleston** *(open Mar–Oct; closed Mon except Bank Hols & Tue)*, an 18th-century farmhouse which became the set's country meeting place. Tours give an inspiring insight to the group's life.
🚗 *Head west on the A27, turn right through Glynde and past Glyndebourne, the opera venue. At the B2192 go left for the A26 to Lewes. After the tunnel, turn left, and left again to park.*

④ Lewes
East Sussex; BN7 2QS

Tom Paine (1737–1809), "Father of the American Revolution", lived in this feisty county town, which today is such a good place to shop that it has its own currency. Spend "Lewes pounds" in galleries and craft shops such as the **Sussex Guild Shop** *(Southover Grange; 01273 479 565)*. Take a break at **Pelham House** *(see right)* for tea in a sculpture garden. Get a taste of history in the medieval **castle** *(closed Mon in Jan)* and walk down the High Street and across the bridge to visit **Harvey's Brewery** shop.
🚗 *Follow signs for A27 (Brighton). Turn left onto B2123 to coast at Rottingdean, and right onto A259, then Marine Drive. At pier turn right, and follow "P" signs to North Laine car parks.*

Where to Stay: inexpensive, under £80; moderate, £80–£150; expensive, over £150

⑤ Brighton & Hove

East Sussex; BN1

There is a lot to see and do in this city of old smugglers' lanes, Bohemian hang-outs, shops, museums, cafés and elegant squares. Time on the beach could easily make a visit last a full day.

Two-hour city walk

Walk down Trafalgar Street under the forecourt of the train station to the **Toy and Model Museum** ① *(closed Sun, Mon)* for a nostalgic return to childhood, then continue to **North Laine** ②. Here is a myriad of laidback cafés and alternative shops selling herbal remedies, fashions, crafts and world food. Go down the fifth right, Sydney St, and almost directly across into Kensington St and then Regent St opposite. Turn left at the end into Church St, past the Dome to **Brighton Museum** ③ *(closed Mon except Bank Hols)*, on the corner, with a great art deco and fashion collection. Continue right into Pavilion Parade for the **Royal Pavilion** ④ *(open daily)*, an Indian-styled folly built in the early 1800s by the Prince Regent (later George IV), with its wonderfully lavish interiors. Cross North St and follow East St down to the seafront and turn left for **Brighton Pier** ⑤ *(open daily)*. Enjoy the arcades and rides, see the fish tanks at the **Sea Life Centre** ⑥ *(open daily)* and ride the **Volks Electric Railway** ⑦ *(Apr–Sep: open*

daily), which goes to the Yellowave Beach Sports venue and café *(closed Mon Nov–Feb)* and Marina. Back at the pier, walk onto the shore and head westwards past the arches. This is the liveliest stretch of seafront, with fish stalls, cafés, funfair rides and the small **Fishing Museum** ⑧ *(open daily)*.

Return to the road, crossing at the traffic lights to go down Ship St by the Ship Hotel. Take the first right, doubling back along Prince Albert St towards the Town Hall. Head left into the maze of alleys known as **The Lanes** ⑨. Once the old fishing town, these are now full of cafés, pubs and shops selling clothes and jewellery.

🚗 **Follow one-way system down through North Laine to bottom of hill and turn left towards A23. Pass to right of St Peter's Church on a huge traffic island, turn left then right up Ditchling Rd. After 6 km (3 miles) or so, at T-junction, go left and right to Ditchling Beacon and village. Car park is just before the main crossroads.**

Top left Jewellers in The Lanes, Brighton **Below right** Indian-style entrance to the Royal Pavilion, Brighton **Below left** Brighton Pier and beach

---

EAT AND DRINK

ALFRISTON

Wingrove House *moderate*
This relaxed yet quality restaurant in the smart, colonial-style Wingrove House has a sunny terrace as well as modern British cuisine that uses locally sourced produce. Lovely rooms available too.
High Street, BN26 5TD; 01323 870 276; www.wingrovehousealfriston.co.uk

LEWES

Pelham House *moderate*
Dine in handsome rooms overlooking the hotel's garden and the Downs.
St Andrew's Lane, BN7 1UW; 01273 488 600; www.pelhamhouse.com

BRIGHTON

The Regency Restaurant *inexpensive*
For excellent fish and chips, this is a good-value spot by West Pier.
131 King's Road, BN1 2HH; 01273 325 014; www.theregencyrestaurant.co.uk

Chilli Pickle *moderate*
Stylish, award-winning Indian restaurant, serving street food, curries and delicious lunchtime *thalis* (platter).
17 Jubilee Street, BN1 1GE; 01273 900 383; www.thechillipickle.com

Terre à Terre *moderate*
Top vegetarian restaurant in The Lanes with an eclectic approach to cooking.
71 East Street, BN1 1HQ; 01273 729 051; www.terreaterre.co.uk

WHERE TO STAY

DITCHLING

The Bull *moderate*
With four smart, themed rooms (with en-suite walk-in showers), this cosy village pub makes a friendly place to stay. It serves good local food, too.
2 High Street, BN6 8TA; 01273 843 147; www.thebullditchling.com

AROUND DITCHLING

Blackberry Wood *inexpensive*
An idyllic rural campsite with pitches in woodland glades 5 km (3 miles) east of Ditchling. All the usual facilities, plus a Gypsy caravan, an old London bus and even a helicopter to rent.
Streat Lane, Streat, BN6 8RS (take Lewes Rd from Ditchling through Westmeston then fourth on the left); 01273 890 035; www.blackberrywood.com

AMBERLEY

Amberley Castle *expensive*
Spend a noble night in this fantastic castle with walled gardens. Four posters, of course, jacket-and-tie fine dining and a portcullis that closes at midnight – so no returning late from the pub.
BN18 9LT; 01798 831 992; www.amberleycastle.co.uk

ARUNDEL

The Swan Hotel *moderate*
There are 14 en-suite rooms with a smart, chic vibe at this 18th-century inn. A great central location too, at the bottom of the High Street.
27–29 High Street, BN18 9AG; 01903 882 314; www.theswanarundel.co.uk

Below Pretty thatched cottage at Amberley, West Sussex

⑥ Ditchling

East Sussex; BN6 8TB

Before reaching this classic Downland village, the road winds up **Ditchling Beacon**, at 270 m (886 ft) the highest point on the Downs with glorious views. The excellent **Ditchling Museum of Art & Craft** *(closed Mon except Bank Hols)* features the work of local artists and craftspeople who lived in the village, including Eric Gill (1892–1940), sculptor and designer of the Gill Sans typeface, and Edward Johnston (1872–1944), creator of the London Underground typeface. More art is on show at the **Turner Dumbrell Workshops**, on the High Street, where work can be bought directly from artists' studios. Take tea in the garden of The General at the crossroads, or visit the Bull pub *(see left)*.

 Go west along **West Street/B2116 to Hurstpierpoint, then south on the B2117, over the A23 and right on the A281 into a left-hand bend. At Henfield, turn left on the A2037 all the way to the A283 (skirting Upper Beeding) and turn left to Steyning. Park on the street.**

⑦ Steyning

West Sussex; BN44 3YE

Half-timbered and quaint, Steyning is a typical Downs market town and worth a stop for a stroll and some tea in the **Steyning Tea Rooms** in the High Street. Take a look in **The Dollshouse Shop** *(closed Sun & Mon)* and don't miss the handsome Norman **church**. The town is a great base for walks to the Iron-Age hill forts of **Cissbury Ring**, the second

Above View of the rolling green countryside of Sussex, from Ditchling Beacon

largest in England, dating from c. 300 BC, and **Chanctonbury Ring**, marked by a beech copse. A round route from Steyning will take about 4 hours, although Cissbury can be reached in under an hour and Chanctonbury can be more easily conquered up an easy track, a short drive west, off the A283.

 Continue west along the A283 **(passing Chanctonbury Lane on the left). At the roundabout, just after Storrington, take the second exit onto the B2139 to Amberley. Park on street.**

⑧ Amberley

West Sussex; BN18 9LT

This small village of honey-coloured cottages is one of the prettiest and most thatched in Sussex. **Amberley Village Pottery** *(closed Wed)*, in an old chapel in Church Street, is where Caroline Seaton makes pots in Amberley Blue, a deep-coloured glaze which she developed in 1964. **Amberley Castle** is actually a manor house and has been turned into an

Below The Steyning Tea Rooms in the old market town of Steyning, West Sussex impressive hotel *(see left)*. There is a useful village shop near the Black Horse pub. Several hours can be spent at **Amberley Museum & Heritage Centre** *(open mid-Mar–early Nov: Wed–Sun; daily during school summer holidays)* in a nearby former chalk pit where there are displays of historic transport, old lime kilns and craftspeople including clay pipe makers.

🚗 *Continue along the B2139 to join the A284 to Arundel. Park by the river on Mill Road, opposite castle entrance.*

Above An example of a half-timbered house, Petworth, West Sussex

🟒 Arundel

West Sussex; BN18 9AB

Dating from the Norman conquest but largely Victorian, **Arundel Castle** *(open Apr–Oct; closed Mon except in Aug & Bank Hols)* dominates this pleasant market town of antiques shops and tearooms – one of the oldest is 16th-century Belinda's in Tarrant Street. Hire a motor boat for a cruise on the River Arun from **The Waterside Tea Garden** *(open Mar–Oct)*. Carry on along Mill Road to **Swanbourne Lake** and hire a rowing boat before visiting Swanbourne Lodge Tea Rooms for a restorative cream tea. Glide through reed beds and waterways on a boat safari at the **Arundel Wildfowl and Wetlands Centre** *(open daily)*. **Bignor Roman Villa** *(open Mar–Oct)*, 9 km (6 miles) north of Arundel, is also worth a visit.

🚗 *Return up A284, then A29 towards Pulborough. At Bury Hill turn left to Bignor (signed) and carry on past Roman Villa and Sutton to A285. Turn right to Petworth and central car park.*

🟒 Petworth

West Sussex; GU28 0AE

Petworth town is dominated by the vast **Petworth House and Park** *(open mid-Mar–Nov: Sat–Wed, Thu & Fri partial*

Right An antiques shop on the steep High Street, Arundel

opening*)* whose extensive grounds were designed by "Capability" Brown. The house holds the National Trust's biggest art collection, with works by J M W Turner. The town is known as an antiques centre. In the High Street is a delightful museum, **Petworth Cottage** *(Apr–Oct: open Tue–Sat & Bank Hol Mon, pm only)*, kept in a time warp at 1910, when it was occupied by Mary Cummings, a local seamstress.

🚗 *Take the A272 to Midhurst. There is a car park on the left as the road enters town, or park on Main Street.*

The South Downs Way

This walking route runs for more than 160 km (100 miles) along the ridge of the Downs from Eastbourne to Winchester in Hampshire. It takes 6–9 days to complete, but can be done in stages at weekends. The route is a bridleway, so horse riders and cyclists enjoy it too. **Footprints of Sussex** does self-guided holidays *(01903 813 381; www.footprintsofsussex.co.uk)*. For shorter loop walks, see *www.nationaltrail.co.uk/south-downs-way*

Above Dominating the skyline, the turrets and towers of Arundel Castle

EAT AND DRINK

DITCHLING

Mister Magnolia's *inexpensive*
This coffeeshop serves breakfasts and simple lunches.
1 High Street, BN6 8SY; 01273 846 638

AMBERLEY

The Sportsman *moderate*
This country pub at the back of the village is popular with South Downs walkers for its views. Serves good food and has five en-suite rooms.
Rackham Road, BN9 9NR; 01798 831 787

ARUNDEL

The Black Rabbit *moderate*
The beautiful setting beside the River Arun with views across to the castle made this pub famous.
Mill Road, BN18 9PB; 01903 882 828; www.theblackrabbitarundel.co.uk

The Town House *moderate*
Dine under a splendid Renaissance ceiling at this fine-dining restaurant.
65 High Street, BN18 9AJ; 01903 883 847; www.thetownhouse.co.uk; closed Sun & Mon

Eat and Drink: inexpensive, under £25; moderate, £25–£50; expensive, over £50

Above left In the heart of the market town of Midhurst, West Sussex Above right Modern art in the woods, Cass Sculpture Foundation

Glorious Goodwood
This huge estate encompasses a motor-racing circuit, aerodrome and "Glorious Goodwood", a flat-racing course. The grounds also include a golf course, the Richmond Arms, and the elegant Goodwood Park Hotel. Art lovers are not forgotten either, with a great collection of paintings at the 18th-century Goodwood House and the separately run Cass Sculpture Foundation, a woodland space with monumental pieces. (www.goodwood.com).

VISITING CHICHESTER

Parking
There are five city-centre long-stay car parks and several short-stay car parks just a few minutes' walk from the centre.

Tourist Information
Town: *Inside the Novium Museum, Tower Street, PO19 1QH; 01243 775 888; www.visitchichester.org*

BOAT TRIPS

Chichester Harbour Water Tours
01243 670 504; www.chichesterharbour watertours.co.uk

Chichester Ship Canal
01243 771 363; www.chichestercanal.org.uk

WHERE TO STAY

MIDHURST

The Spread Eagle Hotel and Health Spa *moderate–expensive*
For top-class pampering, try this hotel and spa. It is comfortable and modern, yet still maintains its Tudor roots.
South Street, GU29 9NH; 01730 816 911; www.hshotels.co.uk

AROUND CHICHESTER

Musgrove House *moderate*
Super-friendly B&B with stylish, contemporary rooms, a 15-minute walk from the centre. Breakfast includes locally sourced bacon and sausages, and home-made jams.
63 Oving Road, PO19 7EN; 01243 790 179; www.musgrovehouse.co.uk

Millstream Hotel *expensive*
In a lovely spot, with a garden and a excellent restaurant serving innovative modern dishes, this small hotel offers apartments as well as B&B rooms.
Bosham, PO18 8HL; 01243 573 234; www.millstream-hotel.co.uk

⑪ Midhurst
West Sussex; GU29 9DS
This attractive half-timbered market town, with more than 100 listed buildings, has a broad main street, plenty of pubs and some top-class hotels. The distinctive yellow paintwork on some houses shows that they belong to the Cowdray Estate. The estate includes the **Cowdray Ruins** *(open mid-May–Aug: Sat, Sun & Bank Hol Mon, pm only)*, once a Tudor mansion built in 1520 and partially destroyed by fire in 1793. **The Cowdray Estate** *(www.cowdray.co.uk)* has a farm shop and holiday cottages. Check for fixtures of Cowdray Park Polo Club *(mid-May–mid-Sep)*.

🚗 *Head out of town on the A286 towards Chichester. After the village of Singleton turn left to the Weald and Downland Museum (signed).*

Below The boat house at Bosham, one of the inlets of Chichester Harbour

⑫ Weald and Downland Open Air Museum
Singleton, West Sussex; PO18 0EU
Allow at least three hours to explore the ancient buildings of this excellent museum *(mid-Feb–Dec: open daily; Jan–mid-Feb: open Wed, Sat, Sun)*. Displays of traditional agricultural methods and crafts – with steam tractors and shire horses – bring the rural past to life. Next door, along the A286, the award-wining **West Dean Estate Gardens** *(open daily)* include a fine kitchen garden and extensive Victorian glasshouses. Nearby, the vast grounds of **Goodwood** offer much of interest *(see above)*.

🚗 *Continue past the museum towards Goodwood. At a tight left-hand bend, a cul-de-sac on the right leads to The Trundle, with great views. Go past Goodwood racecourse and House, turning left on the A286 to Chichester. Park in the town centre.*

Where to Stay: inexpensive, under £80; moderate, £80–£150; expensive, over £150

⑬ Chichester

West Sussex; PO19 1NB

This peaceful county town is centred on a market cross from which North, South, West and East Streets radiate. The **Festival** and **Minerva Theatres** *(www.cft.org.uk; 01243 781 312)* are renowned, and **Pallant House Gallery** *(closed Mon except Bank Hols)*, is a superb modern art gallery. Don't miss **Chichester Cathedral**, consecrated in 1108, with John Piper's dramatic 1966 altar tapestry and Marc Chagall's striking stained-glass window (1978). The recumbent figure of Richard

Above The tapestry designed by John Piper, Chichester Cathedral

Fitzalan, 10th Earl of Arundel, with his wife, Eleanour of Lancaster, inspired Philip Larkin's 1956 poem *An Arundel Tomb*, which can be read alongside it. Finally, the **Novium Museum** *(closed Sun Mar–Nov)*, is a local history museum built above the remains of a Roman bathhouse.

There's also much to see just outside Chichester. Head west on the A27 and turn left on the A259 for the impressive mosaics of **Fishbourne Roman Palace** *(Feb–mid-Dec: open daily; mid-Dec–Jan: open Sat & Sun)*. Further along the A259 lies **Bosham**, one of the many inlets of **Chichester Harbour**. Bosham has a pretty Saxon church; the supposed burial place of King Cnut's daughter, the church is depicted in the Bayeux Tapestry and is one of the oldest Christian sites in Sussex. The harbour inlets are in an Area of Outstanding Natural Beauty, one of the best boating areas on the south coast, so consider taking a boat trip for the scenery or birdlife *(see left)*. Other inlets can be reached by heading south from Chichester on the A286 to charming **Dell Quay** and **Itchenor**. Finish a tour of these wet flatlands with a walk on the sandy beach at **West Wittering** or the more pebbly one at **East Wittering**, a short drive to the south.

Above left Traditional beach huts at sandy West Wittering **Above right** Surfer negotiating the pebbles at East Wittering

EAT AND DRINK

AROUND MIDHURST

Horse Guards Inn *moderate*
Great pub serving locally sourced food, with a cosy, shabby-chic interior and an idyllic garden with hay-bale seating and deckchairs. Three rooms also available.
Upperton Road, Tillington, GU28 9AF; 01798 342 332; www.thehorseguards inn.co.uk; open daily lunch and dinner

CHICHESTER

St Martin's Organic Coffee House *inexpensive*
Home-made snacks, soups and cakes are served in this friendly café. There is a garden and a nice log fire in winter.
3 St Martins Street, PO19 1NP; 01243 786 715; www.organiccoffeehouse.co.uk; open in daytime only; closed Sun

Amelie and Friends *moderate*
This is an excellent restaurant in a handsome Georgian mansion with a pretty walled garden out the back.
31 North Street, PO19 1LY; 01243 771 444; www.amelieandfriends.com; closed dinner Sun

AROUND CHICHESTER

Anchor Bleu *inexpensive*
Good, home-cooked food and real ales in a friendly pub with a terrace overlooking the harbour.
The High Street, Bosham, PO18 8LS; 01243 573 956; www.anchorbleu.co.uk

---

DAY TRIP OPTIONS

Explore the area from buzzy Brighton, arty Lewes or pretty Arundel.

Town and Country
Spend the morning in Brighton ❺ with its museums, arty shops, restaurants and exotic Royal Pavilion. There's plenty for children, with a pier, aquarium and mini-railway. Then drive

up Ditchling Beacon ❻ for views and down to the village for tea.

Follow the drive route to Ditchling.

Arts and crafts
In Lewes ❹, browse the galleries and crafts shops before heading over to Charleston and Berwick ❸ to see the Bloomsbury circle's art.

Follow the drive route in reverse.

Historic Waterland
Explore Arundel ❾ with its castle, antiques shops and wetlands centre. Or head to Chichester ⑬ for the cathedral, ancient Roman mosaics and a boat trip or a walk on the beach.

Follow the A27.

Eat and Drink: inexpensive, under £25; moderate, £25–£50; expensive, over £50

The Garden of England

Ashdown Forest to Battle

Highlights

- **Wildlife and wilderness**
  Spot the natural flora and fauna of Ashdown Forest, Dungeness, Rye Nature Reserve and Bewl Water

- **Produce from the garden**
  Sample fruit-rich jams, saltmarsh lamb, hoppy ales, wine, cider and smoked fish

- **Medieval Winchelsea**
  Walk around the gridded streets of this ancient town with vaulted cellars

- **Gardens in bloom**
  Relax at Great Dixter and Sissinghurst, two of Britain's most celebrated gardens

- **Film-set castles**
  Storm the bastions of the South Coast, the mighty Scotney and Bodiam castles

Shady picnic spot with a view over the high heathland of Ashdown Forest

The Garden of England

Between the North Downs and the coast, this itinerary starts in Ashdown Forest and loops through winding river valleys to the flat wetlands of Romney Marsh and back up to the forests of the High Weald and Bewl Water. The roads twist and turn, diving through woodland and opening into farmlands – so often there are wonderful and unexpected views. Weatherboard villages, elegant windmills, distinctive oast houses and handsome hall houses make it one of Britain's most architecturally diverse regions. Called the Garden of England for its orchards of fruit trees and farmland bursting with produce, the area also contains some of the finest and most original gardens in the country.

ACTIVITIES

Enjoy a cream tea on a glorious country estate at Penshurst

Windsurf on the sea or row on the canal at Hythe

Go birdwatching at RSPB Dungeness or on a walk in Rye

Take a dip in the sea at Camber Sands

Board a vintage train from Tenterden to Bodiam or Hythe to Dungeness

Sample wine from excellent English vintages at Tenterden

Visit the glorious gardens at Sissinghurst and Great Dixter

Hire a bicycle to ride around the forest at Goudhurst

Try a day's tranquil fishing on Bewl Water

KEY

 Drive route

Above Traditional oast houses at Sissinghurst, *see p106*

0 kilometres 8

0 miles 8

PLAN YOUR DRIVE

Start/finish: Ashdown Forest to Battle

Number of days: 3–4, allowing for a half day's walk at Rye.

Distance: Around 280 km (175 miles).

Road conditions: The roads are mostly well maintained. Some lanes are narrow and hedgerows can get wild, so be careful not to scratch your paintwork.

When to go: May to June is a good time to visit, when apple and cherry blossom paints the area pink and white. July and August are often the warmest months but are also the busiest. September is harvest time, when the sea is still warm.

Opening times: Museums and attractions are generally open 10am–5pm, but may close earlier (or are closed altogether) Nov–Easter. Shops are often open longer. Churches are usually open until dusk.

Main market days: Yalding: Farmers' Market: every 3rd Sat; **Hythe**: Farmers' Market: 2nd & 4th Sat of month; Rye: Wed morning.

Shopping: Look out for Winnie the Pooh memorabilia in Ashdown Forest; teapots on Tea Pot Island, Yalding; and pottery and antiques in Rye.

Major festivals: Battle: Arts & Music Festival, Oct; Re-enactment of Battle of Hastings at Battle Abbey, Oct; Hythe: Venetian Fête, Aug 2017 (every two years); Rye: Scallop Festival, Feb; International Jazz Festival, Aug; Arts Festival, Sep; **Tenterden**: Folk Festival, Sep/Oct.

DAY TRIP OPTIONS

For a good family trip, visit the **church** at Hythe and picnic on the **beach** before riding the **steam train** along the coast. Historians will enjoy visiting the **abbey** and **battlefield** at Battle, lunching at the Great Dixter **gardens** and exploring the fairytale **castle** at Bodiam. Another day out might take in the **ghosts** of Pluckley and the **gardens** at Sissinghurst followed by a **castle** at Bodiam and a **lakeside stroll** at Bewl Water. For full details, *see p107*.

Above Fisherman's hut at Rye Harbour, *see pp104–5*

VISITING ASHDOWN FOREST

Getting There
From East Grinstead take the A22 south. After three roundabouts (10 km/6 miles) turn left at traffic lights down Colemans Hatch Rd. The Forest Centre is on the left.

Ashdown Forest Centre
Wych Cross, Forest Row, RH18 5JP; 01342 823 583; www.ashdownforest.org

WHERE TO STAY

AROUND PENSHURST

Charcott Farmhouse *inexpensive*
This B&B in a 16th-century farmhouse has three simple, country-style rooms (two en suite) and a pretty garden.
Leigh TN11 8LG (off the B2027, 5 km/3 miles north of Penshurst); 01892 870 024; www.charcottfarmhouse.com

PLUCKLEY

Elvey Farm *moderate*
This boutique guesthouse is a rural treat, with rooms in an old stable, granary, oast house and barn.
Elvey Lane, TN27 0SU; 01233 840 442; www.elveyfarm.co.uk

HYTHE

The Beach *moderate*
Boutique B&B on the Hythe promenade, with seven stylish en-suite rooms and a sun terrace.
50 Marine Parade, CT21 6AW; 07967 590 732; www.thebeachhythe.co.uk

AROUND HYTHE

Livingstone Lodge *expensive*
Spend a night on safari at this wild animal park, with game drives and overnight accommodation in luxurious tented lodges.
Port Lympne Reserve, Hythe, CT21 4LR; 01303 264 647; www.aspinall foundation.org/livingstone-lodge

Below left Attractive local stores and petrol station, Penshurst **Below right** The fertile Kent countryside near Yalding

① Ashdown Forest
East Sussex; RH18 5JP

Probably most famous as the home of the children's book character Winnie the Pooh, Ashdown Forest is filled with deer and sheep and provides walks, views and picnic spots. Pick up walking maps at the **Ashdown Forest Centre** *(open Sat & Sun; also Mon–Fri pm Apr–Oct)* or continue on to the shop **Pooh Corner** *(open daily)* at Hartfield (along Coleman's Hatch Rd to B2110, right, and then left on B2026). Here you can buy the rule book for Poohsticks to play at **Poohsticks Bridge**, a 40-minute walk away. Nearby Cotchford Farm is where Pooh's creator, A A Milne, brought up his son, Christopher Robin (and also where Rolling Stone Brian Jones drowned in his swimming pool in 1966).

🚗 *From Hartfield, at the end of the High St turn right onto the B2110 all the way to the A264. Turn left, then take the first right down the B2188 to Penshurst.*

② Penshurst
Kent; TN11 8DG

The stone bridge over the fledgling Medway is a delightful approach to this attractive village. Don't miss **Penshurst Place** *(open Apr–Oct)* – one of the grandest estates in the county. Dating from 1346, the pretty crenellated manor house contains the largest original medieval hall outside Westminster as well as some great state rooms and galleries. It also has beautiful walled gardens, a small toy museum and children's playground. Stop off for a cream tea

at the Fir Tree Tea Rooms, once part of the estate. Visit St Mary's church in **Speldhurst**, just off the B2176, to see windows by the 19th-century Pre-Raphaelites William Morris and Edward Burne-Jones. Try the impressive George and Dragon for a top-end pub lunch.

🚗 *Take the B2176 east, turn left on the A26. Keep right, turn right at the second roundabout and left at the third before turning off right onto B2017. Continue to the A228 and turn left. Turn right onto the B2015, then take the B2162 to Yalding.*

③ Yalding
Kent; ME18 6JB

The village lies on the River Beult, which joins the Medway at The Lees, where the medieval **Twyford Bridge** spans the river. Nearby is the 500-year-old, much flooded Anchor pub, opposite Tea Pot Island *(see right)* and Twyford yacht basin. Once a centre of hop-growing, Yalding is an attractive village, with a farmers' market on the third Saturday of each month.

🚗 *Turn left on the B2010, turn right and follow the signs for the B2163, right on the A274. After Headcorn, take the third left to Smarden and then on to Pluckley. Park on the street.*

④ Pluckley
Kent; TN27 0QS

This is apple country, and the hedges along the lanes protect the orchards from winds. Pluckley has two claims to fame: as the most haunted village in England, and as the setting for the UK TV comedy *The Darling Buds of*

Pooh Corner shop sign, Hartfield

Above left Apple orchards are dense around Pluckley **Above right** The medieval Twyford Bridge at Yalding

May, based on the stories of H E Bates (1905–74) who lived in nearby Little Chart. A booklet on sale in the Post Office and the Black Horse pub outlines a tour of the village's dozen supposedly haunted sites, one of them being the pub itself.

🚗 *Turn right to Bethersden, past Pluckley station, right on Kiln Lane, then left onto the A28, then first right to Woodchurch. Turn left here onto the B2067 towards Lympne to Hythe. Use town car parks.*

⑤ Hythe
Kent; TN27 0QS

One of the Cinque Ports, a group of towns formed in 1155 to provide ships for the Crown in return for a beneficial tax status, Hythe is now a breezy, attractive resort. The old town is set back from the sea and topped by **St Leonard's Church**, dating as far back as 1090. Don't miss the fascinating ossuary, with the bones of around 2,000 people. Between the town and the sea, the 45-km (28-mile) **Royal Military Canal** has rowing boats for

Kentish Hops
The flowering part of the hop plant used as a flavouring for beer, hops have given Kent its distinctive red-brick oast houses – kilns used to dry fresh hops. Half a century ago, East Londoners would flock to Kent to spend their summers picking hops. Now only a handful of hop gardens remain. The **Hop Farm Family Park** (www.thehopfarm.co.uk), Beltring – between Yalding and Paddock Wood, explains all things hoppy, and has attractions for kids, too, including play areas and rides.

hire. Hythe is also the terminus for the 22-km (14-mile) **Romney, Hythe & Dymchurch miniature railway** *(open Apr–Oct: daily, also Jan–Mar: Sat & Sun; www.rhdr.org.uk)*. Popular with windsurfers, Hythe's long sandy **beach** is safe and family friendly. Five miles west of Hythe, **Port Lympne Reserve** is home to more than 600 animals; you can even stay overnight *(see left)*.

🚗 *Take the A259, signed to Hastings, to New Romney, then turn off on to the B2071 and follow it to Dungeness.*

EAT AND DRINK

ASHDOWN FOREST
Piglit's Tearoom *inexpensive*
Have a little something in the tearoom that adjoins the Pooh Corner shop.
High Street, Hartfield, TN7 4AE; 01892 770 456; www.pooh-country.co.uk; open in daytime only

PENSHURST
Fir Tree Tea Rooms *inexpensive*
Enjoy cream teas and home-made cakes in a 16th-century building.
Penshurst, TN11 8DB; 01892 870 382; open Apr–Oct: Wed–Sun & Bank Hol Mon, Jan–Mar: Sat & Sun, all pm only

AROUND PENSHURST
George and Dragon *moderate*
Medieval oak-beamed inn that exudes character – local produce includes Ashdown Forest lamb..
Speldhurst Hill, Speldhurst, TN3 0NN (off the B2176, 4.3 km/2.7 miles south of Penshurst); 01892 863 125; www.speldhurst.com

YALDING
Tea Pot Island *inexpensive*
Have a cream tea, a coffee or snack at this riverside setting, filled with over 6,500 teapots at the last count.
Hampstead Lane, ME18 6HG; 01622 814 541; www.teapotisland.com; open in daytime only, daily Apr–Nov, some weekends Dec–Mar

HYTHE
Hythe Bay Seafood *moderate*
On the seafront, this large family-run restaurant is good for seafood. The menu runs from simple fish soup to a Hythe Bay shellfish platter and lobster.
Marine Parade, CT21 6AW; 01303 233 844; www.hythebay.co.uk

Below Windsurfers in Hythe, taking advantage of the open breezy beach

Eat and Drink: inexpensive, under £25; moderate, £25–£50; expensive, over £50

Above Rye Windmill guesthouse, on the pretty Tillingham river, Rye

WHERE TO STAY

DUNGENESS

The Watch Tower *inexpensive*
Lovely B&B with one twin room that comes with its own private, plant-filled conservatory overlooking Dungeness. *Dungeness Road, TN29 9NF; 01797 321 773; www.watchtowerdungeness.com*

RYE

Rye Windmill *moderate*
Near the quay, this hotel offers rooms with character and excellent breakfasts. *Mill Lane, TN31 7DW; 01797 224 027; www.ryewindmill.co.uk; usually minimum two-night stay at weekends*

AROUND TENTERDEN

Barclay Farmhouse *moderate*
This 18th-century farmhouse, off the A262, offers comfort and hospitality. *Woolpack Cnr, Biddenden, TN27 8BQ; 01580 857 127; www.barclayfarm house.co.uk; usually minimum two-night stay at weekends*

Below left The Old Lighthouse (1904), Dungeness **Below right** Film director Derek Jarman's Prospect Cottage, Dungeness

⑥ Dungeness
Kent; TN29 9NB

The windswept headland of **Dungeness** – the largest shingle spit in Europe – lies at the southern end of Romney Marsh, a low-lying area of expansive skies, narrow lanes, water channels and fields dotted with sheep – look out for Romney saltmarsh lamb in restaurants. On your approach along the coast road towards the hulking **nuclear power station** *(closed to visitors)*, stop by **Prospect Cottage**, where film-maker Derek Jarman created an unusual garden from what he found on the beach. At the 45-m (147-ft) **Old Lighthouse** (1924–94), climb to the top to see the view and examine the great glass prisms. The area's special habitat has made it an important **RSPB site** *(open daily)* with trails for kids and regular sightings of bitterns, plovers and wheatears.

🚗 *Take Dungeness Road north to Lydd, then follow signs to Camber and on to Rye. Park at the entrance to the town.*

⑦ Rye
East Sussex; TN31 7LA

It is a pleasure just to stroll around this pretty, ancient and cobblestoned former port. Climb **St Mary's Tower** for excellent views; on the High Street, pop into **Rye Art Gallery** *(open daily)*, buy sweets from jars in Britcher & Rivers' 1920s shop, or pick up delicious picnic snacks from Rye Delicatessen. Head to the waterfront where the tar-black former warehouses are troves of bric-a-brac and antiques. Watch the fishing boats behind the bowling green landing the day's catch.

On the road in to Rye lies **Camber Sands**, a vast sweep of beach revealed when the tide races out across the flat shore. Popular with horse riders and sand yachters, the beach gets busy on summer weekends.

🚗 *Leave Rye on the Winchelsea Road and take the turning signed to Rye Harbour. Drive to the end and park in the car park, by the Nature Reserve Information Centre.*

⑧ Rye Harbour
East Sussex; TN31 7TU

Home to **Rye Harbour Nature Reserve** *(www.wildrye.info)*, these wetlands and reed beds are great for birdwatching. A network of paths cross the area, so it is easy to tailor a walk to the time available. Lime Kiln Cottage by the River Rother is the information centre.

A three-hour country walk

From the car park follow the river past **Lime Kiln Cottage** ① and continue past the bird hide to the sea. Turn right and follow the coast west, past the Ternery Pool on the right – a great place to see wildlife. Walk past the **Mary Stanford Lifeboat House** ② from where, in 1928, a lifeboat with 17 volunteers rowed out to help a storm-stricken ship; all were lost at sea. Turn inland by the marked footpath that runs right by the edge of the larger body of water – Nook Beach – and turn right, veering round to the left past Castle Farm barns. Carry on to a small cluster of houses, to Sea Road and walk up to the

Above Camber Sands has seven miles of award-winning dune-backed beach

roundabout, and take the first exit past the Bridge Inn. Then, turn first left up the steep Strand Hill under Strand Gate into **Winchelsea ③**.

Overlooking the wetlands and sea below, tiny Winchelsea is laid out in the manner of a medieval Bastide town (from Southwest France) – on a grid pattern divided into quarters with wide streets. With little modern development, it feels as if nothing has changed since it was first designed by Edward I in 1288, following a series of storms in which Old Winchelsea all but disappeared. At the town's centre is the large Church of St Thomas the Martyr. Half ruined, its great chancel now serves as the nave, with brilliant stained-glass windows, including one to the victims of the 1928 Rye lifeboat disaster. A feature of Winchelsea's houses is their enormous cellars: look out for the stone steps leading to these vaulted undercrofts where wine was stored; tours are arranged on various dates between April and mid-October (www.winchelsea.net).

Return down to the roundabout and back down Sea Road. Past the Castle Farm barns, just after the footpath begins, follow the signs left, along the track to **Camber Castle ④**, a ruined 16th-century fort. Take the path forking right that skirts the Castle Water. This is another great spot for seeing more birdlife. Follow the path sharp left towards the road, then right, between the ponds and back onto

the road. Turn right here back to the car park by the **Martello Tower ⑤**, one of a series of 74 bastions built along the south coast between 1805–08 during the Napoleonic Wars.

🚗 *Return to Rye, take A268 through the town centre, forking right onto B2082 to Tenterden. Park free for 2 hours at the supermarket just before town.*

⑨ Tenterden
Kent; TN30 6AN

On the road to town, after a series of sharp bends, stop at **Smallhythe Place** (open Mar–Oct: Sat–Wed; www.nationaltrust.org.uk), home of the actress Ellen Terry (1847–1928). Dating from the 16th century, this pretty half-timbered house and cottage garden was the actress's home for nearly 30 years.

Also on the way, look out for award-winning **Chapel Down Vineyard**, the country's biggest producer of English wine (tours Apr–Oct; book in advance on 01580 766 111).

In the handsome town of **Tenterden**, browse the antiques shops and upmarket boutiques, and step back in time at the **Kent & East Sussex Light Railway Station** (www.kesr.org.uk) which runs steam and classic trains to Bodiam and hosts themed weekends several times throughout the year.

🚗 *Drive through Tenterden turning left on the A28, signed to Ashford, then forking left on the A262 to Sissinghurst.*

Below The restored Kent & East Sussex Light Railway Station, Tenterden

Above Rural scenery of wheat fields and hay bales near Sissinghurst, Kent

ACTIVITIES AT BEWL WATER

Bewl Water Outdoor Centre
Bewl Water, Lamberhurst, TN3 8JH; 03000 415 200; www.bewlwater.org

WHERE TO STAY

AROUND BEWL WATER

The Bell *moderate*
South of Bewl Water, this quirkily furnished village pub has seven equally unconventional rooms. Good food, too.
High Street, Ticehust, TN5 7AS; 01580 200 234; www.thebellinticehurst.co.uk

BATTLE

The Powder Mills *moderate*
Gorgeous Georgian country house hotel with fishing lake and grounds. Good restaurant open to non-residents.
Powder Mill Lane, TN33 OSP; 01424 775 511; www.powdermillshotel.com

Below left The gatehouse of Sissinghurst Castle
Below right The splendid gardens and hall house of Great Dixter

⑩ Sissinghurst
Kent; TN17 2AB

One of the great National Trust estates in southeast England, **Sissinghurst Castle Garden** *(open daily)* is not in fact a castle but the remains of a Tudor manor built around 1560. It became a "Castle" in 1756 when it was used to house French prisoners of war who called it "Le Château". The estate was bought by the parliamentarian Harold Nicolson and gardening writer Vita Sackville-West in 1930, who laid out the grounds as a series of "rooms", each with a distinctive theme and colour. The white garden, best in early July, is spectacular, but at any time of year there is something to see. Climb to the top of the tall brick Elizabethan tower in the centre of the gardens for a bird's-eye view of the estate; Vita's old writing room lies halfway up.

Piano at Finchcocks, near Goudhurst

🚗 *Carry along the A262 to Goudhurst. Turn left at the village pond for free parking, just down on the right.*

⑪ Goudhurst
Kent; TN17 1AL

This is an idyllic village with a fine pond and uplifting views. The church tower is sometimes open, for even better views across the Weald. South from Goudhurst on the B2079 lie the green forests of **Bedgebury Pinetum** *(www.bedgeburypinetum.org.uk)*, with

adventure playgrounds, cycle trails and educational activities. Hire some bikes, enjoy a picnic, or just stroll among the tall trees.

Also near Goudhurst, off the A262 is **Finchcocks** *(Apr–Sep: open Sun & Bank Hols; Wed–Thu in Aug; 01580 211 712; www.finchcocks.co.uk)*, a Georgian manor set in beautiful grounds with a museum of early pianos and other instruments. Return to the A262 and follow signs for **Scotney Castle** *(open daily)*. This magical, ruined 14th-century castle has towers, a moat, brightly coloured flower gardens, shady woodland and a hop farm.

🚗 *Take the road out of Scotney Castle to the roundabout, turning left on the A21. Turn right to Bewl Water following the signs – park on site.*

⑫ Bewl Water
Kent; TN3 8JH

Built in the 1970s, the largest inland water in southeast England, **Bewl Water** *(open daily)* is encircled by a 21-km (13-mile) walk and riding path. There is a wide range of activities on offer at **Bewl Water Outdoor Centre**, such as canoeing, windsurfing and rock climbing. Alternatively take a lake cruise, explore an adventure playground, hire a bike or try some fly fishing. After all that, enjoy a snack at the restaurant.

🚗 *Return to the A21, turn right and then left onto the A268 to Hawkhurst,*

Above left Bewl Water, the largest reservoir in southeast England **Above right** The almost complete exterior of Bodiam Castle

then turn right on the A229 and left on the B2244. Turn left to Bodiam Castle, signed and with on-site parking.

⑬ Bodiam Castle
Kent; TN32 5UA

When it comes to castles, few live up to the ideal as well as **Bodiam Castle** *(open daily)*. Built in 1385 beside the River Rother to defend the coast – now some miles away – it saw little action. A square bastion with corner towers and a carp-filled moat, the castle has been the backdrop to films such as *Monty Python and the Holy Grail*. Re-enact swashbuckling movie moments on the battlements, spiral staircases, and gatehouse with original portcullis.

🚗 *From the car park turn left over the river and take first left. At a staggered junction turn left for Great Dixter House and Gardens. Park in the free on-site car park.*

⑭ Great Dixter
Kent; TN31 6PH

A beautiful medieval hall house, **Great Dixter** *(Apr–Oct: open Tue–Sun & Bank Hol Mon; garden 11am–5pm; house 2–5pm)* is an amalgam of two buildings. The original half-timbered house, built between 1440 and 1454, was bought by Nathaniel Lloyd in 1909.

He transported another, similar Tudor house from Benenden nearby and commissioned the Arts and Crafts architect Edwin Lutyens, to meld them together and plan the gardens. Nathaniel's son, the garden writer Christopher Lloyd, was born here in 1906 and made the gardens some of the most inspiring in Britain, using innovative planting techniques. Since his death in 2006, Great Dixter has been managed by a charitable trust.

🚗 *Head back to town and take the A28 south. Turn right and follow the signs to Battle. Park by the Abbey.*

⑮ Battle
Kent; TN33 0AD

At **Battle Abbey** *(open Apr–Oct: daily, Nov–Mar: Sat & Sun; www.englishheritage. co.uk)* stretch your legs with a stroll around the battlefield where, in 1066, the Normans defeated the English: the audio tour is excellent. The Abbey itself was largely destroyed during the 16th-century Dissolution of the Monasteries. The market town of Battle sprang up around the Abbey and merits a short visit. Go down memory lane at **Yesterday's World** *(opening times vary, call 01424 777 226 to check before visiting)*, a museum of social history.

EAT AND DRINK

AROUND GOUDHURST

Halfway House *inexpensive*
Lovely country pub 8 km (5 miles) northwest of Goudhurst, with a big garden, good-value food and real ale served straight from the barrel. *Horsmonden Road, Brenchley, TN12 7AX; 01892 722 526; www. halfwayhousebrenchley.co.uk*

AROUND BODIAM

The Curlew *moderate*
Michelin-starred restaurant serving modern British cuisine in a former coaching inn that is casual and informal. Organic and biodynamic wines from independent producers are on offer too. *Junction Road, Bodiam, TN32 5UY; 01580 861 394; www.thecurlew restaurant.co.uk; closed Mon*

BATTLE

Nobles *moderate*
Good centre of town restaurant with menus featuring local produce – try the Romney Marsh lamb. It has a terrace for sunny days and the set menus are great value. Probably best to book ahead. *17 High Street, TN33 0AE; 01424 774 422; www.noblesrestaurant.co.uk*

DAY TRIP OPTIONS

Discover Kent's history and country-side from Hythe, Battle or Pluckley.

Coastal Marshes

In Hythe, ⑤ see its fine church, then buy provisions and head to the beach with a picnic. Next take the steam railway to New Romney and on to Dungeness ⑥ for a walk on the shingles and some birdspotting.

This trip doesn't require any driving.

War and Peace

At Battle ⑮, see the Abbey and walk the field where the decisive battle in the last successful invasion of England took place. Next, head for a peaceful lunch in the wonderful house and gardens of Great Dixter ⑭, before climbing the battlements of 14th-century Bodiam Castle ⑬.

Retrace the driving directions to Great Dixter and Bodiam Castle. To return, head north-east to A21, then south.

Ghosts, Gardens and Castles

Stay in the haunted village of Pluckley ④, then go to see the wonderful gardens and ancient buildings of Sissinghurst Castle ⑩. Drive through pretty Goudhurst ⑪ to Scotney Castle and if there is time, go to Bewl Water ⑫ for a lakeside stroll or a cycle ride.

Head south out of Pluckley, turn right on A28 and right on the A262. Retrace the journey to return to Pluckley.

Eat and Drink: inexpensive, under £25; moderate, £25–£50; expensive, over £50

The River Cam and Constable Country

Cambridge to East Bergholt

Highlights

- **A world-class university**
  Walk through the historical charms of Cambridge on the picturesque River Cam with its outstanding medieval architecture of college courtyards and churches – and then go punting

- **Galleries and museums**
  Undertake some further education at Cambridge and Saffron Walden's museums, see great art at Audley End, Gainsborough's House and gallery at Sudbury and Sir Alfred Munnings Art Museum at Dedham

- **Constable Country**
  Tour the ancient wool towns, pretty villages, historic churches and rural landscapes captured by John Constable in his paintings

View across the River Cam towards King's College Chapel, Cambridge

The River Cam and Constable Country

This glorious drive begins only 103 km (64 miles) from central London but the places it visits are surprisingly rural, with a flavour and colour that is distinctly local. It traces a route from the venerable university architecture of Cambridgeshire through the unspoiled village greens of Essex to the fertile countryside of the Stour Valley and Dedham Vale, just straying across the border into Suffolk. Here are opportunities to explore a landscape of timeless beauty, immortalized by some of Britain's greatest artists. In this part of East Anglia, history is everywhere present in the ancient market towns, the villages whose cottages – many half-timbered, thatched and washed prettily in pink – seem almost to have sprung from the earth.

KEY

Drive route

0 kilometres 5

0 miles 5

ACTIVITIES

Go punting on the River Cam under the Bridge of Sighs and along the glorious Cambridge Backs

Take tea at "ten to three" at the pretty village of Grantchester, made famous by poet Rupert Brooke

Take your own snap of the village green in Finchingfield, supposedly the most photographed in England

Cross the moat bridge to look around historic Hedingham Castle and maybe watch a joust or two

Take a river cruise beside the lush meadows at Sudbury

Step into a gorgeous Constable painting by the House on Water Lane, Stratford St Mary

Walk along the banks of the Stour at East Bergholt

Below View across the mill pond on the River Cam, Grantchester, *see p113*

Above View across the graveyard to the windmill at Thaxted, built by local farmer John Webb at the turn of the 19th century, *see p114*

Below The Bridge of Sighs built in 1831, St John's College, Cambridge, *see pp112–13*

PLAN YOUR DRIVE

Start/finish: Cambridge to East Bergholt.

Number of days: 3–4 days, allowing at least a half day in Cambridge.

Distance: About 177 km (110 miles).

Road conditions: Good, well-paved and signposted. Off the main roads, lanes are narrow and can be busy.

When to go: Best from April to October as the weather is generally more pleasant and the countryside green and blooming.

Opening times: Museums and attractions are generally open 10am–5pm, but close earlier (or are closed altogether) Nov–Easter. Shop hours are longer. Churches are usually open until dusk.

Main market days: Cambridge: Farmers' Market, Sun; **Saffron Walden**: Market (crafts, farm produce, etc), Tue & Sat; **Thaxted**: Market, Fri am; **Sudbury**: Market Thu & Sat; **Long Melford**: Farmers' Market, 3rd Sat of month.

Shopping: Long Melford is famous for its antiques, arts and crafts shops.

Major festivals: Cambridge: Summer Music Festival, mid-Jul to early Aug; Folk Festival, end Jul/Aug; **Thaxted**: Music Festival, end June/early July; Sudbury: Festival of Performing Arts, mid-Feb to mid-Mar.

DAY TRIP OPTIONS

Cambridge merits the best part of a day to tour its **colleges, galleries, churches** and **picnic** on a **punt**, then head to pretty Grantchester for tea. For quintessential England, see Saffron Walden with its quirky **museum**, then tour the grand **mansion** Audley End, the **church** of Thaxted, Finchingfield **village green** and the **ruins** of Hedingham Castle. **Sources of artistic inspiration** abound here, from **Long Melford**, with its two great halls linked to children's books, to the charming **villages of Constable Country**, which, with their cottages, churches, galleries and beautiful scenery, have all been immortalized in Constable's paintings. For full details, *see p117*.

Above Gothic cloisters at St John's College, Cambridge University

VISITING CAMBRIDGE

Parking
Cambridge is not car-friendly and much of the centre is pedestrianized. Park in one of the five park-and-ride car parks ringing the city or, for the most central car park, follow signs to Grand Arcade.

Tourist Information
Peas Hill, CB2 3AD; 08712 268 006; www.visitcambridge.org

College Opening
Visiting times vary from college to college. Some charge for entrance at certain times. Colleges may be closed to visitors in the exam period (Easter–Jul).

Punting
A plethora of firms offer chauffeur tours and self-punting. Well-established outfits include **Scudamore's** *(01223 359 750; www.scudamores.com)* and **Cambridge Chauffeur Punts** *(01223 354 164; www.punting-in-cambridge.co.uk)*

WHERE TO STAY

CAMBRIDGE

Hotel du Vin & Bistro *expensive*
Choose from 41 rooms in a marvellous old building at the heart of the city. Emphasis on creature comforts, and on bistro classics in the restaurant.
15–19 Trumpington Street, CB2 1QA; 0844 736 4253; www.hotelduvin.com

Hotel Felix *expensive*
This highly regarded hotel offers Victorian elegance overlaid with modern chic. Lovely bedrooms and bathrooms, large grounds, and local produce on the menu in the Graffiti Restaurant.
Whitehouse Lane, CB3 0LX; 01223 277 977; www.hotelfelix.co.uk

❶ Cambridge
Cambridgeshire

This vibrant city – famed the world over for its medieval university – offers enrapturing architecture, a rich historic fabric, green spaces and many activities for the visitor. Cambridge stands on the River Cam, amid beautiful green countryside. Dominated by its 31 colleges, the city enjoys the buzz generated by a large student population.

A three-hour walking tour

From the Grand Arcade car park, turn right into Corn Exchange St and left into Wheeler St to find the **Tourist Information Centre** ①. Turn right, then left onto King's Parade. After St Catharine's College turn right onto Silver St. As you cross the bridge, look right for the **Mathematical Bridge** ②, designed by William Etheridge and first built by James Essex the Younger in 1749. Constructed without nails, this wooden bridge was the first in the world to be designed according to mathematical analysis. To the left, next to the Anchor pub, there is punt hire on the River Cam. On the far side of the bridge, the walk leads via a footpath to the right along **The Backs** ③, with unmissable rear views of the colleges of Queens', King's, Clare and Trinity Hall. At Trinity, where the path ends, continue along Queens Rd, then bear right on Northampton St. On the left, at the junction with Honey Hill, is **Kettle's Yard** ④ *(closed until at least summer 2017; www.kettlesyard.co.uk)*, for 16 years home to Harold Stanley Ede, the Tate Gallery's first modern art curator. The little museum is filled

Wrought-iron gate, Cambridge

with paintings, sculptures and found objects from Ede's collection. Behind is Cambridge St Peter, the city's second-oldest church, and next door is the **Museum of Cambridge** ⑤ *(open Tue–Sat & Sun pm)*, where 20,000 objects and documents recall rural life in Cambridgeshire. Cross Northampton St, turn right onto Magdalene St and cross the bridge (punts for hire here too).

In the Second Court of **Magdalene College** ⑥ on the left is Pepys Library *(call 01223 332 115 for opening times)*, housing the diaries of Samuel Pepys, bequeathed to the college in 1703. Back on Magdalene St by Bridge St, on the right, are some fine half-timbered Tudor houses – erotic carvings hint that one may have been a brothel. At the corner of St John's St stands the **Church of the Holy Sepulchre** ⑦ *(closed Sun am)*, one of four Norman round churches in England, dating from the 12th century. Head down St Johns St for **St John's College** ⑧, founded in 1511 by Lady Margaret Beaufort, mother of Henry VII, and enter First Court, the oldest part of the college. Signs lead to **St John's Chapel**, designed by Sir George

Below Grantchester church, mentioned in one of Rupert Brooke's most famous poems

EAT AND DRINK

CAMBRIDGE

Clarendon Arms *inexpensive*
Popular local town centre, with a terrific selection of ales and delicious pasta.
35 Clarendon Street, CB1 1JX; 01223 778 272

Fitzbillies *inexpensive*
A Cambridge institution established in 1922, this bakery is famed for its Chelsea buns, "probably the stickiest in the world".
52 Trumpington Street, CB2 1RG; 01223 352 500; www.fitzbillies.com; dinner served Fri & Sat only

Cotto *moderate*
This café, deli, restaurant and gallery makes much of local organic produce. Dishes might include seared beef carpaccio or sautéed veal kidney.
183 East Road, CB1 1BG; 01223 302 010; www.cottocambridge.co.uk; dinner served Wed–Sat; closed Sun

Midsummer House *expensive*
Garlanded with awards, including two Michelin stars, this riverside place is recommended for its professionalism and highly imaginative cuisine from its five-, seven- and ten-course menus.
Midsummer Common, CB4 1HA; 01223 369 299; www.midsummerhouse.co.uk

GRANTCHESTER

The Orchard Tea Garden *inexpensive*
Tread in the footsteps of Rupert Brooke and relax over traditional tea or lunch in this idyllic spot, with its historic wooden pavilion and glorious orchard setting.
45–7 Mill Way, CB3 1RS; 01223 551 125; www.orchard-grantchester.com; closed over Christmas

Gilbert Scott in 1863–9. Here a statue of William Wilberforce broods on the evils of slavery. Spanning the Cam is the Bridge of Sighs, designed by Henry Hutchinson in 1827. Turn right out of St John's and enter **Trinity College** ⑨, founded in 1546 by Henry VIII, through its Great Gate. The Wren library was completed in 1695 to designs by the famous architect. Turn right out of Trinity to head back to **King's College** ⑩. Visit the chapel, probably the city's most spectacular building, to marvel at the magical architecture of its ceiling.

🚗 *Follow ring road to Trumpington St, signed M11 south. At Trumpington turn right to Grantchester. Use pay car park and continue on foot.*

② Grantchester

"Stands the church clock at ten to three, and is there honey still for tea?" wrote Rupert Brooke (1887–1915) in his gentle satire of English life, *The Old Vicarage, Grantchester*. It's a pretty village with thatched cottages and historic inns, not yet subsumed by its larger and more lively academic neighbour. See the memorial to the poet Brooke, and the Old Vicarage that was for a time his home; take a snap of the clock at ten to three – and enjoy traditional afternoon tea at the old Orchard Tea Garden.

🚗 *Return to the A1309 at Trumpington, turn right, then left to Great Shelford on A1301. After four roundabouts, take B184 to Saffron Walden. Follow signs for pay parking or look for free short-stay parking in the town centre.*

Below Punters seen from The Backs as they glide past King's College, Cambridge

Kettle's Yard ④ ⑤ Museum of Cambridge
NORTHAMPTON ST
MAGDALENE ST
⑥ Magdalene College
QUEEN'S ROAD
BRIDGE ST
Church of the Holy Sepulchre ⑦
JESUS LANE
St John's College ⑧
ST JOHN'S STREET
SIDNEY STREET
The Backs
Trinity College ⑨
GREEN ST
MARKET ST
HOBSON STREET
Trinity Hall
Clare College
King's College ⑩
KING'S PARADE
Tourist Information Centre 🛈
ℹ
WHEELER ST
CORN EXCHANGE ST
P
QUEEN'S ROAD
River Cam
③ The Backs
Queens' College
St Catharine's College
Corpus Christi College
DOWNING ST
Mathematical Bridge ②
SILVER ST

0 metres 250
0 yards 250

Above left Thaxted's picturesque 19th-century windmill Above top right The Tudor-style town hall in the heart of Saffron Walden, built in 1761 Above right Thatched cottage in traditional Suffolk pink, Thaxted

❹ Audley End

Essex; CB11 4JF

Henry VIII gave Walden Abbey to Sir Thomas Audley, who transformed it into a splendid mansion *(Apr–Oct: open daily, Tue; www.english-heritage.org.uk)*. The third Baron Baybrooke, who came into the property in 1825, brought in works by Holbein, Canaletto and many more. There are 30 rooms to be seen, some designed by Robert Adam, as well as parkland designed by landscape gardener "Capability" Brown, and a Victorian kitchen garden.

🚗 *Return to Saffron Walden and take B184 south (clearly signed) to Thaxted. Park on the street.*

❺ Thaxted

Essex; CM6

A pleasing, small town which does not go out of its way to pull in tourists, but nevertheless boasts ancient, timber-framed houses and a 14th-century **Guildhall** complete with jail *(open Easter–Sep: Sun and for special exhibitions)*. There's also a windmill built in 1804, almshouses and, on the hilltop, the magnificent **Church of St John the Baptist**. Dating to the 14th century, the "Cathedral of Essex" is held by some to be the finest parish church in the country. The town's famous residents have included composer Gustav Holst, who lived here 1914–25, when writing

❸ Saffron Walden

Essex; CB10

A gem of a medieval market town, Saffron Walden sits on the River Cam, in unspoiled Essex countryside. Dating in parts from the 12th century, the town has many half-timbered buildings, although the Tudor-style **town hall** was built as late as 1761. Opened in 1835, **Saffron Walden Museum** *(open Tue–Sun; www.visitsaffronwalden.gov.uk)* is one of Britain's oldest public museums. It stands in a meadow, beside the ruins of 12th-century Walden castle and offers eclectic collections – from Egyptian sarcophagi and mammoth tusks to displays about the people and natural history of the region.

🚗 *From the centre, follow signs on B1383 to Audley End and car park.*

Below Audley End, one of the finest Jacobean houses in England his *Planets Suite*, and highwayman Dick Turpin (1705–39), whose cottage can be seen on the alley up to the church.

🚗 *Take Bardfield Rd right, signed "the Bardfields", to Great Bardfield and B1057 left to Finchingfield. Park on street.*

⑥ Finchingfield
Essex; CM7

A picture-postcard village, reputedly the most photographed in England, with thatched cottages, village green, duck pond, windmill and Norman Church of St John the Baptist. Dodie Smith, author of *The One Hundred and One Dalmatians*, once lived here.

🚗 *Cross the bridge and turn right past church to Wethersfield, head east along the High St to Sible Hedingham. Go left on A1017 and almost immediately right on B1058. Follow signs to the car park.*

Above Ancient mulberry tree in the grounds of Gainsborough's House, Sudbury

⑦ Hedingham Castle
Essex; CO9 3DJ

Cross a dry moat by way of a Tudor bridge to reach the four-storey remains of this 12th-century castle *(Apr–Oct: open Sun–Thu; www.hedinghamcastle.co. uk)*, with its tall keep, banqueting hall and minstrels' gallery. The grounds and surrounding woodlands are especially lovely in spring when carpeted with bluebells. In summer, there may be jousting and other spectacles.

🚗 *Take B1058, then A131 to Sudbury. Join one-way system and follow signs to car park by Tourist Information Centre.*

⑧ Sudbury
Suffolk; CO10

This ancient Suffolk wool town, amid sublime countryside in the Stour Valley, boasts no fewer than three medieval churches, a Victorian corn exchange,

and a **bronze statue** of the painter Thomas Gainsborough (1727–88), which presides over the market square. Modern commercial development has been at some cost to historic charm, but **Gainsborough's House** *(open daily; www.gainsborough.org)*, a typical Suffolk building, has a unique collection of the work of this master of portraiture and landscape. Loaned works and local artists are frequently on display, too. In the walled garden stands a 400-year-old mulberry tree. South of town, there are pleasant meadows to picnic in and river cruise boats operate from the quayside, run by the **River Stour Trust**.

🚗 *Follow signs round one-way system to Bury St Edmunds, A134. Branch onto B1064 to Long Melford.*

Above The imposing keep of 12th-century Hedingham Castle

Above War Memorial by the village green and pond at Finchingfield

EAT AND DRINK

SAFFRON WALDEN

Kim's Coffee House *inexpensive*
Home-baked cakes and scones, sandwiches and filled baguettes, and a vast choice of leaf teas can be enjoyed in the Georgian premises of this friendly establishment or outside, in the gardens. *5 Hill Street, CB10 1EH; closed Sun*

AROUND SAFFRON WALDEN

Cricketers *moderate*
Locally sourced, seasonal, organic food takes pride of place at this 16th-century inn, run by the parents of TV chef Jamie Oliver, 12 minutes' drive from Saffron Walden on the B1383/B10.8. The menu features chicken, "lots of fish" and home-made sausages. *Wicken Road, Clavering; CB11 4QT; 01799 550 442; www.thecricketers.co.uk*

HEDINGHAM CASTLE

Bell Inn *inexpensive–moderate*
Beamed and timbered 15th-century real-ale pub in extensive garden, serving freshly prepared, honest food, much of it locally sourced. Turkish pizzas from the wood-fired oven Wednesdays to Fridays, while Monday night is barbecued fish night – phone ahead to book your fish. *CO9 3EJ; 01787 460350; www.hedinghambell.co.uk*

AROUND SUDBURY

The Henny Swan *moderate*
This inn with garden on the banks of the Stour, south of Sudbury, has numerous awards for its stylish gastropub cooking. For a novelty, book to come here for lunch from Sudbury aboard the eight-seater electric boat, the *Rosette*. *Henny Street, Great Henny, CO10 7LS; 01787 267 953; www.thehennyswan. co.uk*

Eat and Drink: inexpensive, under £25; moderate, £25–£50; expensive, over £50

Above Tudor mansion of Kentwell Hall, built in 1554, Long Melford

Constable Country

"The sound of water escaping from mill dams, willows, old rotten planks, slimy posts and brickwork, I love such things. These scenes made me a painter." So wrote John Constable (1776–1837), who would go on to be recognized, with J M W Turner, as one of the foremost landscape artists of the 19th century. The dramatic vistas, farmlands, water meadows and marshes of the Stour Valley and Dedham Vale, the big skies and distant church spires, all evoke Constable's true spirit.

WHERE TO STAY

LONG MELFORD

Bull Hotel *moderate*
There are 25 comfortable en-suite rooms at this old but friendly and comfortable half-timbered inn set in a central location.
Hall Street, CO10 9JG; 01787 378 494; www.oldenglishinns.co.uk

AROUND LONG MELFORD

Angel *moderate*
Decent pub accommodation and obliging service in this warm and friendly inn (first licensed in 1420). Head north out of Long Melford on the A134 and turn right on Bridge St Rd at Bridge Street to get to Lavenham.
Market Place, Lavenham, CO10 9QZ; 01787 247 388; www.theangellavenham.co.uk

DEDHAM

Dedham Hall and Fountain House *moderate*
This historic manor house hotel and restaurant set in expansive grounds also has an artists' studio and art school housed in a converted Dutch barn. The hotel offers 18 pleasant rooms (13 in an annexe for painting holidays). The place is run with a generous ethos.
Brook Street, CO7 6AD; 01206 323 027; www.dedhamhall.co.uk

Sun Inn *moderate–expensive*
There are seven bedrooms furnished to a high standard in this 15th-century inn. The food on offer is good, too. Expect imaginative breakfasts and a restaurant featuring modern British cooking. Also prepares delicious picnics to order.
High Street, CO7 6DF; 01206 323 351; www.thesuninndedham.com

⑨ Long Melford
Essex; CO10 9AA

This village is aptly named, with its long high street lined with specialist and independent shops, galleries and antiques emporia, bars, restaurants and old inns. **Holy Trinity Church**, dating from the late 15th century, is grand and glorious and the **Old Bull Inn** (c. 1450) once played host to Beatle John Lennon. Delightful Georgian and Queen Anne cottages overlook the green, as does turreted **Melford Hall** (1554) *(open late Mar–late Oct: Wed–Sun pm; www.nationaltrust.org. uk)*, where Queen Elizabeth I once slept and where children's author Beatrix Potter sketched for her books by the fishponds. Then, it's into the car again and – "Parp, parp!" – head north, following tourist signs to the setting for the film *Toad of Toad Hall*. **Kentwell Hall** *(check online calendar for opening times: www.kentwell.co.uk)* is a moated, red-brick Tudor mansion, with gardens and a rare-breeds farm – home to Tamworth pigs, near-extinct Norfolk Horn sheep and huge Suffolk Punch

horses. The humour and hospitality of Patrick Phillips – owner since 1970 – is everywhere in evidence.

🚗 *Head back towards Sudbury on B1064, then follow one-way system to A134 (signed Colchester). Turn off left onto B1068 to Stoke-by-Nayland. Park in the centre.*

⑩ Stoke-by-Nayland
Suffolk; CO6 4QU

Another wonderful Suffolk village, on a hilltop in Constable Country, Stoke-by-Nayland has plenty of attractive half-timbered and traditional pink-washed cottages. **St Mary's Church**, which features in a number of John Constable's paintings, was built from the profits of the local wool trade and dates mainly from the 14th and 16th centuries. It has a fine octagonal font and a well-preserved oak door, adorned with a Tree of Jesse.

🚗 *Rejoin B1068 to Higham. Here, turn right and right to Stratford St Mary. At the village sign turn left to the car park.*

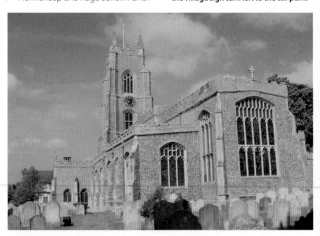

Right St Mary's Church, Stoke-by-Nayland, a typical Suffolk "wool" church

Where to Stay: inexpensive, under £80; moderate, £80–£150; expensive, over £150

Above left 16th-century half-timbered house, Stratford St Mary **Above centre** Sign for a 15th-century coaching inn in pretty Dedham **Above right** View of the River Stour from the bridge, East Bergholt

⑪ Stratford St Mary
Suffolk; CO7 6YG

The southernmost village in Suffolk, Stratford St Mary is another "Constable Country" location. On the road in, look out for the fine pair of striped half-timbered houses, the **Ancient House** and **Priest's House** *(not open to the public)*, opposite the Post Office. Carry on under the A12 to find flint-faced **St Mary's Church**. The building is mainly 15th century, but parts of it may date back to the 1200s. Further along the road (once known as Water Lane) stands **Ravenys**, a private house immortalized in Constable's painting *A House on Water Lane*.

🚗 *Continue on B1029 over A12 to Dedham and park by church.*

⑫ Dedham
Essex; CO7 6AZ

This village retains some fine timber-framed and early-Georgian buildings, and the **Church of St Mary the Virgin**, built in 1492, whose graceful 40-m (131-ft) tower appears in Constable's paintings – his work *The Ascension* is on display inside. The painter attended the **Old Grammar School**, founded by Elizabeth I. Head east on Brook St and follow the road to the **Sir Alfred Munnings Art Museum** *(Apr–Oct: open 2–5pm Wed–Sun;*

www.munningsmuseum.co.uk), a showcase for this artist, famous for his studies of racehorses, who was also an excellent painter of landscapes.

🚗 *From the centre, take Manningtree Rd, left at T-junction, left onto A137 and left at roundabout (still A137). Go left on B1070 to East Bergholt. Park by church.*

⑬ East Bergholt
Suffolk; CO7 6UP

The birthplace of John Constable, this village boasts more pubs than any other in Suffolk. The "ruined" flint towers of the **Church of St Mary the Virgin** were never completed. The bells, however, had already been cast and now hang in a timber bell cage dating from 1531 – they are rung on Sunday mornings. Head down Flatford Rd (clearly signed) to visit **Willy Lott's Cottage** and **Flatford Mill** – settings for two of Constable's famous paintings, *The Hay Wain* and *The Mill Stream*. Nearby, there are lovely walks on both sides of the River Stour and rowing boats can be rented for waterborne adventures. The lovely **East Bergholt Place** *(Mar–Sep: open daily; www. placeforplants.co.uk)*, just off the B1070, described as "a Cornish garden in Suffolk", and laid out 1900–14, features an arboretum and specialist plant centre in a Victorian walled garden.

EAT AND DRINK

LONG MELFORD

Bizzi Beans Café *inexpensive*
Handy for Kentwell Hall, this place offers home-made scones and cakes – including boiled fruitcake. Enjoy baguettes and rolls, filled with free-range chicken and eggs, and speciality coffee too.
Cherry Lane Garden Centre, High Street, CO10 9DH; 01787 464 800; www.bizzibeans.net

Scutchers *moderate*
Tip-top cooking from a fairly short à la carte menu offers dishes such as fillet of turbot with a prawn and chive risotto and pan-fried calves' liver with onion gravy. They offer a very creditable wine card too.
Westgate Street, CO10 9DP; 01787 310 200; www.scutchers.com; open Thu–Sat

STOKE-BY-NAYLAND

Crown Inn *moderate*
A changing menu based on local ingredients includes "catch of the day", Bradfield potatoes and Colchester asparagus, washed down with local ales. Upmarket but friendly. Eleven bedrooms and great breakfasts.
Park Street, CO6 4SE; 01206 262 001; www.crowninn.net

DAY TRIP OPTIONS

Take in the area's wealth of beautiful and historic buildings alongside idyllic English scenery.

A University Education

In Cambridge ❶, enjoy the walk around stunning architecture, some of it over 800 years old. Picnic and punt along the Cam, then drive the short distance to Grantchester ❷ for tea, before returning to Cambridge.

Follow Trumpington St, there and back.

Quintessential England

Staying at Saffron Walden ❸, see its town hall and museum, before touring the mansion at Audley End ❹. Then off to Thaxted ❺, for more half-timbered buildings and church. Drive on to pretty Finchingfield ❻, and finish the day with a visit to Hedingham Castle ❼.

Follow the drive instructions.

Creative Inspiration

From Long Melford ❾, see the two great halls with links to popular children's books. Visit Sudbury ❽, to learn about Gainsborough, then take the Constable tour through Stoke-by-Nayland ❿, Stratford St Mary ⑪, and Dedham ⑫, and East Bergholt ⑬, to see the places and countryside that inspired the great artist.

Follow the drive instructions.

Eat and Drink: inexpensive, under £25; moderate, £25–£50; expensive, over £50

The Broads and the North Norfolk Coast

From Norwich to Heacham

Highlights

- **Historic county town**
  Begin your tour with an exploration of endearing Norwich – the old county town of Norfolk that "has everything"

- **Wonderful waterworld**
  Discover the world-famous Norfolk Broads, filled with history and wildlife under the big skies of East Anglia

- **Seaside secrets**
  Escape the crowds on open sandy beaches, in pretty fishing villages and at quintessentially English seaside resorts

- **Coastal cuisine**
  Eat Cromer crab fresh off the boats, Stewkey Blue cockles on the beach and fish and chips on the pier

Glorious sunrise scenery under the wide open skies of the Norfolk Broads

The Broads and the North Norfolk Coast

This drive begins in the bustling and historic county town of Norwich before cutting through the beautiful Norfolk Broads National Park, where the flat still waters magnify the sunlight streaming from wide skies. Then it heads to the sea, simply following the spectacular coastline west. It's one of the few places in the country where you can see the sun both rise and set in the ocean in a spectacular display of pinks, oranges and mauves. And if the drive ever feels a long way from the sea, simply turn off the main road to find safe, sandy beaches, fishing villages and old-fashioned English resorts. The trip is clearly best enjoyed in fine weather, with glorious opportunities for swimming and sunbathing, but lowering skies and storm-tossed seas also make for dramatic scenery. Walkers, birdwatchers, naturalists and photographers will be in their element among unspoilt salt marshes and wild shores.

KEY

⸺ Drive route

ACTIVITIES

Canoe along the tiny creeks and shallow lakes of the Norfolk Broads from Horning

Hunt for crabs and shrimps in tidal pools at Mundesley

Catch a traditional end-of-the-pier show at Cromer

Walk along the Norfolk Coast Path at Sheringham

See a bittern or marsh harrier in the salt marshes at Cley-next-the-Sea

Take a boat to Blakeney Point to see the migrant terns, dunlin and wigeon and the resident seal colony

Picnic in the glorious sand dunes at Wells-next-the-Sea

Eat a cup of delicious Stewkey Blue cockles doused in plenty of vinegar, while sitting on the beach

Go shopping in Burnham Market, known as "Chelsea on Sea"

Watch the sun sink into the sea from the stripy cliffs of Hunstanton

Below Norwich's Art Nouveau Royal Parade, first opened in 1899, *see p122*

Above View from the pier of Cromer beach, washed by the North Sea, *see p124*

see p124

PLAN YOUR DRIVE

Start/finish: Norwich to Heacham.

Number of days: 3 days.

Distances: Around 160 km (100 miles).

Road conditions: Generally well-maintained and unchallenging.

When to go: From late May to September is best for sun, sand and sea.

Opening times: Galleries, museums and attractions are generally open 10am–5pm, but often close earlier Nov–Easter. Shops are often open longer. Churches are usually open until dusk.

Main market days: Norwich: provisions market, Mon–Sat; **North Walsham**: Farmers' Market, 2nd Sat of month: **Cromer**: Fri; **Sheringham**: Wed and Sat; **Burnham Market**: Farmer's Market, 1st Sat and 3rd Fri of month; **Hunstanton**: Wed.

Shopping: Norwich has some good shops, especially the Royal Arcade, as does Burnham Market. Find great seafood – Cromer crab, Stewkey Blue cockles and samphire – on the coast.

Major festivals: Norwich: Norfolk & Norwich Festival, May; Royal Norfolk Show, late Jun; Food & Drink Festival, Sep; Fringe Festival, Oct; **Cley**: Little Festival of Poetry, Oct; **Wells-next-the-Sea**: Holkham Country Fair, Jul; **Burnham Market**: Flower Show & Carnival, Jul; Concerts, Aug; **Hunstanton**: Arts Festival, Jun, Jul; **Norfolk**: Broads Outdoors Festival, May, within the National Park.

DAY TRIP OPTIONS

Something for everyone. From Norwich spend half a day walking in the **historic centre**, then go to Horning for a **canoe trail** through the Broads. Nature lovers can get close to some **marine animals,** then try a **boat trip** to see the **birds** and **seals** at Blakeney, and go **birdwatching** on the Cley marshes. Families can visit the **animal sanctuary** at West Runton, enjoy a **train ride** from Sheringham and inspect the **tanks** at Weybourne. Alternatively, spend the morning at grand **Holkham Hall** before browsing in the shops of Burnham Market and enjoying the **aromas** of a lavender farm. For full details, *see p127*.

Above View of Norwich Cathedral, built in the 11th and 12th centuries

VISITING NORWICH

Parking
The city centre can be confusing to drivers but the largest central car parks are Chapelfield and Castle Mall, or use park-and-ride facilities around the city.

Tourist Information
The Forum, Millennium Plane, NR2 1TF; 01603 213 999; www.visitnorwich.co.uk

WHERE TO STAY

NORWICH

By Appointment *moderate*
Restaurant with five rooms, lavishly furnished with swags and antiques, in three 15th-century merchants' houses. Breakfast menu includes local sausages, field mushrooms and fresh croissants.
25–29 George Street, NR3 1AB; 01603 630 730; www.byappointmentnorwich.co.uk

Maids Head *moderate*
With en-suite four-star accommodation and guest parking, this is a handy city-centre hotel. It also has a great old bar.
20 Tombland, NR3 1LB; 01603 209 955; www.maidsheadhotel.co.uk

HORNING

Moorhen B&B *moderate*
A delightful old guesthouse with two garden rooms, two rooms overlooking the River Bure and a family "cabin" room.
45 Lower Street, N12 8AA; 01692 631 444; www.themoorhenhorning.co.uk

AROUND MUNDESLEY

Beechwood Hotel *moderate*
This characterful, creeper-covered hotel has 17 en-suite rooms just off the A149 in North Walsham, south of Mundesley. The proprietors are friendly and welcoming. It's worth considering the hotel as a dining option, too.
Cromer Road, NR28 0HD; 01692 403 231; www.beechwood-hotel.co.uk

❶ Norwich
Norfolk; NR2 1TF

"Norwich has everything" wrote architectural historian Nikolaus Pevsner in 1962 – a cathedral and castle, grand halls, cobbled streets lined with ancient buildings, museums, theatres, bars and restaurants, a 900-year-old market, many shops, and two rivers – the Wensum and Yare. The old county town of Norfolk, Norwich makes an ideal base for exploring the East Anglian countryside, the Fens and Norfolk Broads.

Two-hour walking tour

Start at the magnificent **Cathedral** ①, with the second-tallest spire in the UK. It was built by the Normans 1096–1145, although the spire was not completed until 1480. Flanking the West Door, in niches, are two recent figures by David Holgate who used local people for his models. Turn right into Tombland from **Erpingham Gate** ②, where there is a bust of Edith Cavell, a Norfolk nurse executed by the Germans in World War I for helping British and French soldiers to escape. Turn right into Palace St and left and left again to walk down Quayside, along a short stretch of the Wesum. Take a left on Wesum St and right onto cobbled Elm Hill, lined with cottages and antique shops, noting the tiny **Church of St Simon and St Jude** ③, the second most ancient in Norwich. Fork right and right again onto St Andrew's St and take a left on Bridewell Alley to find the **Bridewell Museum** ④, which tells the story of Norwich and its people. To continue, turn right and walk down Bedford St

Stained-glass, Norwich Cathedral

and Lobster Lane, then left onto Lower Goat Lane; continue to find **City Hall** ⑤ lording it over Market Square. Built in the 1930s, this has the longest balcony in England and its sonorous clock bell – Great George – is the largest in Europe. Descend into the square and head to the right to see the 15th-century **Church of St Peter Mancroft** ⑥, dedicated to St Peter and St Paul, whose symbols appear on either side of the north porch. Wander through the market to emerge on to Gentleman's Walk and pass through the Art Nouveau **Royal Arcade** ⑦, designed by George Skipper and opened in 1899. The arcade is lined with traditional old shops. Exit to see **Norwich Castle** ⑧ *(open daily, pm only on Sun; www. museums.norfolk.gov.uk)*, looming above on a mound, with its Norman keep and garden. From 1345, this served as a prison and place of public execution, but since Victorian times it has been a museum with displays of art, archaeology and history. Beyond the castle, go left on Market Avenue

Below Cobbled street and traditional shops in Elm Hill, Norwich

EAT AND DRINK

NORWICH

Ruth's Kitchen *inexpensive*
This daytime-only restaurant offering dishes with a distinct Middle Eastern slant is a terrific spot for lunch.
39 Magdalene Street, NR3 LQ; 07775 964 015

Waffle House *inexpensive*
Enjoy Belgian waffles cooked to order with a variety of toppings – sweet and savoury, plain and wholemeal. Expect to queue at peak times.
39 St Giles Street, NR2 1JN; 01603 612 790; www.wafflehousenorwich.co.uk

Britons Arms Coffee House & Restaurant *inexpensive-moderate*
This charming thatched restaurant, in a medieval setting, has a small terrace and serves good, traditional cooking.
9 Elm Hill, NR3 1HN; 01603 623 367; closed Sun; www.britonsarms.co.uk

La Tasca *inexpensive–moderate*
Yes, it's a chain restaurant, but it's housed in beautiful, spacious premises, with tables outside and with personable service. It's good for tapas at fair prices.
24 Tombland, NR3 1RF; 01603 776 420; www.latasca.co.uk

Bishop's Dining Room *moderate*
Elegant, pink-washed restaurant with short, interesting set lunch and dinner menus that include veggie, meat and fish options and home-baked bread.
8–10 St Andrew's Hill, NR2 1AD; 01603 767 321; open Tue–Sat; www.bishopsrestaurant.co.uk

Last Wine Bar & Restaurant *moderate*
Housed in a former shoe factory, this restaurant offers imaginative cuisine such as home-smoked chicken with truffle mayonnaise or peanut butter parfait, and a good wine list.
76 St George's Street, NR3 1AB; 01603 626 626; www.lastwinebar.co.uk; closed Sun

Below Thatched cottage in the attractive riverside village of Horning

and right on Upper King St, back to Tombland and the cathedral.

🚗 *From the cathedral cross the river to A1151 to Hoveton St John, take a right on A1062; pay parking on the right.*

② Horning
Norfolk; NR12 8AA

This pretty village, downriver from charming but busy Wroxham, is blessed with thatched cottages, good shops, waterside inns and restaurants. The **Galley** deli on Lower Street sells good picnic fare, perfect for an outing on the river. Summer guided canoe tours and trails provide the ideal way to explore the Broads, venturing into peaceful backwaters inaccessible to motor vehicles and walkers – try *01603 783 777; www.thecanoeman.com.*

🚗 *Return to Hoveton St John and turn right on to A1151, turn left on to A149; carry straight on to B1145 to Mundesley.*

③ Mundesley
Norfolk; NR11 8JH

The golden, sandy beaches at this old-fashioned resort, with its gaily painted beach huts, are among the finest in Norfolk. At low tide, children splash around in the sun-warmed tidal pools. Above the beach there's a 3-m (10-ft) bomb-shaped **war memorial** to the 36 men killed clearing mines from the Norfolk coast after World War II and tiny **Mundesley Maritime Museum**

The Norfolk Broads

Britain's largest nationally protected wetland has a network of rivers, lakes (broads) and marshes that abound with rare flora and fauna. It's a haven for birds such as wigeon, teal, marsh harriers or bitterns, plants such as the fen orchid or ragged robin and large butterflies such as the swallowtail. Visitors can fish, take a boat trip, cycle or walk through watery landscapes, admiring the villages, churches and windmills. Contact *Broads Authority, 18 Colegate, Norwich, NR3 1BQ; 01603 610 734; www.broads-authority.gov.uk.*

(May–Sep: open Sun–Fri) in a former coastguards' look-out, possibly the smallest museum in the country.

🚗 *Head northwest on the B1159, the coast road to Cromer.*

BOAT TRIPS

For trips to Blakeney Point to see the seal and seabird colonies, try **Beans Boats** *(01263 740 038; www.beansboattrips.co.uk)* or **Temples Seal Trips** *(01263 740 791; www.sealtrips.co.uk)* at Morston Quay or **Bishops Boats** *(01263 740 753; www.bishopsboats.com)* at Blakeney Quay.

WHERE TO STAY

CROMER

Cliftonville Hotel *moderate*
Enjoy sea views in this Edwardian hotel – there's a good restaurant, open to non-residents – with a fine minstrels' gallery.
Seafront, NR27 9AS; 01263 512 543; www.cliftonvillehotel.co.uk

AROUND SHERINGHAM

Dales Country House Hotel *expensive*
Twenty-one good en-suite rooms are on offer here, in a former rectory in grounds by Sheringham Park, on B1157 south.
Lodge Hill, Upper Sheringham, NR26 8TJ; 01263 824 555; www.dalescountryhouse.co.uk

WEYBOURNE

Weybourne Forest Lodges *moderate*
Well-equipped, comfortable lodges in in a delightful sylvan setting.
Sandy Hill Lane, NR25 7HW; 01263 588 440; www.weybourneforestlodges.co.uk

CLEY-NEXT-THE-SEA

Cley Windmill
This lovely windmill offers B&B or self-catering facilities as well as home-cooked dinner by candlelight in the dining room.
Cley Windmill, NR25 7RP; 01263 740 209; www.cleywindmill.co.uk

AROUND BLAKENEY

Morston Hall *expensive*
A luxurious manor house with great sea views and an award-winning restaurant.
Morston, Holt, NR25 7AA (12km/7miles on the A149); 01263 741 041; www.morstonhall.com

Below Traditional seaside pier with theatre at Cromer beach

Above left Historic station on the North Norfolk Railway Poppy Line, Sheringham **Above top right** Horse grazing at the Hillside Animal and Shire Horse Sanctuary **Above right** Rhododendrons at Sheringham Park

④ Cromer
Norfolk; NR27 0AH

A resort of note since the 18th century, Cromer is best known for its delicious crabs. From April to September, boats ply to and from crab banks out to sea, landing the local delicacy. Along the front, tall Victorian houses look out to the ocean, over the sand-and-shingle beach. Also, overlooking the beach is the **RNLI Henry Blogg Museum** *(closed Mon; Dec & Jan)* offering an interesting history of the RNLI and drinks and cake in the café upstairs. The pier's **Pavilion Theatre** still hosts traditional end-of-the-pier shows. In town, the tower of **St Peter and St Paul Church** soars to a stunning 49 m (160 ft) and may be climbed at certain times for breathtaking views over the area.

🚌 *Head west on A149 to West Runton.*

⑤ West Runton
Norfolk; NR27 9QH

This attractive village is home to the **Hillside Animal and Shire Horse Sanctuary** *(Jun–Aug: open Sun–Fri; Apr–May, Sep–Oct: open Sun–Thu: closed winter; www.hillside.org.uk)*. The rescued animals include some magnificent heavy work horses, ponies, pigs, cattle, goats, alpacas, rabbits, ducks and hens – many of them up for "adoption" (sponsorship). There's much to delight young children, and the wonderful collection of old carts, farm machinery and wooden caravans, will occupy older minds.

🚌 *Keep west on A149 to Sheringham.*

⑥ Sheringham
Norfolk; NR26 8RA

A former fishing village, Sheringham is now a thriving, very English holiday resort, with clifftop gardens, arcades and golden sands. Its situation on the Norfolk Coast Path makes the resort an ideal base for walkers. From the A149 follow signs to **Sheringham Park** *(mid-Mar–Sep: open daily; Oct: open Wed–Sun; Nov–mid-Mar: open Sat & Sun)*, with paths through parks and National Trust gardens landscaped by Humphry Repton (1752–1818). Take a trip by steam or vintage diesel train on the **North Norfolk Railway Poppy Line** *(Jun–Sep: open daily; check at other*

Where to Stay: inexpensive, under £80; moderate, £80–£150; expensive, over £150

times; 01263 820 808; www.nnrailway.co.
uk). With a "Rover" ticket for a day's
travel, board and alight at will. There
is a charming station building,
complete with period furnishings,
at the western terminus, just 8 km
(5 miles) from Sheringham and not
far from the flower-filled Georgian
town of **Holt**, a repeated finalist in
the Anglia In Bloom contest.

🚗 *Carry on A149 west to Weybourne.*

Above Little station on the North Norfolk Railway
Poppy Line, Weybourne

🅐 Weybourne
Norfolk; NR25 7SZ

This attractive village (pronounced
"Webbon'") sits amid farm and heath
land. It has a famously steep, pebbly
beach, a historic station on the Poppy
Line and the **Muckleburgh Collection**
*(Mar: open Sat & Sun; Apr–Oct: open
daily; www.muckleburgh.co.uk)*, Britain's
largest private collection of military
vehicles and equipment.

🚗 *Take A149 west, via Salthouse –
stopping off at Cookies Crab Shop.*

🅗 Cley-next-the-Sea
Norfolk; NR25 7SZ

A thriving port in medieval times, Cley
is now some distance inland. In its
heyday, it exported wool to the
Netherlands – and imported curved
gables, Flemish bricks and pantiles,
which mix happily with Georgian
architecture. **Cley Windmill** is an 18th-
century mill that has been converted
into a B&B with views of the salt marsh
and bird sanctuary. The owners usually
let visitors have a look inside. Visit the
Norfolk Wildlife Trust visitor centre on
the marshes, east of town. Facilities
include a remote camera, a café, hides
for birdwatching, and an audio trail.

🚗 *Carry on west on A149 to Blakeney.*

🅘 Blakeney
Norfolk; NR25 7SZ

Like Cley, this was a busy port in
ancient times but, since the harbour
has silted up, only small craft can
navigate the creeks. The village is
delightful, with attractive flint cottages,
a 14th-century guildhall and places to
shop, eat, drink and stay. However, the
greatest draw for visitors are the boat
trips to **Blakeney Point**, which put out
from here and neighbouring Morston,
to the west. These trips, lasting one to
two hours, provide an excellent way
to view seabirds and basking seals in
their natural environment, without
unduly disturbing them. The seal
colony – a mix of Common and Grey
seals – numbers some 500. Common
seals have their young or pups Jun–
Aug; the Greys Nov–Jan.

🚗 *Take the A149 west via Stiffkey
(pronounced "Stewkey"), famous for its
cockles, with pretty flint cottages, salt
marshes and reed beds.*

Above Sign for the village of Blakeney
painted according to Norfolk tradition

EAT AND DRINK

CROMER

**Rocket House Café and
Restaurant** *inexpensive*
Visit this stylish place above the RNLI
Henry Blogg Museum (with lift access),
for coffee and a cake, or a meal of local
seafood with unsurpassed sea views.
*The Gangway, Promenade, NR27 9ET;
01263 519126; open daily for breakfast,
lunch and tea; also dinner May–Oct: Sat*

WEYBOURNE

The Ship Inn *inexpensive–moderate*
Simplicity is key in this attractive old pub.
The short menu features delicious local
dishes such as seafood chowder.
*The Street, NR25 7SZ; 01263 588 721;
www.theshipinnweybourne.com*

AROUND WEYBOURNE

Cookies Crab Shop *inexpensive*
Try the soups and local fish at this
café/shop. Bring your own alcohol.
*The Green, Salthouse, NR25 7AJ; 01263
740 352; www.salthouse.org.uk; open
9am–6pm daily*

CLEY-NEXT-THE-SEA

The George *inexpensive–moderate*
Good, honest fare with a few flourishes
can be enjoyed in this birdwatchers'
paradise. Consider the rooms, too.
*High Street, NR25 7RN; 01263 740 652;
www.thegeorgehotelatcley.co.uk*

BLAKENEY

The Blakeney White Horse
inexpensive–moderate
Seasonal seafood fresh off the boat,
good local produce and home-made
desserts. There are also a few rooms.
*4 High Street, NR 25 7AL; 01263 740 574;
www.adnams.co.uk*

Left Cley Windmill, set on the salt marshes and
popular with artists

Eat and Drink: inexpensive, under £25; moderate, £25–£50; expensive, over £50

Above Lobster and crab boats at the quayside Wells-next-the-Sea

WHERE TO STAY

WELLS-NEXT-THE-SEA

Globe Inn *moderate*
Seven bright and airy en-suite rooms are available in this refurbished inn. The breakfast menu includes Cley smoked haddock with poached egg, and there are good-value bar snacks all day.
The Buttlands, N23 1EU; 01328 710 206; www.holkham.co.uk/globe

Victoria Hotel *moderate–expensive*
A historic hotel on the edge of the Holkham Estate, this has real-ale bars on the ground floor and an upmarket restaurant. Some of the 10 en-suite rooms have views over the marshes. There are also three glorious self-catering lodges available.
Park Road, NR23 1RG; 01328 711 008; www.holkham.co.uk

BURNHAM MARKET

The Jockey *inexpensive–moderate*
This pub offers four decent bedrooms with en-suite shower rooms in the heart of this lovely village. There are hearty breakfasts and bar meals that make use of local ingredients.
Creake Road, PE31 8EN; 01328 738 321; www.thejockeyburnhammarket.co.uk

HUNSTANTON

Neptune Inn *moderate*
There are six pleasant en-suite rooms at this handsome 18th-century coaching inn. The Michelin-starred restaurant uses mainly Norfolk ingredients in the restaurant and bar.
85 Old Hunstanton Road, PE36 6HZ; 01485 532 122; www.theneptune.co.uk

Right Creek into the harbour at Wells-next-the-Sea

⑩ Wells-next-the-Sea
Norfolk; NR23 1AN
A popular resort town, Wells got its name from the many clear springs in the area. Today, as a result of silting, it is more "near" than "next" the sea – vessels must sail some way up inlets to berth here, but the harbour is still a great attraction. Stroll up to the grassy Georgian square known as The Buttlands, for a drink in either of the village inns, the **Crown** or the **Globe**, or buy a picnic from the **Wells Deli** and head for the beach. Travel in style on the tiny, narrow-gauge, steam or diesel **Wells Harbour Railway** *(seasonal service)*. The beautiful sands are backed by expansive dunes and cooling pines.

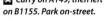

Wells-next-the-Sea village sign

Just west, neighbouring **Holkham Hall Estate** *(open spring–summer; park open daily; www.holkham.co.uk)* is a fabulous Palladian-style country seat amid a deer park, home to Viscount and Viscountess Coke (pronounced "Cook"). It houses a treasury of statues, Old Masters' paintings, antiques and tapestries. The Statue Gallery contains one of the finest private collections of classical sculpture, including a statue of Diana and a bust of Thucydides from the 4th century BC. A notice on the piano on the way in, invites able musicians to sit down and play. The hall was a setting in the film *The Duchess*, starring Keira Knightley as Georgiana Spencer and Ralph Fiennes as the Duke of Devonshire.

🚗 **Carry on A149, then left on B1155. Park on-street.**

⑪ Burnham Market
Norfolk; NR23 1AB
Away from the coast, enjoy the fine Georgian cottages book-ended by two small churches in this riverside town, known as "Chelsea on Sea". Browse the hat and dress shops, art gallery, jewellers, fish shop and delicatessen, then have a deserved drink at the handsome Hoste Arms.

🚗 **Head north on the B1355, then turn left on A149.**

> ### Stiffkey Blues
> Local cockles known as "Stewkey Blues" have been harvested on the Stiffkey marshes for generations. Their blue colour comes from their anaerobic mud habitat. Often used in fancy restaurant dishes, they are best from a seafood stall, smothered in vinegar and eaten on the beach.

Peddars Way

The Norfolk Coast Path forms part of the ancient Peddars Way, a scenic trail that starts at Knetishall Heath, near Thetford, and runs across 74 km (46 miles) of mainly flat fenland to the sea near Hunstanton, following an old Roman road. It hugs the coast eastward to Cromer before turning inland and joining the Weavers Way and Angles Way to Great Yarmouth.

⑫ Hunstanton

Norfolk; PE36 6BQ

An old-fashioned, bucket-and-spade sort of resort, "Sunny Hunny" has two distinct geographical features. Its award-winning sandy beaches are overlooked by cliffs striped red, white and brown and, although an east coast town, it looks west, into glorious sunsets over the Wash. History buffs might like **Old Hunstanton** for its deeper roots and charm, but hidden away among traditional amusements on Hunstanton's Southern Promenade (with pay parking), is the fascinating **Sea Life Sanctuary** *(open daily; 01485 533 576; www.sealsanctuary.co.uk)*. This is dedicated to the rescue, rehabilitation and release back into the wild of sick

and injured seals and other marine animals. Walk through an underwater glass tunnel and be mesmerized by sharks, seahorses, rays and other sea creatures in this safe habitat.

🚌 *Head south on the A149.*

⑬ Heacham

Norfolk; PE31

This seaside village is a popular holiday destination, and the wide open sands attract kite-fliers and windsurfers. Like Hunstanton, Heacham looks west across the vast bay and enjoys the evening spectacle of golden sunsets reflected in the water. In 1614, the Algonquin Indian princess Pocahontas married the Heacham local John Rolfe – commemorated by a carving in the 13th-century Norman St Mary's Church. Just outside the village, located in an old watermill, is **Norfolk Lavender** *(open daily; 01485 570 384; www.norfolk-lavender.co.uk)*, with fragrant meadow garden, plant centre, herb garden and shop. Try lavender and lemon scones in the tearoom, take a minibus tour of the blooming lavender fields in July, or visit the Rare Breeds and Animal Centre on site.

Above left Local produce at Burnham Market
Above centre Resident of the popular Sea Life Sanctuary, Huntstanton **Right** Bronze lioness, Holkham Hall, near Wells-next-the-Sea

EAT AND DRINK

WELLS-NEXT-THE-SEA

Crown Hotel *moderate*
The emphasis here is on local produce, seasonality and sustainability. The result is good, inventive but unfussy cooking.
The Buttlands, NR23 1EX; 01328 710 209; www.thecrownhotelwells.co.uk

BURNHAM MARKET

Hoste Arms *moderate*
Eat in the bar or in comfortable dining-rooms from an imaginative menu of local produce – Brancaster oysters, Cromer crab and Norfolk pork. There are also plenty of good rooms – Horatio Nelson is said to have stayed here.
The Green, PE3 8HD; 01328 738 777; www.hostearms.co.uk

AROUND HEACHAM

Rose and Crown *moderate*
Family-friendly, 14th-century beamed inn with walled garden– try the beef or lamb grazed on the salt marshes at Holkham, and fish and shellfish landed off the Norfolk and Suffolk coast.
Old Church Road, Snettisham, PE31 7LX; 01485 541 382; www.roseandcrownsnettisham.co.uk

---

DAY TRIP OPTIONS

There's lots of choice here for history buffs, nature lovers, families, and even those who like life a little slower.

Norwich and the Broads

Staying at Norwich ❶, explore the town in the morning – see the castle, cathedral, historic centre and shops, then head for Horning ❷, to buy a picnic and spend the afternoon on the Broads in a canoe. Finally, enjoy a fish supper at Mundesley ❸ by the sea.

Follow the instructions in this drive.

Wildlife Adventure

From Hunstanton ⑫, visit the Sea Life Sanctuary to learn about the animals up close. Then drive over to Blakeney ❾ for a boat trip to see the sea birds and seals in their natural environment. Finish up at Cley-next-the-Sea ❽ birdwatching in the salt marshes.

Take the A149 there and back.

Family Fun

Starting at Cromer ❹, enjoy the traditional resort atmosphere then set off for West Runton ❺, to see the farm

animals at the sanctuary. Stop off at Sheringham ❻ for a railway ride and then head to Weybourne ❼ for the amazing collection of military vehicles.

Take the A149 there and back.

A Genteel Day

Take a tour of the grand hall and estate at Holkham. Then drive to Burnham Market ⑪, for some quaint village life and a spot of shopping, before heading for Heacham ⑬ and a visit to the lavender farm.

Take the A149 there and back.

Eat and Drink: inexpensive, under £25; moderate, £25–£50; expensive, over £50

Borderlands to Beacons

From Hereford to Blaenavon

Highlights

- **Ancient and modern treasures**
  Wonder at Saxon and Norman architecture, medieval artifacts and modern ecclesiastic art in Hereford, Kilpeck and Brecon

- **Idyllic valley landscapes**
  Travel through the Vale of Ewyas with its ancient priory, leaning church tower and its pass over the Black Mountains

- **The book capital of the world**
  Rummage through the books in Hay-on-Wye, the world centre for antiquarian and second-hand books

- **Industrial heritage**
  Step back in time and tour the extraordinary collection of Industrial Revolution sites at Blaenavon

Crickhowell countryside, on the eastern edge of the Brecon Beacons

Borderlands to Beacons

Beginning in the compact English borders city of Hereford, with its beautiful cathedral, this drive follows a route through the ecclesiastical highlights of the "Golden Valley" (Abbey Dore) and Vale of Ewyas (Llanthony Priory). It then crosses into Wales to Hay-on-Wye, the book capital of the world, and through the glorious landscape of the Brecon Beacons National Park before finishing in Blaenavon, a sprawling industrial World Heritage Site.

Above From farmland to wilderness – the varied landscape of the Brecon Beacons, *see p134*

Below Pointed, arched doorway at Hereford Cathedral, *see p132*

ACTIVITIES

Map the 13th-century route to Jerusalem on the Mappa Mundi at Hereford Cathedral

Taste some fine cider at Hereford's Cider Museum

Drive over stunning Gospel Pass for views of the Wye Valley

Go fishing, birdwatching or take a boat out on the waters of Wales' second largest lake at Llangorse

Walk glorious trails in the Brecon Beacons

Trace the lineage of Jesus on the medieval Jesse sculpture inside St Mary's Priory Church in Abergavenny

Go down a mine and reflect on South Wales' industrial past – a history which changed the modern world

0 kilometres 5

0 miles 5

KEY

━━ Drive route

HEREFORDSHIRE

ABBEY DORE ❸

①HEREFORD

②KILPECK

❹

LE OF VYAS

ABERGAVENNY

MONMOUTHSHIRE

Below Pastel-painted B&Bs lining the streets in the heart of Brecon, *see p133*

PLAN YOUR DRIVE

Start/finish: Hereford to Blaenavon.

Number of days: 3, allowing half a day to explore Hay-On-Wye.

Distances: 175 km (110 miles).

Road conditions: Good roads in most places and well signposted. Some roads are narrow and quite rural.

When to go: Spring is pleasant but summer is best for outdoor activities.

Opening times: Museums and attractions are generally open 10am–5pm, but close earlier (or are closed altogether) Nov–Easter. Shops are often open longer. Churches are usually open until dusk. Some B&Bs close for winter.

Main market days: Hereford: Indoor Retail Market, Wed & Sat; Butter Market (foods and miscellaneous), Mon–Sat; Hay-on-Wye: Butter Market (food, antiques and bric a brac), Thu am; Brecon: Farmers' Market, second Sat of the month.

Shopping: Look out for apple juice around Crickhowell, as well as produce from the Black Mountain Smokery, Welsh venison, lamb and Penderyn Whisky in the Brecon Beacons.

Major festivals: Hereford: Art Week (open studios, exhibitions – *www. brightstripe.co.uk*), Sep; Hay-on-Wye: Hay Festival, (everything about books – *www.hayfestival.com*), a week from end of May to the start of Jun; Brecon: Jazz Festival (*www.breconjazz.co.uk*), Aug; Green Man Festival (music festival – *www.greenman.net*), end Aug; Abergavenny: Food Festival (*www. abergavennyfoodfestival.com*), late Sep.

DAY TRIP OPTIONS

Church buffs can start at Hereford **cathedral** before heading to the fine **church** at Kilpeck. Visit the **abbey** at Dore and drive through the Vale of Ewyas, past the **priory** and a **church** with a **leaning tower**. Last stop is the **book capital** at Hay-on-Wye. Families might prefer a visit to the **iron works** and a trip down the **mine** at Blaenavon, then the **castle** and **manor house** at Tretower, and **waterside activities** at Llangorse. For full details, *see p135*.

Above Dore Abbey, founded by French Cistercian monks in 1147

VISITING HEREFORD

Parking
One-hour parking at King Street and three-hour disabled-only parking at Broad Street.

Tourist Information
01432 268 430; www.visit herefordshire.co.uk

WHERE TO STAY

HEREFORD

Somerville House *moderate*
This friendly boutique B&B is located in a Victorian villa a short walk from the station. Serves healthy breakfasts.
12 Bodenham Road, HR1 2TS; 01432 273 991; www.somervillehouse.co.uk

HAY-ON-WYE

The Swan at Hay *moderate*
This former coaching inn dates back to Georgian times and has 18 comfortable rooms and pretty gardens.
Church Street, HR3 5DQ; 01497 821 188; www.swanathay.co.uk

AROUND HAY-ON-WYE

The Old Post Office *moderate*
Set in a 17th-century building, southeast of Hay off the B4350, this B&B has three en-suite rooms; vegetarian breakfasts.
Llanigon, HR3 5QA; 01497 820 008; www.oldpost-office.co.uk

AROUND BRECON

Felin Glais *moderate*
Restored 17th-century barn in fields to the west of Brecon. It offers rustic chic and weekend evening meals.
Aberyscir, LD3 9NP; 01874 623 107; www.felinglais.co.uk

Felin Fach Griffin *moderate*
At this lovely terracotta-painted pub off the A470 northeast of Brecon, boutique rooms are stylish and comfortable.
Felin Fach, LD3 0UB; 01874 620 111; www.eatdrinksleep.ltd.uk

1 Hereford
Herefordshire; HR4 9BW
With its gentle hills and gardens, it is easy to forget that in the Middle Ages Hereford saw fierce border skirmishes between the Welsh and English, even after the Saxon King Offa of Mercia (AD 757–96) invaded Wales and built his dyke. For earlier civilizations, visit **Hereford Museum and Art Gallery** *(open Wed–Sat)* on Broad St and see a Roman mosaic and coins, keys and bronzes found locally.

High above the River Wye, **Hereford Cathedral** has Saxon origins and fine Norman pillars, dog-tooth arches and an ancient library. See, too, one of Britain's finest treasures, the Mappa Mundi, a map of the known world, drawn on deer vellum in 1290. Among the modern artworks are Simon Beer's silver corona, above the altar, and John Piper's tapestries. Hereford is a big cider producer, so follow signs to the **Cider Museum** *(open Mon–Sat)* to learn the secrets and history of cider production.
🚗 *Cross the river and take A465 until a sign to the left for Kilpeck; follow signs and park outside the church.*

2 Kilpeck
Herefordshire; HR2 9DN
The crowning glory of this pretty village is the **Church of St Mary and St David**, perhaps the best 12th-century Norman Romanesque church in Britain. Look for exquisite Celtic and Norse-style carving dating from 1140 and the whimsical carved corbels of animals, wrestlers and dancers below the roofline. The church warden can give guided tours *(01981 570 315)*. To see the remains of the **motte and bailey castle** and for good views, walk up behind the churchyard and left over a stile up the hill.
🚗 *Return to A465 and turn left. Drop in to the Galanthus Gallery and café at Wormbridge (open Thu–Sun), then take next right and follow signs to Abbey Dore. Park on road by the abbey.*

3 Abbey Dore
Herefordshire; HR2 0AA
Nestling in the fertile "Golden Valley", this village is home to the remains of the Cistercian **Dore Abbey**, founded in 1147 from wool trade profits. Only the eastern end still stands, but it is an impressive height. The abbey was dissolved in 1537 and reconsecrated in 1634 as an Anglican church. There are fine examples of 13th-century roof bosses, a number of interesting wall paintings and a wooden musicians' gallery, which dates from the 1700s.

Take a relaxing river walk in the **Abbey Dore Court Gardens** *(open Apr–Sep: Tue, Thu, Sat & Sun)*, just north of the church and signposted off the B4347.
🚗 *Take B4347 to A465 and turn right. Turn right to Llanfihangel Crucorney. Just before the Skirrid Inn, Wales's oldest pub, turn right to the priory and follow signs to Cymyoy. Turn left at T-junction by Coach House and right at end of road.*

4 Vale of Ewyas
Llanthony, Monmouthshire; NP7 7NN
This is a beautiful glaciated valley, with woodlands and fertile farmland, offering good horse riding. **Cwmyoy Church** sits on a geologically recent landslip which some say coincided with Christ's crucifixion. The ground is still settling, and the church's tower is said to lean even more than the one at Pisa. There is also a stone cross here similar to an Irish high cross. Return to the valley road and turn right to **Llanthony Priory** by the River Honddu. Legend has it that St Peter and St Paul visited here and that St David, the patron saint of Wales, lived here as a hermit. In the 12th century, the knight William de Lacy was so impressed with its spirituality that he founded a church on the spot – later the site of Wales's

Below Finely sculpted doorway at the Church of St Mary and St David, Kilpeck

Where to Stay: inexpensive, under £80; moderate, £80–£150; expensive, over £150

first Augustinian priory. Carry on north over the Black Mountains to **Gospel Pass** at 542 m (1,778 ft) with dramatic views over the Wye Valley.

🚗 *Keep going north from Gospel Pass to Hay-on-Wye and park in the large car park at the back of the castle on B4348.*

5 Hay-on-Wye
Powys; HR3 5DB
Hay is a characterful Welsh market town with winding streets, built on a hillside beneath the ruins of a Norman castle. It is considered by some the second-hand book capital of the world. The largest bookshop is **Richard Booth**, named after the original owner, who started to promote Hay as a book centre in 1961. The Hay Festival of Literature (*www.hayfestival.com*) is held at the end of May and attracts high-profile poets, writers and politicians.

Take the B4351 from Broad St to **Clyro**, a pretty village on the outskirts of town that was once home to the Reverend Francis Kilvert, a great Victorian diarist, who depicted the rural life of his parish during the 1870s.

🚗 *Leave Hay on B4350 (signed Brecon) and join the A438, then the A479 through Talgarth. Turn right onto the B4560, then right in Llangorse to the lake car park.*

6 Llangorse Lake
Brecon, Powys; LD3 7TR
The largest natural lake in South Wales, **Llangorse Lake** was created during the last Ice Age. In the summer, it is a popular watersports centre with boats for hire from the **Lakeside Caravan & Camping Park** (*www.llangorselake.co.uk*). The lake is also good for fishing and its reedy shallows attract waterfowl which can be viewed from lakeside hides. At the north edge of the lake is the tiny man-made islet, or crannog,

Ynys Bwlc. This was built around AD 900 by piling stones and earth onto brushwood and reeds, and held a royal hall and church and was linked to the shore by a causeway. At the **Llangorse Crannog Centre** visitors can learn more about the lake. Enjoy lakeside walks to Llangorse village – a centre for pony trekking, and a starting point for trails in the Brecon Beacons National Park.

🚗 *From the lake road, turn left back into Llangorse and follow the signs to Brecon on the A40 and B4601.*

7 Brecon
Powys; LD3 9DP
An old market town at the confluence of the Honddu and Usk Rivers in the Brecon Beacons National Park, Brecon contains a mix of medieval, Tudor, Jacobean and Georgian architecture around its central square, **The Bulwark**, and 16th-century Church of St Mary's.

Theatr Brycheiniog (*01874 611 622; www.brycheiniog.co.uk*) offers a rolling programme of drama and comedy.

Visit also the **South Wales Borderers Museum** (*www.royalwelsh.org.uk; open weekdays*) on the Watton (B4601), covering Welsh regimental history including the defence of Rorke's Drift (1879), where 139 soldiers faced 5,000 Zulu warriors.

Founded as a Benedictine priory in 1093, **Brecon Cathedral** has some of the best monastic buildings in Wales – mostly built in the 13th and 14th centuries. The decorated Norman font with its birds, grotesques and beasts is the oldest object. The Havard Chapel has many millitary memorials and the regimental colours from Rorke's Drift. There's also a Heritage Centre and café.

🚗 *Leave on the B4601, then take the A470 towards Cardiff. At Libanus turn right to the Brecon Beacons National Park Visitor Centre (signposted).*

Above left Pastoral landscape in the fertile Vale of Ewyas **Above right** Hereford Cathedral, home to much ancient and modern art

EAT AND DRINK

HEREFORD
Café @ All Saints *inexpensive*
This café in a church offers daily specials such as Hereford pork, leek and butterbean broth.
High Street, HR4 9AA; 01497 370415; www.cafeatallsaints.co.uk

HAY-ON-WYE
Kilvert's Inn *moderate*
This very popular pub serves good bar food, with a mix of traditional and Mediterranean flavours.
The Bullring, HR3 5AG; 01497 821 042; www.kilverts.co.uk

Old Black Lion *moderate*
A historic inn with a reputation for fine food, it serves traditional Welsh produce – sirloin steaks, pulled lamb or venison chilli either at the bar or in the den.
Lion Street, HR3 5AD; 01497 820 841; www.oldblacklion.co.uk

Other options
For delicious low-fat sheep's milk ice cream, try **Shepherds** *inexpensive* (*9 High Town, HR3 5AE; 01497 821 898; www.shepherdsicecream.co.uk*). For wholesome food, with good vegetarian options, try the **Granary** *inexpensive* (*Broad Street, HR3 5DB; 01497 820 790*).

Below The popular Granary Café, by the clocktower in Hay-on-Wye

Eat and Drink: inexpensive, under £25; moderate, £25–£50; expensive, over £50

Above View looking into the hills of the Brecon Beacons National Park **Below** Sheep grazing on the verdant upper slopes of the Brecon Beacons

VISITING BRECON BEACONS NATIONAL PARK

National Park Visitor Centre
Libanus, Brecon, LD3 8ER; 01874 623 366; www.breconbeacons.org

WHERE TO STAY AROUND TRETOWER COURT AND CASTLE

Ty Gwyn *inexpensive*
Beautifully restored Georgian building, with three attractive en-suite rooms and lots of character, in Crickhowell on the A40 from Tretower to Abergavenny. There's a pretty garden and local produce for breakfast.
Brecon Road (A40), Crickhowell, NP8 1DG; 01873 811 625; www.tygwyn.com

⑧ Brecon Beacons National Park
Powys; LD3 8ER

This walk is a figure of eight across a plateau in the shadow of the Brecon Beacons. While enjoying the scenery and waymarked trails, listen out for birdsong – especially the skylarks in summer.

A two-hour walking tour

From the far end of the car park next to the **Visitor Centre** ① carry straight on to the grassy track. A signpost shows the way (do not veer left up the slope). Look out for gorse clumps with yellow flowers – these are popular with songbirds such as stonechats, meadow pipits and chaffinches. The path then leads up a gentle incline with the Brecon Beacons landscape on the right. Follow the broad grassy path straight ahead, past the pond on the right and across a road, past a sign pointing back to the Visitor Centre. After a while the path dips down to a farm road and then up again to the peak ahead. Cross the road and the boggy watercourse and head up the path to the trig point on top of **Twyn y Gaer** ②, the site of an Iron Age hillfort, at a height of 367 m (1,204 ft). From here there are great views around, and all the way down to Brecon. To return, take the worn pathway to the right of the pillar and follow it back round the

Sign from Blaenavon World Heritage Site

hill and down to the farm road again. Look for "pillow mounds" – banks of earth created in the 18th century for rabbits to breed and feed the growing populations of the industrial towns to the south. Cross over the road and head uphill, veering right towards the boundary fence where there is a clear pathway following a Roman road – **Sarn Helen** ③. This was the old route linking the Roman forts between Y Gaer and Coelbren, and is still traceable further along the common. Follow the path beside the fence until the fence turns abruptly right. Leave the fence and walk straight ahead, across gently sloping common land on the path downhill to a road. Cross the road keeping an area of flat land with a **pond** ④ on the left and follow the path back down to the Visitor Centre, enjoying the dramatic vistas on the way.

🚗 *Return to Brecon and take the A40 east. Go left after the Kestrel pub and left at the end of the road, and park outside the gates of Tretower.*

⑨ Tretower Court and Castle
Crickhowell, Powys; NP8 1RF
These two sets of buildings clearly illustrate the transition from castles to houses in the borders, indicating the advent of a more peaceful time. The **tower**, built by Picard c.1100, is one of a number of motte and bailey castles built during the Norman advance into Wales. In the 14th century, the **house** became the main dwelling place. It is a rare intact example of a medieval manor house with a walled front and courtyard. Partly rebuilt in the 15th century by Sir Roger Vaughan, it has wonderful timber work and a garden.

🚗 *Continue along the road to return to the A40 and carry on eastwards to Abergavenny. Park in the town centre.*

⑩ Abergavenny
Monmouthshire; NP7 5ND
Set in the Usk Valley with easy access to the Brecon Beacons, Abergavenny is superbly located. At its heart is **Abergavenny Castle**, a classic motte and bailey structure from the 11th century. It saw three centuries of fierce border fighting and was the scene of the infamous massacre of Welsh chieftains by the Normans in 1175.

Above St Mary's Priory Church, Abergavenny, founded in the 11th century

A 19th-century hunting lodge, on the site of the keep, houses **Abergavenny Museum** *(open Mon–Sat; Mar–Oct also Sun pm)*, with displays of local social history. However, the star attraction is **St Mary's Priory Church**. Founded in 1087 as a Benedictine priory, it is one of the finest churches in Wales. It has a huge 15th-century carved oak "Jesse" sculpture – tracing Jesus' lineage back to Jesse – which is unique in size and craftmanship. Also admire the fine English School Renaissance alabaster tombs in the Herbert Chapel and the adjacent 14th-century Tithe Barn, housing tapestry and exhibitions.

🚗 *Return to A40 east, taking A4143, then B4246 to Blaenavon. Park on site.*

⑪ Blaenavon
Gwent; NP4 9RN
Set on a mountainside in a bleak and awe-inspiring landscape, Blaenavon rose to prominence at the start of the Industrial Revolution and is now a UNESCO World Heritage site. One of several heritage attractions here, **Blaenavon Ironworks** *(Apr–Oct: open daily; Nov–Mar: open Fri–Sun)* was the most advanced ironworks in the world when it was built in 1787. The vast infastructure includes mines, water towers, steam-powered blast furnaces, casting houses and workers' cottages. The works fell into decline with the advent of large-scale steel making.

The **Big Pit: National Coal Museum** *(open daily)* is where the coal that fired the furnaces came from. In this fascinating industrial museum, ex-miners escort groups around the mines, 90-m (300-ft) underground and reveal the harsh lives of the miners (men, women and children) who worked in dark and damp conditions.

Above The ruined Norman tower of Tretower Castle, near Crickhowell

VISITING BLAENAVON

Blaenavon World Heritage Centre
Church Road, NP4 9AS; 01495 742 333; www.visitblaenavon.co.uk

EAT AND DRINK

AROUND TRETOWER COURT AND CASTLE

The Bear Hotel *inexpensive–moderate*
This atmospheric pub in Crickhowell, on the A40 outside Tretower, serves traditional food such as liver and bacon, fishcakes and faggots.
High Street, Crickhowell, NP8 1BW; 01873 810 408; www.bearhotel.co.uk

Nantyffin Cider Mill *moderate*
This lovely old drovers' inn, on the A479 from Tretower to Crickhowell, offers a high standard of cuisine using produce from local farms and estates.
Brecon Road, NP8 1SG; 01873 810 775; www.cidermill.co.uk

AROUND ABERGAVENNY

The Walnut Tree *moderate–expensive*
This well-known restaurant, just off the B4521 northeast of Abergavenny, is part-operated by top chef Shaun Hill. The food is well-flavoured modern British and the set lunch is excellent value.
Llanddewi Skirrid, NP7 8AW; 01873 852 797; www.thewalnuttreeinn.com

---

DAY TRIP OPTIONS
Hereford and Abergavenny make excellent bases for these trips.

Churches, History and Books
Start in Hereford ①, with its cathedral, and head to Kilpeck ② for its church, then on to Abbey Dore ③ and the spectacular Vale of Ewyas

④, stopping off at the church and priory. Drive over Gospel Pass for a stroll around Hay-on-Wye ⑤.

Follow the driving instructions, but return to Hereford on the B4352.

Family Activity Day
Spend the morning touring the industrial sites at Blaenavon ⑪,

before heading to Tretower Court and Castle ⑨, and on to Llangorse Lake ⑥ for a walk and some fishing or birdwatching. If there's still time, take a look around pretty Brecon ⑦.

Follow the driving instructions from Abergavenny to Blaenavon and then follow the A40.

Eat and Drink: inexpensive, under £25; moderate, £25–£50; expensive, over £50

Wonders of West Wales
Llandovery to Newport

Highlights

- **Glorious Welsh gardens**
  Visit two striking, individual gardens: colourful and sculptural planting at Aberglasney and the exotic and futuristic National Botanic Garden

- **Majestic Welsh castles**
  Admire the crumbling bastions of Norman might from Carreg Cennen to Kidwelly and Carew, reminders of a turbulent Welsh history

- **Stunning Pembrokeshire coast**
  Walk along the rugged, splintered cliffs to rocky coves and wide sandy bays washed by the powerful Atlantic

- **One of Britain's oldest cathedrals**
  For over 1,400 years there has been Christian worship at St Davids Cathedral, an astonishing work of religious art

Tenby Harbour overlooked by Prince Albert's monument on Tower Hill

Wonders of West Wales

The drive heads west from Llandovery through some glorious Welsh gardens – The National Botanic Garden and nearby Aberglasney – to the home of Dylan Thomas, one of the great poets of the 20th century, in the sleepy coastal town of Laugharne. The route is studded with solid Norman castles, built to control the land the French invaders had just conquered. Take some time out in the bustling resort of Tenby before visiting Britain's smallest city, St Davids, with its ancient cathedral. Walk the stunning wild clifftops, rich in religious myths in Britain's only National Coastal Park, and visit the seabirds on Ramsey Island. See the Neolithic burial monument of Pentre Ifan and walk the Preseli Hills, source of the mysterious bluestones at Stonehenge (see p68).

Monington
Rosslare
NEWPORT 14
B4582 A487
Nevern
Eglwyswrw
Llanfair Nant-gwyn
Strumble Head
Goodwick
Dinas
Manorowen
13 FISHGUARD Cilgwyn
Pentre Ifan
Blaenffos
Abercastle
Llanychaer
Pontfaen
Brynberian
Crymmych
Porthgain
Mathry
B4313
Mynydd Prescelly
A478
Abereiddy
A487
A40
Letterston
Pinchestone
Maes-yr wyn
Llanfyrnach
Trelech
Croes-goch
B4331
B4299
Whitesands Bay
B4583
A487
PEMBROKESHIRE
Llangolman
Blaen-waun
Middle Mill
Hayscastle Cross
Wallis
B4313
Llanglydwen
Gellywen
Abe
ST DAVIDS
11
Brawdy
Llanycefn
A478
Llanboidy
Ramsey Island
SOLVA
A487
Roch
B4330
Spittal
Clarbeston Road
Llandissilio
Simpson Cross
Keeston
B4329
Wiston
Egremont
Cwmfelin Boeth
Meidrim
St Brides Bay
Portfield Gate
Haverfordwest
Llawhaden
A40
St Clears
Whitland
Little Haven
B4341
Uzmaston
Narberth
B4328
Eber
Skomer Island
St Bride's
Hasguard
A4076
Hook
Templeton
B4314
Crunwear
Red Roses
A4066
LAUGHARNE
6
Marloes
B4327
Johnston
Rosemarket
Yerbeston
A4075
Ludchurch
A477
B4314
A4066
East Marsh
Skokholm Island
St Ishmael's
Dale
Milford Haven
A477
Houghton
CAREW CASTLE
Kilgetty
7
PENDINE
St Ann's Head
Angle
Neyland
Cosheston
Sageston
A478
Saundersfoot
Carmarthen Bay
Rosslare
Pembroke Dock
Pembroke
A4075
Gumfreston
Lamphey
B4318
8 TENBY
Castlemartin
B4320
St Petrox
B4319
Cheriton
A4139
Lydstep
Penally
Caldey Island
Linney Head
Bosherston
ST GOVAN'S CHAPEL 10
St Govan's Head

ACTIVITIES

Cycle (or walk) around the Brecon Beacons from Llandovery

Climb up to the fabulous beauty spot of Carreg Cennen Castle

Take a boat to Ramsey or Caldey Islands to see the seabirds

Picnic in the grounds of Carew Castle and walk to the mill

Count the steps down and up to St Govan's Chapel – it is said the number is never the same

Listen to the sublime evensong at St Davids Cathedral

Surf the Atlantic rollers at Whitesands Bay, St Davids

Hike in the splendid Preseli Hills from Newport

Below Dylan Thomas' Boathouse, overlooking Carmarthen Bay, Laugharne, see p141

Above The mazy clifftop path of the Pembrokeshire Coast National Trail, close to St Davids, *see pp144–5*

0 kilometres 5

0 miles 5

KEY

Drive route

Below Pendine Sands with the tide out, once a favourite location for land-speed record attempts, *see p142*

PLAN YOUR DRIVE

Start/finish: Llandovery to Newport.

Number of days: 4, allowing half a day at St Davids.

Distances: Around 270 km (168 miles).

Road conditions: Well-paved and signposted. In remote areas the country roads can be very narrow.

When to go: Spring is very pretty, with wild flowers, and summer is best for outdoor activities. Many attractions and venues close during the winter.

Opening times: Attractions and museums are generally open 10am–5pm, but close earlier (or are closed altogether) Nov–Easter. Shops are often open longer. Churches are usually open until dusk. Some B&Bs close in winter.

Main market days: Llandeilo: Country Market, Civic Hall, Fri am; Tenby: Country Market, St John's Hall, Fri am; St Davids: Country Market, Cross Square, Thu am; Fishguard: Country Market, Market Hall (within Town Hall), Thu am; Farmers' Market, Sat, Market Hall.

Shopping: Buy natural soaps from the Soap Shed at St Davids produce market, and jams and chutneys from Miranda's Preserves at village stores in Llandovery and many local delis.

Major festivals: St Davids: Cathedral Festival, classical music, last week in May; Fishguard: Folk Festival, 4 days at end of May; International Classical Music Festival, 10 days late Jul; Pembrokeshire's Jazz 'n' Blues Festival, 5 days at end of Aug.

DAY TRIP OPTIONS

Castle and garden lovers can stay at Llandovery to visit the **castle** and the **gardens** at Aberglasney, and climb up to Carreg Cennen **castle** before admiring the **Great Glasshouse** at the National Botanic Garden. **Families** will enjoy the beach at Tenby, Carmarthen Bay, a visit to the **museum** at Pendine, and the **castle** and **Dylan Thomas' house** at Laugharne; finish off with the **castles** at Kidwelly and Carew. For more **coastal fun**, stay at Newport, see Fishguard **harbour**, then on to St Davids for the **cathedral**, **walk**, and time at the **beach**. Enjoy a **fish supper** in Solva. For full details, *see p145*.

Above Aberglasney House set in the famous gardens, near Llandeilo

VISITING LLANDOVERY

Parking
Cheap parking by the castle and TIC.

Tourist Information
Kings Road, SA20 0AW; 01550 720 693; open Apr–Oct

WHERE TO STAY

LLANDOVERY

Kings Head Inn *moderate*
Lashings of history are on offer at this 16th-century inn with nine rooms. There's a cosy bar and restaurant with traditional home-cooked Welsh food.
1 Market Square, SA20 0AB; 01550 720 393; www.kingsheadllandovery.co.uk

LLANDEILO

The Cawdor *moderate*
This relaxed boutique hotel mixes the contemporary with the antique and serves good food.
Rhosmaen Street, SA19 6EN; 01558 823 500; www.thecawdor.com

LAUGHARNE

The Boat House B&B *moderate*
This B&B has four airy, contemporary rooms. It's just a short walk from here to Dylan Thomas's famous Boathouse.
1 Gosport Street, SA33 4SY; 01994 427 263; www.bed-breakfast-holiday.co.uk

Below left Pastel-coloured inn on Market Square, Llandovery **Below right** Yellow daisy-like flowers at Aberglasney Gardens

① Llandovery
Carmarthenshire; SA20 0AP
This is a lovely Welsh market town with neat cottages and Georgian buildings. The ruined **Norman castle** by the river was built in 1110 and sacked by Owain Glyndŵr in 1403. Drive south on Bridge Street out of town over the river and then fork right to the village of **Myddfai**. A family of doctors, the "Physicians of Myddfai", lived here from the 12th to the 18th centuries, and were renowned for their herbal remedies. Walkers can use Llandovery as a base for hikes around the northern edge of the Brecon Beacons National park (*www.breconbeacons.org*). Or hire bikes from **Towy Valley Cycles** (*07576 431 960*), which can arrange a bike pick-up. Maps and leaflets are available at the tourist information centre (TIC).
🚗 *From Llandovery re-cross the bridge and take the A40 west to Llandeilo.*

② Llandeilo
Carmarthenshire; SA19 6BH
This elegant town is perched on a bluff overlooking the Tywi, the longest river to flow entirely within Wales. At its centre is 13th-century **St Teilo's Church**, rebuilt in the 19th century by renowned Victorian revivalist architect George Gilbert Scott. The church has an exhibition on the St Teilo Gospels, a local 8th-century illuminated book,

and the earliest known example of Welsh script. Head west on the A40 turning off left to Llangathen and **Aberglasney Gardens** (*open daily; www.aberglasney.org*), a rare restored cloister garden dating back to the 15th century. It is a planter's paradise, with vast swathes of delphiniums and a yew tunnel. The mansion house has a splendid early Victorian Ionic portico, a shop and a café. Enjoy the colourful profusion of butterflies attracted by the flowers in summer.
🚗 *From Llandeilo take A483 south to Ffairfach, take a left at roundabout, right after a railway bridge, following signs to Trapp, then castle and car park.*

③ Carreg Cennen Castle
Carmarthenshire; SA19 6UA
Just east of Trapp, on the western edge of the Brecon Beacons National Park, **Carreg Cennen Castle** (*open daily*) is a dramatic ruined fortification, set high on a stunning 99-m (325-ft) limestone bluff. There is evidence of prehistoric and Roman activity, but it was the 11th-century Welsh princes who first built on the site. Today's remains are those of the magnificent 13th-century Norman edifice. Walk up the hill to the castle from the car park.
🚗 *Go back to Ffairfach and straight on to A476. Turn right on A48, then right on B4310 to the Botanic Garden (signed).*

④ National Botanic Garden of Wales
Carmarthenshire; SA32 8HG
Occupying the site of a Regency country estate that was once owned by Sir William Paxton, Master of Calcutta Mint, the National Botanic Garden of Wales (*open daily; www.gardenofwales.org.uk*) is the largest garden in Wales. Its centrepiece is

the Great Glasshouse, designed by Lord Norman Foster. It is the largest single-span glasshouse in the world and houses a number of rare and endangered plants. The garden has an unrivalled collection of Mediterranean flora, as well as a unique double-walled garden, an award-winning Japanese garden and a bee garden. There are also woodland and lakeside walks. The garden is wheelchair-friendly, and mobility aids are available (pre-booking advised; 01558 667 149). There are also two cafés, a restaurant, a shop and a plant sales area.

🚗 Head back to the A48 west towards Carmarthen and take the A484 south to Kidwelly (Cydweli). Follow signs to castle.

⑤ Kidwelly Castle
Carmarthenshire; SA17 5BQ

An imposing fortification, built during the 13th–15th centuries on a bluff over the River Gwendraeth, **Kidwelly Castle** (open daily) was part of the Norman strategy to secure south Wales by controlling the river passes here and at Laugharne, Llansteffan and Loughor. The earliest parts of the castle consist of the square inner ward with the four round corner towers and portcullis gates to the north and south. Further concentric defences were added in the mid-13th century by its new owners, the de Chaworth family. The gatehouse is extremely well fortified and was designed so that it could be held independently if the rest of the castle was captured. The castle also contains two bakehouses and the remains of a chapel.

🚗 Return to Carmarthen, head west on the A40 and turn left onto the A4066 south to Laugharne.

Dylan Thomas
Dylan Thomas was one of the world's great 20th-century English-language poets. Born in Swansea, he wrote over half of his poems including "And Death Shall Have No Dominion". He moved west to New Quay and Laugharne to write his masterpiece "Under Milk Wood", a play about a night and a day, in the imaginary Welsh fishing village of Llareggub (which means something entirely different read backwards). He was a big success in America but died in New York aged only 39.

⑥ Laugharne
Carmarthenshire; SA33 4SD

This is a very picturesque coastal town with lovely cottages and Georgian houses set on the expansive Taf Estuary. The town and coastline is dominated by the ruins of **Laugharne Castle**. It was built by the Norman de Brian family in the 13th and 14th centuries and later turned into a grand Tudor Mansion in the 16th century by Sir John Perrot. During the Elizabethan period, the town was bigger than Cardiff and remained an English-speaking village within Wales.

The narrow fishing lane behind the castle leads up to Dylan Thomas's home, the **Boathouse** (01994 427 420; www.dylanthomasboathouse.com) with his modest writing study in the garage. There is a nice café here, so enjoy a cup of tea while gazing out over pretty **Carmarthen Bay**. The poet is buried in a simple grave in the churchyard in the north of the town.

There are several interesting shops behind the clocktower and a jeweller, **Quicksilver**, where you can have a gemstone set in a silver ring within an hour.

🚗 From Laugharne continue on the A4066 to Pendine.

EAT AND DRINK

LLANDEILO

The Angel Hotel moderate
This established inn has a relaxed bar – choose from the blackboard menu, or dine in the more formal bistro. There's always a vegetarian choice available. 60 Rhosmaen, SA19 6EN; 01558 822 765; www.angelbistro.co.uk

AROUND THE NATIONAL BOTANIC GARDEN OF WALES

Y Polyn moderate
On the B4310 south of the A40, Y Polyn offers excellent Welsh produce, such as organic beef, in traditional dishes with a modern twist. Everything is home-made – even the bread. Capel Dewi, Nantgaredig, SA32 7LH; 01267 290 000; www.ypolynrestaurant.co.uk

LAUGHARNE

The Cors Restaurant moderate
Set in beautiful gardens and with a charming interior, this restaurant features local produce such as salt marsh lamb. It also has three "shabby chic" bedrooms. Newbridge Road, SA33 4SH; 01994 427 219; www.thecors.co.uk; open Thu–Sat

Below The imposing Carreg Cennen, in a superb setting **Bottom left** The Great Greenhouse, National Botanic Garden of Wales **Bottom right** Kidwelly Castle, one of a series of 13th-century Norman fortifications

Above left The smaller of Tenby's two lovely sandy beaches **Above top right** Tenby kiosk offering fishing and sightseeing trips **Above right** Fishing and pleasure boats just outside Tenby harbour

VISITING TENBY

Parking
Park in Five Arches, *South Cliff Street, SA70 7AS* or Sainsbury's multi-storey car park, *Upper Park Road, SA70 7LT*

Tourist Information
Upper Park Road, SA70 7LT; 01437 775 603

WHERE TO STAY

AROUND PENDINE

Jabajak *moderate*
This small hotel is set within a vineyard and has an excellent restaurant. To get here, head north at the Whitland roundabout on the A40.
Banc y Llain, Llanboidy Rd, Whitland SA34 0ED; 01994 448 786; www.jabajak.co.uk

AROUND CAREW CASTLE

Cresselly House *moderate*
Enjoy the antique-filled rooms in this grand 18th-century country house just off the A4075, north of Carew Castle, and wander the lovely grounds.
Cresselly, SA68 0SP; 01646 651 992; www.cresselly.com

AROUND TENBY

Wychwood House *inexpensive*
Large en-suite rooms, a pretty garden and lovely views are on offer at this friendly B&B, just outside Tenby, south off the A4139. Also does evening meals.
Penally, SA70 7PE; 01834 844 387; www.wychwoodhousebb.co.uk

⑦ Pendine
Carmarthenshire; SA33 4NY
This coastal town is best known for the flat sandy beach that made it ideal for land-speed record attempts. Malcolm Campbell in *Bluebird* in 1924 reached 146 mph (235 km/h) and then raised it to 174 mph (280 km/h) in 1927. The **Museum of Speed** *(Easter–Sep: open Tue–Sun & Bank Hols)* traces the history of these records. See *Babs*, the car buried in the dunes after crashing and killing its driver, Parry-Thomas, in a record attempt in 1927, now dug out and restored. In a repeat of history, Campbell's grandson set a UK electric car land-speed record here in 2000.
🚗 *Head west on B4314 to Red Roses, turn left onto A477 and left onto A478 to Tenby. Use either of the car parks at the end of South Cliff St or in Upper Park Rd.*

Below The still impressive 14th-century ruins of Carew Castle

⑧ Tenby
Pembrokeshire; SA70 8EU
This 9th-century walled town marks the start of the Pembrokeshire Coast National Park. Sandwiched by two golden beaches, Tenby is a gem of a holiday resort. **St Mary's Church** has a superb roof, and alabaster tombs of Tenby mayors John and Thomas White. The 15th-century **Tudor Merchants House** *(Apr–Oct: open Wed–Mon; Jul & Aug: daily; Nov–Mar: Sat & Sun)* is a living museum with *secco* wall paintings. No visit is complete without a walk up Castle Hill – with its statue of Prince Albert – for the views and to visit **Tenby Museum and Art Gallery** *(open daily; closed Sun & Mon in winter; www.tenby museum.org.uk)*, which has local history exhibitions. The **Wilfred Harrison Gallery** displays original paintings by siblings Gwen John (1876–1939) and Augustus John (1878–1961), who grew up in Tenby. Consider taking a boat trip to **Caldey Island**, run by Cistercian monks *(closed Sun; boats sail Apr–Oct, call 01834 844 453; www.caldey-island.co.uk)*. There are medieval churches, an abbey and quiet sandy bays here.
🚗 *Leave on B4318, turn left onto A477 and then turn right on A4075. Park in free car park on the left next to the cross.*

⑨ Carew Castle
Pembrokeshire; SA70 8SL
This is another magnificent example of the transition from Norman castle to Elizabethan manor house in Wales *(see also p135)*, although the castle is sadly ruined. Nevertheless, there are spectacular views of **Carew Castle** *(open daily; www.carewcastle.com)* from over the millpond and the grounds,

Where to Stay: inexpensive, under £80; moderate, £80–£150; expensive, over £150

where events are regularly held. Take a gentle stroll to the only restored tidal mill in Wales, and inspect the large 11th-century **Carew Cross** nearby, one of the best examples of its type in Wales, with fine Celtic knot work.

🚗 *Head back to A477 and turn right, fork left on A4075 to Pembroke, straight over roundabout and left on B4319 to Bosherston. Drive on to coast (road passes military firing range, closed Mon–Fri except Aug). Park at St Govan's Head.*

⑩ St Govan's Chapel
Bosherston, Pembrokeshire; SA71 5DP

An ancient Christian cell, **St Govan's Chapel** is set into a steep cliff on the southernmost tip of Pembrokeshire. It was probably founded in the 6th century by the followers of St Govan – the chapel is at least 11th century. St Govan's identity is unknown, but most experts favour St Gobham, Abbot of Dairinis in County Wexford, who visited and stayed until his death in AD 586. He is said to have lived as a hermit, keeping a look out for marauding pirates, the scourge of the local population, from Lundy Island. It is said that the number of steps to the chapel (approximately 74) is never the same on the way up as on the way down. Be sure to stop off at the little village of Bosherston to visit the craft shop, teahouse or pub, and admire the gorgeous lily ponds.

Design from Solva Woollen Mill

🚗 *Return to Pembroke and on to A477 across the toll bridge, then A4076 to Haverfordwest. Drive through town on A487 to Solva. Park in the Harbour Inn car park at the near end of town.*

Above The pretty inlet harbour of Solva, once used for smuggling

Above The spectacular cliff coastline, home to St Govan's Chapel

⑪ Solva
Pembrokeshire; SA62 6UU

The jewel of the Pembrokeshire Coast National Park, Solva is the ideal location for walking, sailing or simply relaxing among the galleries, restaurants and shops. Used as a smuggling centre and later a busy port, Solva has a lovely harbour set in a cleft in the coastline. A walk on the cliffs above the inlet is recommended. The summer **Solva Regatta** sees a series of fun events, including a popular raft race. A little way north lies **Solva Woollen Mill** (open Mon–Fri; Jul–Sep: also at weekends; www.solvawoollenmill.co.uk), with a working waterwheel, making flat-weave carpets and coverings.

🚗 *From the Woollen Mill, turn right past the quarry and on to the A487. Turn left for St Davids. Either park on outskirts by the visitor centre and walk in, or carry on and over the roundabout to the cathedral car park on Quickwell Hill.*

EAT AND DRINK

TENBY

The Bay Tree *moderate*
Set in charming Tudor Square, the Bay Tree has an excellent menu of hearty bistro-style food and a cordial ambience.
Tudor Square, SA70 7AJ; 01834 843 516; www.baytreetenby.co.uk

Mews Bar and Grill *moderate*
Freshly cooked food here includes fish caught in the local harbour.
Upper Frog St, SA70 7JD; 01834 844 068

Ocean Restaurant *moderate*
Overlooking the harbour, the Ocean has an Italian bias and serves pizzas, pastas, steaks and fish dishes.
St Julian's Street, SA70 7AY; 01834 844 536; www.tenby-oceanrestaurant.co.uk

AROUND TENBY

St Brides Hotel Restaurant *moderate*
North of Tenby, on the A478, then the B4316, this hotel restaurant has glorious sea views. The menu uses local produce such as Welsh beef and lamb.
St Brides Hill, Saundersfoot, SA69 9NH; 01834 812 304; www.stbrides spahotel.com

SOLVA

Cambrian Inn *moderate*
Pies, burgers, locally caught fish and more adventurous dishes are on offer in this former coaching inn.
6 Main Street, SA62 6UU; 01437 721 210; www.thecambrianinn.co.uk

AROUND SOLVA

The Rising Sun Inn *moderate*
A family-run inn serving food prepared with local produce and real ales, 16 km (10 miles) east on A487.
Pelcomb Bridge, Haverfordwest, Pembrokeshire, SA62 6EA; 01437 765 171; www.therisingsunwest.co.uk

Eat and Drink: inexpensive, under £25; moderate, £25–£50; expensive, over £50

Above St Non's Retreat, on the St Davids coastline, built in 1934

VISITING ST DAVIDS

Parking
Park in the cathedral car park, or by the Visitor Centre.

Visitor Centre
On the A487 on the way into town. Oriel Y Parc, SA62 6NW; 01437 720 392; www.orielyparc.co.uk

Boat trips to Ramsey Island
Book tickets from **Thousand Island Expeditions** *(Cross Square, SA62 6SL; 01437 721 721; www.thousandislands. co.uk)*. Boats leave from St Justinian.

Surfing at Whitesands
Learn to surf, or improve your skills at **Tyf Surf School** *(01437 720 488; www.tyf.com)*.

WHERE TO STAY

AROUND ST DAVIDS

Crug Glas *moderate–expensive*
Just off the A487 to Fishguard, this is a beautiful, elegantly furnished country hotel on a working farm. There's a restaurant for evening meals.
Abereiddy, SA62 6XX; 01348 831 302; www.crug-glas.co.uk

NEWPORT

Llys Medygg *expensive*
Lovely Georgian house in the heart of Newport. Stylish comfy bedrooms with modern artworks and bathrooms. Enjoy fresh fruit and pancakes at breakfast.
East Street, SA42 OSY; 01239 820 008; www.llysmeddyg.com

Below Pretty pastel-painted houses of the village-like city of St Davids

⑫ St Davids

Pembrokeshire; SA62 6RH

More of a village than a city, St Davids' key attractions are its coastline and its cathedral. Set in the Pembrokeshire National Park, it is blessed with glorious beaches. This easy circular walk heads south to the Pembrokeshire Coast National Trail and back to the cathedral.

A two-hour walking tour

Start at the cathedral car park on Quickwell Hill, turning right and right again into Nun Street. Cross Cross Square and turn right into Goat Street and left down St Stephen's Lane. Go left at the end and then first right into Pen-y-Garn. At the end of this road, turn right along a field to a sign for St Non's Chapel. Take a left and keep on this path all the way to the coast. After three right-then-left turns and several gates and stiles, the modern **St Non's Retreat** ①, its chapel built in 1934, is visible. Dedicated to St David's mother, Non, it has lovely windows. Follow the path around the retreat to the remains of the original **Capel Non** ②, actually Non's house. A 7th–9th century creed stone with an incised Latin ring cross marks David's birthplace. See, too, the vaulted well said to have spouted during a storm when St David was born around AD 500 – reputed to have healing powers. There is a small shrine to Mary on the right. Follow the path up steps to the

Pembrokeshire Coastal Path ③ and around the rocky headlands. The path goes up the side of the **Porth Clais** ④ inlet, once St Davids port, with its tiny harbour and boats. At the end of the inlet, follow the path right, up the hill, and head for the campsite, keeping the buildings on the right. Go straight and then take the track inland along the edge of the field. Carry on straight up to the road next to the Warpool Court Hotel entrance. Cross the road, then turn left. Walk down the path into Bryn Rd to a sign for Dinas Tyddewi (St Davids City). Turn left into Mitre Lane, and carry on to the **Farmer's Arms** ⑤ on Goat St and back to the cathedral.

Built with local purple-red stone on the site of the 6th-century monastery of St David, **St Davids Cathedral** ⑥ has long been a major pilgrimage site – two trips to St Davids equalled one to Rome. The present, 12th-century, cathedral has a magnificent interior. Admire the early 16th-century oak ceiling with wooden pendant ceiling bosses and beautiful 14th-century rood screen. Evensong is a delight *(Thu–Tue: 6pm).* Across a little bridge, explore the stone ruins of the **Bishop's Palace** ⑦, built between 1280 and 1350, before returning to the car park, where the Tower Gate House has a display of religious stones.

West of town, on the B4853, lies **Whitesands Bay**, where legend says that St Patrick left Wales to take Christianity to Ireland. It is a stunning sandy surf beach. Visible just offshore lies **Ramsey Island**, an RSPB reserve with choughs, guillemots, razorbills and even peregrine falcons. Boat trips go to the island; look out too for pods of dolphins and even whales.

Stained-glass window, St Davids Cathedral

🚗 *Take the A487 direct to Fishguard and park in the town centre car park or in the Lower Town.*

Pembrokeshire Coast National Trail

Running along Britain's only true coastal park, the Pembrokeshire Coast National Trail *(01646 689 076; www.ntpcnpa.org.uk)* is 300 km (186 miles) and covers some spectacular scenery. The Puffin bus service enables walkers to follow the path and not walk back at the end of the day.

⑬ Fishguard
Pembrokeshire; SA65 9HA
This is a town of three parts: Lower Town, with its fishing harbour; Upper Town, with its shops; and, to the north, Goodwick, with a ferry terminal. Park in the centre to explore the town where the "Last Invasion of Britain" (1797) took place. The tale goes that a French force of 1,400 troops in four warships found

their way, in bad weather, into a cove nearby. However, the invasion was foiled when local women dressed in traditional tall hats and red clothes were taken for British grenadiers – a tapestry in the **Town Hall** portrays the event. St Mary's Churchyard, in Main Street, has a memorial stone to the invasion's heroine, Jemima Nicholas. The **West Wales Gallery** *(closed Sun; www.westwalesartscentre.com)* is one of the best galleries in Wales.

🚗 *Take A487 out of Fishguard, turn right on B4313 and left for Cilgwyn – a hilly drive with stunning views – to Newport.*

⑭ Newport
Pembrokeshire; SA42 0TN
Set on the estuary of the River Nevern, Newport was once a very busy port, but has long since silted up. The town has good access to the Pembrokeshire Coastal Path and is a popular base for walks into the Preseli Hills, famous as the source of the Stonehenge bluestones. For a closer Neolithic site, head east on the A487 and follow the signs right to **Pentre Ifan**, a tomb dating from c. 3500 BC and built from a series of upright stones with a huge 5-m (17-ft) capstone. Return towards the A487 but cross over to the pretty Norman village of **Nevern**. The church is famous for several items: it has a 4-m (13-ft) high, 10th-century, two-piece **Celtic Cross**; a smaller **Vitalian Stone**, possibly from AD 500; an avenue of "bleeding yews" which exude a bright red sap and, inside, the **Maglocunus Stone**, inscribed with a 5th-century example of Ogham script (an ancient southern Irish alphabet).

Above The picturesque harbour in Fishguard's Lower Town

EAT AND DRINK

ST DAVIDS
The Refectory at St Davids Cathedral *inexpensive*
A daily changing menu is served in the cathedral's airy restaurant. Local produce is used in dishes such as mushroom and smoked Pembrokeshire cheese quiche. *St Davids Cathedral, SA62 6RH; 01437 721 760; www.stdavidsrefectory.co.uk*

Cwtch *moderate*
Enjoy relaxed dining at this modern restaurant with seasonal menus and local produce. Enjoy sea trout, cockles or leek and mushroom pudding. *22 High Street, SA62 6SD; 01437 720 491; www.cwtchrestaurant.co.uk*

AROUND ST DAVIDS
The Sloop Inn *moderate*
At Croes-goch, turn left off the A487 to Fishguard, to this perfect 18th-century harbourside pub serving a wide range of bar meals. *Porthgain SA62 5BN; 01348 831 449; www.sloop.co.uk*

NEWPORT
Cnapan *moderate*
Established restaurant serves quality modern British cuisine using local produce such as black beef and Welsh cheeses. Also a B&B with friendly hosts. *East Street, SA42 0SY; 01239 820 575; www.cnapan.co.uk*

DAY TRIP OPTIONS
Castles, gardens, churches and beaches – this drive has it all.

Castles and Gardens
From Llandovery ①, see its castle and Myddfai – famed for its physicians, then pack a picnic and head for Llandeilo ② and the colourful gardens at Aberglasney. Climb the hill to stunning Carreg Cennen Castle ③. Finally, visit the spectacular National Botanic Garden of Wales ④.

Follow this drive's instructions and then retrace the journey.

Camarthen Bay
Visit the beach at Tenby ⑧, skirt the bay to sandy Pendine ⑦ and its Museum of Speed. Head to Laugharne ⑥ for bay views from both the castle and Dylan Thomas' home. Carry on to the stout bastion of Kidwelly Castle ⑤. If there's time, stop off at Carew Castle ⑨, before returning to Tenby for some of its lively nightlife.

Follow this drive's instructions in reverse, taking the A477 to Carew Castle.

Coastal Fun
From Newport ⑭, head down to pretty Fishguard ⑬ to learn about the last invasion of Britain. Then on to St Davids ⑫ to visit the cathedral and enjoy a clifftop walk. Have a bracing swim or surf at Whitesands Bay and finish off with supper in Solva ⑪.

Follow the A487 there and back.

Eat and Drink: inexpensive, under £25; moderate, £25–£50; expensive, over £50

Through Snowdonia National Park

Machynlleth to Llandudno

Highlights

- **Spectacular mountain peaks**
  Enjoy the magnificent scenery around
  Cadair Idris, and take a train or walk up
  to Wales' highest peak, Mt Snowdon

- **Glacial lakes and waterfalls**
  Be stunned by the sparkling jewel-like
  lakes and streaming waterfalls of
  Snowdonia National Park

- **Redoubtable castles**
  Tour the finest 13th-century military
  buildings in Europe – Harlech, Conwy,
  Caernarfon and Beaumaris castles

- **Traditional seaside fun**
  Build a castle (made of sand) on the
  beach at Llandudno, Wales' biggest and
  most beautiful seaside resort

Sweeping valley in Snowdonia
National Park

Through Snowdonia National Park

This drive runs through north Wales past some staggering mountain scenery, with sorties to the peaks of Cadair Idris and Mount Snowdon. Most of the route follows a trail through the pristine Snowdonia National Park, a very special part of the country where many locals speak Welsh as their first language. On the way to the island of Anglesey, there are pretty mountain villages – ideal bases from which to explore the countryside – and frequent stops at some fearsome castles. Returning to the mainland, the drive finishes at lively Llandudno, Wales' largest and most attractive seaside town.

Above Spectacular lakeside scenery around Llyn Gwynant north of Beddgelert, *see p151*

ACTIVITIES

Fish for brown and sea trout on the idyllic waters of Tal-y-Llyn, a glacial lake outside Machynlleth

Climb to the mighty summit of Cadair Idris' beautiful and peaceful southern Snowdonia National Park

Storm the mighty Harlech Castle and walk along the walls, admiring the vertiginous views

Ride one of the most thrilling rail routes in the UK up to the dramatic peak of Mt Snowdon

Take a boat trip to see the seals and seabirds around Puffin Island, from Beaumaris, Anglesey

Swing through the tree tops or go rock climbing in Betws-y-Coed

Soar above Llandudno in a cable car up to the top of the Great Orme, and do some skiing on the way down

0 kilometres 10

0 miles 10

KEY

Drive route

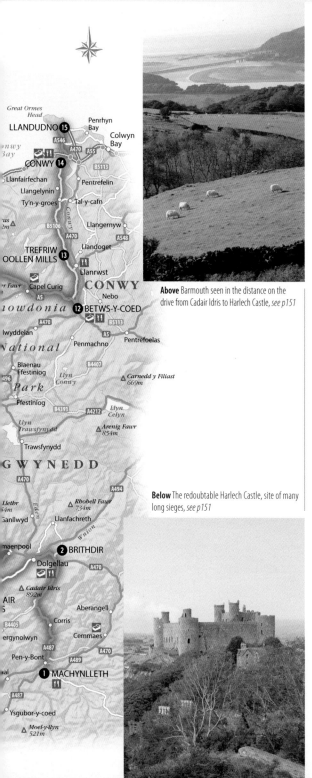

Above Barmouth seen in the distance on the drive from Cadair Idris to Harlech Castle, *see p151*

Below The redoubtable Harlech Castle, site of many long sieges, *see p151*

PLAN YOUR DRIVE

Start/finish: Machynlleth to Llandudno.

Number of days: 4, allowing time to explore Snowdonia National Park and walk on Anglesey Island.

Distance: Around 295 km (183 miles).

Road conditions: Well-paved and signposted – the roads below Cadair Idris are narrow but have passing places.

When to go: Summer is best for outdoor activities, some places in the north close in the winter.

Opening times: Museums and attractions are generally open 10am–5pm, but close earlier (or are closed altogether) Nov–Easter. Shop times are longer. Churches are usually open until dusk.

Main market days: Dolgellau (near Brithdir): Farmers' Market, 3rd Sun of month; Porthmadog (near Harlech): Fri; Anglesey (at Menai Bridge, near Llanfair PG): Farmers' Market, 3rd Sat of month; Conwy: Farmers' Market, last Wed of month.

Shopping: Local crafts, including traditional double-weave blankets.

Major festivals: Llanberis: Snowdonia Marathon, Oct; Anglesey: Oyster and Welsh Food Festival, Oct; Beaumaris: Arts Festival, May; Conwy: Honey Fair, Sep; Feast, Oct.

DAY TRIP OPTIONS

For photographers, stay at Machynlleth, see **glacial lakes,** then Brithdir's **church** and on to the **peaks** of Cadair Idris. Stay at Caernarfon for the **castle**, then go to Llanberis and take the thrilling **train ride** up Mt Snowdon. Tour huge **tunnels** inside a mountain and then see the **pretty village** of Beddgelert. Discover Anglesey from Beaumaris – enjoy the **castle** and a **cruise**; see Moelfre's **maritime memorials** and then tour the **stately home** of Plas Newydd. For family fun, stay at Llandudno with its **sandy beach, tramway** and Great Orme **Neolithic mines**. Head to Conwy for the **castle** and then Betws-y-Coed for some **tree-top fun**. For full details, *see p157*.

Above left Dark stone and painted house façades in Machynlleth **Above right** Welsh hill-farming country on the drive to Brithdir

SHOPPING IN MACHYNLLETH

Park on Maengwyn St. The Spectrum Gallery stocks a wide range of original contemporary pieces, including ceramics, prints, glass and jewellery *(Maengwyn Street, SY20 8EB; 01654 702877; www.spectrumgallery.co.uk).*

VISITING BEDDGELERT

Snowdonia National Park Information Centre
Canolfan Hebog, LL55 4YD; 01766 890 615; www.eryri-npa.gov.uk

WHERE TO STAY

AROUND MACHYNLLETH

Penrhos Arms Hotel *moderate*
Enjoy pleasant rooms with crisp bed linens in this friendly, cosy country inn, 11 km (7 miles) northeast on the A470. *Cemmaes, SY20 9PR; 01650 511 243; www.penrhosarms.com*

AROUND BRITHDIR

Ffynnon *moderate–expensive*
This award-winning boutique hotel is in Dolgellau, 8 km (5 miles) southwest of Brithdir. It has six luxurious rooms. *Ffynnon, Love Lane, Dolgellau, LL40 IRR; 01341 421 774; www.ffynnontownhouse.com*

HARLECH CASTLE

Cemlyn Tea Shop *moderate*
There are just two en-suite rooms above this lovely tea shop. One of them has views of Harlech Castle and the sea. *High Street, LL46 2YA; 01766 780 425; www.cemlynrestaurant.co.uk*

BEDDGELERT

Sygun Fawr *moderate*
Lovely old house in pretty gardens, with friendly atmosphere and lots of character – try for a mountain view. Take A498 north and then first right. *Beddgelert, LL55 4NE; 01766 890 258; www.sygunfawr.co.uk*

❶ Machynlleth
Powys; SY20 8EE

This historic market town is where Owain Glyndŵr first assembled his Parliament and was crowned as Prince of Wales in 1404. Owain started his revolt against the English in 1400 during the reign of Henry IV. In 1412, after the revolt foundered, legends say that Owain went into hiding around Machynlleth, and he was never seen again. A copy of his seal can be seen in the **Old Parliament House** *(Easter–Sep: closed Sun; also closed Mon in term time; closed Jan & Feb).* This low stone house was actually built in the 16th century, but is now a museum about Owain Glyndŵr.

The **Tabernacle**, a Neo-Classical Wesleyan chapel dating from the late 18th century, has been converted to a centre for the performing arts. The **MOMA Wales** *(open Mon–Sat; www. momawales.org.uk)* has evolved around it with seven art galleries displaying the work of Welsh artists from 1900.

Head north on the A487 for the **Centre for Alternative Technology** *(open daily Apr–Oct, call for winter opening; 01654 705 950; www.cat.org.uk)* for the eco-house, organic gardens, cliff railway and hands-on activities.

Below Leafy wooded avenue by the Art Nouveau Church of St Mark's, Brithdir

Continue on the A487 and take a sharp left on B4405 to **Tal-y-Llyn** a stunningly beautiful glacial lake in the shadow of Cadair Idris. Enjoy a walk or take a boat out onto the lake. Its shallow reedy beds are stocked with brown trout, and the lake is visited by sea trout and salmon in October. Obtain permits for fishing at the lake from **Tynycornel Hotel** *(01654 782282; www.tynycornel.co.uk).*

🚗 *Leave on the A487, then turn left on the A470 towards Dolgellau and follow the signs to Brithdir church. Park on the B4416 at the church entrance.*

❷ Brithdir
Gwynedd; LL40 2SB

Brithdir's major attraction is the **Church of St Mark's**. Its dark stone exterior conceals an Italian-style interior *(open most of the year)* with red-ochre walls and a blue-sky ceiling. Designed by Henry Wilson (known for his commissions for department store, Liberty's) and built 1895–98, it is one of the few Art Nouveau churches in Wales. See the ebony and abalone inlay on the doors and naturalistic carvings on the chestnut choir stall pews – squirrels, rabbits, a tortoise and an owl – all created in the Arts and Crafts tradition. Notice, too, the beaten copper panels on the pulpit and altar.

🚗 *Return to the A470 and follow the signs into Dolgellau. Once there, follow*

signs for Tywyn until a sign to Cadair Idris on the left. After 8 km (5 miles), turn right to Llynnau Cregennan, where there is a car park by the lake.

Above One of the many rivers running off the peaks around Beddgelert

③ Cadair Idris
Gwynedd

A huge 11-km (7-mile) long ridge, 892-m (2,927-ft) high, Cadair Idris dominates the surrounding area. The name means "Chair of Idris", after the giant warrior of Welsh legend. It's an area of outstanding scenic beauty and very popular with walkers. The tough paths to the top from the waters of **Llynnau Cregennan** take 4 to 6 hours to complete – on the way there are some standing stones and cairns over 4,000 years old. Climb to the small hill just above the car park for splendid views of Barmouth and Snowdonia.

🚗 *Take the road up and down to the A493 and turn right to Penmaenpool. Here, take a left over the toll bridge to the A496. Turn left for Barmouth and on to Harlech. Park in front of the castle.*

Below Impressive Harlech Castle, looking as though it has grown out of the rocky hillside

④ Harlech Castle
Gwynedd; LL46 2YH

Impressively situated on a bluff over Tremadog Bay, **Harlech Castle** was built between 1283–90 at a cost of £8,190 by Edward I's master mason, James of St George, who was also responsible for Caernarfon, Conway and Beaumaris castles. One of Edward's "iron ring" of castles, Harlech was designed to be supplied by sea, but the waters have since receded, leaving the castle high and dry. In 1404 Owain Glyndŵr took the castle, using it for his parliament. It was retaken after a long siege in 1408 by Harry of Monmouth, later Henry V. In the Wars of the Roses, it endured the longest siege in British history (1461–68) before being taken by the Yorkists, giving rise to the well-known military song "Men of Harlech".

🚗 *Continue on the A496 north and turn left, signed to Porthmadog. In Penrhyndeudraeth, follow the signs on the A4085 to Beddgelert.*

⑤ Beddgelert
Gwynedd; LL55 4YE

Perhaps Snowdonia's prettiest village, Beddgelert has a lovely tea shop and several cafés. The town is centred on a rustic bridge from where, along the south bank of the river, a path leads to the supposed monument to Llywelyn the Great's deerhound, Gelert. The story goes that, while Llywelyn was hunting, the dog saved his child from a wolf. Seeing the blood, Llywelyn thought Gelert had killed his boy and slew him, only to find his son safe and the wolf dead. He set a cairn of stones over the dog's grave, **Beth Gelert**. A short drive east on the A498, **Llyn Gwynant** is a lake in stunning scenery.

🚗 *Turn left out of the car park onto the A498, then left onto the A4086 to Llanberis, left at the roundabout and right to the railway car park.*

Above Stone houses overlooking the river at Beddgelert, crossed by a rustic bridge

EAT AND DRINK

MACHYNLLETH

The Wynnstay *moderate*
Local suppliers provide the ingredients for the dishes here, from pheasant breast to Cardigan Bay fish soup. There's also a separate pizzeria.
Heol Maengwyn, SY20 8AE; 01654 702 941; www.wynnstay-hotel.com

AROUND BRITHDIR

Dylanwad Da *moderate*
This little restaurant and coffee shop in Dolgellau, about 8 km (5 miles) southeast of Brithdir, uses lots of local produce. It's open in the evenings on Friday and Saturday.
2 Ffos-y-Felin, Dolgellau, LL40 1BS; 01341 422 870; www.dylanwad.co.uk

HARLECH CASTLE

Castle Cottage Restaurant *expensive*
An award-winning family-run restaurant in the heart of Harlech, Castle Cottage adds a sophisticated twist to Welsh produce, such as duet of Welsh beef with horseradish potatoes. There's a good wine list, and rooms, too.
High Street, LL46 2YL; 01766 780 479; www.castlecottageharlech.co.uk

BEDDGELERT

Tanronnen Inn *inexpensive*
For a traditional bar meal, head for this busy inn, conveniently situated in the centre of town. The inn has rooms and also does packed lunches for day trips.
Beddgelert, LL55 4YB; 01766 890 347; www.tanronnen.co.uk

Above View of the beautiful countryside of the Snowdonia National Park

VISITING MOUNT SNOWDON

Snowdonia National Park Information *Electric Mountain Centre, Llanberis, LL55 4UR; 01286 870 765; open May–Aug; out of season, use the office in Caernarfon: 01286 672 232*

SHOPPING IN BEAUMARIS

For locally designed items of clothing, try Cole & Co *(42 Castle Street, LL58 8BB; 01248 811 312)*. They also have a gift shop and gallery *(33 Castle Street, LL58 8AP)*.

WHERE TO STAY

AROUND CAERNARFON

Ty'n Rhos *moderate*
Comfortable country hotel less than 8 km (5 miles) northeast of Caernarfon, off the A4866. Guests enjoy elegant rooms, wonderful locally sourced food and peaceful gardens.
Seion, Llanddeiniolen, LL55 3AE; 01248 670 489; www.tynrhos.co.uk

Plas Dinas *moderate–expensive*
Enjoy a taste of country house living at this 17th-century, grade II-listed house on the A487 not far south of Caernarfon. It has lovely gardens and elegant rooms, and serves local bacon for breakfast.
Bontnewydd, LL54 7YF; 01286 830 214; www.plasdinas.co.uk

BEAUMARIS

Ye Olde Bulls Head Inn *moderate*
Country-style bedrooms with a modern touch are on offer at this established inn. Next door, their contemporary town house has stylish colour-themed rooms and luxurious bathrooms.
Castle Street, LL58 8AP; 01248 810 329; www.bullsheadinn.co.uk

Right The award-winning Hafod Eryri visitor centre at the summit of Snowdon

⑥ Mount Snowdon
Gwynedd; LL55 4TY

A popular destination, **Llanberis** has many significant attractions, not least Wales' highest mountain, Snowdon, at 1,085 m (3,560 ft). Walk to the top or take the train. The 7.5-km (4-mile) trip passes through stunning scenery and is perhaps the most exciting train journey in the UK. The **Snowdon Mountain Railway** *(Apr–Oct: open daily; Mar–Apr: partial service; 0844 493 8120; www.snowdonrailway.co.uk)* is weather dependent, so check beforehand.

At the top of Snowdon, **Hafod Eryri**, the railway terminus and visitor centre, awaits. Britain's highest building and possibly one of its most unusual was designed by architect Roy Hole, after the original 1930s café was demolished in 2006. Created from stone and slate and with a large flat roof, Hafod Eryri does not seem out of place in Snowdon's rugged landscape.

Inside the walls are lined in timber and the window affords thrilling views.

Nearby, the **Electric Mountain Centre** *(open daily: tours Easter–end Oct; 01286 870 636; www.electricmountain.co.uk)* has a café and activity rooms, and runs tours of the Dinorwig Power Station, deep in Europe's largest man-made cavern, inside Elidir Mountain (not suitable for wheelchair users or anyone who suffers from claustrophobia).

Don't miss **Dolbadarn Castle** *(open daily)*, perched on the hillside over the main road beside the lake, Llyn Peris. Built in the 13th century by Llywelyn the Great, it is simple but masterful – the 12-m (40-ft) tower once reached three storeys.

Steam buffs will love the **Llanberis Lake Railway** *(May–Sep: open daily; call at other times; 01286 870 549; www.lake-railway.co.uk)*. The narrow-gauge steam railway runs along the pretty wooded lakeside. Nearby is the **National Slate Museum** *(open daily; closed Sat Nov–Easter; 0300 1112 333; www.museumwales.ac.uk)*, telling the story of slate in a series of Victorian workshops with talks and demonstrations.

🚗 *Take A4086 to Caernarfon. Head into the centre and park by the castle.*

⑦ Caernarfon
Gwynedd; LL55 2AY

By the Menai Straits and with sea access, Caernarfon is the ideal site for a castle. **Caernarfon Castle** *(open daily)* was built in 1283 as part of Edward I's ring of castles to subjugate the Welsh. With its polygonal towers and twin-turreted gateway, Caernarfon Castle is a fine example of late 13th- and early 14th-century military architecture. The colour-banded masonry was inspired by Constantinople's walls. King Edward wanted the castle to be a royal residence and seat of government for north Wales. Its symbolic status was emphasized when Edward made sure his son, the first English Prince of Wales, was born here in 1284. It was more recently used for the investiture of the present Prince of Wales in 1969.

On the A4085, on the edge of town, stands the Roman fort of **Segontium** (*open daily*) dating from AD 77–78. The large fort was built to control the approach to Anglesey and see off Irish seaborne raiders. It was in use until AD 395 and its internal layout is still visible.

🚗 *Leave by A487 to Bangor. Take the A5 left across Menai Suspension Bridge (1826). Take the A545 right to Beaumaris. Park by the pier or opposite the castle.*

⑧ Beaumaris
Anglesey; LL58 8AP

With medieval, Georgian, Victorian and Edwardian buildings and a wide range of shops, Beaumaris is an attractive town for visitors. See the **Church of St Mary** for the carved tomb of Joan, Llywelyn the Great's wife. The main draw here is **Beaumaris Castle** (*open daily*), a military masterpiece and the last and largest of Edward I's Welsh castles. Built in 1295 with concentric symmetry and four lines of defence, to a design by Master James of St George, it was meant to control the Menai Straits and there are great views of Snowdonia. The low-lying castle has 16 towers and a chapel with

a vaulted ceiling and lancet windows. However, the money ran out before the fortifications had reached full height.

Seafaring types can take a cruise to see seals and puffins, or go wreck fishing. Book with **Starida Sea Services** (*01248 810 251; www.starida.co.uk*).

Take the coastal road north to the tranquil tip of Anglesey, to **Penmon Priory** at the entrance to the Menai Straits. Founded in the 6th century, it was destroyed by the Danes in the 10th. The present **St Seiriol's church** dates from around 1140. Inside are some beautiful early stone Welsh crosses. The well, outside, is believed to be part of the original 6th-century building, which would make it the oldest ecclesiastical site in Wales.

🚗 *Leave on B5109, turn right onto the A5025, turning right for Moelfre. Drive on to the seafront car park.*

Above left Caernarfon Castle, built to recall the walls of Constantinople **Above top right** A train at Llanberis, on the Snowdon Mountain Railway **Above right** Cosy Beau's Tea Room, in a historic building close to the castle, Beaumaris

EAT AND DRINK

MOUNT SNOWDON

Caban Cyf *inexpensive*
Near Llanberis, this restaurant uses organic produce from its own garden. *Yr Hen Ysgol, Brynrefail, LL55 3NR; 01286 685 500; www.caban-cyf.org; open 9am–4pm daily*

Snowdon Mountain Railway Station Café & Caffi y Copa at Hafod Eryri *inexpensive*
The café at Hafod Eryri on Snowdon's summit offers baked savouries from the Village Bakery, while the café at Llanberis serves all-day brunch, snacks and tea. *Snowdon Summit/Llanberis, LL55 4TY; 01286 870 223; www.snowdonrailway.co.uk*

Heights Bar and Grill *moderate*
This traditional restaurant serves up burgers, jacket potatoes, baguettes and more substantial offerings. *74 High Street, Llanberis, LL55 4HB; 01286 238 235; www.castell-caernarfon.co.uk*

BEAUMARIS

Beau's Tea Room *inexpensive*
This is the place to fill up on tea and fresh *bara brith* served on antique bone china. In a cosy 400-year-old building, the café also sells hot meals. *30 Castle Street, LL58 8AP; 01248 811 010; www.beaustearoom.co.uk*

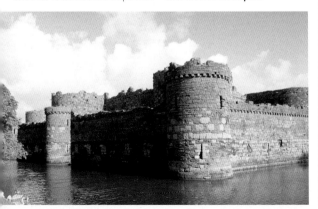

Left Beaumaris Castle, the largest of Edward I's Welsh fortifications

Eat and Drink: inexpensive, under £25; moderate, £25–£50; expensive, over £50

Above Cottages in the coastal village of Moelfre, on the Island of Anglesey

VISITING MOELFRE

Parking
Free parking close to the village and a pay-and-display car park on seafront.

Tourist Information
01248 713 177;
www.visitanglesey.co.uk

WHERE TO STAY

AROUND MOELFRE

Siop y Rhos *inexpensive*
Enjoy sea or mountain views at this sheltered farmhouse 3 km (2 miles) west of Moelfre. The extensive range of breakfast options includes pancakes and smoked salmon. Packed lunches are available too.
Lligy, LL70 9PZ (01248 850 801; www.stayinanglesey.com

Llwydiarth Fawr *moderate*
This Georgian home is at the heart of a working farm about 10 km (6.5 miles) from Moelfre. Its spacious, elegant interior is furnished with antiques and includes a library.
Llanerch-y-medd, LL71 8DF (take A5108 out of Moelfre, at roundabout take second exit onto A5025, turn left, left again and bear left, then take second right towards B5111 and turn left; farm is on left); 01248 470 321; www. angleseyfarms.com/llwydiarth.htm

AROUND LLANFAIRPWLL

Cleifiog Uchaf *moderate*
A 16th-century Welsh longhouse in a superb location, this small hotel has a relaxing interior and its own access to the Anglesey Coastal Path.
Valley, LL65 3AB (take A5/A55 towards Holyhead, exit 3 for A5 to Valley, fourth exit at the roundabout, left at Lon Spencer, then right); 01407 741 888; www.cleifioguchaf.co.uk

⑨ Moelfre

Anglesey; LL72 8LL

The sleepy village of Moelfre looks north into the Irish Sea, over the ships going to and from Mersey port. This walk follows the headland around the village, past memorials highlighting the dangers of the sea and the bravery of the Royal National Lifeboat Institution (RNLI) crews.

A two-hour walking tour

From the seafront car park, walk with the sea on your right to the **RNLI Seawatch Centre** ① *(Apr–Oct: open daily)*, which chronicles the island's maritime and natural history, and the lives of locals such as Richard Evans who saved the lives of two boat crews.

Outside, walk down to the sea to the bronze sculpture of coxswain Evans MBE who retired in 1970. Then turn left and follow the coastal path to the **RNLI Lifeboat Station** ② *(open daily; 01248 410 367; www.moelfrernli. com)*, which has information about the work of the RNLI – run by volunteers – who rescue hundreds of people a year from the sea. Further along the footpath, see terns, gannets and fulmars on the island of Ynys Moelfre, just offshore. Continue along the coast and go through two gates, up a slight hill and some steps and over a stile. Go through another gate, and along a path. Walk down the path towards a small bridge, over a stream, and then up the steps to the top. Here is the

RNLI logo at Moelfre Lifeboat Station

Monument to the Royal Charter ③, a passenger steam clipper returning to Liverpool from Melbourne, which sank off the coast of Anglesey in October 1859 during one of the fiercest storms of the century. It was a catastrophe with 459 lives lost and only 21 passengers and 18 crew surviving. No women or children survived. It was the highest death toll of any shipwreck off the Welsh coast in the days before Moelfre had a lifeboat. Walk back down the steps and up the path and take a right past the caravans. Keep on the track and cross the cattle grid, past a cottage and onto the road. Turn left into a housing estate, past the house Ty Mawr followed by a school, a library and Maes Hydryd. Continue straight on and take a left past Ann's Pantry, a family-run café and restaurant, and the Kinmel Arms Hotel, with fine ales and pub food. The car park is over the road.

🚗 *Drive back on the A5025, through Pentraeth and under the A55 to Llanfair PG. Use the railway station car park beside James Pringle Weavers.*

Left Headland and Monument to the Royal Charter, near Moelfre

⑩ Llanfairpwllgwyngyll-gogerychwyrndrobwll-llantysiliogogogoch

Anglesey; LL61 5UJ

The name means "Church of St Mary in the hollow of the white hazel trees, near a fierce whirlpool and the Church of St Tysilio, near the red cave." Often shortened to Llanfair PG or Llanfairpwll, at 58 letters long it is the longest place name in Britain. It was devised by the Victorians to attract tourists. The train station sign is the usual subject for photos. Nearby is the **Marquess of Anglesey's Column** *(open daily)* a 27-m (89-ft) monument to Henry William Paget who lost his leg at the Battle of Waterloo. Climb the 115 steps for a fabulous panorama. Pose for a picture by the name sign above **James Pringle Weavers** *(open daily; 01248 717 171)*, a thriving knitwear outlet and souvenir shop.

🚗 *Turn right out of the car park onto Holyhead Rd and then right onto A4080 to Plas Newydd (signed) and car park. A minibus shuttles visitors to the house.*

⑪ Plas Newydd

Anglesey; LL61 6DQ

Just outside Llanfair PG, **Plas Newydd** *(open mid-Mar–end Oct: Sat–Wed; 01248 714 795)* is the ancestral home of the Marquess of Anglesey. The house was redesigned in the 18th century by renowned architect James Wyatt in a mixture of Neo-Gothic and Neo-Classical styles. It is set in parkland with beautiful walks and dramatic views over the Menai Straits and Snowdonia. The long dining room features an 18-m (58-ft) mural of a mythological harbour scene by the artist and set designer Rex Whistler c.1936-40, who died in World War II. There is a small military museum about the 1st Marquess of Anglesey, who was the Duke of Wellington's cavalry commander at the Battle of Waterloo.

🚗 *Take the A4085, turn right onto the A5 and right again onto the A55 to cross back to the mainland. Take the A5 at exit 11 signed to Betws-y-Coed. In the town centre, turn left over the bridge to the car park.*

EAT AND DRINK

MOELFRE

Ann's Pantry *inexpensive*
Enjoy fresh locally sourced and Fairtrade produce at this café/bistro with sea views. There is a daily blackboard lunch menu, and the home-made cakes are a speciality.
Moelfre, LL72 8HH; 01248 410 386; www.annspantry.co.uk

Kinmel Arms *moderate*
This pub offers good panoramic seafront views and a wide menu including daily specials, and is popular with the locals.
Moelfre Bay, LL72 8LL; 01248 410 231

LLANFAIRPWLL

Tafarn Ty Gwyn *inexpensive*
Lively village pub with good food at reasonable prices.
8 Holyhead Road, LL61 5UJ; 01248 715 599

Below left Llanfairpwllgwyngyllgogerych-wyrndrobwllllantysiliogogogoch **Below** Neo-Gothic and Neo-Classical Plas Newydd

Above The highest waterfall in Wales, Swallow Falls, Betws-y-Coed

VISITING BETWS-Y-COED

Snowdonia National Park Information Centre
Royal Oak Stables, LL24 0AH; 01690 710 426

Adventure Activities
For rock climbing and canyoning activities, including lessons, try **Seren Ventures** *(Adventure Centre, Vicarage Road, LL24 0AD; 01690 710 754; www.serenventures.com);* for tree-top activities, suitable for all ages, contact **Tree Top Adventure** *(Treetop Lodge, Llanrwst Road, LL24 0HA; 01690 710 914; www.ttadventure.co.uk).*

WHERE TO STAY

AROUND BETWS-Y-COED

St Curig's Church *inexpensive*
Snuggle up in this cosy converted church about 8 km (5 miles) west on the A5. There are original stained-glass windows, and a hot tub in the garden. *Capel Curig, LL24 0EL; 01690 720 469; www.stcurigschurch.com*

Pengwern Guesthouse *moderate*
Welsh-speaking hosts run this immaculate country house, a short distance south on the A5. Local produce for breakfast, free Wi-Fi and fine views. *Allt Dinas, LL24 0HF; 01690 710 480; www.snowdoniaaccommodation.co.uk*

CONWY

Sychnant Pass House *moderate*
Situated about 3 km (2 miles) west of Conwy this is a friendly and relaxed country guesthouse, with comfortable rooms, highly rated food, and a swimming pool and hot tub. *Sychnant Pass Road, LL32 8BJ; 01492 596 868; www.sychnant-pass-house.co.uk*

⑫ Betws-y-Coed
Conwy; LL24 0HD
The principal village in the Snowdonia National Park, **Betws-y-Coed**, the "prayer house in the wood", is a popular tourist spot along with the nearby **Swallow Falls**, the highest continuous waterfall in Wales. Nestled in a wooded valley at the confluence of the rivers Conwy, Llugwy and Lledr, it is well-appointed with galleries, cafés, shops, pubs and hotels. Its oldest building is the 14th-century **St Michael's Church** *(Easter–Nov: open daily)* with a stone effigy of Gruffydd ap Dafydd Goch, related to Llywelyn, the last free Welsh Prince of Wales. The countryside around Betws-y-Coed offers rivers, pools and

Traditional designs at Trefriw Woollen Mills

waterfalls. Several walks start from the ancient Pont-y-Pair bridge, built in 1468, in the town centre. Those looking for more extreme activities can go rock climbing, abseiling or canyoning, or try an adventure obstacle course among the tree tops.

🚗 *From the car park, take B5106 north to Trefriw. Park across the road from the mills by the war memorial.*

⑬ Trefriw Woollen Mills
Conwy; LL27 0NQ
Established in 1859 and run ever since by the Williams family, **Trefriw Woollen Mills** *(museum open Apr–Oct: Mon–Fri; shop open daily in summer, closed Sun in winter; 01492 640 462; www.t-w-m.co.uk)* use 50-year-old machines and do their own blending, spinning dying and weaving. The mill is best known for its double-weave blankets. There is a weavers' garden with a display of the plants that provide fibres, soap and natural dyes and, in summer, there are weaving demonstrations. Walk or drive alongside the river that supplies the mill, to the lakes of Llyn Geirionydd and **Llyn Crafnant**. A café beside Llyn Crafnant has great cakes and ice cream *(open Mar–Oct).*

🚗 *Turn right out of the car park to leave Trefriw on the B5106 north to Conwy, and pass through the break in the city wall. At the roundabout, turn left into Rose Hill Street and park next to the castle.*

Below Betwys-y-Coed, nestled in a deep wooded valley at the confluence of three rivers

⑭ Conwy

Conwy; LL32 8AY

At the mouth of an estuary spanned by Telford's 1826 suspension bridge, Conwy is best known for its **Castle** *(open daily)*. It was built by Master James of St George in four years (1283–87) using local stone. The castle and the medieval town walls have World Heritage status and are Britain's finest example of a *bastide* or fortified town, with 21 towers, three double gateways and a 1280-m (4,200-ft) long wall.

There are other interesting historic buildings in the town. **Aberconwy House** *(Mar–Oct: open daily; Nov & Dec: open Sat & Sun)* is a 14th-century merchant's house with period displays; **Plas Mawr** *(closed Mon)* is one of the finest surviving Elizabethan town houses (1558–1603). Admire its symmetry, the crow-stepped gables and pedimented windows. **The Potters Gallery** *(www.thepottersgallery.co.uk)*, further down the High Street has a great collection of local ceramics. And finally, on Conwy Quay, squeeze into the **Smallest House in Britain** *(Apr–Oct: open daily)* – it is 2.75 m (9 ft) high and 1.5 m (5 ft) wide and was last owned by a 2-m (over 6-ft) tall fisherman!

🚗 *Leave Conwy on A547 over the bridge and take A546 left to Llandudno. Head for the seafront and promenade.*

⑮ Llandudno

Conwy; LL30 2RP

Wales' largest seaside resort, Llandudno lies in a wide bay sheltered by two limestone headlands, the Ormes. Most of the town was laid out in 1849 with grand buildings, a promenade – the Parade and the longest pier in Wales. The Great Orme is a 207-m (679-ft) high promontory reached by road, **cable car** *(Apr–Oct: open daily)* and a **funicular tramway** *(open daily)* with spectacular views from the top.

Explore the **Great Orme Mines** *(Mar–Oct: open daily; www.greatormemines.info)*, the world's largest Bronze-Age copper mine, through tunnels dug over 3,500 years ago. The Great Orme is a good place for walking following the signed nature trails, and winter sports fans will enjoy skiing or tobogganing at the **Llandudno Ski and Snowboard Centre** *(open daily; www.jnllandudno.co.uk)*.

Among the town's other attractions is the outstanding contemporary art gallery **Oriel Mostyn** *(01492 879 201; www.mostyn.org)* in Vaughan Street.

Above left Inside the impressive outer ward in World Heritage status Conwy Castle **Above centre** The Knights Shop, selling suits of armour opposite Conwy Castle **Above right** Small fishing station on pretty Conwy Estuary

EAT AND DRINK

BETWS-Y-COED

Ty Gwyn Hotel *moderate*
This former coaching inn offers a range of restaurant and bar meals.
Betws-y-Coed, LL24 0SG; 01690 710 383; www.tygwynhotel.co.uk

AROUND TREFRIW WOOLLEN MILLS

The Tannery *moderate*
This restaurant on the A470 near Trefriw serves imaginative modern Welsh cuisine on a riverside terrace.
Willow Street, Llanrwst; LL26 0ES; 01492 640 172; www.ytanerdy.co.uk

CONWY

The Mulberry *inexpensive–moderate*
This pub on the Marina serves a range of dishes and traditional ales.
Ellis Way, Marina; LL32 8GU; 01492 583 350; www.themulberry.robinsons brewery.com

Watsons Bistro *moderate*
Enjoy contemporary Welsh fare at this bistro tucked under the old town walls.
26 Chapel Street, LL32 8BP; 01492 596 326; www.watsonsbistroconwy.co.uk

---

DAY TRIP OPTIONS

Several stops along the route make ideal bases from which to explore the area's spectacular scenery, historic sites and visitor attractions.

A Photographers' Treat

Starting from historic Machynlleth ❶, visit beautiful Tal-y-Llyn and enjoy boating or fishing on the lake. Carry on to Brithdir ❷, to see the church and head to Llynnau Cregennan for a walk in the shadow of Cadair Idris ❸.

Follow the drive's instructions.

Exploring Snowdonia

From Caernarfon ❼, see the castle before heading for Llanberis, and a train ride up Mt Snowdon ❻. Then travel through a mountain with the Electric Mountain Centre. Finally, drive to pretty Beddgelert ❺ for the stunning scenery.

Take the A4086 and A498; but return to Caernarfon via the A4085.

Anglesey Adventure

Staying at Beaumaris ❽, see the castle and enjoy a morning cruise around Puffin Island. Head to Moelfre ❾, and

learn about the island's maritime history. Then tour the beautiful home of the Marquess of Anglesey, Plas Newydd ⓫.

Follow the drive's instructions.

Family Fun

Explore the beach, take the tram up the Great Orme to see the copper mines at Llandudno ⑮, then head to Conwy ⑭ to tour the castle and have lunch. Drive into the heart of Snowdonia to Betws-y-Coed ⑫, for a walk to Swallow Falls or thrilling tree-top adventure.

Take the A470 and A55.

Eat and Drink: inexpensive, under £25; moderate, £25–£50; expensive, over £50

Along Offa's Dyke

From Ludlow to Holywell

Highlights

- **England's finest market town**
  Wander through Ludlow's historic centre with its half-timbered buildings, medieval street plan, ancient church and mighty castle

- **Stately castle homes**
  Explore the beautiful residences of Powis, Chirk and Bodelwyddan castles, packed full of interesting artifacts and set in magical grounds

- **Heaven on earth**
  Spend some time at Llangollen, with its society haunts, looming hilltop castle, ancient ruined abbey and spectacular canal and aqueduct

- **The Lourdes of Wales**
  Take the waters at Holywell – probably the oldest pilgrimage site in Britain, and appreciate its air of piety and faith

View of the Long Mynd, a series of dramatic hills in Shropshire

Along Offa's Dyke

This drive takes the visitor from the English borders over Wenlock Edge and around the Long Mynd, an ancient hog's-back ridge, into the beautiful Welsh countryside. The route now runs parallel to Offa's impressive but ultimately ineffective dyke, heading north to the estuary of the River Dee. On the way, the drive winds past the remains of once-mighty castles and still grand country houses, and Thomas Telford's fabulous feat of engineering, the aqueduct on the Llangollen Canal at Pontcysyllte, which dates from 1805. There are cultural and spiritual highlights, too. See a copy of William Morgan's first translation of the Bible into Welsh in the Cathedral at St Asaph and the "Jesse Tree" window of St Dyfnog's Church, and experience the tranquillity of St Winefride's Well in Holywell.

Above Ruins of Denbigh Castle, overlooking the surrounding countryside, *see p166*

ACTIVITIES

Learn about old rural crafts at Acton Scott Farm Museum

Look out for distinctive red kites hovering over Powis Castle

Be pulled by a historic steam locomotive through the Welsh countryside on the Welshpool & Llanfair Light Railway

Clamber up to Castell Dinas Bran for the astonishing views

Glide over the 38-m (125-ft) high Pontcysyllte Aqueduct in a canal barge

Step through 600 years of housing history in Ruthin

Follow a nature trail in the grounds of Bodelwyddan Castle

Take the healing waters at the Lourdes of Wales, Holywell

Below Bodenham's, one of many striking half-timbered buildings in Ludlow, *see p162*

Above Beautiful lakeside woodland at Dingle Nursery and Garden, *see p163*

KEY

—— Drive route

0 kilometres 10

0 miles 10

PLAN YOUR DRIVE

Start/finish: Ludlow to Holywell.

Number of days: 4, allowing half a day at Ludlow and half a day at Llangollen.

Distance: About 207 km (129 miles).

Road conditions: Good, well-paved and signposted.

When to go: Spring and summer is best for walks in the hills.

Opening times: Galleries, museums and attractions are generally open 10am–5pm, but often close earlier Nov–Easter. Shops are often open longer. Churches are usually open until dusk.

Main market days: Ludlow: 4 days a week, Castle Square; **Welshpool**: 1st Sat of month, Farmers' Market, Coed-y-Dinas; **Llangollen**: Fri am, Town Hall; **Denbigh**: last Fri of month, Town Hall; **Holywell**: Thu & Sat am.

Shopping: Plenty of Shropshire produce and local foods around Ludlow and pottery at St Asaph. Carved wooden lovespoons can be found all over Wales.

Major festivals: Ludlow: Arts festival, Jun–Jul; Food Festival, mid-Sep *(www.foodfestival.co.uk);* St Asaph: North Wales International Music Festival, end Sep *(www.nwimf.com);* Llangollen: International Musical Eisteddfod, Jul.

DAY TRIP OPTIONS

Families will enjoy staying at Ludlow to visit the **castle** and a **farm museum** for a **picnic**, before heading to Welshpool for the **steam train** and maybe a tour of the **castle**. Alternatively, spend a day near Llangollen – climb a hill to the **castle**, walk along a **canal**, see the **aqueduct**, admire the **views** at Horseshoe Pass, visit an **abbey**, then drive to Chirk Castle for its **interiors** and **gardens**. For those interested in cultural and religious treasures, see Denbigh's **castle** and **churches**, the **Welsh Bible** at St Asaph, **treasures** and **gardens** at Bodelwyddan Castle, the **pilgrimage site** and **well** at Holywell, and the **Jesse window** at St Dyfnog's. For full details, *see p167*.

Above Carved wooden façade of the Feathers Hotel, Ludlow

VISITING LUDLOW

Parking
Follow signs to town centre and park as near as possible to Castle Square: there is pay-and-display parking on Mill Street and Dinham, down the side of the castle, and a car park off Castle Street.

Tourist Information
1 Mill Street, SY8 1AZ; 01584 875 053; www.shropshiretourism.co.uk

WHERE TO STAY

LUDLOW

The Feathers *moderate–expensive*
Choose a room in the oldest part of this picturesque and central hotel for the most original features. Local produce features on the restaurant menu.
21 Bull Ring, SY81AA; 01584 875 261; www.feathersatludlow.co.uk

AROUND LUDLOW

The Clive *moderate*
This former farmhouse, north of Ludlow on the A49, has 15 immaculate en-suite rooms and serves fresh produce for breakfast. It also has a superb restaurant and bar, open to non-residents.
Bromfield, SY8 2JR; 01584 856 565; www.theclive.co.uk

WELSHPOOL

The Royal Oak Hotel *moderate*
Once a Georgian coaching inn, this hotel has comfortable boutique-style rooms with a contemporary or classic decor.
The Cross, SY21 7DG; 01938 552 217; www.royaloakwelshpool.co.uk

① Ludlow
Shropshire; SY8 1AS

The market town of Ludlow is a great base for exploring the glorious Marches countryside. Growing from the wealth of the medieval wool trade, Ludlow became an important political centre. Much of its medieval street pattern has survived almost intact and there are some fine examples of timber-framed buildings and a ruined castle. This walk gives a good introduction to the town.

A two-hour walking tour

From Mill St, turn left to 11th-century **Ludlow Castle ①** *(open daily)*, one of a series of Norman castles built in the Marches to control the Welsh. Return to Castle Square, and across Mill St on the right to the **Assembly Rooms ②** – a Tourist Information Centre and museum with local history and geology exhibits. Continue down the narrow Market St and turn right into the fine **Broad Sreet ③**. Appreciate the seamless mix of timber-framed Tudor and elegant brick buildings. Return back up Broad St and turn right into King St towards the restored 15th-century toll house, **The Tolsey ④**. Now occupied by solicitors' offices and shops, this is where tax was collected for every head of cattle brought for sale at market. At the Old Bull Ring pub, turn left onto Bull Ring and continue to the **Feathers Hotel ⑤**,

Carved stone arch at Ludlow Castle

built in 1619, with its skilfully carved half-timbered frontage. The balconies were added in the 19th century. Return back up the street, admiring the woodwork on the buildings. Turn right and head back to the **Butter Cross ⑥**, which was rebuilt in 1744 in Neo-Classical style as a town hall and served as a butter market. Take a right past Barclays Bank to **St Laurence's Church ⑦**. Established in the 11th century, this was rebuilt in 1199 and heavily modified in the 15th century. Look out for the tomb of Arthur Tudor (Henry VII's son) and the carved misericords of medieval scenes. Climb the 42-m (138-ft) tower for fabulous views. Admire the stained glass – the Palmer's window tells of King Edward the Confessor's visit to the Holy Land. The cherry trees in the graveyard commemorate the poet A E Housman (1859–1936), author of *A Shropshire Lad*,

Above View of the Shropshire countryside around Ludlow

whose ashes are buried in the church wall near the West Door. Exit the church and return to King St. Turn right and carry on down Church St to Castle Square, turning left to return to Mill St.

🚗 *Take A49 towards Shrewsbury, then B4365 right to a T-junction (B4368). Turn left, then first right to Ticklerton and the museum, 2 km (1½ miles) beyond.*

② Acton Scott Farm Museum
Shropshire; SY6 6QN

This living history farm museum *(Apr–Oct: open daily)* recreates life on a Shropshire farm at the turn of the last century. Visitors are returned to the days of shire horses, hay ricks and milkmaids, and the farm is stocked with pigs, poultry, cows and sheep, including some rare breeds. Kids will enjoy the daily demonstrations by farm workers dressed in period costumes. There are also waymarked walks starting from the farm.

🚗 *Turn left from car park and straight across to A49. Turn right, then left onto B4370, then take A489 right. Next take the B4385 to castle and car park.*

③ Montgomery Castle
Powys; SY15 6HN

It was the Norman knight Roger de Montgomerie (the very first Earl of Shrewsbury) who built the first fort here in c.1070 – the motte-and-bailey Hen Domen, at the bottom of Castle Hill. The present castle *(open daily)* was built in 1223 during the reign of Henry III to defend the border against the Welsh Prince, Llywelyn the Great (1173–1240). It was demolished during the Civil War. There are great views out over a wide expanse of countryside to the north and east.

🚗 *Head northwest on the B4385, join-ing the A483 north, with the floodplain of the Severn flowing south on the right. Fork left onto the A490 into Welshpool. Park in Church St in the town centre.*

④ Welshpool
Powys; SY21 8RF

Set in the picturesque countryside of the Severn Valley, Welshpool makes an excellent base for exploring the surrounding area. The big attraction, off the A490 into town (with car park, or a 1-km/2-mile walk across parkland), is stunning **Powis Castle** *(open daily except Christmas Day)*. Originally a 13th-century fort, it is the only Welsh castle to have remained a residence from the medieval to the modern period. The castle's golden age was in Stuart times, when it was acquired by the Herbert family (1587) and altered extensively. In 1784, Henrietta Herbert married Edward Clive, the son of Clive of India. Clive's collection in the museum is probably the greatest display of Indian Mughal art outside the subcontinent.

The "red castle" (Castell Coch in Welsh) sits in a delightful Baroque 17th-century Italianate terraced garden dotted with sculptures and manicured hedges. Look out, too, for sentinel red kites that hover above.

At the western edge of town, the **Welshpool & Llanfair Light Railway** *(Aug: open daily; Mar–Oct: times vary; 01938 810 441; www.wllr.org.uk)*, built in 1903, takes visitors on a 26-km (16-mile) round trip through rural Powys on a narrow-gauge steam railway. The **Dingle Nursery and Garden** *(open daily; www.dinglenurseries.co.uk)* at Frochas, north of Welshpool on the A490, has a superb small garden.

🚗 *Continue along the A490, then A483 and A5, taking the B5070 to Chirk. Follow signs left for Chirk Castle (with car park).*

EAT AND DRINK

LUDLOW

Koo *inexpensive–moderate*
It's a welcome surprise to find such good-value Japanese cuisine in Ludlow. Enjoy sparkling fresh food that looks too good to eat. The service is friendly and the restaurant is very popular.
127 Old Street, SY8 1NU; 01584 878 462; www.koo-ook.co.uk

The French Pantry *moderate*
This tiny, unpretentious restaurant offers a taste of France with friendly service. Try Normandy pork with prunes and brandy, followed by delicious desserts.
15 Tower Street, SY8 1RL; 01584 879 133; www.thefrenchpantry.co.uk

Mr Underhills *expensive*
In a glorious setting beside the weir, this Michelin-starred restaurant offers friendly service and superb food: the 7-course tasting menu changes daily. Booking essential (also does rooms).
Dinham Weir, Ludlow SY8 1EH; 01584 874 431; www.mr-underhills.co.uk

WELSHPOOL

Corn Store *moderate*
This bright and buzzing restaurant in the heart of town is family-friendly and serves a wide-ranging menu with dishes to satisfy both carnivores and vegetarians.
4 Church Street, SY21 7DL; 01938 554 614; closed Sun & Mon

AROUND WELSHPOOL

Seeds *moderate*
Quirky little restaurant in a cottage 18 km (11 miles) north of Welshpool on the A490, with a reputation for serving great food. The menu features gems such as home-potted shrimps and rack of Welsh lamb, and also vegetarian dishes.
5 Penybryn Cottage, High Street, Llanfyllin, SY22 5AP; 01691 648 604

Below The imposing red Powis Castle, set in exquisite terraced gardens

Above left Decorative topiary in the grounds of Chirk Castle Top right Pub sign, Llangollen Bottom right The ruins of Valle Crucis Abbey, set in glorious countryside

WHERE TO STAY

AROUND CHIRK CASTLE

The West Arms Hotel *moderate*
The drive to this ancient inn set in the tranquil Ceiriog Valley is long – but a real treat. The hotel is 18 km (11 miles) west of Chirk on the B4500 with pretty en-suite rooms and lovely views.
Llanarmon Dyffryn Ceiriog, LL20 7LD; 01691 600 665; www.thewestarms.co.uk

LLANGOLLEN

Gales of Llangollen *moderate*
This hotel has 15 en-suite rooms with original features, plus antique and brass beds. Some rooms are over the wine bar, others in a timber-framed building.
18 Bridge Street, LL20 8PF; 01978 860 089; www.galesofllangollen.co.uk

RUTHIN

Firgrove Country House *moderate*
This charming Georgian house, just west of Ruthin on the B5105, has extensive gardens, two attractive B&B rooms plus a self-catering suite. Can do evening meals.
Llanfwrog, LL15 2LL; 01824 702677; www.firgrovecountryhouse.co.uk

Manorhaus *moderate*
This boutique hotel has eight modern, stylish rooms. There are luxurious touches like fine bedlinen, sleek bathrooms, a sauna, and there's even a private cinema for guests.
Well Street, LL15 1AH; 01824 704 830; www.manorhaus.com

Right The colourful hills and valley of Horseshoe Pass, near Llangollen

⑤ Chirk Castle
Wrexham; LL14 5AF
Built as a border fortress at the end of the 13th century by Roger Mortimer, a warlord of Edward I, Chirk Castle *(open daily Mar–Oct; grounds: open daily all year)* is full of beautiful furniture and paintings. It was bought in the 16th century by Sir Thomas Myddleton; his descendants hired Augustus Pugin (1812–52), Gothic revivalist and architect of the Houses of Parliament, to carry out major alterations. There are also some wonderful Neo-Classical rooms by Joseph Turner. The library has many fine books, and the garden, with dramatic clipped yews, is another highlight. There is also an impressive set of intricate iron-lacework gates.
🚗 *Return to Chirk, taking B5070 north to A5 and on to Llangollen. Park in the centre, or cross the bridge and turn right into Mill St for the long-stay car park.*

⑥ Llangollen
Denbighshire; LL20 8AW
British Prime Minister and Welshman, David Lloyd George (1863–1945), described the area around Llangollen as "a little bit of heaven on earth". Llangollen itself is best known for the International Musical Eisteddfod. This was set up in 1947 to encourage good relations between all nations after World War II. The town gets very busy during the festival in July. Visit the black and white, ornately half-timbered **Plas Newydd** *(Apr–Sep: open Wed–Mon)*, the former home of the "Ladies of Llangollen", Lady Eleanor Butler and Miss Sarah Ponsonby, who ran away from Ireland together to live here between 1780 and 1829. Famed in Regency society, their visitors included the Duke of Wellington, Wordsworth, Byron, Shelley and the Darwins. Above the town looms 213-m (700-ft) the ruins of **Castell Dinas Bran**. Follow the path marked from the Canal Wharf bridge up to the top for superb views. The 74-km (46-mile) **Llangollen Canal**,

Offa's Dyke
The Anglo-Saxon King Offa of Mercia (AD 757–96) is best known for his dyke, a defensive earthwork, running north to south, built to protect the border between Mercia and Wales. Built from AD 780–90, it was up to 27 m (88 ft) wide and 8 m (26 ft) high, with probably a wall or palisade at the top. However, it was of limited success and was soon overrun. Today, the 285-km (177-mile) **Offa's Dyke Footpath** *(www.nationaltrail.co.uk/offasdyke)* is a pretty national trail passing close to Montgomery, Powis Castle, Chirk Castle and Castell Dinas Bran.

over the Dee valley, is a beautiful spot for a walk. It crosses the stunning 38-m (125-ft) high **Pontcysyllte Aqueduct**, designed by Thomas Telford and William Jessop. Completed in 1805, it is the longest and highest aqueduct in the UK. For a better look, head 5-km (3-miles) east on the A539. Here visitors can hire a barge for the day to cruise the canal from **Trevor Wharf Services** (*Canal Wharf, LL20 7TX; 0117 304 1122*).

West of Llangollen, along the A542 (with car park), lies **Valle Crucis Abbey**, a ruined Cistercian abbey dating from 1201. Walk further along the road to **Eliseg's Pillar**, set up in the 9th century by the King of Powys in memory of his great-grandfather. Driving further on, the road rises up to **Horseshoe Pass** (416 m/1,367 ft, often snowbound in winter) and the Ponderosa Café – worth a stop for the views, but beware of crisp-snatching mountain sheep.

🚗 *Take the A542, then A525 to Ruthin. Park in the centre off Station Road.*

Above Barges cruising serenely along the Llangollen Canal

⑦ Ruthin
Denbighshire; LL15 1YN

This town's historic centre is filled with timber-framed buildings. **Nantclwyd y Dre** (*Apr–Sep: open Fri–Sun and Bank Hols*) is a c.1435 historic house in Castle Street displaying rooms from seven periods from the 15th to the 20th century. The **Ruthin Craft Centre** (and TIP) shows crafts from across the British Isles. **Ruthin Gaol** (*Apr–Sep: open Wed–Mon; www.ruthingaol.co.uk*), opposite the Watergate Tea Room, has been restored as a prison museum.

🚗 *Leave on the A525 for Denbigh. Look out for a sign to Llanrhaeadr on left (easy to miss) and park by church.*

Above Half-timbered houses line the street in the market town of Ruthin

⑧ St Dyfnog's Church
Denbighshire; LL16 4NN

In the tiny village of Llanrhaeadr, St Dyfnog's Church holds one of the most important Welsh ecclesiastical treasures. It is the most complete "Jesse Tree" window (showing Jesus' descent from Jesse, King David's father). The work dates from 1544 and was paid for by pilgrims seeking the healing powers of the holy well of St Dyfnog – visible in the woods behind the church. It is regarded as the finest pre-Reformation stained glass in Wales. Admire its powerful depth of colour, revealed in 23 portraits from Jesse, reclining at the base, to other figures associated with Jesus' lineage. Next door is the **Anvil Pottery**, in an old smithy, where the two potters make beautiful but functional glazed stone and earthenware pots.

🚗 *Take the A525 north to Denbigh, then the A543 – car park is on the right.*

Above Plas-Newydd, the pretty home of the "Ladies of Llangollen"

EAT AND DRINK

AROUND CHIRK CASTLE

The West Arms Hotel *moderate*
Cosy fireplaces and low beams add character to this historic inn, 18 km (11 miles) west of Chirk on the B4500. There's a restaurant and bar, serving Welsh lamb, local trout and vegetarian dishes.
Llanarmon Dyffryn Ceiriog, LL20 7LD; 01691 600 665; www.thewestarms.co.uk

LLANGOLLEN

The Corn Mill *moderate*
Gorgeous riverside setting at this converted corn mill, now an award-winning pub. Come for delicious beef sandwiches, ploughmans' lunches, fishcakes and sticky toffee pudding.
Dee Lane, LL20 8PN; 01978 869 555; www.brunningandprice.co.uk

AROUND LLANGOLLEN

Ponderosa Café *inexpensive*
The splendid views are the selling point here, more than the food. It's cheap, cheerful and child-friendly.
Horseshoe Pass, LL20 8DR; 01978 790 307; www.ponderosacafe.co.uk

The Britannia Inn *moderate*
Located at the foot of the Horseshoe Pass, this inn is famed for the hearty meals served in its beamed bar rooms. Good ales and wines, too.
Horseshoe Pass, LL20 8DW; 01978 860 144; www.britinn.com

RUTHIN

On the Hill *moderate*
The husband-and-wife team here work with the best of local produce. Try the trio of pork with port and honey glaze, plum and apple crumble, and Shropshire blue cheese.
1 Upper Clwyd Street, LL15 1HY; 01824 707 736; www.onthehillrestaurant.co.uk

Eat and Drink: inexpensive, under £25; moderate, £25–£50; expensive, over £50

Above The former St Asaph Union Workhouse and H M Stanley Hospital building

WHERE TO STAY

AROUND DENBIGH

Tan-yr-Onnen *moderate*
In the country just south of Junction 28 on the A55, this B&B offers modern rooms, a sunny conservatory, and serves home-made bread for breakfast.
Waen, LL17 0DU; 01745 583 821; www.northwalesbreaks.co.uk

Pentre Mawr Country House *expensive*
Head east from Denbigh on the Ruthin Rd, taking the minor road further east to the B5429. Turn left and left again to this historic family home. It has beautiful bedrooms, some with four-poster beds and free-standing baths. There are lovely views, a swimming pool and hot tubs and home-cooked dinners, if required.
Llandyrnog, LL16 4LA; 01824 790 732; www.pentremawrcountryhouse.co.uk

AROUND ST ASAPH

Bach y Graig *inexpensive*
This 16th-century farmhouse is set in quiet countryside, south of St Asaph off the A541. It has five cosy en-suite rooms and a beamed lounge with a log fire.
Tremeirchion, LL17 0UH; 01745 730 627; www.bachygraig.co.uk

HOLYWELL

Pantasaph Farm B&B *inexpensive*
Just off the A55, this highly rated and peaceful B&B is set in 6 acres of farmland. Enjoy full Welsh breakfasts, and evening meals on request.
Pantasaph Farm, CH8 8PL; 01352 713 138; www.pantasaphfarm.co.uk

Right One of the towers of Denbigh Castle, built to subdue the Welsh

9 Denbigh

Denbighshire; LL16 3DE
Dominating the town, **Denbigh Castle** *(open daily)* was built in 1282 under Henry de Lacy, Edward I's councillor. Marvel at the triple-towered Great Gatehouse with a statue of King Edward – only grand Caernarfon Castle has something similar. Even the town walls were built to integrate with the castle. Walk north down to the **Burgess Gate**, the main gate of the town wall with chequered stonework. On the way, look out for the tower of **St Hilary's Chapel**, built in 1300, and **Leicester's Church**, the remains of Robert Dudley, Earl of Leicester's unfinished church. It was important because it was the only large church built (1578–80) between the Dissolution of the Monasteries and the rebuilding of St Paul's Cathedral in London.

🚗 *Leave on the A525 to St Asaph. Park next to the cathedral (on the A525).*

Item from Earthworks Pottery, St Asaph

10 St Asaph

Denbighshire; LL17 0RD
This tiny city, set amid glorious scenery with views over the Vale of Clwyd, is home to Britain's smallest cathedral. **St Asaph's Cathedral** *(open daily)* was founded in AD 560 by exiled Scottish bishop Saint Kentigern. However, its turbulent history – it was sacked by Henry III in 1245, Edward I in 1282 and Owain Glyndŵr in 1402 – means that the current building is mostly 14th century with more modern additions made by the Victorian architect Sir George Gilbert Scott (1867–75). Importantly, it houses a copy of the 1588 translation of the Bible into Welsh by William Morgan who later became bishop here. The revised version, published in 1620, enabled the survival of the Welsh language and its continued everyday use in the face of pressure from English. The cruciform **St Asaph Union Workhouse** *(access may be limited)* was built in 1838. One of its inmates was five-year old orphan John Rowlands, who later changed his name to Henry

Far left The bathing pool at St Winefride's Well, Holywell **Left** Stained-glass window, from a chapel at St Winefride's Well, Holywell

Morton Stanley and, as a journalist, found missing explorer Dr Livingstone. 🚗 *Leave on B5381 towards Betws-yn-Rhos, over roundabout and sharp right. Follow brown signs to castle.*

⑪ Bodelwyddan Castle
Denbighshire; LL18 5YA
A "fortified" house and museum set in expansive grounds, **Bodelwyddan Castle** *(open weekends; open weekdays, summer and school holidays; 01745 584 060; www.bodelwyddan-castle.co.uk)* was named after Elwyddan, a 5th-century Romano-British chieftain. Although the estate dates back to the 15th century, most of what is visible today – the limestone turrets and battlements – was created by John Hay Williams between 1830 and 1852 with the architects Hansom and Welch. As an outpost of the National Portrait Gallery, it is a real trove of art treasures, and also houses furniture from the V&A Museum and sculptures from the Royal Academy of Arts. The interiors are sumptuous and there are galleries on the upper floor. Outside, there are formal gardens and parkland with woodlands walks and nature trails. The grounds also have trenches used to train soldiers for World War I.

🚗 *Turn right out of castle, over the flyover, and onto A55 towards Chester. Turn off for A5026 on the left, turning left at the sign for St Winefride's Well.*

⑫ Holywell
Flintshire; CH8 7PN
Close to the estuary of the River Dee, Holywell is a historic market town whose name derives from its main attraction, **St Winefride's Well** *(open daily)*. Legend has it that in AD 660, the son of local chieftain, Caradoc, beheaded the young Winefride after she refused his advances. Water sprang from the earth at the spot where her head fell, and she was restored to life by her uncle, St Beuno. The spring rises in the crypt of a 16th-century hall and flows into a large bathing pool. Look out for the sculpture of a pilgrim being carried to the well on a friend's back. The waters of the "Lourdes of Wales" have been said to cause miraculous cures since the 7th century and today, pilgrims travel from all over the world to worship at the shrine and take the water. In the Middle Ages, the Holywell to St David's road linked the two most important Welsh shrines and was known as "The Pilgrims Road" right up to the 19th century.

SHOPPING IN ST ASAPH

Wendy Gill at **Earthworks Pottery** *(Lower Street, LL17 0SG; 01745 583 353; www.earthworks-pottery.co.uk)* creates attractive handmade slipware ceramics. Browse the individual jugs, teapots, vases, jars and hand-decorated pots with planetary themes. There is parking nearby on Lower Street.

EAT AND DRINK

ST ASAPH

The Bridge *moderate*
This 16th-century former brewery is now a modern gastropub serving light lunches alongside a varied dinner menu, including pie of the day.
Lower Street, LL17 0SG; 01745 536 725; www.thebridgestasaph.co.uk

AROUND HOLYWELL

Red Lion Inn *inexpensive*
Take the A5026 northwest, then the A5151, turning right for Llanasa to find this cosy country pub. Enjoy a wide range of bar meals, including traditional fish and chips.
Llanasa, CH8 9NE; 01745 854 291

DAY TRIP OPTIONS
Ludlow, Llangollen and Denbigh are all excellent bases for exploring the treasures of Wales.

One for the Kids
From Ludlow ❶, see the castle and buy food for a picnic, then head to Acton Scott Farm Museum ❷ to see the animals and enjoy lunch in the country. On to Welshpool ❹, for a ride on the steam train and a visit to Powis Castle, if there's time.

Follow the drive route but return on the A490, A489 and A49 for speed.

Local Llangollen
Start at Llangollen ❻ with a visit to the society ladies' house of Plas Newydd, then a climb up Dinas Bran for some stunning views. After a visit to the canal and aqueduct, have lunch at Horseshoe Pass, and see Valle Crucis Abbey. Drive south to Chirk Castle ❺ to admire its interiors and gardens.

Follow the drive's instructions in reverse.

Cultural and Religious Treasures
Staying at Denbigh ❾, see the castle and churches before heading to St Asaph ❿ to see the William Morgan Bible; head on to Bodelwyddan Castle ⑪, filled with fine treasures, and on to the pilgrimage site of Holywell ⑫. Return towards Denbigh, going past it and on to Llanrhaeadr and St Dyfnog's Church ❽ for the Jesse Tree window.

Follow the drive's instructions all the way there and back.

Around the Peak District

Ashbourne to Matlock Bath

Highlights

- **The Peak landscapes**
  Travel through some of England's most scenic country – walk up to the lofty crags of Stanage Edge, drive through winding Winnats Pass and enjoy sheltered Dovedale

- **Towns and villages with character**
  Discover Georgian Buxton, quaint Bakewell with its courtyards, and soak up the local atmosphere in the old village pubs of Edale and Eyam

- **Grand mansions**
  Admire one of the most majestic of aristocratic palaces at Chatsworth, set in sublime grounds, and one of the most intact medieval manor houses in England at Haddon Hall

View across the River Wye from Haddon Hall, England's finest medieval manor house

Around the Peak District

The Peak District has long been renowned as a place of beauty, becoming the country's first national park in 1951. Despite being in the heart of industrialized England, the Peak area's villages and towns have a remote feel and retain an individuality often lost elsewhere – within minutes of parking the car, visitors can be exploring secluded valleys, or striding up over hills with fabulous views. The Peak District divides in two, between the limestone White Peak to the south, where water has scooped out the soft rock into deep caves and sheltered valleys, and the Dark Peak north of Buxton, where the harder millstone grit has created a dramatic landscape of ridges and windswept moorland.

Above Typical Peak District scenery on the lovely road to Edale, *see p173*

ACTIVITIES

Cycle along the beautiful Tissington Trail from Ashbourne

Walk through amazing Peak District scenery at Ilam

Take the waters at the handsome spa town of Buxton

Hike the Pennine Way, or at least part of it, from Edale

Climb down into Castleton's watery caverns to see the area's unique Blue John stone

Get lost in the maze at Chatsworth and marvel at the sheer grandeur of the country house and gardens

Feast on an original Bakewell Pudding and other goodies on a stroll around Bakewell's shops and markets

Travel back in time to the Middle Ages at Haddon Hall

Look down on the world from the cable car at Matlock Bath

KEY

Drive route

0 kilometres 10

0 miles 10

Above Wild-garlic-lined steps off Lover's Walk, above Matlock Bath, *see p175*

Below The cable car at the Heights of Abraham, Matlock Bath, *see p175*

PLAN YOUR DRIVE

Start/finish: Ashbourne to Matlock Bath.

Number of days: 2–3, allowing half a day for the Dovedale walk.

Distances: Around 97 km (60 miles).

Road conditions: The roads are in good condition.

When to go: Peak District weather is notoriously changeable, but from May to September is usually when there is the best chance of good weather.

Opening times: Museums and attractions are generally open 10am–5pm, but close earlier (or are closed altogether) Nov–Easter. Shops are often open longer. Churches are usually open until dusk.

Shopping: For the area's most famous dish, try the Old Original Bakewell Pudding Shop on Bridge St, Bakewell. Look out, too, for David Mellor's cutlery at Hathersage, and Blue John, as pure stone or jewellery, in Castleton and Bakewell.

Main market days: Ashbourne: Thu, Sat; **Buxton**: Tue, Sat, Farmers' Market 1st Thu of month; **Castleton**, Farmers' Market, 1st Sun of month; **Bakewell**: Mon, Farmers' Market last Sat of month; **Matlock**: Market Hall open Tue, Fri & Sat, Farmers' Market Wed.

Main festivals: Ashbourne: Shrovetide Football Match, Shrove Tuesday and Ash Wednesday; **Buxton**: Festival, Jul; Castleton: Garland Day, 29 May; Bakewell: Bakewell Show (farming show), 1st week Aug; **Matlock**: Matlock Bath Illuminations, Sep–Oct.

DAY TRIP OPTIONS

Tour the White Peak from Ashbourne with its **pub** and **church**, go on to Ilam for a **walk** in the prettiest of **dales** and finish in the **spa town** of Buxton. Or, to see the Hope Valley, try a **hike** in Edale and then visit the **caves** at Castleton before eating **sweet treats** at Bakewell. History lovers should start at Bakewell, buy a **picnic** and tour the grand **house and estate** at Chatsworth, then visit the medieval **manor house** Haddon Hall and ascend the **cable car** at Matlock Bath. For full details, *see p175*.

Above One of several pretty "Swiss chalet-style" houses in Ilam

VISITING ASHBOURNE

Parking
Park in the Market Place or nearby
Shawcroft Car Park off Park Road.

Tourist Information
Pavilion Gardens, St John's Road,
Buxton, SK17 6XN; 01298 25106;
www.visitpeakdistrict.com

Ashbourne Cycle Hire
Mapleton Lane, DE6 2AA; 01335 343 156;
www.peakdistrict.org/cycle

WHERE TO STAY

ILAM AND DOVEDALE

Hillcrest House *inexpensive*
Charming B&B on the road from Ilam to
Ashbourne, with spacious rooms and
modern comforts. Generous breakfasts.
*Thorpe, DE6 2AW; 01335 350 436;
www.hillcresthousedovedale.co.uk*

BUXTON

Buxton Hilbre *inexpensive*
A welcoming three-room B&B known
for its quality organic breakfasts.
*8 White Knowle Road, SK17 9NH; 01298
22358; www.buxtonhilbre.co.uk*

Old Hall Hotel *moderate*
Perhaps the oldest hotel in England, this
now has modern facilities to add to its
character. There's a bar and cosy lounges
and the restaurant uses top local produce.
*The Square, SK17 6BD; 01298 22841;
www.oldhallhotelbuxton.co.uk*

AROUND CASTLETON

Losehill House Hotel & Spa *moderate*
This hotel is intimate, luxurious and has
comfortable, light rooms. Hotel is on the
A6187, take the Edale Rd north, forking
left down a track and keeping right.
*Edale Road, Hope, S33 6AF; 01433 621
219; www.losehillhouse.co.uk*

❶ Ashbourne
Derbyshire; DE6 1EX
This charming market town is full of
fascinating corners, such as the 15th-
century half-timbered **Ashbourne
Gingerbread Shop** and the **Green Man
& Black's Head Royal Hotel**, whose
extraordinary pub sign runs across the
main street. Ashbourne is famed for its
yearly Shrovetide Football Match – a
chaotic ancestor of modern soccer,
played all day and with half the village
on each side. A walk along Church St,
past the beautiful 1585 **Grammar
School** and 1640s almshouses, leads
to the magnificent Gothic **St Oswald's
Church**, with finely sculpted tombs
from the 14th to the 18th centuries in
the Cockayne-Boothby chapel.

To explore the stunning countryside,
get a bike from **Ashbourne Cycle Hire**
and ride along the flat 21-km (13-mile)
Tissington Trail, a disused railway line.

🚗 *Leave by the A515 north and turn left
at the sign for Thorpe, Ilam and Dovedale. Park near the obelisk in Ilam village.*

❷ Ilam and Dovedale
Staffordshire; DE6 2AZ
Starting from quaint Ilam, this bracing walk explores Dovedale, a
winding, hidden gorge of dramatic rock formations and woods by the
sparkling River Dove. Its beauty has been long celebrated – so it's
popular – but during the week, it's still possible to avoid the crowds.

A three-hour walk
From the **obelisk at Ilam** ①, walk up
the road beside the river until you
pass the last cottage. Go through a
gate on the left into fields. Climb up
to a wider footpath, turn left and at a
green footpath sign go right on the
path for **Stanshope**. This goes up the
side of **Bunster Hill** ②, the giant peak
between Ilam and Dovedale. At a dry-
stone wall, do not go through the gate
but head up the steep path, with the
wall to the left, to the top of the hill.

At the top, rest and enjoy the views.
Return to the path and go through a
gate and the next field to a large five-
bar gate onto a broad track between
stone walls. Outside **Ilamtops Farm**
③, turn right to walk down to **Air
Cottage** ④. Just before the cottage,
follow the sign leading off to the right.
Stop on the crags nearby to enjoy the
full view of Dovedale below.

Below the cottage, the signed path
curves through the woods before it
climbs up again to the small gate into

Dovedale Wood ⑤. The path goes through the wood before a right turn starts a very steep winding descent to the bottom of Dovedale itself, to a stone pillar known as **Ilam Rock** ⑥.

Turn right, and cross a footbridge to the main path down the east side of the dale. Compared to the windswept hills, it feels sheltered here. On the walk through the woods, look out for cave entrances and natural landmarks, such as the rock arch to **Reynard's Cave** ⑦, the stone towers of the **Twelve Apostles** ⑧ (through the trees), **Lover's Leap** ⑨ and the dale's most picturesque sight, the **Stepping Stones** ⑩ to the west bank. Here, the Dove turns, below another hill, **Thorpe Cloud** ⑪. Follow the path back to the Dovedale car park, and beyond it, take the footpath to the right back to Ilam.

🚗 *Go up hill to Stanshope, through the village and at next junction left through Wetton. Take left fork at bottom of hill, next right, then left signed Hulme End. After tunnel, turn left for Hulme End, left again at junction and right at Manifold Inn (B5054). Take left to Sheen and Longnor, then B5053 and A515 to Buxton. Park near the Crescent.*

③ Buxton
Derbyshire; SK17 6BD
Famous for its mineral waters since Roman times, Buxton was transformed in the 1780s, when the fifth Duke of Devonshire decided to create a stylish spa here in imitation of Bath, and commissioned Neo-Classical buildings such as the elegant **Crescent** and giant domed **Stables**, now Derby University. Buxton remained popular in the 19th century, gaining the lovely **Pavilion Gardens** and the ornate 1905 **Opera House** (www.buxtonoperahouse.org.uk) – the centre of the Buxton Festival of Music and Arts (July). The water from

St Ann's Well, in the town centre, is still valued. The baths are now a shopping centre, still with beautiful Victorian tiles.

🚗 *Leave on A6 north, turn right onto A623. At Sparrowpit, take left to Edale (B6061). At junction keep left for Barber Booth, then left again towards Chapel-en-le-Frith. Turn sharp right for Barber Booth and car park on left in Edale.*

④ Edale
Derbyshire; S33 7ZA
Nestling in a broad valley, pretty Edale is a magnet for hikers as the start of the **Pennine Way**, the 412-km (256-mile) footpath to Scotland – but there are many shorter walks in the area. Visit the Peak District National Park's **Moorland Centre**, for maps, information and walking routes. The **Rambler Inn** and **Old Nag's Head** pubs are favourite spots for a restorative drink after a hike.

🚗 *Retrace the route back to the B6061 and turn second left for Edale (Winnats Pass) to Castleton.*

⑤ Castleton
Derbyshire; S33 8WQ
Winnats Pass, a spectacular gash in the landscape, leads to lovely **Castleton**, overlooked by the romantic ruins of 11th-century **Peveril Castle** (open mid-Mar–Oct daily; Nov–mid-Mar: closed Sat & Sun), which gave Castleton its name. This old stone village is also close to dramatic **caves** (open daily) from which minerals such as Blue John, a unique local purple fluorspar, were mined for centuries. The best caves to visit are **Blue John Cavern** at the top of Winnats Pass, **Peak Cavern**, **Treak Cliff Cavern** and **Speedwell Cavern**, a "drowned mine" reached by boat. Further down the valley, **Hope** is another attractive village, with a fine 14th-century church.

🚗 *Continue down the Hope Valley Rd (A6187) to Hathersage.*

EAT AND DRINK

ASHBOURNE
St John Street Gallery & Café *inexpensive*
A former magistrates' court has been turned into a contemporary art gallery and licensed award-winning café serving home-made food with a Mediterranean slant, cakes and local artisanal bread. Special dietary needs are catered for. Free Wi-Fi.
50 St John Street, DE6 1GH; 01335 347 425; www.stjohngalleryandcafe.co.uk

AROUND ILAM AND DOVEDALE
The Manifold Inn *moderate*
This classic stone coaching inn, on the route from Ilam to Buxton, has a garden terrace and serves good pub food including roasts, steaks, set buffet meals, and lighter options – it also has rooms and a two-bedroom cottage.
Hulme End, Hartington, SK17 0EX; 01298 84537; www.themanifoldinn.co.uk

BUXTON
Pavilion Gardens *inexpensive*
Occupying the magnificent Victorian conservatories in Buxton's grand park, this café makes the most of its space and light. Choose between the main café, or the Art Café above, decorated by local artists. The menu, based on local produce, runs from breakfasts and snacks to larger dishes for lunch.
St John's Road, SK17 6BE; 01298 23114; www.paviliongardens.co.uk

AROUND BUXTON
Vanilla Kitchen *inexpensive*
Take the A6 east, then the B6049 north to Tideswell to find this bright, award-winning café. Ingredients are seasonal and local, whether used in tasty lunches or the scrumptious range of cakes. Beers, wines and great Fairtrade coffee are also served.
Queen Street, Tideswell, SK17 8PF; 01298 871519; www.vanillakitchen.co.uk

---

Eat and Drink: inexpensive, under £25; moderate, £25–£50; expensive, over £50

Above Glorious Chatsworth Park, created by "Capability" Brown in the 1760s

Peak District Pubs

Snug old stone pubs are among the jewels of the Peak District, and many provide well-priced food. As well as the **Manifold Inn** *(see p173)*, other pubs to look out for are **Smith's Tavern** and the historic **Green Man & Black's Head Royal Hotel** *(see p172)* in Ashbourne, the **Bluebell Inn** in Tissington near Ilam, the **Old Nag's Head** and the **Rambler Inn** in Edale, the **Cheshire Cheese** in Hope near Castleton, the **Miners Arms** in Eyam and the **Plough Inn**, just south of Hathersage.

WHERE TO STAY

EYAM

Crown Cottage *inexpensive*
This former pub in the centre of Eyam has four spacious rooms, a piano, and plenty of maps and local information. Derbyshire oatcakes and sausages are on the breakfast menu.
Main Road, S32 5QW; 01433 630 858; www.crown-cottage.co.uk

AROUND EYAM

Bretton Cottage *moderate*
This distinctive guesthouse in a 17th-century hillside farmhouse, off Sir William Hill Rd just north of Eyam, offers huge rooms with sitting areas and stunning views. The organic breakfasts are substantial, too. There are also two self-contained cottages for rent.
Bretton, near Eyam, S32 5QD; 01433 631 076; www.peakholidayhomes.com

AROUND CHATSWORTH

Bubnell Cliff Farm *inexpensive*
Enjoy two characterful rooms with large bathrooms and lovely views on all sides in this homely farmhouse B&B in Baslow off the A619 on the edge of the Chatsworth estate. As usual in the Peaks, generous breakfasts of hearty farm produce make a great start to the day.
Wheatlands Lane, Baslow, near Bakewell, DE45 1RF; 01246 582 454; www.bubnellcliff.co.uk

AROUND HADDON HALL

East Lodge Hotel and Restaurant *expensive*
In Rowsley, off the A6, south of Haddon Hall, this fine old house has been beautifully restored with a blend of country-house and modern boutique-hotel style. It has just 12 sumptuous rooms and the gourmet restaurant, looking out onto the gardens, provides seasonal modern menus to match.
Rowsley, Matlock, DE4 2EF; 01629 734 474; www.eastlodge.com

⑥ Hathersage
Derbyshire; S32 1DD

On the drive down the Hope Valley, a dramatic wall of red rock, **Stanage Edge**, is visible to the northeast of Hathersage. Head up to the "Edge" from town for fabulous views – many walking paths begin near Hathersage's tranquil 14th-century church. In the churchyard lies **Little John's Grave** where, according to local legend, Robin Hood's best friend is buried. Off the village's main road is the **Round Building**, the workshop and shop of the celebrated cutlery designer David Mellor (1930–2009).

🚗 *Take B6001 through Grindleford, then right (B6521) to Eyam. Follow signs to Eyam museum for large car park.*

⑦ Eyam
Derbyshire; S32 5QP

Eyam became famous as an amazing example of self-sacrifice. In 1665, when the Great Plague was raging in London, the disease also took hold of Eyam. The village agreed to cut off all contact with the outside world until the plague had run its course, to avoid infecting the surrounding villages. They maintained this for nearly a year, during which 257 people died. The story is told in the **Eyam Museum** *(late Mar–Oct: open Tue–Sun)* and through monuments around the village, such as the **Riley Graves**, where all seven of the Hancock family were buried in a field. Despite this grim history, today Eyam is a charming village of old stone houses. The imposing mansion of **Eyam Hall** *(for opening times, see www.nationaltrust.org. uk)* hosts a craft centre *(open Tue–Sun)*.

🚗 *Take the B6521 south and then the A623 left to Baslow, where Chatsworth is well signposted. The B6012 leads through the Chatsworth estate.*

⑧ Chatsworth
Derbyshire; DE45 1PP

One of the grandest of Britain's great houses and a model of 18th-century elegance, the Palladian mansion of Chatsworth *(open daily)* has been home to the Dukes and Duchesses of Devonshire since the early 1700s. Truly palatial, the house has sumptuous furnishings and works of art, but is made still more magnificent by its setting, as the centrepiece of a majestic park created by "Capability" Brown in the 1760s with huge formal gardens, fountains, a maze and cascading waterworks. There's also an adventure playground, shops, a farmyard, restaurants and exhibitions. Opposite the Chatsworth entrance, **Edensor** is a pretty model village, built in the 1830s when the then Duke decided the original Edensor village was too close.

🚗 *Turn right from Chatsworth, back towards Baslow, then left on a road signed for Pilsley and Bakewell (B6048). Turn left again onto A619 into Bakewell. Use pay car park off main street.*

Below The church at Eyam, a village decimated during the Great Plague of 1665

9 Bakewell
Derbyshire; DE45 1BT

A bustling market town at the heart of the Peak District, Bakewell is a charming place just to wander and window-shop. It's also known for good food, with food stores in the courtyards off the main street and plenty of tea shops offering the local speciality, Bakewell Pudding – it's never called a tart in its home town. In addition to its weekly market, the town hosts a monthly **Farmers' Market** attracting many local food producers. The **Old House Museum** (*Apr–Oct: open daily*), Bakewell's oldest house, begun in 1543, has been made into a fascinating museum of everyday life.

🚗 *Take the A6 south. Haddon Hall is on the left but park on the right.*

Above Extravagant topiary in the grounds of Haddon Hall

10 Haddon Hall
Derbyshire; DE45 1LA

The most complete medieval and Elizabethan manor house in England, Haddon Hall (*Apr, Oct: open Sat–Mon; May–Sep: open daily; www.haddonhall.co.uk*) has remained virtually unaltered, except for upkeep, since the 1600s, and is still owned by the Manners family. Original features include massive medieval kitchens, flagstoned courtyards, a 12th-century chapel with 15th-century wall paintings and a Long Gallery with exquisite wood panelling.

🚗 *Turn right out of the car park and continue down A6 to Matlock Bath. Pay-and-display parking along main street.*

11 Matlock Bath
Derbyshire; DE4 3AT

Matlock developed in the 19th century as a spa with mass-market appeal. It is still a popular destination, especially **Matlock Bath** to the south of the main town, where the River Derwent runs through an impressive narrow gorge. The main street (A6) beside the river is lined with budget restaurants and ice-cream and souvenir shops. The most popular family attraction is the **Heights of Abraham** (*Mar–Nov: open daily; www.heightsofabraham.com*) at the top of the gorge – reached via a dramatic cable car ride – with caverns, gardens, nature trails and dramatic views.

Above left Stone houses in the hilly market town of Bakewell **Above centre** Pretty gardens and medieval manor house of Haddon Hall **Above right** Matlock Bath, perched beside the River Derwent

EAT AND DRINK

HATHERSAGE

Coleman's Deli *inexpensive*
A lively deli café in a renovated coach house building serving sandwiches, salads and sumptuous cakes.
The Square, S32 1BB; 01433 650 505; www.colemansdeli.com

AROUND CHATSWORTH

Rowley's Restaurant *moderate*
This stylish bar-restaurant in Baslow, on the A619 just north of Chatsworth, serves creative modern British food.
Church Lane, Baslow, DE45 1RY; 01246 583 880; www.rowleysrestaurant.co.uk

BAKEWELL

Piédaniel's *moderate*
Chef Eric Piédaniel combines his own French skills and culinary traditions with local produce, and his restaurant is a beautifully calm, relaxing space.
Bath Street, DE45 1BX; 01629 812 687; www.piedaniels-restaurant.com

MATLOCK BATH

Stones Restaurant *moderate*
In an enviable riverside location, Stones offers both set menu and à la carte options. Try the duo of seafood.
1c Dale Road, Matlock, DE4 3LT; 01629 56061; www.stones-restaurant.co.uk; closed Sun & Mon

---

DAY TRIP OPTIONS
Take in stunning countryside, historic houses and pretty towns.

Through the White Peak
Explore Ashbourne ❶ and then take a long walk in the country at Dovedale ❷ before driving north through quaint Peak District villages to relax in Buxton's elegant Georgian pavilions ❸.

Follow the drive route north but return via the A515 to save time.

Along the Hope Valley
Staying at Buxton ❸, drive to Edale ❹ for a walk above the village, and then visit the caves at Castleton ❺. Drive on through Hathersage ❻, with views of Stanage Edge and finally stop at Bakewell ❾ for some food shopping.

Follow the drive route but return via A6.

Great houses in the Peaks
From Bakewell ❾, buy some treats for lunch and visit majestic Chatsworth ❽ to enjoy a picnic in the park. Drive round to the smaller but older Haddon Hall ❿ and end the day with some family fun at Matlock Bath ❿.

Take the A6 there and back.

Eat and Drink: inexpensive, under £25; moderate, £25–£50; expensive, over £50

Yorkshire Dales and Abbeys

Harrogate to Bolton Abbey

Highlights

- **Health-giving Harrogate**
  Test the restorative waters in this gracious Victorian spa resort with its fine architecture and pretty parks

- **Crumbling abbeys**
  Wander through the historic, romantic ruins of these once-great Yorkshire abbeys, set in marvellous countryside

- **Gorgeous gardens**
  Admire a charming kitchen garden, orderly civic flowerbeds, a national hyacinth collection and a beautiful ornamental water garden

- **Great dale views**
  Walking or driving, there are always breathtaking views over the beautiful Yorkshire Dales National Park

Rolling green Wensleydale, perfect for sheep whose milk is used to make cheese

Yorkshire Dales and Abbeys

Departing from the beautiful spa town of Harrogate, this drive follows a circuit through the Yorkshire Dales National Park, with some truly sublime stretches that demand to be taken at an easy pace. Along the way are the estate village of Ripley with its castle, the small cathedral city of Ripon, the pretty market towns of Middleham and Leyburn, linked by an ancient bridge across the Ure, and Hawes, home of Wensleydale cheese. Star features of the tour are the ruins and grounds of Jervaulx, Fountain and Bolton abbeys. Plundered in the 16th century on the orders of Henry VIII, these once-glorious monastic buildings are now poignant monuments to the transience of power.

Above Middleham castle, dating from 1170, favourite home of the young Richard III, *see p182*

ACTIVITIES

Take the plunge in a steamy Turkish bath in the beautiful spa town of Harrogate

Set your watch in Ripon when the Hornblower blows in the market place at 9pm every evening

Explore the poignant ruins of Jervaulx Abbey, laid waste by Henry VIII's henchmen

Watch the young racehorses galloping out in the morning on the moors outside Middleham

Walk into the beautiful Yorkshire Dales having packed a delicious Wensleydale picnic from Hawes

Learn how to fly fish at Bolton Abbey, or ride a steam train, pet the farm animals or just enjoy the scenery

KEY

Drive route

Above Glorious Yorkshire Dales' scenery between Hawes and Bolton Abbey, *see p183*

PLAN YOUR DRIVE

Start/finish: Harrogate to Bolton Abbey.

Number of days: 3 days, taking it at a gentle pace.

Distance: Around 160 km (100 miles).

Road conditions: The roads are in good condition and not challenging.

When to go: The best time is between spring and early autumn – Harrogate, with its green spaces, is especially wonderful at blossom time.

Opening times: Museums and attractions are generally open 10am– 5pm, but close earlier (or are closed altogether) Nov–Easter. Shop opening hours are longer. Churches are usually open until dusk.

Main market days: Harrogate: Farmers' Market, 2nd Thu of month; **Ripon**: Thu; **Leyburn**: Fri; North Dales Farmers' Market, 4th Sat of month; **Hawes**: Produce and Antiques Market, Tue.

Shopping: Stock up on some Harrogate toffee and various types of Wensleydale – young, mature, smoked etc. Look out, too, for produce from Nidderdale farms, such as beef or chicken. And there is also good local beer to be enjoyed along the way.

Major festivals: Harrogate: Music Festival, Jul; **Ripon**: Ripon International Festival (music, arts, architecture and nature), Sep; **Leyburn**: Dales Festival of Food, May.

DAY TRIP OPTIONS

Families can enjoy a day **shopping** in Harrogate, then head for the **steam railway** and visit the **children's farm** and **parkland** at Bolton Abbey. Garden lovers and history buffs will enjoy the **market town** of Ripon, the magnificent **ruined Fountains Abbey** and **water gardens** nearby, as well as the **castle** and **gardens** at Ripley. Follow the steps of royalty through the **picturesque Dales**, from Middleham with its **castle**, to Leyburn with its **great views**, on to Hawes for its famous **cheese** and then to Jervaulx Abbey for its enchanting **ruins**. For full details, *see p183*.

Above Pretty flowers of Crescent Gardens in front of the Royal Hall, Harrogate

VISITING HARROGATE

Parking
Follow signs for centre, for parking on Montpellier Road or Union Street

Tourist Information
Royal Baths, Crescent Road, HG1 2RR; 01423 537 300; www.yorkshire.com

WHERE TO STAY

HARROGATE

April House *moderate*
This small, friendly B&B in a Victorian house in a quiet avenue offers rooms run by friendly hosts.
3 Studley Road, HG1 5JU; 01423 561 879; www.aprilhouse.com

Balmoral Hotel *moderate*
Plush boutique hotel in an old building with opulent rooms and en-suite Victorian bathrooms at good prices.
16–18 Franklin Mount, HG1 5EJ; 01423 508 208; www.balmoralhotel.co.uk

Grants *moderate*
In a quiet but central location, this Victorian town house has smart en-suite rooms and its own steakhouse.
3–13 Swan Road, HG1 2SS; 01423 560 666; www.grantshotel-harrogate.com

RIPLEY

The Boar's Head *moderate*
Friendly hotel owned by the Ingilbys has "olde worlde" but comfortable rooms that include access to the castle.
Ripley Castle Estate, HG3 3AY; 01423 771 888; www.boarsheadripley.co.uk

RIPON

The Old Deanery *moderate*
This small historic, central hotel offers individually designed en-suite rooms. There's also a decent restaurant.
Minster Road, HG4 1QS; 01765 600 003; www.theolddeanery.co.uk

❶ Harrogate
North Yorks; HG1 1BS

This vibrant and elegant spa town, on the edge of the Dales, grew up around a sulphur well, enclosed within the Royal Pump Room built in 1842. Modern visitors will find a wide choice of boutiques, antique shops, restaurants and bars, and plenty of green spaces in Crescent Garden and Valley Gardens. The vast open park, "The Stray", was created in 1778 so that the people of Harrogate could access the springs.

A two-hour walking tour

From the car park walk up Montpellier Road to the tourist office, housed in the **Royal Baths** ① on Crescent Rd. Dating from 1897, the baths were once a key destination for the health-conscious super-rich, who came for the sulphur water, peat baths and other delights. Inside, the Turkish baths, with original Victorian tiles, have been restored to their 19th-century glory. Facing away from pretty Crescent Gardens, and with the baths on the right, turn left into Ripon Road past the Royal Hall, built in 1903, and take Swan Rd on the left. It was at the **Old Swan Hotel** ② that crime writer Agatha Christie was found after crashing her car and going missing in 1926. Booked in as Theresa Neele – her husband's mistress – she claimed amnesia, but it is not known what really lay behind it all. Visit the **Mercer Art Gallery** ③ *(closed Mon except Bank Hols; Sun, pm only)* on Swan Rd, with its fine art collection of some 2,000

works, mainly from the 19th and 20th centuries. At the 19th-century **Royal Pump Room Museum** ④ *(open daily)* on Crown Place, built around the Old Sulphur Well, try some of the strongest sulphur water in Europe. Head into **Valley Gardens** ⑤ *(open daily)* opposite and follow the stream to see the restored 1930s Colonnade, Sun Pavilion and Magnesia Pump Room. Return to the Royal Pump Room and head right up Royal Parade and right at the roundabout, past the stately Crown Hotel, up Cold Bath Rd, noting the fine Georgian houses. Turn left into Queens Rd and left into Lancaster Rd to West Park Stray. Turn right down Beech Grove and left onto Otley Rd towards the Prince of Wales roundabout. Turn right onto Trinity Road. Admire the Gothic-style, 19th-century **Trinity Church** ⑥, then cross Leeds Road and enter the marvellous public amenity of **The Stray** ⑦. The tree-shaded path across the park leads to the domed Tewit Well, England's oldest spa. Here, in 1571, William Slingsby came upon a spring, and, tasting from it, was reminded of the health-giving waters of European spas. Either follow Slingsby Walk across the railway to appreciate the size of the park – or head back to town along West Park Street for refreshments at Yorkshire's famous tearooms, **Bettys** ⑧, on the left, before heading back to the car park.

🚗 *Head north along Parliament St (the A61), and take the left fork to enter Ripley. There is free parking by the castle.*

② Ripley

North Yorks; HG3 3AY

Home to the Ingilby family since the 14th century, **Ripley Castle** *(Apr–Sep: open daily; Nov & Mar: closed Mon, Wed, Fri; Dec–Feb: closed Mon–Fri)* is set among walled gardens and wooded walks, lakes and a deer park with venerable oaks. The kitchen garden grows many herbs and rare vegetable varieties and the castle also houses a National Hyacinth Collection – from March to October the flower borders are spectacular. Inside, seven rooms are open to the public for guided tours. Explore a family history of political, military, religious and social turbulence, from the Renaissance to the Industrial Revolution. The delightful **estate village of Ripley**, adjoining the castle, was built in the 1820s on the whim of Sir William Ingilby, who, inspired by his European travels, endowed it with a *Hôtel de Ville* (town hall) on a square with stocks, a market cross and a war memorial.

🚗 *Exit the village, bearing right on the A61. After 10 km (6.3 miles), take the first exit off the roundabout onto the A6108; follow signs to the centre.*

③ Ripon

North Yorks; HG4 1QT

Small but perfectly formed, Ripon is centred on its market square and has plenty for the visitor – including an impressive 7th-century **cathedral**. On the square, the Hornblower "sets the watch" by blowing his horn in each corner at 9pm – a tradition dating from the 11th century.

Stained-glass window, Ripon Cathedral

Take the B6265 west, turning left for **Fountains Abbey and Studley Royal** *(open daily)*. This World Heritage Site contains a Cistercian abbey founded in 1132, the most complete abbey ruins in the country, and a truly spectacular and ornate Georgian water garden.

🚗 *Head northwest on the A6108 and follow signs for Jervaulx Abbey. There is on-site parking with an honesty box.*

Above left Agatha Christie's hideout, the Old Swan Hotel, Harrogate **Above centre** The East end window of Ripon Cathedral **Above right** Ripley Castle, still the Ingilby family home after 700 years

EAT AND DRINK

HARROGATE

Bettys Café Tea Rooms
inexpensive–moderate
The original Bettys has been tempting visitors since 1919, with the promise of "something fresh and dainty". There is an extensive choice of cooked food, as well as over 300 breads, cakes and 50 different teas and coffees.
1 Parliament Street, HG1 2QU; 01423 814 070; www.bettys.co.uk

Hales Bar *moderate*
The town's oldest pub has retained its Victorian character using mirrors and working gas lights, and has friendly staff, real ale and good simple food. The odd whiff of sulphur wafts from the springs that flow below the cellar.
1 Crescent Road, HG1 2RS; 01423 725 570; www.halesbar.co.uk

Norse *moderate–expensive*
At night Baltzersen's café turns into a relaxed restaurant serving Nordic-influenced cuisine. Fresh, seasonal produce is used to create a menu of eight savoury and two sweet dishes. A tasting menu is also available.
22 Oxford Street, HG1 1PU; 01423 202 363; www.norserestaurant.co.uk

RIPON

Lockwoods *moderate–expensive*
This is a popular family-run lunchtime café bar and evening restaurant just off the square, serving sandwiches, light lunches and more ambitious dinners from an eclectic menu.
83 North Street, HG4 1DP; 01765 607 555; www.lockwoodsrestaurant.co.uk

Left The wrought iron Art-Deco canopy of Bettys Café Tea Rooms, Harrogate

Above Jockeys taking the young racehorses out for exercise, Middleham

WHERE TO STAY

JERVAULX ABBEY

Park House *expensive*
Set in the grounds of the abbey, this is a perfectly situated small B&B housed in two converted former workers' cottages. It is also home to the Abbey's owners, who welcome guests with tea and delicious home-made cake.
Jervaulx Abbey, HG4 4PH; 01677 460 184; www.jervaulxabbey.com

MIDDLEHAM

The Black Swan *moderate*
This charming "olde worlde" 17th-century real-ale inn right by the castle comes complete with log fires and oak beams. The garden is perfect for breakfasts in summer.
Market Place, DL8 4NP; 01969 622 221; www.blackswanhotelmiddleham.co.uk

Domus House *moderate*
One of a number of decent options clustered around the town's square. This Virginia creeper-clad Georgian house offers three en-suite rooms.
Market Place, DL8 4NR; 01969 623 497; www.middlehamonline.com

The White Swan *moderate*
Overlooking Market Square, the White Swan subsumed the old post office and underwent refurbishment, adding a smart brasserie.
Market Place, DL8 4PE; 01969 622 093; www.whiteswanhotel.co.uk

BOLTON ABBEY

Devonshire Arms *expensive*
This country house has been in the Devonshire family since 1753. Furnished with antiques, it is gloriously situated and offers every comfort, including a spa, sauna, tennis courts, and a range of good restaurants.
Bolton Abbey, BD23 6AJ; 01756 710 441; www.thedevonshirearms.co.uk

④ Jervaulx Abbey
North Yorks; HG4 4PH
Founded in 1156, this once-great Cistercian monastery is today in private hands, but allows public access. Declared forfeit to the Crown under Henry VIII *(see p192)*, its roof was stripped of lead and the church destroyed by gunpowder. What survived such vandalism is a place of utter peace and charm, in a beautiful wildflower meadow amid the Yorkshire Dales. Tour the remains of this enchanting building including the dormitory, kitchen, parlour, infirmary and cloister. The home-made cakes in the tearooms are excellent, too.

🚗 *Continue on A6108 to Middleham; park for free on the cobbled square.*

⑤ Middleham
North Yorks; DL8 4QG
This historic town boasts an impressive castle, two market places and a racehorse training stables. Visitors can watch the jockeys riding out in the morning on the moors beyond **Middleham Castle** *(Oct–Mar: closed Thu & Fri)*. This castle was from 1461 home to Richard, Duke of York, who would ascend to the throne for a brief reign as Richard III in 1483. Chambers and lodgings were added over time to the 12th-century keep to create a more luxurious palace.

Take the A6108 northwest across a 19th-century bridge over the River Ure to pretty **Leyburn**, filled with craft shops, galleries, a chocolatier and a tea pottery. It's also an excellent place for walking. At the top of the market place, follow signs for the **Leyburn Shawl**, supposedly where Mary Queen of Scots dropped her shawl in her flight from Bolton Castle, where she was imprisoned in 1538–9. Climb the escarpment for a short walk and great views across Wensleydale. Power walkers can try the 11-km (7-mile) walk to Bolton Castle (and get the bus back) – for instructions, visit *www.dalesbus. info/richmond/walk_5.htm.*

🚗 *From Leyburn take the A684 west through the Yorkshire Dales National Park to Hawes. Aysgarth Falls, on the way, is a good place to stop for a picnic.*

Above Aysgarth Falls in the picturesque Lower Wensleydale valley

Wensleydale

This wonderful cheese is handmade using milk from cows grazing on the sweet pastures in Upper Wensleydale. White Wensleydale is a young cheese, with a clean, mild, slightly sweet flavour. It can be bought, along with mature and oak-smoked and ewes' milk versions at the **Wensleydale Creamery** shop and visitors' centre on the left on Gayle Lane on the way out of Hawes *(www.wensleydale.co.uk).*

Below The haunting ruins of Jervaulx Abbey in beautiful bucolic surroundings

Where to Stay: inexpensive, under £80; moderate, £80–£150; expensive, over £150

6 Hawes

North Yorks; DL8 3NT

Pretty, bustling Hawes, at the head of Wensleydale, valley of the waterfalls, is Yorkshire's highest market town. There are some fine walks to be enjoyed from here; visit *www.wensleydale.org* for directions. Pick up picnic supplies from the **Wensleydale Creamery** *(open daily)* and see how they make the famous cheese. Tuesday is market day and stalls of produce line the streets. **Dales Countryside Museum** *(open daily)* is also well worth a visit, with displays about the history, people and landscape of the region, housed in the converted railway station.

Wensleydale Creamery sign, Hawes

🚗 *Head south on Gayle Lane to Buckden. Turn right on the B6160 all the way to Bolton Abbey. Use on-site car parks.*

7 Bolton Abbey

Skipton; N Yorks; BD23 6EX

Now owned by the Duke and Duchess of Devonshire, Bolton Abbey *(open daily; www.boltonabbey.com)*, located on the banks of the River Wharfe, was founded by Augustinian monks in 1154. Although the priory buildings were partially destroyed during the Dissolution of the Monasteries, the Parish Church of St Mary and St Cuthbert survived, and continues to this day. The ruins are best explored in the company of a volunteer guide or by downloading a detailed map from the website and planning a visit.

Bolton Abbey offers a very different experience from dreamy Jervaulx; there is so much to do in its 12,140 hectares (30,000 acres), including over 130 km (80 miles) of paths for riverside or moorland walks, a steam train for a nostalgic trip to *Embsay*, stocked rivers for fly fishing (with lessons available, if needed), woods and parkland for picnics, a children's farm and a range of visitors' shops and places to eat.

Above (all) Bolton Abbey, extensively damaged during the Dissolution of the Monasteries in 1539

EAT AND DRINK

AROUND MIDDLEHAM

George and Dragon *moderate*
This 17th-century coaching inn on the A684 between Hawes and Leyburn, serves soup, sandwiches and full meals, using local ingredients in season such as roast Nidderdale chicken breast with smoked applewood risotto.
Aysgarth, DL8 3AD; 01969 663 358; www.georgeanddragonaysgarth.co.uk

The Sandpiper Inn *moderate*
Well-kept ales and inventive cooking from a changing menu are on offer at this traditional inn. Try some home-made soup, a Wensleydale sandwich, fish and chips or pressed Dales lamb.
Market Place, Leyburn, DL8 5AT; 01969 622 206; www.sandpiperinn.co.uk

---

DAY TRIP OPTIONS

Choose from family fun around Harrogate, touring the beautiful gardens of Fountains Abbey and Ripley Castle, or a day out in the Dales.

Town and Country

Explore Harrogate ❶, taking in its pretty flower gardens, fine architecture and spa facilities. Head to Bolton Abbey ❼ to ride a steam train, see some farm animals, go fishing and just enjoy the glorious countryside.

From Harrogate take the scenic A59, then B6160 to Bolton Abbey.

Gardens and History

Staying at Ripon ❸, visit its cathedral before heading off to Fountains Abbey and Water Gardens. After walking around the best-preserved Cistercian abbey in England, go on to historic Ripley ❷ for a picnic in the castle's deer parks, gardens or the estate village, or just make use of the tearooms. Then return to Ripon for dinner and to hear the Hornblower.

Take the B6265 to Fountains Abbey; head down Fountains Lane to B6165 to Ripley. Return via the A61 and A6108.

Royalty in the Dales

Visit the castle at Middleham ❺, former haunt of Richard III; pop across to quaint Leyburn and walk in the steps of Mary Queen of Scots up to Leyburn Shawl to see the great views. Enjoy the drive to Hawes ❻ to stock up on cheese for a picnic on the way through the Dales to the graceful ruins of Jervaulx Abbey ❹, destroyed by King Henry VIII.

Follow the instructions in the drive to Hawes and on to the B6160, but turn off left at Kettlewell back to Middleham.

Eat and Drink: inexpensive, under £25; moderate, £25–£50; expensive, over £50

North Yorkshire Moors & Coast

York to Sutton Park

Highlights

- **Historic York**
  Walk through this living museum of a city with its great Minster, medieval streets and Georgian town houses

- **The grandest stately homes**
  Admire the splendours of Castle Howard and lovely Sutton Park

- **Wild North York Moors**
  Explore this airy expanse of heather, woodland and rollercoaster dales on foot, by bike or by steam train

- **Atmospheric abbeys**
  See the poignant ruins at Rievaulx and Gisborough, and Gothic Whitby, an inspiration for the story of Dracula

- **Fun and fishing on the coast**
  Make a splash in the fishing towns and seaside resorts on this beautiful coast

Heather adds colour to the hills and valleys of the North York Moors, Rosedale, Yorkshire

North Yorkshire Moors and Coast

England's largest county, North Yorkshire is strewn with picturesque villages, old market towns, stately homes and castles, historic churches, romantic ruins, and so much more. Its coastline is variously quaint, bustling and unspoilt. Its high, heather-clad moorland is stirringly beautiful with great vistas where sheep graze peacefully. There are some purely scenic stretches of dramatic road. This drive, which passes through the Howardian Hills and the centre of the North York Moors National Park, before reaching the seaside, provides more than a glimpse of all these aspects. The trip takes the historic city of York for its point of departure, with a walk at the heart of this wonderful city.

Above Sandsend, just north of Whitby, a small town with a long sandy beach, *see p191*

ACTIVITIES

Climb York Minster's 275 steps and look out over the delightful warren of medieval streets and buildings

Enjoy a warm Yorkshire Fat Rascal – a traditional rich fruit and nut scone – at Bettys Tea Rooms, York

Revisit Brideshead, actually Castle Howard, the palatial home used as a setting in the TV series and film of Evelyn Waugh's classic novel

Cycle through beautiful Yorkshire forests near Pickering

Walk through time in historic buildings chronicling 400 years of rural history at Hutton-le-Hole, one of the country's prettiest villages

Hop aboard a steam train on the Rail Trail over the Yorkshire moors from Grosmont to charming Goathland, and stroll back

Go deep-sea fishing in Whitby, a centre of Yorkshire coastal fishing

Look down on Rievaulx Abbey from above – England's foremost Cistercian abbey looks fabulous when seen from Rievaulx Terrace

Walk along the Cleveland Way National Trail from the pretty town of Helmsley

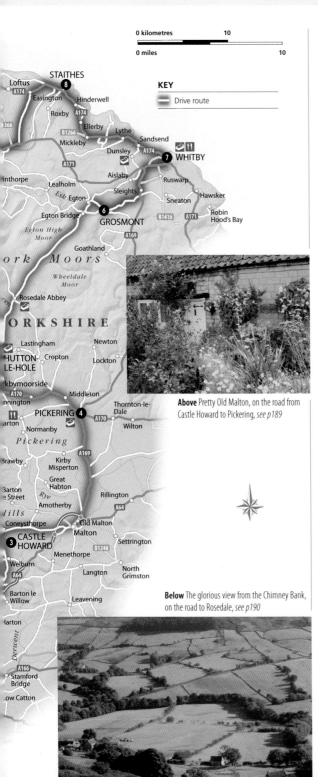

0 kilometres 10

0 miles 10

KEY

Drive route

STAITHES
Loftus
A174
Easington   Hinderwell
Roxby   A174
366
Ellerby   Lythe
B1266   Sandsend
Mickleby   A174
Dunsley   WHITBY
A171
inthorpe   Aislaby   Ruswarp
Lealholm   Sleights
Esk   Egton   Sneaton   Hawsker
Egton Bridge   Robin
GROSMONT   B1416   A171   Hood's Bay
Egton High   A169
Moor
Goathland
ork Moors
Wheeldale
Moor
Rosedale Abbey
ORKSHIRE
Lastingham   Newton
HUTTON-   Cropton   Lockton
LE-HOLE
kbymoorside
A170   Middleton
nnington   Thornton-le-
PICKERING   Dale
arton   A170   Wilton
Normanby
Pickering
Brawby   Kirby   A169
Misperton
Great
Barton   Habton   Rillington
e Street   Rye   Amotherby   A64
lills
Coneysthorpe   Old Malton
CASTLE   Malton
HOWARD   Settrington
Menethorpe   B1248
Welburn   North
A64   Langton   Grimston
Barton le
Willow   Leavening
larton
Derwent
A166
Stamford
Bridge
.ow Catton

Above Pretty Old Malton, on the road from Castle Howard to Pickering, *see p189*

Below The glorious view from the Chimney Bank, on the road to Rosedale, *see p190*

PLAN YOUR DRIVE

Start/finish: York to Sutton Park.

Number of days: 4 allowing half a day in York.

Distances: 233 km (145 miles).

Road conditions: The roads are generally well-maintained. The steepest routes over the high moors require the use of low gears.

When to go: Best from late April through to mid-September. In summer the heather covering the moors blooms a rich purple.

Opening times: Galleries, museums and attractions are generally open 10am–5pm, but often close earlier Nov–Easter. Shops are often open longer. Churches are usually open until dusk.

Main market days: York: open market, Newgate, daily; **Pickering**: street market, Mon; **Whitby**: Tue & Sat; Helmsley: Fri; Gisborough: Thu & Sat.

Shopping: Look out for Whitby jet jewellery and local smoked kippers; chocolate in York; heather honey from the Yorkshire moors; and knitwear made with wool from local sheep breeds.

Major festivals: York: Spring Festival of New Music, May; Early Music Festival, July; National Book Fair, Sep; Food and Drink Festival, Sep; **Whitby**: Regatta and Carnival, mid-Aug; Folk Week, late Aug.

DAY TRIP OPTIONS

See the **Minster** and **medieval streets** of York, then explore the **palace** and **grounds** of Castle Howard, enjoy some **aromatic lavender** and finish at the **Georgian mansion** of Sutton Park. From Pickering, explore the **moors** by **foot**, **bike** or **steam train** and marvel at some **frescoes**; in Hutton-le-Hole, see **historic buildings** and a take a thrilling **high moor drive**. From Whitby, see the **ruined abbey**, take a **fishing trip**, visit Grosmont for a **steam-train ride**, then **walk** home. For full details, *see p193*.

Above Example of Georgian architecture at the heart of the city of York

① York

Yorkshire; YO1 7JN

A walled city on the River Ouse and spiritual capital of the North of England for 2,000 years, York is best explored on foot. Its rich architectural tapestry mixes the medieval with half-timbered Tudor and elegant Georgian. Amid the high culture of churches, galleries and museums, cool bars, smart restaurants and open spaces abound.

A three-hour walking tour

Start at the **Minster** ① *(open daily)*, York's most striking landmark. Built of magnesian limestone between 1220 and 1470, this is the largest Gothic cathedral in Northern Europe, with awe-inspiring stained-glass windows. Climb the tower's 275 steps to take in the views. In Minster Yard nearby lie the National Trust's **Treasurer's House and Garden** ② *(closed Fri)*, covering 2,000 years of history. From the Minster, go left up Deangate. Carry on along Goodramgate, by Lady Row, the oldest houses in York, dating back to 1316. These are fine examples of jettied houses, where the upper storey overhangs the lower. Ahead, in the tallest of York's four medieval gatehouses, is the **Richard III Experience** ③ *(open daily)*, stripping away the myths around the last Plantagenet king. Next, turn left along Lord Mayor's Walk, then left again down Gillygate. Cross to Exhibition Square and **York Art Gallery** ④ *(open daily)*, with an impressive collection of paintings and ceramics. Cross back to the gateway into the old shopping street of High Petergate. Stop in Café Concerto for possibly the best cappuccino in town. Carry on down Low Petergate, and after Church St bear right for the higgledy-piggledy **Shambles** ⑤. This is one of the best-preserved medieval streets in Europe, lined with timber-framed buildings dating from 1350. Once home to York's butchers, it is named for the "shammels" or shelves used to display the meat. From here, turn right down The Pavement and onto Coppergate, then left into Castlegate. At its end

Sign for Bettys Café Tea Rooms

stands a fine Georgian town house, **Fairfax House** ⑥ *(open daily; closed Jan–early Feb)*, home to a world-class collection of furniture and clocks. Walk down Tower St, right onto Clifford St, then Coney St, then right again into St Helen's Square for yet another York tradition – tea and cakes in the Art-Deco **Bettys Café Tea Rooms** ⑦. Cross Davygate and halfway up Stonegate turn right down Coffee Yard to **Barley Hall** ⑧ *(open daily)*, which recreates life in a 15th-century house. Cross High Petergate back to the Minster.

🚗 *Take the A64 north from the outer ring road, After 11km (7 miles) take the left signed Castle Howard. Pass the monument and branch left. Tourist signs lead through Terrington to the farm.*

② Yorkshire Lavender
Terrington, North Yorks; YO60 6PB

This lavender farm and herb nursery *(closed mid-Oct–Feb; www.yorkshire lavender.com)* grows hundreds of different lavender varieties, creating a haze of blue in summer on its south-facing slopes. Admire the gardens,

buy plants, herbs, scented candles and essential oils and feast on blueberry and lavender jelly with herb scones in EJ's tearoom.

🚗 *Return to Terrington and take the Malton Road, following signs to Castle Howard (with car park).*

③ Castle Howard
North Yorks; YO60 7DA

Vast gardens dotted with lakes and fountains surround this veritable palace *(grounds: open daily; house: open daily Mar–Oct; www.castlehoward.co.uk)* built over three centuries from 1699 by the Howard family, who still live here. In 1981, Castle Howard was Brideshead in the TV series of Evelyn Waugh's *Brideshead Revisited* (and again in 2007 for the film). Admire the sumptuous Great Hall under the dome, wander in the Rose Garden or Potager and visit the striking Turquoise Drawing Room.

🚗 *Return to the Malton Road and continue east, passing through Malton and sedate Old Malton; take the A169 to Pickering. Use the car park over the roundabout in the centre of town.*

Above left Pubs along the river Ouse, York
Above centre Yorkshire Lavender farm, overlooking the Vale of York **Above right** The magnificent stained glass of York Minster

SHOPPING IN YORK

For beautiful soft knitwear, made from the wool of rare-breed sheep saved from slaughter, try **Responsibly Gorgeous** *(1 Peter Lane, York; 01904 675 987)*. The shop also sells other ethical and fairtrade designer fashions.

EAT AND DRINK IN YORK

Bettys Café Tea Rooms *inexpensive*
One of a small, venerated chain of Yorkshire tearooms, Bettys' menu is a unique mix of Swiss and Yorkshire specialities – try the Fat Rascal, a plump, warm fruit scone, or the chicken and mushroom rösti. Cooked meals and snacks all day.
6-8 St Helen's Square, YO1 8QP; 01904 659 142; www.bettys.co.uk

Café Concerto *moderate*
This is an attractive, modern-European café-bistro, whose walls are papered with sheet music. Great coffee, wraps, salads, baguettes, club sandwiches, and more substantial dishes.
21 High Petergate, YO1 7EN; 01904 610 478; www.cafeconcerto.biz

Melton's *moderate*
Excellent restaurant with a firm commitment to home-cooking and Yorkshire ingredients such as rare breed Thirsk pork and local cheeses.
7 Scarcroft Road, YO23 1ND; 01904 634 341; www.meltonsrestaurant.co.uk

Walmgate Ale House & Bistro *moderate*
In a historic 17th-century building, enjoy Yorkshire Brewery ale, snacks, a great range of local cheeses and hearty meals either in the bar or bistro.
25 Walmgate, YO1 9TX; 01904 629 222; www.walmgateale.co.uk

Left Castle Howard, one of Britain's finest historic houses and gardens

Eat and Drink: inexpensive, under £25; moderate, £25–£50; expensive, over £50

VISITING WHITBY

Parking
Park on Whitby Station forecourt or turn
right and pass between the Co-op and
Tourist Office for plenty more spaces.

Tourist Information
*Langborne Road, YO21 1YN; 01723 383
636; www.discoveryorkshirecoast.com*

WHERE TO STAY

PICKERING

Bramwood Guest House *inexpensive*
Eight rooms in a very attractive 18th-
century stone house. Hearty breakfasts
are cooked to order with local produce.
*19 Hallgarth, YO18 7AW; 01751 474
066; www.bramwoodguesthouse.co.uk*

White Swan Inn *moderate*
Former coaching inn offers comfortable
accommodation in the main hotel and
more modern rooms in the stables.
*Market Place, YO18 7AA; 01751 472
288; www.white-swan.co.uk*

HUTTON-LE-HOLE

Burnley House *moderate*
Georgian farmhouse set on the green,
with trout stream nearby – the owners
welcome guests in with tea and cake.
*Hutton-le-Hole, YO62 6UA; 01751 417
548; www.burnleyhouse.co.uk*

White Horse Farm Hotel *moderate*
A 16th-century inn with 11 rooms, a bar
with real ales, and views of the valley.
*Rosedale Abbey, YO18 8SE; 01751 417
239; www.whitehorserosedale.co.uk*

WHITBY

White Horse and Griffin *moderate*
This hotel has good rooms and a great
breakfast menu of local kippers, wild
mushroom omelettes and Bloody Marys.
*87 Church Street, YO22 4BH; 01947 604
857; www.whitehorseandgriffin.com*

Dunsley Hall *moderate–expensive*
This lavish country house built in 1900,
offers 26 rooms, extensive grounds
and an excellent restaurant.
*Dunsley, YO21 3TL (north of the A171
into Whitby); 01947 893 437; www.
dunsleyhall.com*

④ Pickering
North Yorks; YO18 8DY

This market town is an excellent base
for exploring the North Yorkshire Moors
National Park. Do it on foot *(find walks at
www.northyorkmoors.org.uk)* or by bike:
the **Purple Mountain Bike Centre**
*(01751 460 011; www.purplemountain.co.
uk),* in Dalby Forest, hires out bikes and
has details of trails for all abilities. A
more sedate way to see the moors is
by steam train: the **North York Moors
Railway** *(Apr–Oct; www.nymr.co.uk)* runs
all the way to Whitby. There's a lot to
see in Pickering, too. The charming
12th- to 13th-century **Church of St
Peter and St Paul** contains striking
frescoes, discovered in 1852, that were
hidden under limewash during the
16th-century Reformation. Explore
Pickering Castle *(Apr–Oct: open daily)*;
it was first built of wood in 1079 and
rebuilt in stone in the 13th century.

🚗 *Head west on A170, turning right to
Hutton-le-Hole. Park at top of the village.*

⑤ Hutton-le-Hole
North Yorks; YO62 6UA

Hutton is built around a series of
greens on which local Swaledale and
Blackface sheep graze. Hutton Beck
runs through the village, spanned by
pretty bridges and perfect for a picnic.
The Ryedale Folk Museum *(open daily)*
is an amazing village within a village.
Twenty-one buildings reveal the lives
of local folk over the centuries to the
1950s. Look inside an Elizabethan
manor, a thatched cottage, a 1950s
village store – even a witch's hovel.

Leaving the village, turn right on
the road signed to Lastingham and
then fork left (unsuitable for caravans)

Above Charming houses of Hutton-le-Hole, built
around a series of sheep-grazed greens

on the stunning road to **Rosedale**. This
crosses the Chimney Bank, from the
top of which the valley spread below
resembles a vast green patchwork
quilt. Check the brakes before
attempting this drive – the descent to
the village of Rosedale Abbey is said to
be the steepest road in England.

🚗 *In Rosedale Abbey, take the road by
the Milburn Arms, opposite the green,
signed to Egton. Turn right at sign for
Grosmont. Park at Grosmont station.*

⑥ Grosmont
North Yorks; YO22 5QE

In the beautiful Esk Valley, this village
is known for two reasons; the first is
Grosmont Station *(Apr–Oct; www.nymr.
co.uk)*. Volunteers run this delightful
old station for the North York Moors
Railway from Pickering to Whitby. Hop
aboard for a nostalgic journey and
visit the village of Goathland. Walk

Below left North York Moors Railway steam train at Grosmont Station **Below right** Shop selling
traditional beach equipment and that sugary seaside staple – rock

back via the 5-km (3-mile) **Rail Trail**. Its other claim to fame is as the setting for popular UK TV drama series *Heartbeat*.

🚗 *Leave on Front St, turning left at Sleights on A169 and right onto A171. Veer left onto Prospect Hill and take 3rd exit at the roundabout for seafront.*

🕖 Whitby

North Yorks; YO21 1YN

Visually dramatic, the buzzing fishing port and resort of Whitby clings to the hills on the banks of the River Esk, its hilltop abbey ruins silhouetted against the sky. Other architectural highlights include fine Georgian houses and humbler white fishermen's cottages, linked by ginnels (alleys). **Whitby Abbey** *(open daily)* was founded by St Hilda in AD 655, but today's ruins are the 13th-century buildings destroyed by Henry VIII and further damaged by German battleships in 1914. Sharing the windswept hillside is **St Mary's Church** *(open daily)* and its graveyard, reached by 199 steps. The two edifices provided a dramatic setting in Bram Stoker's Gothic vampire novel *Dracula* (1897). Leeds-born artist Frank Sutcliffe set up a studio in Whitby in 1876, taking photos of fishermen, farmers, ships and moorland. See his work at the **Sutcliffe Gallery**, *(Flowergate; www.sutcliffegallery.co.uk)*.

It's a short walk to **Sandsend** which has a nice, sandy beach and plenty of surf; or a longer one to family-friendly **Robin Hood's Bay**; or just climb up past the Abbey and explore the

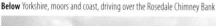

Whitby fudge shop sign

Cleveland Way *(www.clevelandway.co.uk)*. And why not catch a fish supper on the high seas with a half-day fishing trip *(01287 660 118 or 07790 955604; www.whitbyfishingtrips.co.uk)*.

🚗 *Head inland, turning right on the A174 through Sandsend and right to Staithes; use the pay-and-display car park.*

🕗 Staithes

North Yorks; TS13 5BH

As a young man, the explorer James Cook (1728–79) once worked in the draper's shop in this fishing village, and it is here that he first dreamt of becoming a sea captain and navigator. Still ringed by cliffs offering spectacular walks, this pretty harbour village has probably changed little to this day. To the north lie the dramatic **Boulby Cliffs**, the highest on England's east coast.

🚗 *Go west on the A174. Turn left at Easington on a minor road to the A171. Turn right and follow signs to Guisborough.*

Above Crab and lobster pots in Whitby, still a busy fishing centre

SHOPPING IN WHITBY

Whitby Jet
Mourning for Prince Albert, Queen Victoria set a fashion for lustrous black jet jewellery. Whitby's shore proved a rich source of this beautiful gemstone. Buy it from **Whitby Jet Heritage Centre** and **W Hamond** *(both on Church St)*.

Whitby Kippers
W R Fortunes *(22 Henrietta St)* produces richly flavoured kippered herrings, smoked using oak and beech shavings.

EAT AND DRINK

AROUND PICKERING

The Blacksmiths Arms Hartoft *moderate*
This dining pub serves traditional pies, steaks, and fish and chips along with smoked eel and lavender cheesecake. *Hartoft End, YO18 8EN (take Cropton Lane, left off the A170); 01751 417 331; www.blacksmithscountryinn.co.uk*

WHITBY

Elizabeth Botham & Sons *inexpensive*
This family-run teahouse is delightfully old fashioned. Choose a speciality tea to wash down gingerbread with Wensleydale cheese or plum bread. *35 Skinner Street, YO21 3AH; 01947 602 823; www.botham.co.uk*

Magpie *inexpensive–moderate*
This Whitby portside institution serves tip-top fish dishes, including oysters, chowders, prawn cocktail and Whitby crab – it can get busy at lunchtime. *14 Pier Road, YO21 3PU; 01947 602 058; www.magpiecafe.co.uk*

Green's Seafood Bistro and Restaurant *moderate*
Serves seafood fresh from the quay each morning, as well as local meat and game. Relax downstairs or enjoy the same menu in the more formal upstairs. *13 Bridge Street, YO22 4BG; 01947 600 284; www.greensofwhitby.com*

Below Yorkshire, moors and coast, driving over the Rosedale Chimney Bank

Eat and Drink: inexpensive, under £25; moderate, £25–£50; expensive, over £50

WALKING THE CLEVELAND WAY NATIONAL TRAIL

The 176-km (109-mile) Cleveland Way National Trail crosses the North Moors National Park in a horseshoe-shaped route from the market town of Helmsley to Saltburn on the coast and along to Filey. Several companies offer a luggage-transfer service for long-distance walkers, or there are many possibilities for shorter, circular walks. Information can be found on the trail website *(www.nationaltrail.co.uk/ClevelandWay)*.

WHERE TO STAY

AROUND GISBOROUGH PRIORY

King's Head *moderate*
Award-winning B&B comprising two adjoining 17th-century cottages at the foot of Roseberry Topping. Eight en-suite rooms. Breakfast of local bacon, black pudding, sausages and Whitby kippers. *The Green, Newton-under-Roseberry TS9 6QR; 8 km (5 miles) on A171 and A173; 01642 722 318; www.kingsheadinn.co.uk*

AROUND HELMSLEY

Pheasant Hotel *expensive*
Stylish country hotel 5 km (3 miles) from Helmsley, with an award-winning restaurant and a quiet setting overlooking the village duck pond. Fifteen rooms, indoor pool and comfortable lounge and bar areas. *Harome, Helmsley YO62 5JG; 01439 771 241; www.thepheasanthotel.com*

Below Rievaulx Abbey, once one of the great abbeys in Yorkshire **Below right** Statue of James Cook the explorer, Great Ayton

Above The splendid Gothic east gable of Gisborough Priory

⑨ Gisborough Priory
North Yorks; TS14 6HG

Little remains of this 14th-century **Augustine monastery** *(closed Mon, Tue)*, but the towering skeleton of the eastern gable gives an idea of what a masterpiece the building must have been. Founded in AD 1119 by the Bruce family, who became kings of Scotland, the priory was twice rebuilt. After the Dissolution of the Monasteries under Henry VIII, the priory was acquired by the Chaloner family, who created a magnificent garden on the site. Volunteers are working to restore it as a public space. In summer, plays are staged here.

🚗 *Go west on the Middlesbrough Road (A171), then left on the A173 to Great Ayton.*

The Dissolution of the Monasteries

When the Pope refused to annul his marriage to Catherine of Aragon in 1531, Henry VIII had himself declared Head of the Church of England. As well as helping solve his marriage problems, this enabled him and his minister, Cromwell, to sieze power from the Catholic Church in England. Taking his lead from the Protestant Reformation in Europe, Henry VIII claimed to be fighting the greed and corruption of the Church. By 1540, over 850 monasteries and shrines had been closed and their wealth and property diverted to the Crown.

⑩ Great Ayton
North Yorks; TS9 6NB

For eight years the boyhood home of explorer Captain James Cook, this is a delightful village with views of the distinctively shaped sandstone hill, the Roseberry Topping. The High Green has a statue of 16-year-old Cook looking towards Staithes and the sea. Low Green, on the banks of the Leven, is a great picnic spot. The Postgate School is now the **Captain Cook Schoolroom Museum** *(Apr–Oct: open daily pm)*. The 12th-century **All Saints Church** on Low Green, where Cook's family is buried, is still used for candlelit worship *(Sun pm, Wed am)*.

🚗 *Carry on along the A173, taking the B1257 left for a fabulous 32-km (20-mile) drive. Turn right at the sign for Rievaulx Abbey. Park by the entrance.*

Above Flowers outside a pub in the attractive
market town of Helmsley

⓫ Rievaulx Abbey

North Yorks; YO62 5LB

This partially ruined building *(Apr–Oct:
open daily; Nov–Mar: open Sat & Sun;
www.english-heritage.org.uk)* is widely
regarded as England's foremost
Cistercian abbey. The atmospheric
remains of soaring pillars and graceful
arches set on a slope in a quiet valley,
fire the imagination. Founded in 1131,
by the 13th century it was home to
140 monks and over 500 lay brothers.
An indoor exhibition explores the
farming, commercial and spiritual
aspects of the abbey. The café serves
fresh locally sourced food – and cider
from Ampleforth Abbey. Nearby, and
close to the main road, **Rievaulx
Terrace and Temples** *(open daily)* has
two classical Georgian temples and
fabulous views over Rievaulx Abbey.

🚗 *Drive on the B1257 to Helmsley. Park
on the market square or Cleveland Way.*

Above Unspoiled Helmsley, a favourite
destination for walkers on the North York Moors

⓬ Helmsley

North Yorks; YO62 5AB

This small but bustling market town
on the River Rye is dominated by the
ruins of 13th-century **Helmsley Castle**
*(Mar–Oct: open daily; Nov–Feb: open Sat
& Sun)*. Against this backdrop,
Helmsley Walled Garden *(open Apr–
Oct)* is a pretty 18th-century fruit and
vegetable garden and a nice place
for a picnic. At the start of the
Cleveland Way National Trail, the
town is a popular base for walkers.

🚗 *Leave on B1257, then A170, then
B1257 again. Turn right onto B1363
south towards York. At Sutton-on-the-
Forest, follow signs to Sutton Park.*

⓭ Sutton Park

Sutton-on-the-Forest, N Yorks; YO61 1DP

The home of Sir Reginald and Lady
Sheffield *(house open Jun; gardens open
May & Jun; ring ahead, 01347 810 249)*,
this is a fine early Georgian stately
home (1730) set in pretty parkland.
The furniture came from Buckingham
House (before it became a palace).
There are woodland walks, a Georgian
ice house and the gardens – especially
the roses – are stunning in summer.

EAT AND DRINK

AROUND HELMSLEY

Star Inn *expensive*
Award-winning pub restaurant offers
imaginative cooking using fresh, local
produce flavoured with herbs from the
garden. Venison cooked over charcoal
with honey-roast black figs, Filey turbot
with oxtail carpaccio, and Yorkshire
rhubarb with gingerbread cheesecake.
*High Street, Harome, YO62 5JE (5 km/3
miles southeast of Helmsley); 01439
770 397; www.thestaratharome.co.uk*

SUTTON PARK

Hare at Scawton *moderate*
This rustic country pub offers creative
fine dining in three tasting menus –
dishes may include sea trout with
quails eggs, venison with liquorice,
and strawberries with buttermilk.
*Scawton YO7 2HG (take the B1257
and then first left); 01845 597 769;
www.thehare-inn.com*

DAY TRIP OPTIONS

Wherever you stay, history is not far
away, and neither are the moors.

Architectural Indulgence

In York ❶, see its Minster and medieval
"shambles". Tour the splendid Castle
Howard ❸ and go on to Yorkshire
Lavender ❷ for aromas, fresh air and
lunch. Finish off with the exquisite
interiors and gardens of Sutton Park ⓭.

*Take the A64 north. Turn off for Castle
Howard and Yorkshire Lavender, then
continue west to the B1363 and south.*

Moorland Adventures

Staying at Pickering ❹, see the church
frescoes before enjoying a few hours
of energetic cycling in the Dalby
Forest. Next head for Hutton-le-Hole
❺ and explore the historic rural
buildings of Rydale Folk Museum.
Finish the day with a thrilling roller
coaster of a drive over Rosedale
Chimney Bank, enjoying the views.

*Head west on A170, turning right to
Hutton-le-Hole, then follow the signs
to Rosedale. Take Moor Lane south.*

Coastal Fun

Be scared by the Gothic ruins of the
abbey and spooky graveyard at
Whitby ❼. If the vampires aren't
biting, maybe the fish will be, so try to
catch some on a boat trip. If there is
time, drive to Grosmont ❻ to take
the restored steam train to pretty
Goathland. Those feeling fit can walk
back to Whitby on the Rail Trail.

*I lead out of Whitby on the A171, turn
left on the A169, turning right down
Eskdaleside to Grosmont.*

Eat and Drink: inexpensive, under £25; moderate, £25–£50; expensive, over £50

The Poetry of the Lakes

Carlisle to Coniston

Highlights

- **Handsome Carlisle**
  Tour the border county town of Cumbria, with its splendid cathedral complex and historic castle

- **Natural wonders**
  Drive through luxuriant forests and mountain passes; see nesting ospreys, lofty waterfalls and an enormous rock brought from Scotland by a glacier

- **Jewels of the Lakeland**
  Make the most of the Lake District's prettiest and most unspoiled waters – cruise, row, go trout fishing or just relax by their lapping shores

- **Literary landscapes**
  Visit the home of Wordsworth, the celebrated lake poet; the marvellous house of John Ruskin; and Beatrix Potter's charming cottage

Rowing boat on the still, clear waters of Derwent water, Lake District

The Poetry of the Lakes

This tour winds its way around the Lake District, starting with gentle miles through green, open pastures grazed by sheep. There are also a few long stretches to cover, amid some of the most stupendous natural scenery in all of Britain. The route entails two lovely, unchallenging passes; taking in scattered slate-roofed farms, it runs alongside lakes great and small, touristy and tranquil. Stop-offs along the way include the small town of Cockermouth, bustling Keswick on Derwent Water and the famous Dove Cottage in Grasmere, once home to the poet William Wordsworth, who drew his inspiration from the surrounding natural beauty.

Above Typical Lake District cottage built with local stone, matching the dry-stone walls

ACTIVITIES

Soak up the history of Carlisle, close to the Scottish borders, taking in the magnificent cathedral and the doughty castle

Visit a traditional brewery to see Cockermouth beer in production and sample the real ales in the brewery's bar

Watch ospreys nesting via CCTV at the Whinlatter Forest Park

Go walking, hiking, off-road biking, sailing, canoeing – the Lake District is one vast adventure playground

Go underground in the last working slate mine in Britain at the stunning Honister Pass

Spend an evening at the theatre in Keswick and emerge to find Derwent Water lapping the shore before you

Try and work out Sarah Nelson's secret recipe by eating her traditional Cumbrian gingerbread in Grasmere

Watch skilled glassblowers at work and buy a memento from Ambleside

Tour the inside of the lakeside Victorian home of John Ruskin the poet, artist, commentator and conservationist

Take a pleasure cruise across Coniston on a steam yacht

KEY

═ Drive route

Below Traditional cruiser skimming across the surface of Ullswater lake near Keswick, see p201

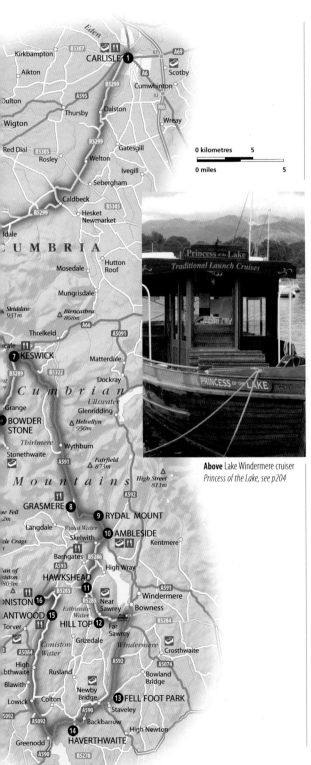

Above Lake Windermere cruiser *Princess of the Lake, see p204*

PLAN YOUR DRIVE

Start/finish: Carlisle to Coniston.

Number of days: 5, including a half day at Carlisle.

Distances: Approximately 217 km (135 miles).

Road conditions: The roads are good, but watch out for straying sheep.

When to go: Spring is the ideal time to see hosts of golden daffodils; May–Jun is when the azaleas are ablaze; summer is fun but busy; and Oct has the blaze of autumn colour.

Opening times: Galleries, museums and attractions are generally open 10am–5pm, but often close earlier Nov–Easter. Shops are often open longer. Churches are usually open until dusk.

Main market days: Keswick: Sat; Carlisle: Farmers' Market, first Fri of month; Victorian Market Hall, closed Sun.

Shopping: Look out for gingerbread in Grasmere, ice cream in Buttermere, fine relishes in Hawkshead and fudge in Coniston. There are also wool products and glass products from Ambleside.

Major festivals: Cumbria-wide: Lake District Summer Music Festival, Aug; **Carlisle:** Music City, late May; International Summer Festival, Jul; Northbound, Aug; Taste Cumbria Food Festival, Sep; **Keswick:** Film Festival, Feb; Words by the Water, Mar; Jazz Festival, May; **Grasmere:** Lake Artists' Society Summer Exhibition, Aug.

DAY TRIP OPTIONS

Families will love discovering Carlisle with its **fortifications** and **cathedral**, followed by a visit to Cockermouth with its **castle ruins**. Continue to Whinlatter Forest Park for a **walk** or **bike ride**. Learn about Lakeland stone at Keswick's **ancient stone circle**, climb the **Bowder Stone**, cross **Honister Pass**, go down a **slate mine** and take in the **scenery** on a **walk** by Buttermere Lake. Poetry lovers will relish seeing Wordsworth's **cottage** and **burial place** at Grasmere; his home at **Rydal Mount**, as well as Ambleside and Hawkshead – and enjoy a **walk** or **go fishing.** For full details, *see p205.*

Above Ancient wooden door at Carlisle's 12th–14th-century castle

VISITING CARLISLE

Parking
Exit M6 at junction 43, then drive down A69 Rotary Way to Warwick Rd until you see Lowther St. Turn right to The Lanes car park on the left, or follow signs to station for short- and long-stay parking (pay-and-display car parks clearly signed). There is street parking at the Lanes Shopping Centre, in Botchergate, West Walls and Castle Way among others.

Tourist Information
Old Town Hall, Market Square, CA3 8JE; 01228 598 596; www.visitcumbria.com

WHERE TO STAY

CARLISLE

Cornerways Guest House *inexpensive*
A conveniently situated and good value B&B. Not all rooms are en suite. Serves full English and Continental breakfasts.
107 Warwick Road, CA1 1EA; 01228 521 733; www.cornerwaysbandb.co.uk

Mount Farm *inexpensive*
Spacious rooms in a barn or stable conversion on a working farm, with great views and delicious breakfasts.
Blackford, CA6 4ER; 5 km (3 miles) north off A7; 01228 674 671; www.mount-farm.co.uk

AROUND CARLISLE

Willowbeck Lodge *moderate*
A purpose-built Scandinavian-style lodge offering breakfast with Craster kippers, free-range eggs and Scotch pancakes.
Lambley Bank, Scotby, CA4 8BX; 5 km (3 miles) east on A69; 01228 513 607; www.willowbeck-lodge.com

Where to Stay: inexpensive, under £80; moderate, £80–£150; expensive, over £150

① Carlisle
Cumbria; CA3 8JA
Streets of handsome terraces surround the ancient centre of this border city, which is still intact, atmospheric and accessible behind the bland store fronts of the pedestrian precinct. Carlisle is characterful, with a strong sense of civic pride and the small but beautiful cathedral at its spiritual heart. Visitors won't go hungry in town, since a range of tasty options awaits here and in the countryside beyond.

A two-hour walking tour
Start at the **Railway Station** ① with its imposing Tudor-Gothic-style façade. It was designed in 1847 by Sir William Tite, designer of the Bank of England and London's Royal Exchange. From the station it is impossible to miss the **Citadel** ② *(closed to the public)*; its oval East and West Towers were begun in 1810–11 to a design by Thomas Telford and contained courts and a prison. The West Tower has oak-panelled courtrooms, a grand jury room and cells. Walk between the towers up English St towards the city's shopping centre. At the centre of the pedestrianized area is Carlisle Cross, dated 1682. The tourist office is here, housed in the **Old Town Hall** ③ which was founded in 1122 and has been rebuilt many times. Just outside stands a "Victorian" pillar box marking the fact that England 's first such box was erected in Carlisle in 1853. Turn right out of the tourist office and enter grey and red stone **Carlisle Cathedral** ④. Its glorious interior is lit by exquisite stained-glass windows, some dating from the 14th century. Beneath a stunning barrel-vaulted, starred ceiling are excellent paintings, a carved oak

Antwerp triptych dating back to 1510 and 15th-century choir stalls.

Clustered around the cathedral are some fine 17th-century buildings, such as the Old Registry, dated 1699, The Deanery with its defensive pele tower *(see p209)*, and the Fratry, a 13th-century monastic dining room. Turn left and left into Abbey Street and go through the wrought-iron gates to **Tullie House Museum & Gallery** ⑤ *(open daily)*, housed in a Jacobean mansion dating from 1689. Its collections are devoted to local social history, archaeology, wildlife, geology and fine arts. Leave by the rear exit to find the **Millennium Walkway** ⑥, a bright subway displaying artifacts celebrating the city. These include the 16th-century cursing stone, recording the scathing words of the Bishop of Glasgow aimed at the marauding reivers of the borders *(see p209)*. Enter the **Castle** ⑦ by its 14th-century gatehouse and portcullis onto the 12th-century keep, with the dank dungeons that once held Mary Queen of Scots. Walk around the outside of the castle and enter Bitts Park at the junction with Castle Way. Cross the park to the River Eden and climb the steps of Eden Bridge. To the

Below The remains of what was an earlier, larger version of Carlisle Cathedral

Above Colourful and quirky independent coffee shop, Cockermouth

EAT AND DRINK

CARLISLE

Alexandros *moderate*
Small, intimate restaurant offering an authentic Greek menu with a few imaginative modern twists.
68 Warwick Road, CA1 1DR; 01228 592 227; www.thegreek.co.uk

David's *moderate*
Lakeland beef and lamb feature on the imaginative menu at this Victorian town house, as well as grilled mackerel served on sourdough. There's a good wine list too.
62 Warwick Road, CA1 1DR; 01228 523 578; www.davidsrestaurant.co.uk

La Pergola *moderate*
Family-run Italian restaurant offering tried and trusted fare in a great location.
28 Castle Street, CA3 8TP; 01228 534 084; www.la-pergola.net

Thin White Duke *moderate*
Warm and inviting, with a stripped-back interior, this bar and restaurant is a lively spot for dinner and drinks.
1 Devonshire Street, CA3 8LG; 01228 402 334; www.thinwhiteduke.info

COCKERMOUTH

The Bitter End *inexpensive*
This friendly real-ale pub with in-house brewery serves traditional sandwiches, steak-and-ale pie and fish and chips.
15 Kirkgate, CA13 9PJ; 01900 828 993; www.bitterend.co.uk

Old Stackyard Tearooms *inexpensive*
A lovely place to enjoy award-winning home-made snacks and light meals.
Wellington Farm, CA13 0QU (just off the A66/A5086 roundabout); 01900 822 777; www.wellingtonjerseys.co.uk

Quince & Medlar *moderate*
Offering an inventive vegetarian menu with organic wines and great fruit drinks, this restaurant is located close to the castle in a superb Georgian building.
13 Castlegate, CA13 9EU; 01900 823 579; www.quinceandmedlar.co.uk

right stands the high-rise Civic Centre; to the left, hidden to all but historical imagination, the course of **Hadrian's Wall**, along Stanwix Bank on the far side of the Eden. Head back into the town centre along Rickergate to pass the glass-roofed **Victorian Market Hall ⑧**, built in 1890, and return through the precinct to the station.

🚗 *Leave via the A6 (Lowther Street). Take the first exit on the roundabout onto the A595, turn left at B5299, following signs for Dalston, then Caldbeck, Uldale and Bassenthwaite. Take B5291 and A66 for Cockermouth. At the roundabout take the B5086 into Cockermouth; park in the town centre.*

② Cockermouth
Cumbria; CA13 9NP

At the meeting of the rivers Derwent and Cocker, this small market town, the birthplace of William Wordsworth (1770–1850), is easily explored on foot. Step inside the Georgian **Wordsworth House** *(closed Fri)* town house, where the poet spent his early years, to see what life was like in the 1770s. Cooking demonstrations and tastings are held in the kitchen, and the walled garden is planted with traditional varieties of flowers, fruit and vegetables. The mostly ruined

Cockermouth Castle, best viewed from the riverside, is only opened to the public during the Summer Festival in July. There are antiques shops on Station Street, and real-ale drinkers should book a tour of 19th-century **Jennings Brewery** *(www.jenningsbrewery. co.uk; 01900 820 362)*.

🚗 *Leave on the B5292 for Lorton. Take left branch to stay on the B5292 to Whinlatter Forest.*

Whinlatter Forest Park sign

③ Whinlatter Forest Park
Cumbria; CA12 5TW

The road climbs through England's only true mountain forest (planted from timber after WW1), affording fabulous views of the Lake District and across the water of the Solway Firth into Scotland. See breeding ospreys via CCTV, or feeding siskins and the shy red squirrels scampering over the feeding station. The **Visitors' Centre** *(www.forestry.gov.uk/whinlatter; 01768 778 469)* has details of woodland walks, or go mountain biking on the longest purpose-built trail in the Lake District, the Altura Trail. Hire bikes and clothing from Cyclewise Whinlatter *(www.cyclewise.co.uk; 017687 78711)*.

🚗 *Return through High Lorton and turn left on to B5289 to Buttermere. There is a car park in the village.*

Above left Traditional water launch, Derwent Water, near Keswick **Above right** Panoramic view over Keswick, Derwent Water and the Fells

VISITING KESWICK

Parking
There is pay parking by the theatre on the lake and at various well-signed sites around the town.

Boating
At **Derwent Water Marina**, west off the A66, hire kayaks, rowing boats, sail boats and windsurfers, or have some lessons. *(Portinscale, CA12 5RF; 01768772 912; www.derwentwatermarina.co.uk)*

WHERE TO STAY

AROUND BUTTERMERE

New House Farm *expensive*
This top-notch 17th-century guesthouse located on B5289 to Buttermere offers impressive rooms. *Lorton, Cockermouth, CA13 9UU; 07841 159 818; www.newhouse-farm.com*

AROUND HONISTER PASS

Langstrath Country Inn *moderate*
There are eight very nice en-suite rooms in this relaxed, attractive, walker-friendly inn just off the B5289 after Honister Slate Mine. It has bags of personality and serves great food – try the local lamb, Cumbrian cheeses and ales. *Stonethwaite, Borrowdale, CA12 5XG; 017687 77239; www.thelangstrath.com*

AROUND KESWICK

Swinside Lodge *moderate*
This Georgian country house, near Stair on the west shore of Derwent Water, offers seven good rooms with great views. The daily changing menu based on fresh local ingredients includes home-made bread, soups, ice cream and Cumbrian cheeses. *Newlands, CA12 5UE; 017687 72948; www.swinsidelodge-hotel.co.uk*

④ Buttermere
Cumbria; CA13 9UZ
This hamlet is scenically situated beneath looming lakeland pikes and crags between tranquil Buttermere Lake and larger Crummock Water. Try the eminently walkable footpath – allow 2–3 hours – around Buttermere (meaning "lake of the dairy pastures"); usually there's a welcome ice-cream van at the end of the walk. It is also a short walk from the village to the spectacular **Scale Force**, the highest waterfall in the Lake District, with a single drop of 52 m (170 ft).

🚗 *Continue along the B5289 over Honister Pass to the mine.*

⑤ Honister Pass
Cumbria; CA12 5XN
The drive across **Honister Pass** is simply glorious, passing skipping streams and rushing torrents, tough grass slopes and rock-studded scree patches, and everywhere shaggy Herdwick sheep.

On the B5289, **Honister Slate Mine** *(open daily; 017687 77230; www.honister. com)* is Britain's last working slate mine and produces traditional Westmoreland green slate. It offers

four daily 90-minute guided tours within the 18 km (11 miles) of tunnels. See the vast caverns being worked, and learn about the extraction and processing of slate (booking essential).

🚗 *Carry along B5289 to Bowder Stone. Note the double stone bridge into Grange village, but don't cross in high summer, when the village is packed.*

The Lady of the Lake

Mary Robinson, the pretty daughter of the landlord at the Fish Hotel, was widely known as the "Beauty of Buttermere". In 1802 she married the Hon. Alexander Augustus Hope, Lieutenant-Colonel of the 14th Regiment of Foot. However, he was really John Hatfield, an imposter and bigamist and was hanged in 1803 in Carlisle for forgery. Her story was the inspiration for the novel by author and broadcaster Lord Melvyn Bragg, *The Maid of Buttermere*.

---

⑥ Bowder Stone
Grange, Cumbria
Weighing 2,000 tons and standing some 9 m (30 ft) high, this stone, you might suppose, had simply broken loose from the rock face – but it is not

Below A visitor from Scotland, the colossal Bowder Stone, Grange local rock, and was probably carried here all the way from Scotland by the glaciers of the Ice Age. It is traditional to shake hands with a friend under the stone and climb to the top.

🚗 *Carry along B5289 into Keswick.*

⑦ Keswick
Cumbria; CA12 5JR

A tourist magnet, this buzzy town has a stunning setting on Derwent Water, surrounded by the fells of Saddleback, Helvellyn and Grisedale Pike. Attractions include the beautifully situated **Theatre by the Lake**, (www.theatrebythelake.com with its professional drama company and art galleries. Alternatively, take to the water in a rowing boat or kayak, or on a cruise. East of town, on the A591, stands the enigmatic **Castlerigg Stone Circle** with distant views of Skiddaw, Blencathra and Lonscale Fell. With an astronomically significant alignment, the circle of 38 stones holds a rectangle of 10 more and dates from around 3,000 BC.

🚗 *Head south on A591 to Grasmere.*

The Hardy Herdwick

Incredibly enduring, Herdwick sheep are native to the Lake District, where they have grazed since the 12th century or earlier. The meat is prized by Cumbrian gourmets. It gets its distinctive taste from a diet of fell grasses and heather. The wool is tough, wiry and long-lasting.

---

⑧ Grasmere
Cumbria; LA22 9SH

On the Wordsworth trail, Grasmere has the sturdy little village church of **St Oswald's**. Inside, there is a glass case holding the poet's prayer book and outside are eight yew trees that he planted. One now marks the grave that Wordsworth shares with his wife, Mary. Nearby are buried his sister Dorothy, four of his children, Mary's sister, and Samuel Taylor Coleridge's son, Hartley. Just beyond the village, on A591 there is free parking on the left for **Dove Cottage** *(closed Dec 24–26 and Jan)*, home to William, and Dorothy from 1799 to 1808. Here, the poet enjoyed a golden age of creativity, and the whitewashed walls, flagged floors and dark panelling resonate with his presence. Here, too, Dorothy wrote her *Grasmere Journals*. In 1802 William married Mary Hutchinson, who joined the household. Guests included fellow poet Samuel Taylor Coleridge, and novelists Sir Walter Scott and Thomas de Quincey. The garden, a "domestic slip of mountain", has been restored to the semi-wild state planned for it by William and Dorothy.

🚗 *Follow A591 alongside glorious Rydal Water to Rydal Mount.*

Sign for local ice cream, Buttermere

Far left The old stone bridge over the River Greta at Keswick **Left** Dove Cottage, home of celebrated Lakes poet William Wordsworth

SHOPPING IN GRASMERE

Sarah Nelson's Grasmere gingerbread is sold at **Grasmere Gingerbread Shop**, in what was once the Lych Gate village school where Wordsworth taught. *(Church Cottage, Ambleside, LA22 9SW; 015394 35428)*

EAT AND DRINK

KESWICK

Square Orange *inexpensive*
Continental-style café-bar offering great coffee, stone-baked pizzas and tapas. It also has indoor games for rainy days. *20 St John's Street, CA12 5AS; 017687 73888; www.thesquareorange.co.uk*

Luca's Ristorante *moderate*
This bills itself as Keswick's premium Italian restaurant and has a loyal local following. It has an extensive menu and a riverside location. *High Hill, Greta Bridge, CA12 5NX; 017687 74621; www.lucasristorante.co.uk*

Highfield Restaurant *expensive*
With a menu that draws on local seasonal produce, this hotel-restaurant serves Cumbrian beef, wild venison and award-winning Cumbrian cheeses. *The Heads, CA12 5ER; 017687 72508; www.highfieldkeswick.co.uk*

GRASMERE

The Jumble Room *moderate*
This quirky restaurant with a changing menu serves delights such as traditional Graythwaite game pie and less traditional Hungarian street food. *Langdale Road, LA22 9SU; 015394 35188; www.thejumbleroom.co.uk*

Below The enigmatic Castlerigg Stone Circle, one of the earliest stone circles in Britain

VISITING AMBLESIDE

Parking
Pay-and-display car park on the right
on the drive into town.

Tourist Information
*Central Buildings, Market Cross
LA22 9BS; 015394 32582;
www.visitcumbria.com*

WHERE TO STAY

AMBLESIDE

Elder Grove *moderate*
This friendly guesthouse has
knowledgeable hosts and is renowned
for extensive and delicious breakfasts.
*Lake Road, LA22 0DB; 015394 32504;
www.eldergrove.co.uk*

High Wray Farm *moderate*
Peaceful and traditional farmhouse
B&B 5 km (3 miles) south of Ambleside,
with brass beds in all three rooms.
Lovely views.
*High Wray, LA22 0JE; 015394 32280;
www.highwrayfarm.co.uk*

HAWKSHEAD

Yewfield *moderate*
Peaceful vegetarian guesthouse set
in extensive grounds. The Tower suite
has the best views.
*Hawkshead Hill LA22 0PR; 015394
36765; www.yewfield.co.uk*

Below top left Terrace of Victorian stone
B&Bs, Ambleside **Below top right** Rydal
Water, one of the smallest lakes in the area
Below left The Old Corn Mill, Ambleside,
dating back to 1680 **Below right** Rydal
Mount, Wordsworth's final home

⑨ Rydal Mount
Rydal, near Ambleside; LA22 9LU
William and Mary Wordsworth moved
to 16th-century **Rydal Mount** *(closed
Jan; Mon & Tue in winter & Dec 25–26;
015394 33002; www.rydalmount.co.uk)* in
1813, with three of their children (two
had died the previous year), William's
sister Dorothy, and sister-in-law Sara. It
was to be his home for the last 37 years
of his life. Use a guide leaflet to tour the
house and garden and see touching
relics such as the poet's leather picnic
box, and correspondence concerning
his appointment as Poet Laureate.
Walk to nearby Rydal Water, one of
Wordsworth's favourite places.

🚗 **Continue on the A591 to Ambleside,
find pay parking on right.**

⑩ Ambleside
Cumbria; LA22 9BS
A favourite destination for walkers,
Ambleside lies at the heart of the
Lake District National Park and
abounds in pubs, restaurants and
hotels. It was here that Wordsworth
carried out his job as distributor of
stamps. Visit **Ambleside Sheepskins**
(see right), and the tiny 17th-century
Bridge House, built on the old
packhorse bridge. In this 4 x 2 m
(13 x 6 ft) former apple store, Mr
and Mrs Rigg brought up six children
in the 1850s.

🚗 **Start off on the A591, turn right for**

the A593 towards Coniston, fork left
onto the B5286 to Hawkshead. Park in
the pay car park outside the village.

The Lake Poets
The first mention of the Lake School
of poetry – Romantic poets who
lived in the Lake District – appeared
in 1817. These were Samuel Taylor
Coleridge, Robert Southey and
William Wordsworth, although
Wordsworth alone was born here.
Much of his poetry was confessional
and autobiographical – highly
original in its day. His *Daffodils*, a
delirious evocation of spring beauty
in the Lakes, is probably his best-
known poem and one of the most
loved in the English language.

---

⑪ Hawkshead
Cumbria; LA22 0NT
This is a charming village, with pretty
cottages, an old Court House, and
the **Beatrix Potter Gallery** *(closed Fri)*
devoted to the children's author, with
some of her original artwork. For
eight years from 1779, Wordsworth
was one of 100 boys attending
Hawkshead Grammar School *(closed
Nov–Mar; Sun am)*. You can see where
he (allegedly) carved his name on a
desk. Nearby is the vast Esthwaite
Water, described in Wordsworth's
Prelude as "our little lake", stocked with
fish and popular with anglers. Permits,

Where to Stay: inexpensive, under £80; moderate, £80–£150; expensive, over £150

tackle, tuition and boat hire are available from the **Esthwaite Water Trout Fishery** *(015394 36541; www. hawksheadtrout.co.uk)* on the southwest shore. Walkers should head for **Tarn Hows**, 5 km (3 miles) to the northwest, a beautiful body of water, with splendid views. Set in woods, it is skirted by a good 2.5-km (1½-mile) path, suitable for wheelchairs. Visit *www.lakedistrict. gov.uk/visiting/ thingstodo/walking* or buy a map from the tourist office.

There are five walking routes from **Grizedale Forest Park Visitor Centre** *(01229 860 010; www. forestry.gov.uk/grizedale)* where a guide map can be bought. To find it, travel south on Main Street, then take the first right at the sign for Grizedale Forest. Alternatively, hire some mountain bikes and enjoy some safe off-roading.

🚗 *From Main St, turn left on B5285 to Near Sawrey (small car park available).*

Hill Top
Near Sawrey, Ambleside; LA22 0LF
Home to children's author Beatrix Potter from 1905, **Hill Top** *(015394 36269; www.nationaltrust.org.uk; closed Fri)* was bought by the author with the proceeds from five of her books. The 17th-century farmhouse and cottage garden with flowers, vegetables and herbs have been kept as they were at the author's wish. Fans of her work will recognize elements from her stories such as the long-case clock from *The Tailor of Gloucester* and the dresser from *The Tale of Samuel Whiskers*. In the village, note the flower-filled gardens of Buckle Yeat Guesthouse, inspiration for Potter's *Tale of Tom Kitten*.

🚗 *Continue on the B5285 to Far Sawrey and Lake Windermere and take the 15-minute ferry journey to the eastern shore (open daily; queues in high season). Travel down the A592 along lake shore to Fell Foot Park.*

WORDSWORTH STREET
FORMERLY LEATHER, RAG & PUTTY STREET
Hawkshead street sign

Above left Colourful Buckle Yeat Guesthouse, Near Sawrey **Above centre** Tower Bank Arms, Near Sawrey, which features in some of Beatrix Potter's stories **Above right** Eccentric teapot topiary in Hawkshead, Cumbria

SHOPPING IN AMBLESIDE

Buy sheepskin slippers and rugs from **Ambleside Sheepskins** *(Bark Mill, Bridge Street, LA22 9DU; 015394 32060; www.amblesidesheepskins.co. uk)*. The shop also sells reindeer and goatskin products.

SHOPPING IN HAWKSHEAD

The **Hawkshead Relish Company** produces home-made preserves, on sale at the Hawkshead Relish Shop *(The Square, LA22 0NZ)*, and outlets in the area. For Beatrix Potter memorabilia and figurines, try the "official stockist", Haddows Gifts *(The Car Park, LA22 0NT)*.

EAT AND DRINK

AMBLESIDE
The Giggling Goose *inexpensive*
This riverside terrace and upstairs tea-room serves good coffee, home-made soups, sandwiches and cakes. Enjoy the alfresco seating by the mill race. *The Old Mill, LA22 9DT; 015394 33370; www.gigglinggoose.co.uk*

The Fulling Mill *moderate*
Choice sandwiches and wraps are offered here at lunchtime, and sharing platters and salads in the evening. *Ryedale Road, LA22 9AN; 015394 32137; www.thefullingmill.com*

AROUND HAWKSHEAD
Drunken Duck *moderate*
On the route to Hawkshead – turn right off B5286 opposite Outgate Inn – this acclaimed gastropub and inn serves quality sandwiches and inventive food. *Barngates, LA22 0NG; 015394 36347; www.drunkenduckinn.co.uk*

Below Hawkshead Grammar School, founded by the Archbishop of York in 1585

Eat and Drink: inexpensive, under £25; moderate, £25–£50; expensive, over £50

Above left Part of the Lakeside & Haverthwaite Railway **Above right** Britain's earliest working locomotive, Haverthwaite Station

WHERE TO STAY

AROUND FELL FOOT PARK

Newby Bridge Hotel *moderate*
Grand hotel in lovely setting on the shores of Windermere (just off the A590 south of Fell Foot), with leisure centre including pool and steam room. Daily changing menu, with fresh produce from their kitchen garden and farm.
Newby Bridge, LA12 8NA; 015395 31222; www.newbybridgehotel.co.uk

Punch Bowl Inn *moderate*
After the ferry, take the A5074 south, turning off to Crosthwaite for nine distinctive rooms in this 18th-century country inn. Imaginative cooking extends to breakfast – freshly squeezed orange juice, potato and dill pancakes with quails' eggs and hollandaise.
Crosthwaite, Lyth Valley, LA8 8HR; 015395 68237; www.the-punchbowl.co.uk

AROUND CONISTON

Old Rectory *moderate*
This hotel, south of Coniston on the A593 – take first left after Little Arrow – is in a 19th-century house set in extensive gardens and woodland. Close to Coniston Water, the Old Rectory offers nine individually styled rooms and traditional Cumbrian breakfasts cooked to order, using local meat and eggs.
Torver, Coniston, LA21 8AX; 015394 41353; www.theoldrectoryhotel.com

Right Sheep grazing in fields with morning mist rising off Coniston Water beyond

Lake Windermere

Running north to south for 18 km (11 miles), Windermere is the largest lake in England and has been an important waterway since Roman times. It is fed by the Rivers Brathay and Rothay at the northern head and feeds into the River Leven at Newby Bridge in the south. On its eastern shore, sprawling Bowness-on-Windermere is the main resort town with many hotels, shops, pubs and attractions, as well as plenty of access to the lake. In high season the town is full to bursting with visitors. The glorious lakeside road south passes along thickly wooded banks holding covetable houses with some truly sublime views.

⑬ Fell Foot Park
Cumbria; LA12 8NN

A late-Victorian park of sweeping lawns, rhododendrons, oaks and pines at the south end of Windermere, Fell Foot Park *(open daily; 015395 31273; www.nationaltrust.org.uk)* has great shoreline access and splendid views of the Fells. There are good picnic areas, rowing-boat hire and a lovely

tearoom housed in an old Victorian boathouse, which serves light lunches.
🚗 *Carry on to Newby Bridge, turning right on to A590 and left on B5278.*

⑭ Haverthwaite
Cumbria; LA12 8AL

This is where children's book author and spy Arthur Ransome *(Swallows and Amazons)* ended his days, but the main reason to visit Haverthwaite is the nearby **Lakeside & Haverthwaite Railway** *(open daily, trains run late May–Oct; 015395 31594; www.lakesiderailway. co.uk)*. The station is on the A590 (on right from Newby Bridge). Once used to carry goods to the steamers on Windermere, the service closed in 1967. But thanks to enthusiasts, the locomotives once more ply alongside the River Leven. See the engines or try the short run to **Lakeside**, which offers lake cruises. Also, visit the **Lakeland Motor Museum** *(open daily)* here.
🚗 *Rejoin the A590, turn right on the A5092, fork right on the A5084 and turn right at Lowick (signed Nibthwaite/ east of lake) then left for Brantwood.*

Far left Peaceful yachts on Coniston Water, in the heart of the Lakeland Fells **Left** Kayaking lesson on Coniston Water

SHOPPING IN CONISTON

Buy some delectable fudge – hand-made from local dairy ingredients – from the **Coniston Fudge Co** *(Post Office, LA21 8DU; 015394 41259; www.conistonfudge.com)*. Flavours include Coniston Cookie Crunch and Ginger. Best of all, visitors can taste before buying.

EAT AND DRINK

BRANTWOOD

Jumping Jenny Coffee House and Restaurant *inexpensive*
Enjoy lunch on the terrace with sublime views over Coniston in this restaurant-café, located in the former stables in Brantwood grounds. The menu includes home-made soups, flans, salads, pasta, cakes and pastries. *Brantwood, LA21 8AD; 015394 41715; www.jumpingjenny.net*

CONISTON

Black Bull Inn *moderate*
This old coaching inn has played host to poet Samuel Taylor Coleridge, artist J M W Turner and the late Donald Campbell, who died on Coniston in an attempt to set a new water speed record. On offer are sandwiches, baked potatoes and hearty cooked meals such as Cumberland sausage, shoulder of lamb, and fish of the day. Wash it all down with ales such as its own Bluebird. It also has a few rooms. *1 Yewdale Road, LA21 8DU; 015394 41335; www.blackbullconiston.co.uk*

⑮ Brantwood

Cumbria; LA21 8AD;

John Ruskin (1819–1900), artist, writer, poet, critic and social reformer, lived at Brantwood *(open daily; mid-Nov–mid-Mar: closed Mon–Tue; 015394 41396; www.brantwood.org.uk)* from 1871. The house is so imbued with his personality that it feels as though he has just gone out for a stroll. His own watercolours and drawings are hung with those of other prominent painters. Views across Coniston, especially from the turret, are sublime and there are wonderful gardens. The best time to visit is in late May, when the azaleas are at their showiest. Aged 81, Ruskin died of influenza and is buried at St Andrew's Church, Coniston.

🚗 *Head north, turning left around the lake to join the B5285 to Coniston and pay parking at Coniston Pier.*

Railway insignia, Haverthwaite Station

⑯ Coniston

Cumbria; LA21 8AJ

Situated at the head of Coniston Water – third-largest of the central Cumbrian lakes – this village was once a centre for the local copper-mining industry, which boomed in the 18th and 19th centuries. It is overlooked by the 802 m (2,631 ft) fell, the Old Man of Coniston, and is also close to **Tarn Hows**. The graceful Victorian steam yacht the *Gondola* (Apr–Oct; www.nationaltrust.org.uk) – so called because of its high prow – glides across the water from Coniston Pier to Brantwood jetty. The 45-minute round trip gives passengers the chance to appreciate the beauty of the lake amid the surrounding Coniston Fells. Or hire a kayak, canoe or rowing boat from **Coniston Boating Centre** *(015394 41366)*, also located near the pier, to explore the lake.

DAY TRIP OPTIONS

Carlisle, Keswick and Ambleside are all good bases for exploring the sublime countryside and following in the footsteps of the Lakeland poets.

War and Peace

Take a tour around Carlisle ❶, a border city often attacked by raiders from the north. See the citadel, castle and cathedral. Then set out on the glorious drive southwest to Cockermouth ❷, having a look at the castle and an ice cream at the Old Stackyard Tearooms. Time permitting, head to Whinlatter Forest Park ❸ for a walk or a bike ride in the quiet woodland countryside.

Follow driving instructions to Whinlatter Forest Park. Continue towards Keswick

on B5292 and return to Carlisle up the east side of Bassenthwaite Lake.

Lakeland Stone

Based at Keswick ❼, enjoy the lake location and Castlerigg Stone Circle, then set off to climb the Bowder Stone ❻. Head for Honister Pass ❺ and Honister Slate Mine, the last working slate mine in the UK. Drive on to Buttermere ❹; enjoy a picnic and walk around the lake admiring the pikes and crags. Head north to Lorton and through Whinlatter Forest Park ❸ to return to Keswick.

Follow the drive's instructions in reverse from Keswick to Whinlatter Forest Park. Then head east back to Keswick.

Wander o'er Vales and Hills

Follow the Wordsworth trail from Grasmere ❽, for the church and cottage with links to the poet, then continue to Rydal Mount ❾ and the nearby lake – two of his favourite places. Ambleside ❿, where the poet worked – is a good place for lunch. Next go on to Hawkshead ⓫, where Wordsworth was schooled, to enjoy a walk or go fishing, before pushing on past Hill Top ⓬, across the lake on the ferry and returning up Windermere's eastern shore.

Follow the drive's instructions to Hill Top and across Lake Windermere. Turn left on A592 through Bowness to return to Ambleside or Grasmere.

Eat and Drink: inexpensive, under £25; moderate, £25–£50; expensive, over £50

Wild Northumbria

Kielder Water to Lindisfarne

Highlights

- **Lakeside adventures**
  Enjoy a wealth of exciting activities beside northern Europe's largest man-made expanse of water at Kielder Water

- **Castles galore**
  See medieval strongholds, romantic coastal ruins, an island's defence and a magnificent ducal home

- **Nature close up**
  Look out for elusive otters and shy deer in Kielder Forest; colourful puffins and terns off Amble, and migrating sea birds and seals on Lindisfarne Island

- **Cradle of Christianity**
  Cross the tidal causeway to Holy Island (Lindisfarne), a special place of pilgrimage with an ancient monastery

Alnwick Castle, familiar to Harry Potter fans as the exterior of Hogwarts

Wild Northumbria

Sparsely populated and with a large pristine moorland habitat, Northumberland is a county of wild beauty. The long and low coastline has seen more development than the wilder, more hilly interior, but as much as a quarter of the county is protected as part of the Northumberland National Park. This makes the area one of the best in the country for a driving holiday – the roads are generally empty and the scenery simply stunning. Architecturally, the area is also surprisingly rich. Sharing a border with Scotland and facing the North Sea, Northumberland was often subjected to attacks from marauding Scots and pillaging Vikings. As a result the coast and interior is studded with more castles than any other county.

Above Sand dunes at Beadnell Beach, near Bamburgh Castle

PLAN YOUR DRIVE

Start/finish: Kielder Water to Lindisfarne Island.

Number of days: 2, including a wait for the tide.

Distances: 126 km (79 miles).

Road conditions: Roads are well-maintained.

When to go: From late May to early August – but the weather can be windy at all times of year.

Main market days: Alnwick: Market Square, Sat & Thu (Mar–Sep); Farmers' Market last Fri of the month.

Festivals: Alnwick: International Music Festival, Aug; Cragside: Rothbury Traditional Music Festival, Jul; Brinkburn Priory Music Festival, early Jul.

Above On the approach road to the impressive Bamburgh Castle

① Kielder Water
Northumberland; NE48 1BX

With 43 km (27 miles) of shoreline set among cool pine forest and heather moorland, Kielder Water is northern Europe's largest man-made lake. Visit the **Tower Knowe Visitor Centre** *(closed Nov through Mar; www.visitkielder.com)* to find out about the activities on offer, such as walking, fishing, lake cruises, mountain biking and horse riding. Further west along the shoreline is the **Leaplish Waterside Park** *(01434 240 436; www.leaplish.co.uk)* with lodges for rent, Bird of Prey Centre, swimming pools, saunas, boat hire and ferry rides.

The forest teems with wildlife such as otters, roe deer, osprey and red squirrels, but also has the least light pollution in the country. You can view the dark skies at the **Kielder Observatory** *(0191 265 5510; www.kielderobservatory.org)*.

🚗 *Turn left out of the visitor centre, following the minor roads towards Greenhaugh. Turn right just before this hamlet then left on B6320 to Otterburn. Turn right on A696 and left on B6341 to Rothbury and Cragside.*

② Cragside
Rothbury, Northumberland; NE65 7PX

One of the great Victorian houses of the northeast and the first to be lit by hydro-electricity in 1880, **Cragside** *(open Mar–Oct: Tue–Sun; www. nationaltrust.org.uk)* was commissioned by scientist and arms manufacturer Sir William Armstrong. It is best seen from below, looming over its woodland estate, and the largest hand-made rock garden in Europe. The sumptuous interiors also contain a wealth of gadgetry. There is some rough going in the grounds, so wear walking shoes and keep a lookout for glimpses of red squirrels

and magnificent firs in the pinetum. Children will enjoy the play area and exploring tunnels and pathways in the rhododendron labyrinth.

🚗 *Return towards Rothbury on B6341, turn left on B6344; turn left on A697 and right on B6345, then A1068 to Amble.*

③ Amble
Northumberland; NE65 0DA

A key centre for coal distribution in the 19th century, Amble's fortunes declined along with the mining industry. Sitting at the mouth of the River Coquet, Amble is now a pleasant and relaxed town. Head north along the Coquet to **Warkworth** to see the **castle** – a former stronghold of the mighty Percy family – with its cross-shaped keep, and enjoy lunch in the Mason's Arms *(see right)* or picnic on the wide sandy beach. In summer, take a boat from the marina to **Coquet Island** with its 24-m (80-ft) high lighthouse, and watch nesting seabirds – puffins, eider ducks and the rare roseate tern. Or walk south along the coast and picnic in the dunes at lovely **Druridge Bay Country Park**.

🚗 *Take the A1068 north for 14.5 km (9 miles) to Alnwick. Turn right onto Greenwell Road for the car park.*

A Man's House is his Castle
Over the centuries, Northumberland has been the site of many battles and border raids with the Scots, so it is no surprise that it boasts more castles than any other part of England. There are also many smaller houses fortified with square bastions or pele towers, which were virtually impregnable. In Elizabethan times these oddities also harboured raiding clans known as the Border Reivers *(see p198)*.

Above left Cragside towering above its large rock garden **Above right** The technologically advanced Victorian manor house at Cragside

GETTING TO KIELDER WATER

From the south, take the A1, turning left on the A68 after Darlington, then left to Bellingham and the road to Kielder.

WHERE TO STAY

AROUND KIELDER WATER
Pheasant Inn *moderate*
On the road (1 km/half a mile) from Kielder Water, this peaceful farmhouse-inn has eight rooms and a garden. *Stannersburn, Falstone, NE48 1DD; 01434 240 382; www.thepheasantinn.com*

AROUND AMBLE
Roxbro House *moderate*
This boutique B&B in a stone house 3 km (2 miles) north of Amble, on the A1068, has six rooms and three log cabins. It serves great locally sourced breakfasts. *5 Castle Terrace, Warkworth, NE65 0UP; 01665 711 416; www.roxbrohouse.co.uk*

EAT AND DRINK

AROUND KIELDER WATER
Old School Tea Room *inexpensive*
Attractive tearooms and craft shop housed in a Victorian school building, ideal for inexpensive snacks. *Falstone, NE48 1AA; 01434 240 459*

AROUND CRAGSIDE
Angler's Arms *moderate*
This 1760s coaching inn is on the River Coquet, off the A697 around 10 km (6 miles) east of Cragside. The menu features kipper salad and steak pie. *Weldon Bridge, Longframlington, NE65 8AX; 01665 570 271*

AROUND AMBLE
Mason's Arms *moderate*
Home-cooked meals at this pub in Warkworth, 3 km (2 miles) north of Amble on the A1068, include pulled pork and Northumbrian/local cheeses. *3 Dial Place, Warkworth, NE65 0UR; 01665 711 398*

Eat and Drink: inexpensive, under £25; moderate, £25–£50; expensive, over £50

Above The Bailey at Alnwick Castle, used in the Harry Potter films

VISITING ALNWICK

Parking
Turn right just before Bondgate archway onto Greenwall Road for car park.

Tourist Information
The Shambles, NE66 1TN; 01665 511 333; www.visitnorthumberland.com/alnwick

VISITING LINDISFARNE ISLAND

Tide Information
Look for tables displayed on posts or call the priory (01289 389 200) for details.

WHERE TO STAY

ALNWICK

Tate House B&B *inexpensive*
Three rooms, two in a late-Victorian house just outside the centre.
11 Bondgate Without, NE66 1PR; 01665 604 661; www.stayinalnwick.co.uk

Oaks Hotel *moderate*
There are 13 comfortable rooms in this friendly pub-hotel on the mini roundabout on leaving Bondgate.
South Road, NE66 2PN; 01665 510 014; www.theoakshotel.co.uk

White Swan *moderate*
This 300-year-old coaching inn, with 55 bedrooms, has a handy central location, good food and guest parking.
Bondgate Within, NE66 1TD; 01665 602 109; thewhiteswan.classiclodges.co.uk

AROUND DUNSTANBURGH

Old Rectory Howick *moderate*
Luxury B&B with a country-house feel set in its own grounds and close to a secluded beach. Award-winning breakfast includes Craster kippers.
Craster, Alnwick, NE66 3LE; 01665 577 590; www.theoldrectoryhowick.co.uk

④ Alnwick
Northumberland; NE66 1TN

This attractive market town is a compact warren of cobbled streets, old stone buildings and narrow alleys tucked between its main attractions, Alnwick Castle and Garden. It is also ideally located for countryside or coastal trips. Allow at least half a day to tour the town and its sights.

A two-hour walking tour

From the car park head down Greenwell Road to the 15th-century **Bondgate Tower** ① (or Hotspur Tower), originally one of four town gateways. Walk up Bondgate Within, past the Market Place and Cross and Northumberland Hall on the left, into Narrowgate, curving round to the right. Turn left down Bailiffgate, with its charming old houses, and visit the **Bailiffgate Museum** ② *(closed Mon; www.bailiffgatemuseum.co.uk)*, in the former St Mary's Church and dedicated to the people and places of the area. Keen walkers can continue down Ratten Row for 1 km (half a mile) to explore **Hulne Park** ③, a vast area of estate forestry, farm and sawmills. Head for 13th-century Carmelite Hulne Friary, in the distance. Otherwise, turn left onto Northumberland St and pass Pottergate Tower into Dispensary St. Go left on Clayport St, up Market St, and right to arrive back on Bondgate Within. Return through the Tower, down Bondgate Without. After passing the War Memorial on the left, across from the Percy Tenantry Lion Column is the 19th-century Alnwick Station building, home to **Barter Books** ④ *(open daily)*, a second-hand bookshop with a café and a model train that tours the top of the shelves. Return to the car park on Greenwell Road.

A path from behind the Greenwell Road car park leads up to **Alnwick Castle** ⑤ *(Apr–Oct: open daily; www.alnwickcastle.com)*, the second-largest inhabited castle in the country and seat of the Dukes of Northumberland since 1309. Fans of the first two Harry Potter films will recognize the exterior as Hogwarts school. Dominating the town, the castle dates from the 11th century but has seen major expansion since the 14th century. Visitors can tour the grand state rooms, a library, a fabulous Renaissance drawing room and an art collection that includes works by Van Dyke and Canaletto.

Walk back down the path to delightful **Alnwick Garden** ⑥ *(open daily; www.alnwickgarden.com)*. In 1997 Jane Percy, Duchess of Northumberland, decided to bring an overgrown garden close to the castle back to life. It is still an ongoing project, created by Belgian garden designers Jacques and Peter Wirtz. The Grand Cascade, visible on entry, is the largest water feature of its kind in the UK. From the sweet to the sinister, the Rose Garden to the Poison Garden, and the Treehouse Restaurant, there is much to enjoy. Return down the path to the car park.

🚗 *Leave Alnwick on Bondgate Without turning left on B1340. After Denwick, follow signs to Dunstanburgh, fork right to Craster to park. Walk to the castle.*

Where to Stay: inexpensive, under £80; moderate, £80–£150; expensive, over £150

Above left Bistro restaurant Lilburns in the centre of Alnwick **Above right** The imposing Bamburgh Castle, the Armstrong family home

5 Dunstanburgh Castle

Craster, Alnwick; NE66 3TT

From the fishing village of Craster the massive, brooding ruins of this grand edifice are visible rising out of the sands atop a cliff. Wear strong, waterproof shoes to walk along the beach and be prepared for a scramble up to Dunstanburgh Castle. It was begun in the 14th century by the Earl of Lancaster, and enough survives of its walls, watchtower and gatehouse to fire the imagination and transport the visitor back some 700 years.

🚗 *Return inland, turning right on the B1339 and then B1340 to Bamburgh.*

6 Bamburgh Castle

Bamburgh, Northumberland; NE69 7DF

On a stunning basalt crag, Bamburgh Castle *(open daily; www.bamburgh castle. com)* looks across the sea to the Farne Islands. Originally built by the Normans, it was all but destroyed in the 15th-century Wars of the Roses by Edward IV. Restoration began in the mid-18th century, and was later continued by Sir William Armstrong *(see p209)* in 1894. It is still the Armstrong family home, but visitors can tour 16 rooms of armour, antiques and paintings, including the magnificent King's Hall and Cross Hall, and the torture chamber, armoury, bake house and scullery. There is also a small museum.

🚗 *Take the B1342, then right on A1 and right for Lindisfarne. Park on the island.*

7 Lindisfarne Island

Northumberland; TD15 2SH

Also known as Holy Island, this tidal islet is inaccessible by car at high tide *(see opposite)*, adding to the thrill of a visit to the cradle of English Christianity. Lindisfarne Monastery was founded in AD 635, and was a powerful centre of Christianity. Prepare to be captivated by this place of pilgrimage. Tour the ruined priory and clamber up to the castle and walled garden, walk around the headland and harbour, and sample the famous crab sandwiches and Lindisfarne Mead. A nature reserve, the island is a great place to see migrating birds and grey seals.

SHOPPING

Craster Kippers
At Craster, the Robsons produce their famous oak-smoked kippers, using the best herrings and traditional methods.
L Robson & Sons Ltd, NE66 3TR; 01665 576 223; www.kipper.co.uk

EAT AND DRINK

ALNWICK

The Art House *moderate*
Restaurant and Gallery in Bondgate Tower serving soups, sandwiches, burgers and salads at lunch time, and more ambitious food for dinner.
14 Bondgate Within, NE66 1TD; 01665 602 607; www.arthouserestaurant.com

Lilburns *moderate*
With a handy location just off Bondgate Within, this bistro has a pleasant family atmosphere and serves good food.
7 Paikes Street, NE66 1HX; 01665 603 444; www.lilburns.co.uk

AROUND DUNSTANBURGH

Dunstanburgh Castle Hotel *moderate*
This hotel restaurant, 3 km (2 miles) north of Craster on the B1339, serves home-made soups, local meat, Whitby scampi and plenty for vegetarians.
Embleton, NE66 3UN; 01665 576 111; www.dunstanburghcastlehotel.co.uk

Left The crumbling ruins of Dunstanburgh Castle, north of Craster village

---

DAY TRIP OPTIONS

Kielder Water and Alnwick make ideal bases for exploring the area.

Family Day by the Lake
Kielder Water ① is the perfect place for a day trip or to stay in a lodge, learn to fish, sail or horse ride; go cycling or walking by the lake and then soak tired muscles in the spa.

Castles and Coast
Staying at Alnwick ④, see the Castle and Garden, then head to Amble ③ for a walk to Warkworth Castle and a beach picnic. Return to Alnwick via the ingenious Cragside Estate ②, with its grand interiors and outside adventures.

Reverse the driving instructions to get to Amble and Cragside; return on B6341.

Castles and Christianity
Walk to see the ruins of Dunstanburgh Castle ⑤, then drive to the impressive Bamburgh Castle ⑥. Carry on to Lindisfarne Island ⑦ for a walk around the island, castle and priory. Vary the order of these, depending on the tide.

Follow the instructions for the drive. Return via the A1.

Eat and Drink: inexpensive, under £25; moderate, £25–£50; expensive, over £50

DRIVE **21**

History and Romance in the Borders

Edinburgh to Rosslyn Chapel

Highlights

- **Cultural capital**
  Wander round Edinburgh, Scotland's stunning capital city, filled with history and grand architecture, where the medieval mingles with the modern

- **Coastal pleasures**
  Watch the myriad seabirds and rich marine wildlife from the rugged cliffs on the glorious East Lothian coast and enjoy the surprisingly sandy beaches

- **Historical romance**
  Visit ancient crumbling abbeys and grand historic houses in the spectacular and wild countryside of the Borders, the land that inspired the novels of Sir Walter Scott

Glorious view of the Borders, seen from Scott's View, on the road to Abbotsford

History and Romance in the Borders

The city of Edinburgh may be the jewel in Scotland's crown, but just a short drive south is a glorious landscape that many people have yet to discover. This circular route takes in coastal towns and villages standing on rugged cliffs by inviting golden sands, as seabirds screech and wheel overhead. It then sweeps inland to the Borders, where mighty rivers like the Tweed flow past bustling towns and ancient abbeys, and where grand historic houses sit in tranquil countryside. The route finally heads north to its last stop at Rosslyn Chapel, famous for its extraordinary – and mysterious – carvings.

Above North Berwick Law, the hill south of the Scottish Seabird Centre, *see p217*

ACTIVITIES

Go ghost hunting in Mary King's Close, the warren of alleys under Edinburgh

Sup a few drams of whisky in the Scotch Whisky Experience, Edinburgh

Take a Seafari in a boat to see puffins and guillemots, from the Scottish Seabird Centre

Walk along the Berwickshire Coastal Path to the lighthouse at St Abb's Head

Sample a Jacobite Ale in the historic 18th-century brewery at Traquair House

Decipher the secret code in the mysterious carvings at Rosslyn Chapel

0 kilometres 10

0 miles 10

Above Princes Street as seen from Calton Hill, Edinburgh, *see p216*

PLAN YOUR DRIVE

Start/finish: Edinburgh to Rosslyn Chapel.

Number of days: 2–3 days, with at least half a day in Edinburgh.

Distance: Approx 362 km (225 miles).

Road conditions: Generally good roads and signposting; some Border roads can be very narrow and the scenic B709 to Traquair House often gets snowbound in winter.

When to go: Best for birdlife in spring and early summer, best for colour in the autumn.

Opening times: Museums and attractions are generally open 10am–5pm, but may close earlier (or are closed altogether) Nov–Easter. Shops are often open longer. Churches are usually open until dusk.

Main market days: Kelso: Farmers' Market, 4th Sat of month; **Traquair House**: Peebles Farmers' Market, 2nd Sat of month.

Shopping: Shop for fine cashmere and woollens in the Borders – especially around Selkirk and Kelso, the heart of Scotland's knitwear industry.

Main festivals: Edinburgh: Festival and Festival Fringe, mid-Aug–early Sep; **Manderston House**: Duns Summer Festival, Jul; **Dryburgh Abbey, Abbotsford & Traquair House**: Selkirk, Melrose & Peebles: Common Ridings, Jun.

DAY TRIP OPTIONS

Familes staying in Edinburgh will enjoy looking around a **royal palace** and some **haunted alleyways**, before exploring the **ancient bastion** of Edinburgh Castle. Then drive off to North Berwick to see the **puffins** and **seals** at the Scottish Seabird Centre and go on an **island boat trip**, before relaxing on the **beach**. History-lovers should head to Kelso to see the local **abbey** and magnificent **castle**, then on to the **abbey** at Dryburgh and Sir Walter Scott's characterful **house**, Abbotsford, before enjoying the glorious **countryside** on the way to a historic **country house**, dating back to 1107. For full details, *see p219*.

Right Field of rapeseed on the drive from St Abb's Head to Manderston House, *see p217*

Map labels

North Sea

dhame
Whitekirk
Tynninghame — Dunbar
Broxburn
prain
B6370 — Spott — Skateraw
Stenton — A1 — Dunglass
Innerwick — Cove
Halls
OTHIAN — Cockburnspath
Hills
Ecclaw
B6355 — Grantshouse — Houndwood
Harchead — Quixwood — A6112
Abbey St Bathans — Auchencrow
Ellemford — Marygold — B6438
B6355 — Preston — Lintlew
Longformacus — Edrom — Chirnside
MANDERSTON HOUSE 4 — Allanton — Hutton — Foulden
Duns — Blackadder — A6105 — Paxton
Gavinton — B6437 — B6460 — Fishwick
estruther — B6456 — Polwarth — Whitstone — B6461 — Horncliffe
BORDERS — Fogo — A6112 — Swinton
A697 — A6105 — Swintonmill — Norham
Houndslow — B6460 — B6437 — A698
Greenlaw — A697 — Simprim
Gordon — Leitholm — Tweed
Hume
6105 — A6089 — B6364 — Coldstream — Cornhill on Tweed
B6397 — Stichill — B6461 — Birgham
Nenthorn — A698 — Learmouth
Smailholm — Ednam — B6350
56 — B6404
DRYBURGH ABBEY — Floors Castle — 5 KELSO
6 — Clintmains — A699 — Roxburgh — B6352
t Boswells — Rutherford
A68 — A698

ST ABB'S HEAD 3 — St Abb's
A1107 — B6438
Coldingham
Eyemouth
A1 — Reston — Ayton
B6355

LOTHIAN — Hills

KEY

▬▬ Drive route

Above *Princes St, Edinburgh with the Balmoral Hotel and Scott's Monument on the left*

VISITING EDINBURGH

Parking
There are car parks by Waverley Station, at Castle Terrace and at Greenside Place.

Tourist Information
3 Princes Street, EH2 2QP; 0131 473 3868; www.edinburgh.org

WHERE TO STAY

EDINBURGH

The Bonham *moderate–expensive*
This chic town house in a leafy corner of the West End has boutique rooms.
35 Drumsheugh Gardens, EH3 7RN; 0131 274 7400; www.townhousecompany.com

NORTH BERWICK

The Glebe House *moderate*
This lovely mansion has four charming rooms and picturesque views.
Law Road, EH39 4PL; 01620 892 608; www.glebehouse-nb.co.uk

AROUND NORTH BERWICK

The Castle Inn *inexpensive*
There are five beautiful bedrooms at this coaching inn on the A198 to Edinburgh.
Manse Road, Dirleton, EH39 5EP; 01620 850 221; www.castleinndirleton.com

❶ Edinburgh
Lothian; EH1

With its brooding castle, dramatic crags and rich history, Edinburgh is Scotland's most romantic city as well as its capital. Visitors have long been fascinated by the medieval streets of the Old Town and charmed by the Georgian squares of the New Town, before being entertained in the city's many bars and restaurants. It's no wonder that it has inspired generations of writers, from Robert Louis Stevenson to J K Rowling.

A three-hour walking tour

Start from Waverley Station car park. Walk uphill on New Street, turn right onto Market St, and then left at a roundabout up Cockburn St. Traverse the medieval Old Town, with its cobbled streets, wynds (alleys) and high buildings – the city was once enclosed by a wall, so built upwards. At the top, turn left and walk down the High Street – the Royal Mile. Pass **John Knox House** ① *(open Mon–Sat; Jul–Aug also Sun pm)*, a distinctive 16th-century building said to have been home to the religious reformer. Next is **Canongate Kirk** ② *(open daily):* the 18th-century economist Adam Smith and David Rizzio, the secretary to Mary Queen of Scots killed by her jealous husband, Lord Darnley, are both buried here. At the end of the Royal Mile is the new Scottish Parliament, opposite the Queen's official residence in Scotland, the **Palace of Holyroodhouse** ③ *(open daily, except royal visits).*

Head back up the Royal Mile, past Cockburn St to **St Giles' Cathedral** ④ *(open daily),* which was founded in the 12th-century. It was from here that Knox led the Scottish Reformation. Nearby is **Mary King's Close** ⑤ *(open daily),* a warren of ancient, supposedly haunted streets beneath the city.

Beyond the cathedral, turn left onto George IV Bridge, then right down charming Victoria St, lined with specialist shops. At the bottom, bear right into the **Grassmarket** ⑥ – now bustling with pubs and shops, but once the haunt of 19th-century body-snatchers Burke and Hare. They lured their victims here and sold the bodies to a local surgeon. Part way down the Grassmarket, turn right up Castle Wynd South. Go up the steep steps, cross the road at the top and up more steps to Castle Hill. Edinburgh's great **castle** ⑦ *(open daily)* is on the left. Set on an extinct volcano, it dates back to the 12th century, but has been a fortress since AD 600. Its treasures include the Honours of Scotland (the Scottish Crown Jewels) and Mons Meg, one of the world's oldest cannons.

Walk down Castle Hill, stopping to sample a few "drams" at the **Scotch Whisky Experience** ⑧ *(open daily)* on the right. At Bank St, turn left and go down The Mound, then walk down Playfair Steps. The **National Gallery of Scotland** ⑨ *(open daily)* is on the left, and good views of the monument to Sir Walter Scott, to the right. Cross Princes St, then walk up Hanover St, to the grand avenues and buildings of the 18th-century Georgian New Town, built so the wealthy could escape the squalor of the Old Town.

Continue to George St, the city's smartest shopping area. Turn left to Charlotte Square, designed by Robert Adam, and bear right to the north side of the square to **The Georgian House** ⑩ *(open daily)*, a fine example of an Edinburgh town house. Retrace the route to Princes St, turn left back up to the station car park.

🚗 *From station car park, turn left onto New Street, left along Calton Rd to a T-junction, left on Leith St and then left onto A1. Beyond the fringes of the city turn left onto A198, taking coastal road to North Berwick. Park on streets near harbour and seabird centre.*

❷ North Berwick
The Harbour, North Berwick; EH39 4SS
With hi-tech cameras on its islands, the **Scottish Seabird Centre** *(open daily; www.seabird.org)* allows visitors to view wildlife all year round. In summer, there are puffins and gannets rearing their young; in winter, grey seals and their dark-eyed pups. Visitors control the cameras, and there are telescopes on the viewing deck. Seabird Seafaris also runs trips around the islands in fast boats. Head to the town's seafront for a game of crazy golf or just take it easy on the sandy beach.

🚗 *Continue on A198 to rejoin A1. After Cockburnspath, turn left onto A1107 and then left on B6438 to St Abb's. The Reserve is to the left just before town.*

❸ St Abb's Head
Nr Eyemouth, Berwickshire; TD14 5QF
The **St Abb's Head National Nature Reserve** has an interactive exhibition and visitor centre detailing various coastal walks, which offer dramatic clifftop views. The most interesting walk goes to the remote lighthouse, built in 1862 by the Stevenson family (relatives of author R L Stevenson):

once lit by an oil lamp it's now fully automated. Next to the visitor centre is a little café *(May–Aug: open daily)*. Continue into **St Abb's** to see the charming harbour.

🚗 *Leave on B6438, cross the A1 (right then left), staying on B6438, and turn left on B6437. Then right on A6105 to the main gates, from where signs lead to the car park and entrance.*

❹ Manderston House
Duns, Berwickshire; TD11 3PP
A superb Edwardian country mansion, Manderston *(May–Sep: open Thu & Sun pm; www.manderston.co.uk)* was built by Sir James Miller, a wealthy baronet, to impress society. Its most extravagant feature is the silver staircase. The house is now home to Lord and Lady Palmer, of Huntley and Palmers biscuits.

🚗 *Drive into Duns and take A6112 to Swinton, then take B6461 to Kelso. Park in or around the main square.*

Below View of the craggy coastline looking north from St Abb's Head

Above left The grand façade of Manderston House, remodelled in 1871 **Top right** View south across the grass terrace at Manderston House **Above right** The hi-tech Scottish Seabird Centre, North Berwick

EAT AND DRINK

EDINBURGH

David Bann *moderate*
Delicious, imaginative vegetarian food such as roast aubergine chickpea cake or risotto with asparagus, fennel and peas.
56–8 Street Mary's St, EH1 1SX; 0131 556 5888; www.davidbann.com

NORTH BERWICK

The Grange *moderate*
The seasonal menu at this popular restaurant might include steak from the local butcher and garden herbs.
35 High Street, EH39 4HH; 01620 893 344; www.grangenorthberwick.co.uk

Osteria No 1 *moderate*
Excellent Italian food at this acclaimed restaurant, which serves a good value 3-course lunch. Mains might feature chicken breast stuffed with pancetta. Try the creamy pannacotta for dessert.
7 High Street, EH39 4HG; 01620 890 589; www.osteria-no1.co.uk

AROUND NORTH BERWICK

Ducks at Aberlady *moderate*
This award-winning restaurant on the A198 to Edinburgh has 23 rooms too.
Main Street, Aberlady, EH32 0RE; 01875 870 682; www.ducks.co.uk

ST ABB'S HEAD

The Old Smiddy Cafe *inexpensive*
Pleasant little café in a former cottage on the outskirts of St Abbs. Serves soups, baguettes and cakes and has seats outside for fine days.
By Nature Reserve Visitor Centre, TD14 5QF; 01890 71707; open daily May–Aug; Mar & Apr weekends only

Eat and Drink: inexpensive, under £25; moderate, £25–£50; expensive, over £50

Above Characterful Abbotsford House, once home to Sir Walter Scott **Above top right** Floors Castle, still home to the Duke of Roxburghe **Above right** Ruined stone archway of 12th-century Kelso Abbey

VISITING KELSO

Parking
If there are no spaces on the square, there are several small car parks nearby, just off the B6461 in Bowmont St, East Bowmont St and Jamieson's Entry.

Tourist Information
Town House, The Square, TD5 7HF; 01835 863 170; www.visitscotland.com

WHERE TO STAY

AROUND KELSO

The Roxburghe Hotel *expensive*
A little way south of Kelso, just off the A698, this imposing historic house has real fires in winter and is set in extensive grounds. As well as luxurious rooms and suites, the hotel also boasts its own golf course, sporting estate and a fine, candlelit restaurant.
Heiton, TD5 8JZ; 01573 238 116; www.roxburghe.net

AROUND ABBOTSFORD

Glen Hotel *moderate*
This handsome Victorian mansion overlooking the River Ettrick has nine rooms, plus a bar and restaurant. Local outdoor activities include fishing.
Yarrow Terrace, Selkirk, TD7 5AS; 01750 20259; www.glenhotel.co.uk

Below The pretty gardens at 15th-century Rosslyn Chapel, Roslin

⑤ Kelso
Roxburghshire; TD5

Kelso is a handsome town on the River Tweed. Near the main square are the ruins of 12th-century **Kelso Abbey**, once one of Scotland's richest abbeys, still with traces of beautifully carved stonework. On the edge of town is **Floors Castle** *(May–Oct: open daily; www. floorscastle.com)*, a grand stately home (1721) set in vast grounds and still home to the Duke of Roxburghe. The sumptuous rooms boast vibrant tapestries and paintings by masters such as Turner, Gainsborough and Hogarth. Golfers may want to try the **Roxburgh Hotel Golf Course** *(see left)*.

🚗 *Leave on A6089 towards Edinburgh, exit left onto B6397, then turn left on B6404. Turn right on B6356 through Clintmains and then left to Dryburgh Abbey and car park.*

⑥ Dryburgh Abbey
St Boswells, Melrose; TD6 0RQ

Founded in the 11th century and built in soft red sandstone, **Dryburgh Abbey** *(open daily)* was frequently damaged in the Border wars between the Scots and the English. However, its beauty is still evident, making for a delightful stroll around the ruins: the refectory's ornate rose window, for example, is still intact. Two famous Scots are buried here: the historical romance writer Sir Walter Scott, and WWI commander Field-Marshal Earl Haig. Their graves are in the ruined north transept chapel.

🚗 *Take B6356 marked Earlston up to Scott's View, with views of the Eildon Hills. Beyond, turn left and left again at two unmarked junctions and onto B6360. Pass under a viaduct, through Gattonside and turn left on B6374. Go right towards A7 and A68, straight over roundabout onto A6091, then left on B6360 to Abbotsford and car park.*

⑦ Abbotsford
Melrose; TD6 9BQ

There's more than a touch of drama about Abbotsford *(mid-Mar–Nov: open daily; www.scottsabbotsford.co.uk)*, which was the home of 19th-century novelist Sir Walter Scott, the author of classic tales such as *Ivanhoe*. He commissioned the house himself and it's full of character, with suits of armour in the oak-panelled hall, his battered leather writing chair in the study and thousands of books crammed onto the shelves of his well-used library. The windows of the house overlook the Tweed, the river he loved. A visitor centre explores Scott's life.

🚗 *From car park go left on B6360, then A7 into Selkirk. Here take A707, then A708 through dramatic scenery, turning right onto B709. This is the remote Borders: there's not a settlement to be seen. Follow signs for Traquair House.*

⑧ Traquair House
Innerleithen, Peeblesshire; EH44 6PW
Scotland's oldest inhabited house, Traquair *(Apr–Oct: open daily; Nov: open Sat & Sun; www.traquair.co.uk)* dates back to at least 1107. It is home to the Maxwell-Stuart family and is steeped in history. The house boasts relics such as Mary Queen of Scots' son's cradle, as well as a concealed room with secret stairs – a means of escape for priests, when Catholics were persecuted in the 16th to 18th centuries. The family were loyal supporters of James II and VI and the Stuart monarchs,

and today make a Jacobite Ale, based on an 18th-century recipe, in their historic brewery.

🚗 *From Traquair, go left on B709 towards Innerleithen, then take A72 towards Peebles. On the outskirts of the town pick up A703 going north; at Leadburn turn right on A6094 to Rosewell, then descend steeply left on B7003. Turn right on B7006 and right again to Rosslyn Chapel.*

⑨ Rosslyn Chapel
Chapel Loan, Roslin; EH25 9PU
Stepping inside Rosslyn Chapel *(open daily; www.rosslynchapel.com)*, it is hard to decide where to look first, there are so many extraordinary – and mysterious – carvings. An angel plays the bagpipes; pagan "Green Men" peer down from pillars; there is even maize, carved here years before the New World was "discovered". The chapel, built for the St Clair family in 1450, is perhaps best known for the lavishly carved Apprentice Pillar, thought by some to conceal the Holy Grail, brought here by the Knights Templar – a theory popularized in the book and film *The Da Vinci Code*.

🚗 *Drive north on B7006, then turn right onto A701 to central Edinburgh.*

DAY TRIP OPTIONS

Edinburgh and Kelso would make good bases for families and history-lovers to explore the area.

Ghosts and Coasts
Staying in Edinburgh ❶, walk around the city, visit the Palace of Holyroodhouse and listen to tales of how people lived cheek-by-jowl in Mary King's Close and the Grassmarket, before stocking up on picnic supplies

and heading to North Berwick ❷ for the Scottish Seabird Centre and a Seafari to see the birds up close. Finish the day relaxing on the beach.

Follow the A1, then the A198. Retrace the route to return.

Border Romance
From Kelso ❺, see Kelso Abbey and Floors Castle. Next, head for the romantic ruins of Dryburgh Abbey ❻, burial place of Sir Walter Scott,

before heading to his former home, Abbotsford ❼. Tour Scott's home, evocative of his dashing fictional tales, with suits of armour and memorabilia, before visiting Traquair House ❽, steeped in history and drama. Drive back through the wild and beautiful Scottish Border countryside.

Follow the drive instructions to get to all the stops, but return via the A72 and A699, if pressed for time.

Eat and Drink: inexpensive, under £25; moderate, £25–£50; expensive, over £50

The Kingdom of Fife

St Andrews to Culross

Highlights

- **The home of golf**
  Explore the ancient university town of St Andrews, with its tightly packed medieval street plan, cathedral and castle, and the oldest golf course in the world

- **Pleasures of the East Neuk coast**
  Stride out along the coastal walking path, take to the seas to watch the abundant wildlife, or stroll around a pretty fishing village

- **Royal retreats**
  Tour fabulous Renaissance Falkland Palace, built for James IV of Scotland, and the romantic ruins of the castle in beautiful Loch Leven where Mary Queen of Scots was imprisoned

Fishing paraphernalia at pretty Pittenweem in the East Neuk of Fife, along the coast from Anstruther

The Kingdom of Fife

Squeezed between the Firth of Tay and the Firth of Forth, Fife was for centuries isolated from the rest of Scotland and still retains its distinctive character. The region was once the seat of Scottish kings and this tour includes some of its most fascinating sights. From St Andrews, with its hallowed golf courses, ancient university – and bracing North Sea winds – the route leads to a former military bunker, hidden deep underground. This subterranean secret is followed by a succession of picturesque fishing villages that line the Fife coast. The route then winds inland past fertile fields, castles and palaces, before returning to the coast in the immaculately preserved mercantile town of Culross.

Map showing the Kingdom of Fife region with locations including:

A92, Moonzie, Lindores, Letham, Bow of Fife, B937, Collessie, Springfield, B936, Auchtermuchty, Dunshalt, A92, A912, Strathmiglo, Ladybank, Kingskettle, A912, A914, Glenfarg, Gateside, A91, FALKLAND PALACE 6, B936, Kettlebridge, PERTH AND KINROSS, Freuchie, Muirhead, Lomond Hills, F I F E, Dalqueich, Milnathort, B919, Kinesswood, B996, Kennoway, Canbo, A91, A922, Kinesswood, Leslie, Markinch, Loch Leven Castle, A977, Kinross, A911, Windygat, Pool of Muckart, Drum, 7 LOCH LEVEN, B920, Glenrothes, Coldrain, B996, B9097, Leven, Coaltown of Balgonie, Devon, B9097, Kinglassie, B922, Cleish, Ballingry, Thornton, Blairingone, A823, Lochore, East Wemyss, Devonside, A908, Loch Glow, Auchterderran, A92, Sauchie, Mill, A977, Loch Ore, Glencraig, Wes, Wen, Alloa, B913, Kelty, A92, Chapel, Gallatown, Saline, Lochgelly, A910, Dysart, A907, Loch Fitty, A909, Kingseat, Cowdenbeath, B917, Kirkcaldy, Kennet, B914, Auchtertool, B925, A921, Comrie, Wellwood, Denibristle, Airth, Kincardine, A985, Dunfermline, Fordell, A909, Kinghorn, New Mills, A994, 2A, A823, M90, 8 CULROSS, Torryburn, Mastertown, A921, Aberdour, Burntisland, Charlestown, A985, Rosyth, Bo'ness, Bridgeness, Inverkeithing, North Queensferry, FORTH ROAD BRIDGE, South Queensferry, F i r t h

Below Lower Largo, home of Alexander Selkirk, the real Robinson Crusoe, *see p226*

ACTIVITIES

Play a round of golf on the famous Old Course in St Andrews

Walk the invigorating Fife Coast Path from Anstruther

Go canoeing, abseiling, or mountain biking in the East Neuk of Fife

Take a boat trip to see the wildlife on the Isle of May

Go birdwatching to spot the lapwings and pink-footed geese at Loch Leven

Take a ferry to the island on Loch Leven to see Mary Queen of Scots' prison

Walk up the hill to the abbey overlooking Culross

KEY

███ Drive route

0 kilometres   5

0 miles   5

Below Fertile farmland on the East Neuk of Fife, near Anstruther, *see p225*

PLAN YOUR DRIVE

Start/finish: St Andrews to Culross.

Number of Days: 1–2 days, possibly 3, if spending more than a day at St Andrews.

Distances: Approx. 148 km (92 miles).

Road conditions: Generally good, though the roads can be busy – signposting is reasonable.

When to go: Late spring and early autumn are good times to visit, though golfers might prefer the long summer days for endless hours on the links.

Opening times: Museums and attractions are generally open 10am–5pm, but close earlier (or are closed altogether) Nov–Easter. Shop times are longer. Churches are usually open until dusk.

Main market days: St Andrews: Farmers' Market, 1st Sat of month.

Shopping: Pick up hand-thrown items from Crail Pottery; local art from the Fisher Studio in Pittenweem; and golf clubs and apparel from Auchterlonie's in St Andrews.

Major festivals: St Andrews: Golf Week, Apr; Anstruther: East Neuk Festival (arts), Jun–Jul; Pittenweem Arts Festival, late Jul/early Aug; Ceres: Highland Games (last Sat of Jun); Crail: Food Festival (mid-Jun); Culross: Culross Festival (arts), Jun.

DAY TRIP OPTIONS

St Andrews makes a great base for exploring Fife and there is plenty to guarantee happy families. In St Andrews, see the **home of golf** at the Old Course, visit the **ancient university** and the **cathedral**, and take a stroll on the **beach**; then head off to Ceres for the **folk museum** and finish off at Falkland for a **royal palace**. Alternatively, visit **St Andrews castle**, with its dungeon, and then head to Scotland's **secret underground bunker**. Continue to Anstruther for **canoeing**, **abseiling**, **cycling**, **walking** or watching the wildlife on a **boat trip**. Finally, do some **ghost hunting** on a tour of a spooky castle. For full details, *see p227*.

Above Victorian bandstand in the seafront park at St Andrews

VISITING ST ANDREWS

Parking
There is parking by the harbour.

Tourist Information
70 Market St, KY16 9NU; 01334 472 021

Playing golf
There are seven links (seaside) golf courses. A daily ballot decides who plays on the Old Course. For all courses, contact **St Andrews Links** (*01334 466 718; www.standrews.org.uk*).

WHERE TO STAY

ST ANDREWS

Doune House *inexpensive*
Close to the Old Course and the centre, this Victorian town house B&B has modern rooms with tartan touches.
5 Murray Place, KY16 9AP; 01334 475 195; www.dounehouse.com

The Macdonald Rusacks Hotel
moderate–expensive
The Rusacks is set beside the Old Course and West Sands, the beach featured in the film *Chariots of Fire*.
Pilmour Links, KY16 9JQ; 0844 879 9136; www.macdonaldhotels.co.uk/rusacks

ANSTRUTHER

Crichton House *inexpensive*
Close to the coastal path, this B&B has light-filled, unfussy en-suite bedrooms, some with superb views.
High Street West, KY10 3DJ; 01333 310219; www.crichtonhouse.co.uk

Craw's Nest Hotel *moderate*
Ask for a room with a sea view at this 3-star hotel, which is close to the 9-hole golf course. It's also a good choice for families, with its attractive gardens and friendly staff.
Bankwell Road, KY10 3DA; 01333 310 691; www.crawsnesthotel.co.uk

Where to Stay: inexpensive, under £80; moderate, £80–£150; expensive, over £150

① St Andrews
Fife; KY16
The **Old Course**, the oldest golf course in the world, attracts thousands of visitors to St Andrews each year. Yet it was religion that first made the city famous. Legend tells that, in the 4th century, St Rule brought the relics of St Andrew from Constantinople to Scotland and kept them in a chapel here, founding the city. They were moved to **St Andrews Cathedral** (*open daily*), after it was built in 1160. Nearby **St Andrews Castle** (*joint ticket with cathedral*) was the residence of senior clergy. Both buildings are now ruined but they still make an imposing pair. Visitors can peer into the castle's bottle-shaped dungeon, into which prisoners were dropped with no hope of release. The **university**, founded in 1410, is the oldest in Scotland and brims with artifacts. It is possible to visit two of the college quads – St Salvator's in North St and St Mary's in South St. The latter has a thorn tree, supposedly planted by Mary Queen of Scots.

🚗 *From harbour car park drive uphill to North St (A917) and turn left. Turn right onto B9131, then left onto B940 following signs for Scotland's Secret Bunker. There is parking on site.*

Below Anstruther Harbour, once busy with the Scottish herring fleet **Below top right** The Isle of May, seen from the cliffs at Anstruther **Below right** Anstruther beach, sheltered by the harbour walls

Highland Fling
Highland Games are an established part of the summer scene in Scotland. Contestants take part in events such as "tossing the caber" (throwing a large wooden post), swinging the hammer, and piping and dancing competitions. They have their origins in ancient gatherings such as *wappinschaws* – where clans gathered to test their military skills. Modern, formal Games date to 1820 and the revival of Highland culture encouraged by writer Sir Walter Scott.

② Scotland's Secret Bunker
Crown Buildings, Troywood; KY16 8QH
Enter the secret world of surveillance in this former military bunker, hidden far beneath an isolated farmhouse. Scotland's Secret Bunker (*Mar–Oct: open daily; www.secretbunker.co.uk*), encased in thick concrete, was to have been the HQ of operations, had the UK come under nuclear attack during the Cold War. In the vast labyrinth, visitors can see the basic dormitories, communications equipment and the little chapel.

🚗 *Return to the B940 and turn right, then right again to take A917. Drive along coast road to Anstruther. Park by harbour.*

❸ Anstruther

Fife; KY10

A charming fishing village typical of the East Neuk (corner) of Fife, Anstruther was once one of the busiest ports in Scotland. The harbour now mainly holds yachts, but the town still has plenty of character with its pubs, award-winning fish and chip shop, and charming buildings. Visitors can also walk the Fife Coastal Path, enjoy a multitude of outdoor activities, or take a boat to the Isle of May to see the wildlife.

A two-hour walking tour

From the car park, bear left (if facing the harbour) and walk past the RNLI lifeboat station to visit the **Scottish Fisheries Museum** ① *(open daily; www. scotfishmuseum.org)* telling the history of the local fishing industry. Walk along James St by the shore. When the 16th-century Tolbooth and council chamber is visible, carry on along John St and then George St, keeping the sea to the right. Look for clues that the houses were for fishermen: some upper windows have posts used for drying fishing nets. Other properties have external staircases (good for drying nets and creels) and Dutch-style gables on the roofs (Holland was a historic trading partner).

Walk past **Cellardyke Harbour** ②, after which there is a caravan park on the left-hand side. Out to sea lies the Isle of May, on which stands a ruined 12th-century monastery and the oldest lighthouse in Scotland (1635). A National Nature Reserve, the island is home to seals and colonies of puffins, guillemots and razorbills.

Soon after Cellardyke, the path turns into a grassy track and passes a pig farm on the left. Go through a gate next to a seat, then another gate. Look out for fishing boats bobbing on the sea. To the left are fields where, in summer, the long grasses and wild flowers come alive with clouds of bees, butterflies and other insects.

Eventually, climb a few steps over a low wall, and go straight ahead – look out for the cormorants that often perch on rocks by the shore. Cross a tiny bridge above a brook and carry on beside the sea. Climb a few more steps over a wall, and follow the shore to a large **outcrop of rocks** ③ – the layers of sediment deposited over the centuries can be seen in the exposed stone. Around a corner, the path enters a grassy area with lots of gorse growing on the left.

Cross another bridge over a brook to see the village of Crail in the distance. If the tide is out, the pretty **shell beach** ④ here is a good place for a breather, with large rocks as convenient seats. For those with stamina, the path goes on to Crail, otherwise retrace the walk back to the car park for some well-earned fish and chips by the harbour.

🚗 *Drive back to A917 and follow to Pittenweem. Then turn right into Charles St; follow the road taking the right fork and then turn left onto B9171. Turn right for castle and car park.*

ANSTRUTHER ACTIVITIES

For canoeing, abseiling, climbing, cycling and archery, try **East Neuk Outdoors** *(01333 311 929; www.eastneukoutdoors. co.uk)*. For boat trips to the Isle of May buy tickets from **Anstruther Pleasure Trips** from the harbour *(07957 585 200; www.isleofmayferry.com)*.

EAT AND DRINK

ST ANDREWS

The Glass House *inexpensive*
This laid-back restaurant in the centre of town serves pizzas, pastas and salads. *80 North Street, KY16 9AH; 01334 473 673; www.houserestaurants.com*

The Doll's House *moderate*
Popular restaurant serving Scottish-French dishes such as Scottish lamb with puy lentils, and sticky toffee pudding. *3 Church Square, KY16 9NN; 01334 477 422; www.houserestaurants.com*

ANSTRUTHER

Anstruther Fish Bar *inexpensive*
This legendary fish and chip shop consistently wins awards for its food. *42–4 Shore Street, KY10 3AQ; 01333 310 518; www.anstrutherfishbar.co.uk*

The Cellar *moderate*
This restaurant serves modern Scottish dishes, with an emphasis on seafood. *24 East Green, KY10 3AA; 01333 310 378; closed Sun; lunch served Fri & Sat; www.thecellaranstruther.co.uk*

Below Beautiful scenery on the Anstruther to Crail coastal path

Above Victorian-style gardens surround the ancient home of Kellie Castle, rumoured to be haunted **Above top right** Imposing walls and turrets of Kellie Castle **Above right** Falkland Palace, once a royal hunting lodge

⑤ Fife Folk Museum
Fife; KY15 5NF

The attractive village of Ceres is home to the **Fife Folk Museum** *(Apr–Oct: open daily; www.fifefolkmuseum.org)*, which sheds light on the history of the working people of Fife. Housed in a 17th-century building, the museum contains a vivid array of items, from agricultural implements to patchwork quilts and a Victorian "bone-shaker" bicycle. A cottage living room has been reconstructed to recreate the feel of a home in the pre-industrial age.

🚗 *Return on B939 to A916. Turn right, then after Scotstarvit Tower, fork left down a minor road. At A914, turn left (signed Glenrothes), then right on a minor road beyond Kettlebridge, crossing A92 onto B936 through Freuchie and on to Falkland. Turn right briefly onto A912, then left into East Port to High St, palace and town car park.*

The Real Robinson Crusoe

Alexander Selkirk, born in Lower Largo in the 17th century, was the inspiration for Daniel Defoe's novel *Robinson Crusoe*. Selkirk went to sea as a youth and in 1704 was serving as a sailing master on the vessel *Cinque Ports*. He quarrelled with the captain and asked to leave the ship. His wish was granted, and he was put ashore on Juan Fernandez, an uninhabited island off Chile. He lived there for over four years until being rescued in 1709.

④ Kellie Castle
Pittenweem; KY10 2RF

Kellie Castle *(Apr, May, Sep & Oct: open Thu–Mon; Jun–Aug: open daily)* dates as far back as the 14th century and is said to be haunted. It was largely rebuilt by the Lorimer family in the 19th century, after it had almost fallen into ruin. The rooms contain fine paintings, grand plaster ceilings and furniture designed by Arts and Crafts architect Sir Robert Lorimer. There are superb views of the Bass Rock and a Victorian-style garden, with roses and herbaceous plants.

🚗 *Turn right onto B9171, then left at B942 to A917. Turn right and at Upper Largo, go straight onto A915 (or detour to Lower Largo – see box), then turn right onto B927 to travel away from the coast. Turn right on A916 north, then right onto B939 into Ceres. The museum is on High St, on the right.*

⑥ Falkland Palace
Falkland; KY15 7BU

The magnificent Renaissance **Falkland Palace** *(Mar–Oct: open daily)* dominates the village. Built as a royal hunting lodge for James IV of Scotland in the 15th century, it became the Stuart monarchs' favourite retreat – Mary

Right RSPB Vane Farm, set on the beautiful shores of Loch Leven

Where to Stay: inexpensive, under £80; moderate, £80–£150; expensive, over £150

Queen of Scots was also very fond of it. As well as touring the palace itself, with its Flemish tapestries and painted ceilings, visitors can visit the gardens and the Real Tennis court, built in 1539.

🚗 *Return to A912, turn left to A91. Turn left again, then merge onto B996 to Milnathort. Turn left onto A922, then straight onto B996 into centre of Kinross. Turn left onto Burns Beggs St, then right onto Pier Rd to the car park for the ferry to Loch Leven Castle.*

Above Falkland Palace gardens, home to Britain's oldest tennis court

7 Loch Leven
By Kinross; KY13 8UF
Loch Leven is famed for the lonely **castle** *(Apr–Oct: open daily)*, perched on an island in its waters, only accessible by ferry. Mary Queen of Scots was imprisoned here on the order of Elizabeth I. While here, Mary was forced to abdicate in favour of her son, James VI. She escaped after a year with the help of her jailer, but was locked up again at Fotheringay in England. The 14th-century castle is now a ruin, but full of atmosphere.

The loch is also noted for its rich bird life. Head south on B996, then left on B9097 to the **Royal Society for the Protection of Birds Vane Farm** *(open daily)*, with nature trails and viewing points – from here look for regular visitors such as pink-footed geese.

🚗 *From Loch Leven Pier, return to B996 and turn right, then left onto Station Rd. Continue on to the A977 and follow it all the way to Kincardine, then head left to join A985 (towards Forth Road Bridge). After 6 km (4 miles) turn right down Gallows Loan to Culross. Park in the town centre near the palace.*

8 Culross
Culross; KY12 8JH
Culross (pronounced "koo-ross") was one of Scotland's largest ports in the 16th century: ships took coal and salt from Fife to the Low Countries and returned with red pantiles, which were used as roofing. This once prosperous town, with its Dutch-influenced architecture and cobbled streets, is almost perfectly preserved. Main sights include **Culross Palace** *(Apr, May & Sep: open Thu–Mon; Jun–Aug: open daily; Oct: open Fri–Mon)*, which was built for a local merchant; and **The Study** *(joint adm with palace)* a 17th-century tower house. It is also worth walking up to the ruined **abbey**, founded by the Cistercians in the 13th century, which can be found on the hills above town.

Above The 17th-century Town House, an example of Dutch-style architecture in Culross

EAT AND DRINK

AROUND KELLIE CASTLE
The Inn at Lathones *moderate*
This former coaching inn has a popular restaurant, serving traditional dishes such as game suet pudding with root vegetable mash. Take B942, then B941 to Largoward, then right on A915.
Largoward, KY9 1JE; 01334 840 494; www.innatlathones.com

Sangsters *moderate–expensive*
This Michelin-starred restaurant serves fine Scottish produce such as venison, crab, beef and salmon. Vegetarians catered for with notice. Take the coastal road (A917) from Pittenweem to Elie.
51 High Street, Elie, KY9 1BZ; 01333 331 001; www.sangsters.co.uk; closed Mon & Tue–Sat lunch; best to book

AROUND FIFE FOLK MUSEUM
The Peat Inn *moderate–expensive*
Michelin-starred food at this country inn, with the focus on fresh Scottish produce. Enjoy imaginative dishes such as cannelloni of langoustines and scallops. From Ceres, head north on B939, then right on B940 to Peat Inn.
Peat Inn, KY15 5LH; 01334 840 206; www.thepeatinn.co.uk; closed Sun & Mon

---

DAY TRIP OPTIONS
St Andrews is an excellent base from which to explore Fife.

Royal and Ordinary Fife
Spend the morning in St Andrews ①, with its famous royal golf course, university and ancient cathedral. Stroll along the golden beach, then drive to pretty Ceres to visit the Fife Folk Museum ⑤ and gain an insight

into the lives of the locals. Drive on to the Stuart monarchs' wonderful Renaissance Falkland Palace ⑥.

From St Andrews take A915, then B939 to Ceres. Follow drive instructions to Falkland. Retrace journey to return.

Family Fun in the East Neuk
In St Andrews ①, visit the castle dungeon and then drive to Scotland's

Secret Bunker ②, with lots for kids to enjoy. Next, visit Anstruther ③ for canoeing, cycling, a boat trip or just relaxing on the beach. If more excitement is needed, carry on to go ghost hunting at Kellie Castle ④.

Follow the drive instructions as far as Kellie Castle. To return, head back to B9171, turn left and carry on to B9131. Then turn left here to St Andrews.

The Wild West Coast of Scotland

Inveraray to Plockton

Highlights

- **Meeting the locals**
  See abundant wildlife: grey and common seals, playful otters, shy pine martens, majestic red deer and rare eagles

- **Natural splendour**
  Travel through some of the most stunning landscapes in Europe – deep sea lochs framed by wild, craggy mountains, and tumbling rivers running through steep-sided glens

- **Historic adventures**
  Visit Glencoe, scene of an infamous betrayal; take a boat to the cave that sheltered Bonnie Prince Charlie, and explore ancient castles with many colourful and historic connections

Glenelg Bay in the distance, seen from the road to Kylerhea Otter Hide

The Wild West Coast of Scotland

Scotland's west coast is the most dramatic, jagged coastline in Great Britain. The route starts on the shores of Loch Fyne, at the pretty town of Inveraray, whose grand castle is still a family home. It continues past stunning mountains and woodland, and through Glencoe, scene of a terrible massacre in 1692. Every now and then you'll see a mighty castle, testimony to the turbulent history of the area. Winding coastal routes lead to the remote Ardnamurchan Peninsula, before heading north to take the ferry across to the craggy mountains and sandy beaches of the Isle of Skye. The final stop is back on the mainland, among the palm trees of Plockton, warmed by the waters of the Gulf Stream.

Above White sand made of crushed seashells on the fabulous beach at Sanna, Ardnamurchan Peninsula, *see p234*

KEY

Drive route

ACTIVITIES

Travel deep inside a mountain at Cruachan Power Station

Climb up McCaig's tower at Oban for views of the Isle of Mull

Come eye-to-eye with an inquisitive stingray at the aquarium in the Scottish Sea Life Sanctuary

Explore the waterfalls and mountains at Glencoe and see the sites of the infamous massacre

Watch for rare pine martens and eagles in the remote Ardnamurchan Peninsula

Take a boat trip from Elgol to see Bonnie Prince Charlie's cave

Watch the otters that inspired the book *Ring of Bright Water* at the Kylerhea Otter Hide

Below Boats moored in the still waters of the port of Oban, *see p233*

Above Narrow, winding coast road on the Isle of Skye, *see pp234–5*

0 kilometres   10

0 miles   10

PLAN YOUR DRIVE

Start/finish: Inveraray to Plockton.

Number of days: About 5–6 days.

Distances: Approx. 478 km (297 miles).

Road conditions: Generally good, but with long stretches of single track roads (with passing places) which should be driven with care. The scenic track to Glenelg, on Skye, is not useable in snow or ice – use Skye Bridge.

When to go: High summer (Jul–Aug) offers long hours of daylight, but can get surprisingly busy. May, Jun, Sep and Oct are ideal. Please note, routes likely to get snowbound in winter.

Opening times: Museums and attractions are generally open 10am–5pm, but close earlier (or are closed altogether) Nov–Easter. Shop times are longer. Churches are usually open until dusk.

Main market days: Oban: Farmers' Market at Benderloch, near Oban, 1st and 3rd Thu of month.

Shopping: Skye has plenty of craft outlets, selling sheepskins, Celtic jewellery, pottery and knitwear. The island and other parts of the west coast, also attracts many artists, whose studios can be visited.

Major festivals: Inveraray: Highland Games, Jul; **Oban**: Highland and Islands Music & Dance, 4 days at the end of Apr; **Skye**: Highland Games, Aug.

DAY TRIP OPTIONS

With beautiful countryside and wildlife, Scotland is great for children. Stay at Inveraray to see its **castle**, before heading off to the **power station** at Cruachan and going deep inside the **mountain**. Picnic by the **loch** at the **iron furnace** at Bonawe and then see the **seals**, **rays** and other **fish** at a **sea life sanctuary**. Older romantics might prefer to stay at Plockton with its **palms** and **harbour** and then visit the **gardens** at Armadale. Carry on to Elgol to see the craggy Cuillin **mountains** and relive the **exploits** of a prince Then take a **ferry** and drive to dreamy **castle ruins**. For full details, *see p235*.

Above View of Argyll Hotel and church tower from Loch Fyne

VISITING INVERARAY

Tourist Information
Front Street, PA32 8UY; 08452 255 121; www.inveraray-argyll.com; Apr–Oct: open daily; Nov–Mar: closed Sun.

Parking
There is parking off The Avenue, in the centre of Inveraray, and by the castle.

WHERE TO STAY

INVERARAY

Creag Dhubh *inexpensive*
A large, detached house set in neat gardens, this family-run B&B has five bedrooms and great views over Loch Fyne.
Main Street South, PA32 8XT; 01499 302 430; www.creagdhubh.com

Loch Fyne Hotel and Spa *moderate*
Near the harbour, with stunning views of Loch Fyne, this hotel has comfortable, stylish rooms, a swimming pool and spa.
Main Street South, PA32 8XT; 01499 302 980; www.crerarhotels.com

Rudha-Na-Craige *moderate*
This handsome house was built in the 19th century by the Duke of Argyll. Now it is a 4-star B&B, with six unfussy, stylish bedrooms, all with views of Loch Fyne.
Inverarary, PA32 8YX; 01499 302 668; www.rudha-na-craige.com

BONAWE IRON FURNACE

Ardanaiseig Hotel *expensive*
Wildly romantic hotel on the shores of Loch Awe (take B845 from Taynuilt), this historic house has luxurious bedrooms.
Kilchrenan, by Taynuilt, Argyll, PA35 1HE; 01866 833 333; www.ardanaiseig.com

OBAN

Ranald Hotel *moderate*
Modern hotel just off Oban's main street with 17 en-suite rooms of varying sizes, including rooms for a small family.
41 Stevenson Street PA34 5NA; 01631 562 887; www.theranaldhotel.com

Where to Stay: inexpensive, under £80; moderate, £80–£150; expensive, over £150

① Inveraray
Argyll; PA32

Sitting on the banks of Loch Fyne, Inveraray is small but imposing. The town was built by the 3rd Duke of Argyll in the 18th century and has two main visitor attractions – its 19th-century jail and castle. The walk explores the surrounding woodland and starts with a visit to the castle.

A one-and-a-half-hour walking tour

From the car park, visit **Inveraray Castle** ① *(Apr–Oct: open daily; www.inveraray-castle.com)*. The building belongs to the Duke of Argyll, and the family are head of the Campbell clan – the 1st Duke's regiment carried out the notorious massacre at Glencoe *(see p234)*. It is crammed with tapestries, silverware and porcelain and unusual items such as Rob Roy's sporran.

From the castle entrance, look for the "Dun na Cuaich walk" signs and follow the blue arrows along a tarmac track. This soon passes a **monument** ②, commemorating the execution of 17 Campbell leaders by the 1st Marquis of Atholl in 1685. This was punishment for rising against the Stuart King James II in protest at his assertion that he was divine head of the church.

Cross the charming 18th-century **stone bridge** ③ – built by John Adam – that spans the River Aray, then bear right to go through the woods. At a gate, go straight ahead on the grassy track to reach another gate, which leads into woodland – in springtime the ground is carpeted with bluebells. The track soon passes a ruined former **lime kiln** ④ on the left hand side. Continue uphill, then branch right after a few minutes, still following the blue arrows.

Eventually the path bears to the right and flattens out a little, and the fresh scent of pine trees fills the air. After passing the remains of a wall, the woodland opens out, providing a glimpse of the surrounding hills. Zig-zag uphill now, to reach the summit, which is covered with wild flowers in summer and also has a welcome seat. The views of the castle, the town and the loch spread out far beneath are wonderful. **Dun na Cuaich** ⑤ means something like "fort of cups" in Gaelic and this peak was the site of an Iron-Age hillfort. The summit is topped with a monument, built by another of the famous Adam family of architects. Some say it was used as a watchtower by the Campbells, others that it was simply built to enhance the landscape.

After enjoying the views and taking a well-earned rest, simply follow the path back down to Inveraray. The

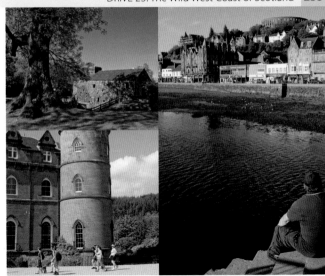

castle at the bottom has a café, where walkers can refuel on tea and cakes.

🚗 *Take the A819 north (signed for Oban) then, after views of Kilchurn Castle, turn left on the A85 to reach Cruachan Power Station and car park.*

② Cruachan Power Station
Dalmally, Argyll; PA33 1AN
Hidden deep inside Ben Cruachan, this hydro-electric power station, *(Apr–Oct: open daily; Nov–Mar: open Mon–Fri; closed Jan)* runs on water fed from a reservoir high on the mountain. Tours take visitors on a bus into a vast cavern in the heart of the mountain. Seeing the workings of this mighty structure feels like entering the world of James Bond. After a visit, try a brisk walk around the loch or to the top of Ben Cruachan, for views of the dam.

🚗 *Carry on A85, then turn right (signed Brochroy), when road splits, bear right to Bonawe Iron Furnace. Park on site.*

③ Bonawe Iron Furnace
By Taynuilt, Argyll; PA35 1JQ
It is hard to imagine industry in this tranquil spot by Loch Etive, but Bonawe *(Apr–Sep: open daily)* was once a flourishing iron furnace and what remains is Britain's best example of a charcoal-fuelled ironworks. The ironworks were built here in the 18th century because of the vast supply of wood from which charcoal could be made. Bonawe produced large numbers of cannonballs – some used by Lord Nelson in his sea battles.

🚗 *Return to the A85 and follow the road to Oban and park on street.*

④ Oban
Oban, Argyll; PA34
Attractive Oban is a bustling working port, with fishing boats bobbing amid the passenger ferries running to the Hebridean islands. Overlooking the town is **McCaig's Tower**, a monument

resembling the Colosseum in Rome. It was intended as a family memorial and to provide work for local masons. Started in 1897, it remained unfinished when McCaig died in 1902. Climb up for fine views to the islands.

Just outside town, on the A85, stand the romantic ruins of **Dunstaffnage Castle** *(Apr–Sep: open daily; Oct–Mar: open Sat–Wed)*, one of Scotland's oldest stone fortifications. It was built in the 13th century to defend against marauding Norsemen and was the stronghold of the MacDougall lords until it fell to the kings of Scotland. Centuries later, Flora MacDonald was imprisoned here for helping Bonnie Prince Charlie escape after the Jacobite rebellion. She was later removed to the Tower of London.

🚗 *Head north on A85, turn right onto A828 across the Connel Bridge. Follow signs to Sea Life Sanctuary and car park.*

⑤ Scottish Sea Life Sanctuary
Barcaldine, Argyll; PA37 1SE
Situated on the shores of Loch Creran, the Scottish Sea Life Sanctuary *(open daily; www.sealsanctuary.co.uk)* rescues seal pups found on the coast, nursing them and rehabilitating them for return to the wild – there are resident seals to admire. The aquarium holds sea creatures from starfish to stingrays and there is an adventure playground and woodland trail – it's a fascinating place for both adults and children.

🚗 *Drive north on A828 along the coast, take A82, signed Crianlarich. Turn right for Glencoe Visitor Centre and car park.*

Above top left 18th-century Bonawe Iron Furnace **Above** Oban, overlooked by the imposing McCaig's Tower **Above left** Tower at Inveraray Castle, home to the Duke of Argyll **Below left** Popular attraction of Inveraray Jail

EAT AND DRINK

INVERARAY
The George Hotel *inexpensive*
This popular seafront pub serves a wide range of traditional and vegetarian dishes. Look out for fresh mussels and chips, Scottish steak pie or haggis. *Main Street East, PA32 8TT; 01499 302 111; www.thegeorgehotel.co.uk*

OBAN
Oban Chocolate Company *inexpensive*
Relax into sofas and enjoy sea views at this modern café for coffee, cakes and ice cream – or hand-made chocolates. *34 Corran Esplanade, PA34 5PS; 01631 566 099; www.obanchocolate.co.uk; closed Jan*

Oban Seafood Hut *inexpensive*
Popular green hut serving the freshest seafood straight off the boat. Enjoy a great-value platter on the quayside. *Calmac Pier, PA34 4DB; www.obanseafoodhut.co.uk*

Coast *inexpensive–moderate*
Contemporary restaurant in a former bank, specializing in locally caught seafood. Try Loch Linnhe langoustines. *102–104 George Street, PA34 5NT; 01631 569 900; www.coastoban.co.uk*

Temple Seafood *moderate*
This small restaurant has great waterside views and offers scallop chowder, lobster and seafood platters. Booking essential. *Gallanach Road, PA34 4LW; 01631 566 000; www.obanseafood.co.uk; open Thu–Sun*

Eat and Drink: inexpensive, under £25; moderate, £25–£50; expensive, over £50

Above The lush Ardnamurchan Peninsula, a haven for Scottish wildlife

CROSSING TO SKYE

Car ferry services
The ferry crossing to Skye from Mallaig takes about 30 minutes and is run by **Caledonian Macbrayne** *(08000 665 000; www.calmac.co.uk)*. The **Glenelg–Skye Ferry** *(Easter–Sep: runs daily every 20 mins; www.calmac.co.uk)* crosses from Kylerhea to Glenelg.

WHERE TO STAY

AROUND GLENCOE

Kilcamb Lodge Hotel *expensive*
Peaceful hotel in a stunning lochside location on the A861, beyond Strontian on the drive to Ardnamurchan Peninsula. Combines luxury with friendliness and attention to detail. Excellent food, too.
Strontian, Argyll, PH36 4HY; 01967 402 257; www.kilcamblodge.co.uk

AROUND ARMADALE CASTLE GARDENS

Tigh an Dochais *moderate*
Sleek rooms at this spotless B&B by the beach, with views of Broadford Bay. Home-made bread and jam for breakfast.
13 Harrapool, Isle of Skye, IV49 9AQ; 01471 820 022; www.skyebedbreakfast. co.uk; closed Dec–Feb

Kinloch Lodge *expensive*
Cosy atmosphere at the home of the chief of the Macdonald clan and his cookery-writer wife. A log fire burns in the drawing room and the charming bedrooms are individually furnished.
Sleat, Isle of Skye, IV43 8QY (on A851); 01471 833 333; www.kinloch-lodge.co.uk

PLOCKTON

The Plockton Hotel *moderate*
This hotel sits right on the seafront in Plockton, so try and get a room with a view across the loch. Bedrooms are en suite and there's a busy bar and restaurant downstairs.
41 Harbour View, IV52 8TN; 01599 544 274; www.plocktonhotel.co.uk

Right Splendid waterfall in Glencoe, scene of the brutal massacre in 1692

⑥ Glencoe
Glencoe; PH49 4LA
The mountains of Glencoe, described by Queen Victoria as: "stern, rugged, precipitous", are truly dramatic and home to wildlife as varied as mountain hares and golden eagles. But it is for the brutal massacre of 1692 that this sombre place is best known. **Glencoe Visitor Centre** *(open daily; www.nts.org.uk)* has an excellent exhibition and film on the history and wildlife of the glen; a viewing platform, and information on walks and climbs in the area.
🚗 *Follow A82 towards Fort William. After Onich, follow signs for Corran Ferry and cross to Ardgour. Then follow the A861 to Salen, and take B8007 to the Natural History Centre and car park.*

⑦ Ardnamurchan Peninsula
Argyll; PH36 4JG
This remote peninsula has a wet but mild climate and is home to a wide array of plants and wildlife. **Nàdurra** *(Apr–Oct: open daily)* introduces visitors to the flora and fauna with displays, remote CCTV cameras, specially constructed pine marten dens and a live "eagle cam". Continue on B8007 to Ardnamurchan

The Glencoe Massacre
The Macdonalds of Glencoe were supporters of the Stuart kings. The government offered an amnesty to Highland chiefs who swore an oath of allegiance to the new monarchs, William and Mary. However, the Macdonald Chief was late making his declaration. So the Earl of Argyll's regiment, led by Captain Campbell, was sent to Glencoe. After enjoying the local hospitality for 10 days, on 13 February 1692, the soldiers attacked their hosts, killing 38 Macdonalds.

Point, generally regarded as mainland Britain's most westerly point. Built in 1849 and automated in 1988, the **lighthouse** *(Apr–Oct; 01972 510 210; www. ardnamurchanlighthouse.com)* is also a museum – climb the 152 steps to the top to enjoy glorious views. Just below there's also a fabulous beach at **Sanna**, where the white sand is made of shells.
🚗 *Follow B8007 back to Salen, go left on A861 and left on A830 to Mallaig. Take the ferry to Skye. Once on the island, take A851 to the castle.*

⑧ Armadale Castle Gardens
Armadale, Isle of Skye; IV45 8RS
Now largely ruined, the castle was once home to members of the Clan Donald, former rulers of this area – Jacobite heroine Flora Macdonald was married here. Visitors can stroll in the **Castle Gardens** *(Apr–Oct: open daily; www.clandonald.com)* and woodlands. There's also a **Museum of the Isles** *(same hours)*, full of history of the area and the Clan Donald. The library helps those tracing their family history.
🚗 *Continue on A851 and A87 into Broadford, then turn left onto B8083. Follow this scenic single track road into Elgol. Park above the harbour.*

9 Elgol

Isle of Skye; IV49 9BJ

Elgol offers fine views of the Cuillins of Skye, a fierce craggy mountain range that challenges even experienced climbers. Bonnie Prince Charlie was hidden here in a remote cave, by loyal members of the Mackinnon clan, after defeat at Culloden in 1746. He was then rowed across to Mallaig and taken to France. Visitors can take a boat trip to the cave, or join a trip to Loch Coruisk in the heart of the Cuillins.

Follow B8083 back to Broadford, turn right on A87 and right to Kylerhea, turning left to Otter Haven Hide car park.

10 Kylerhea Otter Hide

Kylerhea, Isle of Skye; IV42 8

This forest hide *(open daily)* offers great views across the Kylerhea waters to Glenelg. Visitors can watch otters on the shore, common and Atlantic grey seals in the water and even the occasional white-tailed sea eagle. The otters here inspired Gavin Maxwell's famous novel, *Ring of Bright Water.*

From Kylerhea take ferry to Glenelg, take the coast road then turn left to Shiel Bridge. Stop at viewpoint for Five Sisters of Kintail mountains above Loch Duich. In Shiel Bridge, turn left on the A87, then left to castle. In winter, when ferry is not running, leave Skye on A87, cross bridge to Kyle of Lochalsh, turn left for Plockton.

11 Eilean Donan Castle

Dornie, by Kyle; IV40 8DX

This gloriously romantic, castle *(open daily; closed Jan; www.eileandonancastle. com)* reached by an arched stone bridge sits on a rocky island, settled in the 6th century by Saint Donan. The castle was built much later, to defend against invading Vikings. The building was carefully restored in the 1930s – visitors can now see the grand halls, bedrooms and kitchens. Eilean Donan may well look familiar: it has featured in many films, including the James Bond thriller, *The World is Not Enough.*

Continue on the A87 – at Balmacara turn right onto a pretty country road into Plockton. Park on street.

12 Plockton

Plockton, Ross-shire; IV52

The warm winds of the Gulf Stream give the little village of Plockton a surprisingly lush appearance: there are palm trees, colourful flowers and all sorts of exotic plants flourishing in the gardens that line the harbour. It started life as a fishing village, planned in the 18th-century by the Earl of Seaforth. It makes a relaxing base and is popular with sailors, who moor their yachts in the harbour. Visitors can enjoy loch and hill walks or go on a sea cruise to see the coast with **Calum's Boat Trips** *(01599 544 306; www.calums-sealtrips.com).*

Above left Craggy mountains around Elgol **Above centre** Female red deer on the shore, Ardnamurchan Peninsula **Above right** The pretty village of Plockton in its lush setting

EAT AND DRINK

AROUND ARMADALE CASTLE GARDENS

Harbour View *moderate*
This former fisherman's cottage is now a popular restaurant specializing in fish and seafood. Try the fish pie or *moules.*
7 Bosville Terrace, Portree, Isle of Skye, IV51 9DG (on A87 north); 01487 612 069; www.harbourviewskye.co.uk

The Three Chimneys *expensive*
Acclaimed restaurant in the north of Skye, serving modern Scottish cuisine. The menu might include saddle of wild rabbit, or pan-fried sea trout, followed by hot marmalade pudding.
Colbost, Dunvegan, Isle of Skye (on A87 north), IV55 8ZT; 01470 511 258; www.threechimneys.co.uk

PLOCKTON

Harbour Fish Bar *inexpensive*
Fabulous chip shop serving the freshest locally caught fish (and chips), as well as veggie dishes, pizza and pasta.
Innes Street, IV52 8TW; open daily Apr–Oct

Plockton Shores *moderate*
This is part-grocer's shop, part-restaurant, on the waterfront in Plockton. Locally sourced food might include scallops, or venison cooked with juniper and thyme.
30 Harbour St, IV52 8TN; 01599 544 263

DAY TRIP OPTIONS

This route can easily be split into day trips from Inveraray and Plockton.

Family Adventure

From Inveraray ①, buy some picnic provisions and visit the castle, with its splendid interiors, then head north to Ben Cruachan Power Station ②, to go deep inside the mountain. Next, it's a short drive to Bonawe Iron Furnace

③, for a picnic in the idyllic grounds before driving to the Scottish Sea Life Sanctuary ⑤, to see the seals, the aquarium and walk in the woods.

Follow A819, then join A85 north. Turn off right on A828. Reverse to return.

Castles and Skye

Enjoy Plockton's ⑫ temperate climate and pretty palm-lined harbour, then cross the bridge to the Isle of Skye and

walk around pretty Armadale Castle Gardens ⑧. Go to Elgol ⑨, close to the cave that hid Bonnie Prince Charlie and cross back to the mainland on the Glenelg-Skye ferry to visit the romantic ruins of Eilean Donan Castle ⑪.

From Plockton head to the Kyle of Lochalsh and take A87, then A851 to the castle gardens. Then follow the drive instructions all the way back.

Eat and Drink: inexpensive, under £25; moderate, £25–£50; expensive, over £50

The Heart of Scotland

Perth to Loch Lomond

Highlights

- **Fairytale castles**
  Visit the great Scottish castles at Blair Atholl and Glamis, as well as historic Scone Palace, where the kings of Scotland were once crowned

- **Rivers and lochs**
  Enjoy the beautiful scenery from the great River Tay as it flows from Dunkeld down to Perth; from slender Loch Voil to the largest expanse of freshwater in the UK, Loch Lomond

- **Literary associations**
  Follow the literary links: see the home of JM Barrie; Birnam Wood mentioned in Shakespeare's *Macbeth* and visited by Beatrix Potter; and the highland glens and grave of Rob Roy, hero of Sir Walter Scott and Daniel Defoe

A sun-dappled road through Argyll Forest Park, west of Loch Lomond

The Heart of Scotland

This tour characterizes perfectly the variety that Scotland has to offer. It takes visitors through the very heart of the country: where the Lowlands meet the Highlands, where famous figures like Rob Roy once lived and historic battles were fought. Here the landscape – which encompasses Loch Lomond and the Trossachs, Scotland's first National Park – is a picturesque mixture of brooding hills, open glens, ancient trees and tranquil lochs. It is superb walking country, offering trails for all abilities. Food lovers will enjoy the chance to taste some of Britain's finest food – soft fruit from Angus and fresh salmon and trout caught in the River Tay.

Above Balfour Castle in the Kirkton of Kingoldrum, near Kirriemuir, *see p240*
Below Ben Lomond seen in the distance over Loch Lomond, *see p243*

ACTIVITIES

Go on a ghost hunt at spooky Glamis Castle

Enjoys a day's trout fishing on the Tay at Dunkeld

Walk through the wooded gorge, the scene of the Battle at Killiecrankie

Watch for red squirrels in the woods of Blair Castle

Take the ferry across to the island of Inchmahome Priory in the Lake of Menteith

Paddle a kayak on beautiful Loch Lomond or explore via a cruise boat

0 kilometres   10

0 miles   10

KEY

Drive route

Below The spectacular rocks at Bracklinn Falls, near Callander, *see pp242–3*

PLAN YOUR DRIVE

Start/finish: Perth to Loch Lomond.

Number of days: Around 3–4 days.

Distances: Approx 400 km (248 miles)

Road conditions: The roads are mostly good and well signposted, although there are some winding, hilly sections and narrow single-track roads. The road to Bridge of Balgie is unsuitable for caravans, and impassable in bad weather, icy conditions and snow; use A827 as an alternative.

When to go: Spring is a pleasant time to visit. Summer brings better weather, but also more visitors and the Scottish midge. Autumn is beautiful when the trees change colour. Sections of the drive may be snowbound in winter.

Opening times: Museums and attractions are generally open 10am–5pm, but close earlier (or are closed altogether) Nov–Easter. Shops are often open longer. Churches are usually open until dusk.

Main market days: Perth: Farmers' Market, 1st Sat of month.

Shopping: Jams made from local berries; woollens, Celtic jewellery and fine foods at Loch Lomond Shores, the National Park Gateway, Balloch.

Main festivals: Perth: Scottish Game Fair (Scone Palace), Jul; Glamis: Strathmore Highland Games, 2nd Sat in Jun; Dunkeld: Birnam Highland Games, last Sat in Aug; Blair Castle: International Horse Trials, Aug; Glenfiddich Piping and Fiddling Championships, Oct; Balloch: Loch Lomond Highland Games, Jul.

DAY TRIP OPTIONS

Staying at Perth, visit its fine **gardens**, **church** and **gallery** and the **palace** at Scone. Then head to Dunkeld for a walk by the **river**, with its huge stone **bridge**, ruined **cathedral** and mighty **trees**. Romantics can walk beside the **river** at Callander, see the **shops** and then drive by a **loch** to Balquhidder **glen** to see Rob Roy's **grave**, then head south to visit the **island priory** at Inchmahome. For full details, *see p243*.

VISITING PERTH

Parking
There is long-stay parking by the railway station, on the High St and on South St.

Tourist Information
Lower City Mills, West Mill St, PH1 5QP; 01738 450 600; www.perthshire.co.uk

VISITING DUNKELD

Parking
There is a large car park in the town centre, behind the High Street.

Tourist Information
The Cross, PH8 OAN; 01350 727 688; www.perthshire.co.uk

WHERE TO STAY

PERTH

Ardfern House *inexpensive*
Enjoy pretty rooms at this comfortable Victorian house. There's a fire in the lounge and many options for breakfast.
15 Pitcullen Crescent, PH2 7HT; 01738 637 031; www.ardfernguesthouse.co.uk

Beechgrove Guest House *inexpensive*
Attractive B&B overlooking the Tay, just outside the centre, offers traditional en-suite rooms and has its own grounds.
Dundee Road, PH2 7AQ; 01738 636 147

Salutation Hotel *moderate*
Reputed to be one of Scotland's oldest hotels, the Salutation has 84 rooms, a bar and a restaurant.
34 South Street, PH2 8PH; 01738 630 066; www.strathmorehotels.com

AROUND DUNKELD

Kinnaird Estate *expensive*
A superb 18th-century country house in tranquil countryside by the River Tay. Elegantly furnished rooms offer stunning views. Delicious breakfasts of fresh fruit, pastries and pancakes.
Kinnaird Estate, by Dunkeld (on B898 north of Dunkeld); PH8 0LB; 01796 482 440; www.kinnairdestate.com

1 Perth
Perthshire; PH1

The "Fair City", as Sir Walter Scott dubbed Perth, sits on the banks of the River Tay – Scotland's longest river. It's a lovely green city: **Branklyn Gardens** *(Dundee Rd; open daily)* are famed for their brilliant blue Himalayan poppies; and **Cherrybank Gardens** *(Glasgow Rd; open daily)* contain the National Collection of heathers. The **Museum and Art Gallery** *(closed Sun)* contains watercolours by Beatrix Potter, creator of Peter Rabbit *(see opposite)*.

Just north of the city, off the A93, stands **Scone** (pronounced "scoon") **Palace** *(Apr–Oct; open daily; www.scone-palace.co.uk)*. In the grounds lies Moot Hill where ancient Scottish kings such as Macbeth and Robert the Bruce were crowned. The Stone of Destiny stood here until Edward I took it to London in 1296: it sat under the Coronation Chair until 1996. It's now in Edinburgh Castle.

🚗 *Continue on the A93, past the 30-m (100-ft) high Meiklour beech hedge, planted in 1745. Soon after, turn right onto the A984 signed Coupar Angus and at crossroads go right on the A923. At Coupar Angus take the A94 to Meigle.*

2 Meigle Museum
Meigle, Perthshire; PH12 8SB

Meigle Museum *(Apr–Sept; open daily)* contains a superb collection of Pictish stones, dating back to the 8th century. Amongst the images carved on these mysterious stones by the Picts are a camel, a bear and mythical beasts.

🚗 *From Meigle, continue on the A94, turning left to reach Glamis Castle.*

Above The wonderful Italian Garden at Glamis Castle, laid out in 1910

3 Glamis Castle
Glamis, Angus; DD8 1RJ

With its grand towers, turrets and tiny windows, **Glamis Castle** *(Apr–Oct: open daily; guided tours only; www.glamis-castle.co.uk)* looks like a French château or something out of a fairytale. The seat of the Earls of Strathmore since 1372, it was the childhood home of the late Queen Elizabeth the Queen Mother: visitors can see her sitting room and bedroom. The castle is said to be the most haunted building in Scotland and the creepy crypt contains a secret room: according to legend, it was where one of the lords of Glamis played cards with the Devil. The room was later sealed up. In summer, the Strathmore Highland Games are held in the grounds.

🚗 *Take A928 north and park in centre.*

4 Kirriemuir
Angus; DD8

Known in the 19th century for its jute factories, Kirriemuir is now more famous as **J M Barrie's Birthplace** *(Easter–Oct: open Sat–Wed; Jul, Aug: open daily; www.nts.org.uk)*. The museum is signposted, just off the central square. The creator of Peter Pan was the 9th of 10 children and it's hard to imagine how they all squeezed into the tiny upper rooms. Barrie's father, a weaver, worked downstairs. Outside is the little wash house, in which the 7-year-old author acted out his first plays – it inspired Wendy's House in Peter Pan.

🚗 *Pick up A926 towards Blairgowrie, then take A923 past the Loch of the Lowes Visitor Centre (ospreys can be seen in late spring) and into Dunkeld.*

Far left The compact and pretty city of Perth, set beside the River Tay **Left** The elegant tea garden and peacock at 14th-century Scone Palace, Perth

⑤ Dunkeld

Perthshire; PH8

This charming market town, with shops, restaurants and a 14th-century cathedral makes a relaxing place to stop. It stands on one bank of the River Tay, with the town of Birnam on the other. As well as excellent salmon and trout fishing on the Tay, the nearby woods and hills offer plenty of fine walks – ask about these activities in the Tourist Office.

A one-and-a-half-hour walking tour

From the car park, walk down Bridge St and over **Dunkeld Bridge** ① across the Tay. It was built in the early 19th century by Thomas Telford, and cost £15,000 (about £1m today). It's a magnificent structure over 200 m (685 ft) long. Keep to the left and, just over the bridge, take the steps down to the river – a sign says Birnam Walk. Once under the bridge, go left to follow a path which offers picturesque views of **Dunkeld Cathedral** ②, much of which is in ruins, the result of damage during the Reformation in the 16th century.

The most scenic and enjoyable option from here is to retrace the walk route under the bridge, keeping the river now on the left-hand side.

After crossing a small footbridge, there's a mighty sycamore tree and the **Birnam Oak** ③, its lower branches propped up with posts, like an elderly gentleman leaning on a stick. This is the last survivor of Birnam Wood, mentioned in Shakespeare's *Macbeth*.

Follow this lovely tree-lined path along the river to a blue painted **fishing hut** ④ by the waters of the Tay. Then return the same way along the riverside but, just before reaching the Birnam Oak, turn left up a set of steps. Follow the path to the road in Birnam, and cross over to visit the **Beatrix Potter Exhibition** ⑤ *(open daily)*. The children's author Beatrix Potter used to holiday in Birnam as a child, and spent

hours exploring with a local naturalist, Charles Macintosh. The wildlife and countryside inspired Beatrix to create such enduring characters as Peter Rabbit and Mrs Tiggy Winkle, years later. The exhibition includes a Victorian schoolroom, information panels and a Beatrix Potter Garden – the museum is an ideal place for young children. There's also a café.

To return to Dunkeld, either walk back along the river or follow Perth Rd in Birnam to cross the bridge again. 🚗 *Take the A9 north, after Pitlochry turn left, onto the B8019, then right onto the B8079 to Killiecrankie. The Pass Visitor Centre is clearly signposted.*

Left to right Dunkeld: Neo-Gothic fountain at the market cross; part of the ruined wing of Dunkeld Cathedral; the impressive Dunkeld Bridge, spanning the River Tay

EAT AND DRINK

PERTH

63 Tay Street *moderate*
There's a contemporary feel to this fine restaurant in the heart of Perth. Enjoy risotto of Scottish lobster and scallops.
63 Tay Street, PH2 8NN; 01736 441 451; www.63taystreet.com; closed Sun, Mon

MEIGLE

The Joinery Coffee Shop *inexpensive*
Lovely little café in a former joinery in Meigle. Come for home-made soups, freshly made *panini* and delicious cakes.
The Square, PH12 8RN; 01828 640717; www.meiglecoffeeshop.co.uk

KIRRIEMUIR

Lands of Loyal *moderate*
Seasonal produce, game and fish are served in the restaurant of this grand hotel just outside Alyth. After lunch, enjoy a walk in the fabulous grounds.
Alyth, Blairgowrie, PH11 8JQ; 01828 633 151; www.landsofloyal.co.uk

VISITING CALLANDER

Tourist Information
Ancaster Square, FK17 8ED; 01877 330 342; www.visitscotland.co.uk

WHERE TO STAY

PASS OF KILLIECRANKIE

Killiecrankie House Hotel *expensive*
Enjoy crisp white bedlinen and tasteful furniture at this small country hotel with rural views and locally sourced breakfasts.
Pass of Killiecrankie, PH16 5LG; 01796 473 220; www.killiecrankiehotel.co.uk

CALLANDER

Arden House *inexpensive*
This handsome Victorian house has comfortable, good-sized rooms.
Bracklinn Road, FK17 8EQ; 01877 339 405; www.ardenhouse.org.uk

Leny Estate *moderate*
This peaceful estate on the edge of Callander has six attractive, heated lodge-style cabins and a flat in the castle.
Leny House, FK17 8HA; 01877 331 078; www.lenyestate.com

Roman Camp Country House *moderate–expensive*
A 17th-century hunting lodge, this country house with wood panelling and ornate ceilings offers traditional comforts.
Off Main Street, FK17 8BG; 01877 330 003; www.romancamphotel.co.uk

INCHMAHOME PRIORY

Lake of Menteith Hotel *expensive*
This hotel looks across the water towards Inchmahome Priory and has bright rooms. Breakfast on Scottish produce.
Port of Menteith, FK8 3RA; 01877 385 258; www.lake-hotel.com

⑥ Pass of Killiecrankie
Pitlochry, Perthshire; PH16 5LG

On the evening of 27 July 1689, the wooded gorge at Killiecrankie became a bloody battleground, when Highland troops led by John Graham of Claverhouse routed government forces in the first battle of the Jacobite rebellion. The **Visitor Centre** *(Apr–Oct: open daily)* tells the story of the battle and also has displays on the wildlife and natural history of the gorge, which looks particularly beautiful when the trees turn russet and gold in autumn. A path leads down to a viewpoint over **Soldier's Leap**, where a government soldier, leapt 5.5 m (18 ft) across the River Garry to escape the Highlanders.
🚗 *Turn left out of car park and follow B8079 to Blair Castle and car park.*

⑦ Blair Castle
Blair Atholl, Pitlochry; PH18 5TL

Strategically situated to defend the highland passes, imposing Blair Castle *(Apr–Oct: open daily; www.blair-castle.co.uk)* was the ancestral home of the Dukes of Atholl. It dates back to the 13th century but has been greatly expanded over the years. In summer, a uniformed piper may well be playing outside – an Atholl Highlander, the only private army in Europe, raised by the 4th Duke in 1778. Highlights here include the furniture used by Queen Victoria and an ivory compass carried

by Bonnie Prince Charlie. The grounds include a deer park, gardens and woods, the haunt of red squirrels.
🚗 *Return past Killiecrankie on B8079, then go right on the scenic B8019. At Tummel Bridge, go left on B846 and turn right to Fortingall. Park at the church.*

⑧ The Fortingall Yew
Fortingall, Aberfeldy; PH15 2NQ

In a corner of the churchyard stands the Fortingall Yew: probably the oldest living thing in Europe, it is thought to be 5,000 years old. Legend has it that Pontius Pilate knew this tree, not so unlikely as his father, an army officer, was stationed here during the Roman occupation.
🚗 *Continue down the road to Bridge of Balgie and turn left signed to Killin. Turn right on the A827, go through Killin, then pick up the A85 towards Perth. At Lochearnhead, take the A84, then turn right to Balquhidder.*

⑨ Balquhidder
Perthshire; FK19 8PA

This small village is set by Loch Voil under spectacular mountains. In its **churchyard** is the grave of one of Scotland's most famous figures: Rob Roy Macgregor (1671–1734). Rob Roy, whose nickname came from his red hair ("roy" comes from the Gaelic for red), fought at Killiecrankie. After a dispute with the Duke of Montrose, he embarked on a campaign of cattle rustling and eventually became an outlaw. Avoiding capture, he became a romantic hero, immortalized by writers Sir Walter Scott and Daniel Defoe.
🚗 *Return to the A84 south to Callander and park in the centre.*

⑩ Callander
Callander, Stirling; FK17

Popularly known as the "gateway to the highlands", Callander, with its shops and restaurants, makes an excellent base for exploring. In the 1960s and 70s it gained fame as Tannochbrae in the UK TV version of *Dr Finlay's Casebook* by A J Cronin. Visitors can enjoy signed walks along the River Teith and to

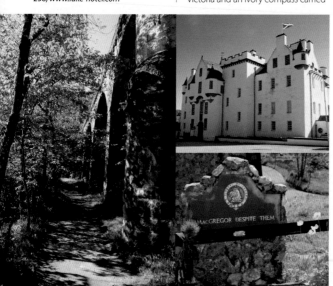

Far left Shaded woods in the gorge at the Pass of Killiecrankie **Top left** The magnificent white-painted exterior of 13th-century Blair Castle **Bottom left** The grave of Rob Roy bearing its defiant motto

Where to Stay: inexpensive, under £80; moderate, £80–£150; expensive, over £150

Bracklinn Falls, climbs up nearby Ben Ledi and bike rides on the national cycleway – see Tourist Information *(left)*.

🚗 *Take A81 signed Glasgow. Go left at B8034 to Port of Menteith ferry car park.*

⑪ Inchmahome Priory
Lake of Menteith; FK8 3RA

There can be few more picturesque places than **Inchmahome Priory** *(Apr–Sep: open daily; www.historic-scotland.gov. uk)*. This Augustinian monastery sits on a small island in the Lake of Menteith, and can only be reached by ferry. The priory, built in 1283, was home to a small religious community for 300 years. Visitors can stroll around the tranquil ruins, which once provided a refuge for young Mary, Queen of Scots.

🚗 *Continue along B8034, turning right on A811. At Drymen, turn right on B837 to Balmaha and car park.*

⑫ Balmaha
Loch Lomond; G63 0JQ

Balmaha is a tiny village on the east bank of **Loch Lomond**, nestling amid ancient oak woods. These support so much wildlife they are a Site of Special Scientific Interest. Walk the **Millennium Forest Path** through the woods or take a ferry from the boatyard to visit the island of **Inchcailleach**. At 39 km (24 miles) long and 8 km (5 miles) wide, Loch Lomond is the largest expanse of freshwater in Britain. The loch is dotted

with thickly wooded islands, including **Inchconnachan**, which is home to an unlikely colony of wallabies, introduced in the early 20th century.

🚗 *Return to Drymen, then take A811 towards Glasgow to Balloch. Follow signs to Loch Lomond Shores car park.*

⑬ Loch Lomond Shores
Ben Lomond Way, Balloch; G83 8QL

Visitors to Balloch should head for **Loch Lomond Shores** *(open daily; www. lochlomondshores.com)*, gateway to the Loch Lomond National Park, to pick up local crafts and walk maps. Here, it is also possible to hire bikes, canoes and kayaks, or book tickets to take a cruise on the loch itself. Visitors with children will enjoy a visit to the aquarium, which offers close up views of creatures such as starfish and sharks.

Above left Unspoilt Callander, set in the beautiful Trossach hills **Above right** Boats on serene Loch Lomond as seen from Balmaha **Below** Lake cruise ship on Loch Lomond awaiting passengers, Balloch

EAT AND DRINK

AROUND BLAIR CASTLE

Loch Tummel Inn *inexpensive*
This inn by Loch Tummel is on the B8019 about 15 minutes from Killiecrankie. Bar meals include big sandwiches, mussels in wine or Aberdeen Angus burgers. *Strathtummel, PH16 5RP; 01882 634 272; www.lochtummelinn.co.uk*

THE FORTINGALL YEW

Fortingall Hotel *moderate*
Beside the famous Fortingall Yew, this hotel restaurant serves good Scottish produce, such as fresh salmon from the Tay and locally raised lamb. *Fortingall, PH15 2NQ; 01887 830 367; www.fortingall.com*

BALQUHIDDER

Monachyle Mhor *moderate–expensive*
Enjoy chic eating on the north shore of Loch Voil. The menu is modern Scottish, and there are vegetarian dishes, too. Also has superb rooms. *Balquhidder, FK19 8PQ; 01877 384 622; www.mhor.net*

CALLANDER

Ciro's *moderate*
This popular Italian restaurant in the centre of town, serves pasta and pizza dishes, as well as Scottish rib-eye steak. *114 Main Street, FK17 8BG; 01877 331 070; www.cirositalianrestaurant.co.uk; closed Wed*

DAY TRIP OPTIONS

Perth and Callander are excellent bases for day trips.

Gardens and River Tay

Staying at Perth ❶, spend the morning enjoying its sights – the river, gardens and galleries – and then enjoy a tour of Scone Palace, where Scotland's kings were crowned. Drive

to Dunkeld ❺ to see its cathedral, and historic trees beside the River Tay, and walk into Birnam.

Take A93 to Scone Palace and then return to Perth centre and take the A9. Return to Perth on the A9.

Romance of the Lochs

From Callander ❿, explore the town and enjoy a walk by the river, before

driving up the loch to Balquhidder ❾ to see Rob Roy's grave and the glens. Then return to Callander and head south to take a boat to romantic Inchmahome Priory ⑪, set on an island in Lake Menteith.

From Callander take A84, then follow signs to Balquhidder. Retrace route and then take A81 to Inchmahome Priory.

On the Highlands Whisky Trail

Inverness to Aberdeen

Highlights

- **Fairytale castles**
  Visit some of Scotland's finest castles, including Cawdor, immortalized in Shakespeare's *Macbeth*, and clifftop Dunnottar Castle, once the keeper of the Scottish Crown jewels

- **Spectacular Speyside**
  Watch dolphins on the Moray coast, then follow the River Spey to sample the finest malt whiskies, made among the heather-clad hills

- **Cities of stone**
  Explore Inverness, notable for its pink sandstone buildings by the River Ness, and historic Aberdeen, the grey granite city on the North Sea

The wild shoreline of Spey Bay, at the WDCS Wildlife Centre

On the Highlands Whisky Trail

This drive is Scotland distilled: the route runs through a landscape of brooding mountains and sparkling rivers, dotted with picture-book castles, barrel-makers and world famous whisky producers. Starting from Inverness, the drive visits Culloden to see the site of the famous battle, continues to Cawdor Castle, then heads north to enjoy some dolphin watching on the Moray coast. Heading south through Speyside, the home of whisky, visitors get the chance to taste a dram or two, before travelling back in time at the Grampian Transport Museum. On reaching the east coast, there are spectacular craggy cliffs at Dunnottar Castle, before the drive ends at the historic granite city of Aberdeen.

ACTIVITIES

Go on a monster hunt with a boat cruise over the mysterious depths of Loch Ness

March across a battlefield and see the memorial at the poignant meadows of Culloden

Watch for wildlife at the Whale and Dolphin Conservation Society Wildlife Centre, Spey Bay

Walk along the Speyside Way in Craigellachie

Climb aboard a vintage train on the Keith & Dufftown Railway

Taste a dram or two of single-malt whisky on a tour of the Glenfiddich Distillery

Enjoy a picnic in the grounds of Leith Hall

Watch the salmon leaping on the waters of the Feugh

Below Archway in the pretty Flower Garden, Cawdor Castle, *see p248*

Above Peaceful boating pond in the park close to the centre of Elgin, *see p249*

KEY

🟫 Drive route

PLAN YOUR DRIVE

Start/Finish: Inverness to Aberdeen.

Number of days: Around 3–4 days, with half a day in Aberdeen.

Distances: Approx. 291 km (181 miles).

Road conditions: Good roads, liable to become snowbound in winter.

When to go: This drive is lovely in the autumn, when the trees are changing colour. In summer, the roads will be busier – but the weather can be fine and the days will be long.

Opening times: Museums and attractions are generally open 10am–5pm, but close earlier (or are closed altogether) Nov–Easter. Shops are often open longer. Churches are usually open until dusk.

Main market days: Inverness: Farmers' Market, 1st Sat of month; Aberdeen: Farmers' Market, 1st and last Sat of month.

Shopping: Scottish whisky is famed the world over, so take the chance to buy a good-quality single malt here. Look out for excellent jams, tablet (the Scottish version of fudge) and buttery shortbread, too.

Main festivals: Inverness: Highland Games, Jul; **Dufftown**: Spirit of Speyside Whisky Festival, May; **Dunnottar Castle**: Stonehaven Folk Festival, Jul; Stonehaven Fireballs Ceremony, Dec; Aberdeen: Highland Games, Jun.

DAY TRIP OPTIONS

History lovers will enjoy the **cathedral** and **museum** at Inverness, before walking on Culloden **battlefield** and exploring the **dungeons** at Cawdor Castle. Finish the day at Nairn on its **sandy beach**. **Whisky buffs** should stay at Craigellachie, watch **dolphins** in Spey Bay and see coopers at work at Speyside Cooperage. End the day with a visit to Dufftown to taste **whisky** and ride on a **heritage train**. Staying at Aberdeen, visit the **transport museum** at Alford, the **waterfalls** and **castle** at Banchory, and the **cliffside castle** at Dunnottar, then return for Aberdeen's **beach funfair**. For full details, *see p253*.

Above St Mary's Catholic Church by the River Ness, Inverness

VISITING INVERNESS

Parking
For long-term parking close to the castle try the Rose St car park, off A82/B865.

Tourist Information
Castle Wynd, IV2 3BJ; 01463 234 353

WHERE TO STAY

INVERNESS

Trafford Bank Guest House *moderate*
Enjoy chic, designer rooms at this 5-star B&B. There are features such as Victorian roll-top baths, DVD players and luxury toiletries – and sherry decanters.
96 Fairfield Road, IV3 5LL; 01463 241 414; www.traffordbankguesthouse.co.uk

Rocpool *expensive*
This boutique hotel offers luxurious rooms and a high-end French bistro endorsed by Albert Roux.
Culduthel Road, IV2 4AG; 01463 240 089; www.rocpool.com

AROUND CAWDOR CASTLE

Sunny Brae Hotel *moderate*
Follow B9090 to the seafront in Nairn for comfortable en-suite rooms, some with views of the Moray Firth, a restaurant, and an attractive guest lounge with a sea view.
Marine Road, Nairn, IV12 4EA; 01667 452 309; www.sunnybraehotel.com

AROUND ELGIN

Milton of Grange Farmhouse *inexpensive*
There are three en-suite rooms and lovely views of the countryside at this working arable farm. Guests can enjoy a full Scottish breakfast, or a fruit and cheese platter. From Elgin, take A96 to Forres, then turn right on B9011.
Forres, Moray, IV36 2TR; 01309 676 360

① Inverness
Highland; IV1
Sitting serenely on the River Ness, Inverness is acknowledged as the capital of the Highlands. The river is flanked on one side by a substantial pink stone **castle**, built in the 19th century on the site of a much earlier structure destroyed by the Jacobite army after 1746. On the other side stands **Inverness Cathedral**, with some fine stained-glass windows. *The* **City Museum** *(open Mon–Sat)* contains a variety of items associated with the Highlands. Visitors can also enjoy a cruise on **Loch Ness** *(www.jacobite.co.uk)* and learn more about Loch Ness wildlife including, of course, the mythical monster. Buses to the boats leave from Inverness Bus Station.

🚗 *From Rose St car park drive onto A82 roundabout, turning right, then join A9 south for a short distance, turning left on B9006. The Culloden Visitor Centre is just off the road and clearly signposted; there is a car park.*

② Culloden
Culloden Moor, Inverness; IV2 5EU
The wind never seems to stop blowing across the bleak expanse of Culloden Moor where, on 16 April 1746, the last battle of the Jacobite Risings took place. It lasted only an hour, but heralded the end of the distinctive clan system, bringing many changes to Highland Scotland. The excellent **Visitor Centre** *(open daily; www.nts.org. uk)* gives the historical context to the battle, together with memorabilia such as Jacobite medals and first-

hand accounts from those involved in the events. Visitors can also walk the battlefield for a soldier's-eye view.

🚗 *Continue on B9006, bearing right onto B9091. Turn right onto B9090 to Cawdor Castle.*

The Mystery of Loch Ness
Stories of a monster lurking in Loch Ness date back to St Columba, who is said to have saved a man from the beast. However, modern sightings started in 1933, when a creature with a long neck was reported in the loch. Murky photographs and film of the creature have appeared: many consider them to be hoaxes, others are sure that Nessie exists. Scientific expeditions have been unable to find the beast, and the mystery lingers on.

③ Cawdor Castle
Cawdor, Nairn; IV12 5RD;
Although Cawdor Castle's *(May–Sep: open daily; www.cawdorcastle.com)* only associations with the real Macbeth were in Shakespeare's imagination, that does not lessen its appeal. It was built in the late 14th century, long after Macbeth had died, and retains a medieval feel with stone staircases, atmospheric passageways and a dungeon. It is still home to the Cawdor family and photos mingle with Flemish tapestries, four-poster beds and artworks by Landseer and Edward Lear. There are several colourful gardens – Walled, Flower and Wild – which are delightful places to explore .

🚗 *Continue on B9090 to Nairn (consider a detour to the beach). Then*

Below The imposing west towers of Gothic Inverness Cathedral, built in 1866

take A96 east and branch off onto
B9011 in Forres, to turn right on B9010.
Drive through fertile fields and turn left
on a signed unclassified road to reach
the abbey, and car park on the left-
hand side.

④ Pluscarden Abbey
Elgin, Moray; IV30 8UA

Sitting serenely in a sheltered valley
surrounded by trees, Pluscarden Abbey
(open daily; www.pluscardenabbey.org)
seems to radiate tranquillity. Founded
in the year 1230 by King Alexander II of
Scotland, this venerable building is still
home to a community of Benedictine
monks – the only such medieval
monastery in Britain still used for its
original purpose. The abbey church
contains contemporary stained-glass
windows, most of which are made in
the abbey workshop by monks.

🚗 *Continue on the minor road to
turn left onto B9010 near Elgin. A 24-m
(80-ft) high column, erected in memory
of the 5th Duke of Gordon in 1839, can
be clearly seen rising above the town.
Take B9010 into Elgin; there is parking
near the cathedral, off the High Street
and also by North Street.*

⑤ Elgin
Elgin, Moray; IV30

With historic buildings, a medieval
street plan and pretty park, Elgin is a
pleasant town for a stroll. Undoubtedly,
its finest sight is the ruined **Elgin
Cathedral** (Apr–Oct: open daily; Nov–Mar;
open Sat–Wed), which was once so large

it was known as the Lantern of the
North; intricate carvings on the exterior
and its almost complete Chapterhouse
provide a glimpse of its former glory.
Elgin Museum (Apr–Oct. open Mon–Sat;
www.elginmuseum.org.uk) has a vast
collection of fascinating items from
ancient Pictish stones, Roman coins,
fossils, paintings by local artists and a
display on the county and its people.

🚗 *Leave Elgin on the A96, towards
Keith. After crossing the River Spey,
turn left onto the B9104 and follow it
to Spey Bay. The WDCS visitor centre
and car park is at the road's end.*

Above left The ruins of Elgin Cathedral, once one
of the finest in Scotland **Above top right** The
field where the decisive Battle of Culloden was
fought in 1746 **Above right** Detail of Pluscarden
Abbey, still home to Benedictine monks

EAT AND DRINK

INVERNESS

Riva *inexpensive*
This smart Italian restaurant offers
classic dishes such as mushroom
risotto, pasta with meatballs and pizzas.
*4–6 Ness Walk, IV3 5NE; 01463 237 377;
closed Sun lunch*

The Kitchen on the River
inexpensive–moderate
This relaxed, contemporary restaurant
beside the River Ness serves modern
Scottish food. Imaginative dishes
include pheasant and venison patties,
or breast of chicken stuffed with haggis.
There are vegetarian options, too.
*15 Huntly Street, IV3 5PR; 01463 259
119; www.kitchenrestaurant.co.uk*

The Rocpool *moderate*
This cool city centre brasserie offers
fusion food, made with as much local
produce as possible. Come for dishes
such as Venetian-style calves' liver, sea
bream with chorizo, or venison with
Parma ham and black pudding.
*1 Ness Walk, IV3 5NE; 01463 717 274;
www.rocpoolrestaurant.com*

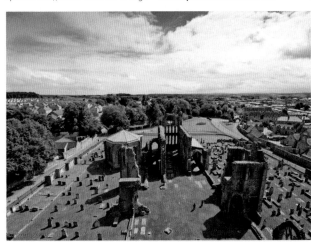

Above Impressive ruins at Elgin Cathedral with an almost intact Chapterhouse

Eat and Drink: inexpensive, under £25; moderate, £25–£50; expensive, over £50

Above *Statue of an osprey outside the WDCS Wildlife Centre, Spey Bay*

VISITING DUFFTOWN

Parking
Park at the top of Balvenie Street under the clock – although most of Dufftown's sights are outside the village.

Tourist Information
2 The Square, AB55 4AD; 01340 820 501

WHERE TO STAY

AROUND SPEYSIDE COOPERAGE

Craigellachie Hotel *moderate*
Built in 1893, the Craigellachie Hotel offers country house accommodation on the River Spey, just north of the Speyside Cooperage. It makes a good stop on the whisky trail, especially as its Quaich Bar has over 700 whiskies to choose from. It's also handy for walks as the Speyside Way runs beside the hotel. The restaurant is worth visiting, too.
Craigellachie, Speyside, AB38 9SR; 01340 881 204; www.craigellachiehotel.co.uk

AROUND LEITH HALL

Castle Hotel *moderate*
Built in the 18th century as a home for the Dukes of Gordon (powerful Scottish nobles), the hotel is set in quiet parkland and has comfortable, traditionally furnished rooms. It's a delightful place for a relaxing break.
Huntly, Aberdeenshire, AB54 4SH (follow driving instructions from Dufftown to Leith Hall); 01466 792 696; www.castlehotel.uk.com

⑥ WDCS Wildlife Centre
Spey Bay, Moray; IV32 7PJ
Perched beside the unspoilt sands of Spey Bay, the Whale and Dolphin Conservation Society Wildlife Centre *(Apr–Oct: open daily; Mar & Nov: weekends; www.wdcs.org)* constantly monitors the water for dolphin activity. This part of the coast is noted for its bottlenose dolphins and visitors have a good chance of spotting them – especially with the help of the wildlife wardens. This area is also home to minke whales, ospreys, otters and wildfowl. The staff here offer informative talks, as well as guided walks on the nature reserve.

🚗 *Return to A96 and turn right, then left on B9015 to Rothes. There, take A941 south, passing the Glen Grant Distillery. Stay on A941 through Craigellachie and on to Speyside Cooperage, with parking.*

⑦ Speyside Cooperage
Craigellachie, Banffshire; AB38 9RS
Nearly all the casks in Scotland are made at this family-run cooperage. The **Visitor Centre** *(open Mon–Fri; www. speysidecooperage.co.uk)* introduces this ancient industry, explaining how they make the oak casks, and how sherry and bourbon casks are repaired, and then used to give distinctive flavours to whiskies. Visitors can watch the coopers and apprentices at work – it's a four-year apprenticeship – using the traditional tools of their trade.

There are also some good walks on the Speyside Way from Craigellachie.

🚗 *Turn right from the cooperage onto A941. Before Dufftown, on the left-hand side, is the Keith & Dufftown Railway, with parking.*

The Honours of Scotland
After Charles I was executed, the Scots crowned his son, Charles II, at Scone Palace. Then in 1650 Oliver Cromwell, (the anti-monarchist leader) ordered an invasion of Scotland. To prevent him destroying the country's Crown Jewels –the Honours of Scotland – they were taken to Dunnottar Castle and later to Kinneff Old Church – where they lay under the floor for eight years. Eventually they were taken to Edinburgh Castle and hidden again – too well, in fact, for everyone forgot where they were until Sir Walter Scott rediscovered them.

⑧ Dufftown
Keith, Banffshire; AB55
Dufftown is popularly known as "the town that was built on seven stills", a reference to the distilleries that dot the surrounding countryside. Founded in 1817, the so-called malt whisky capital of the world is a pleasant town with an imposing central clock tower.

Just outside Dufftown is the **Keith & Dufftown Railway** *(Easter–May & Sep: open weekends; Jun–Aug: open Fri–Sun; www.keith-dufftown-railway.co.uk)*, run by volunteers, which makes a great family expedition (a round trip lasts an hour and a half). A restored diesel train chugs through stunning Highland scenery, crossing the Fiddich Viaduct, passing distilleries and ruined castles, before reaching the market town of Keith, home of the Strathisla Distillery.

Immediately south of the railway station stands the family-owned **Glenfiddich Distillery** *(Easter–Oct: open daily; Nov–Easter: open Mon–Fri; www. glenfiddich.com)*, which has been

Below *Looking out to sea from the WDCS Wildlife Centre, Spey Bay*

producing single malt whisky since 1887, using water from local springs. Visitors can join an informative tour of the buildings, see the shiny copper stills and the warehouses where the whisky is stored in traditional oak barrels. Tours end with a delicious free dram. Whisky buffs might prefer to join a connoisseurs' tour (with an entry charge) which includes a tutored tasting of more whiskies.

🚗 *Continue through Dufftown on A941, then bear left on A920 to Huntly, to pick up the A96, then A97 south. Follow this through fertile farmland, eventually turning left on the B9002. After 1.6 km (1 mile), look out for Leith Hall, with parking, on the left.*

⑨ Leith Hall
Nr Kennethmont, Huntly; AB54 4NQ
This 17th-century mansion house *(grounds open daily)* has been home to the Leiths – a family that long supported the Jacobite cause – for hundreds of years. Although the house (reputed to be haunted) is now closed to the public, the gardens

Below Impressive Leith Hall, home to the Leith family for 350 years **Below right** Whisky barrels at the Glenfiddich distillery, near Dufftown **Bottom right** The pretty gardens at Leith Hall, perfect for a picnic

make a lovely place for a picnic on a fine day. There are also several easy walks to follow. In the grounds, visitors can see an old sycamore tree known as a "dule tree" (gallows tree) – said to have been used to hang criminals.

🚗 *From Leith Hall continue along the B9002, then turn right onto the B992 to Whitehouse. Turn right on the A944 to Alford. Park by the museum.*

⑩ Grampian Transport Museum
Alford, Aberdeenshire; AB33 8AE
This excellent museum *(Apr–Oct: open daily; www.gtm.org.uk)* contains a fascinating variety of vehicles, ranging from a horse-drawn mail coach to the electric "car", the Sinclair C5. There are early bicycles and motorbikes, an eccentric steam tricycle built by a postman in 1895, gleaming vintage cars and a green Jaguar from the James Bond film *Die Another Day*, with a missile launcher in the front grille. Visitors even get the chance to sit in the saddle of a penny farthing bicycle. Great fun for all ages.

🚗 *Leave Alford on A944 west, soon bearing left on A980, then at the junction with the A93, turn right to Banchory. Take B974 off the High Street to Bridge of Feugh car park.*

Above Glenfiddich Distillery – the name means "Valley of the Deer" in Gaelic

SHOPPING IN DUFFTOWN

For a genuine whisky education visit **The Whisky Shop Dufftown** *(1 Fife Street, AB55 4AL; 01340 821 097; www. thewsd.co.uk)* for "talk and taste" sessions. The shop will also help organize whisky tours and tell prospective buyers everything they need to know about *Uisge Beathe* (The Water of Life).

EAT AND DRINK

DUFFTOWN

A Taste of Speyside *moderate*
This is the place to come to try classic Scottish dishes made from fresh local ingredients. There is cullen skink (a fish soup), fillet steaks and fresh salmon. Desserts include a fruit dumpling with Glenfiddich liqueur cream. *10 Balvenie Street, AB55 4AN; 01340 820 860; www.dufftown.co.uk; closed Mon*

Dufftown Glassworks *inexpensive*
A welcoming place for sweet treats such as homemade cakes and scones – plus a choice of decent coffee and tea infusions. *16 Conval Street, AB55 4AE; 01340 821 534; www.dufftownglassworks.com*

Eat and Drink: inexpensive, under £25; moderate, £25–£50; expensive, over £50

Above The dramatic 15th-century ruins of Dunnottar Castle **Above centre** The Triple Kirk spire and Union Terrace Gardens, Aberdeen **Above right** St Mark's Church, Aberdeen, modelled on St Paul's Cathedral

VISITING ABERDEEN

Parking
Park in College Street near the railway station, or Bon Accord shopping centre.

Tourist Information
23 Union Street, AB11 5BP; 01224 288 828; www.aberdeen-grampian.com

WHERE TO STAY

BANCHORY

Tor-na-Coille Hotel *moderate*
A country house hotel set in beautiful grounds near the Banchory golf course and River Dee fishing beats. There are 22 elegant bedrooms, some with original open fireplaces.
Inchmarlo Road, AB31 4AB; 01330 822 242; www.tornacoille.com

AROUND BANCHORY

Raemoir House Hotel *expensive*
Head north from Banchory on the A980 and keep on going to this impressive Georgian mansion set large grounds. There are 16 comfortable rooms and some have fine views.
Banchory, AB31 4ED; 01330 824 884; www.raemoir.com

ABERDEEN

The Marcliffe Hotel and Spa *expensive*
Lovely hotel with luxurious rooms that blend contemporary style with traditional comfort. Expect fluffy white towels in spotless bathrooms, plasma screen televisions and an excellent selection of local produce for breakfast.
North Deeside Road, AB15 9YA; 01224 861 000; www.marcliffe.com

⓫ Banchory

Aberdeenshire; AB31 6NL
A popular holiday spot since Victorian times, Banchory is in Royal Deeside, known for its beautiful countryside and castles. Just south of town on the A974 stands the 18th-century stone **Bridge of Feugh**, over a tributary of the mighty River Dee. The waters foam furiously down below and there is a good chance of spotting salmon leaping over the rocks to reach the calm waters beyond. The best times to see them are Sep–Nov and Feb–Mar. Take the A93 east to the fairytale **Crathes Castle** *(Apr-Oct: open daily; Nov–Mar: open Sat & Sun)*, built in the 16th century. With exquisite interiors – original painted ceilings – and delightful gardens, this is a must-see visitor attraction.

🚗 *Return to the A93, turn right, then take the A957 to Stonehaven. Follow this road through Stonehaven town centre, then turn left onto the A92 signed for the castle. There is a parking area (which gets busy in summer) a short walk from the castle itself.*

⓬ Dunnottar Castle

Nr Stonehaven; AB39 2TL
Perched dramatically on the clifftops with gulls swirling overhead and waves crashing below, **Dunnottar Castle** *(open daily; www.dunnottarcastle.co.uk)* makes a compelling sight. The castle, built in the 15th century, was once home to one of Scotland's most powerful families. Visited by William Wallace, Mary Queen of Scots, the Marquis of Montrose and the

future King Charles II, it gained its place in history when the Honours of Scotland *(see p250)* were hidden here following Oliver Cromwell's invasion. The castle was under siege for eight months, but the Honours were smuggled away to Kinneff Old Church further along the coast. Today, Dunnottar is a picturesque ruin, reached by a steep set of steps.

🚗 *Rejoin the A92/A90 north to Aberdeen, turning onto the A956 to the city centre. Go straight over two roundabouts and the River Dee into College Street to park beside the railway station.*

Where to Stay: inexpensive, under £80; moderate, £80–£150; expensive, over £150

⑬ Aberdeen

Aberdeen; AB11

Known as the Granite City because of its silvery granite buildings, Aberdeen faces out to the North Sea and, not surprisingly, is a city with a strong maritime tradition. For centuries it had firm trading links with Scandinavia and is still an important fishing port. Its historic buildings are interspersed with shops, lively bars and restaurants.

A two–three-hour walking tour

Start at the Tourist Information Centre on Union St. Turn right and walk down Shiprow to the **Maritime Museum** ① *(open Tue–Sun)*, which gives a fascinating insight into the city's maritime heritage, as well as good views of the harbour. Leaving the museum, turn left up Shiprow, then left along Union St, the city's main shopping area. Turn right up Belmont St to the **Art Gallery** ② *(Tue–Sun)*, with a large collection of portraits, Impressionist paintings and works by the Scottish Colourists and the Victorian artists known as the Glasgow Boys. Turn right and walk along Schoolhill, continuing into Upper Kirkgate – look out for the imposing Neo-Gothic **Marischal College** ③, part of Aberdeen University.

Turn left up Gallowgate to the large roundabout, cross to the right; walk a short distance up Mounthooly Way, then go left up Kings Crescent which soon becomes Spittal, then College Bounds, a nice street lined with fine old houses. Go past magnificent King's College, on the right, part of the university, founded in the 15th century. **King's College Chapel** ④ *(open Mon–Fri)* is topped with a distinctive "crown tower", symbolizing the authority and independence of the Scottish king.

Carry on to see a Georgian townhouse up ahead, once a meeting place for the city's trade organizations. Cross over the road ahead. Walk up the historic cobbled Chanonry where the university **Botanic Gardens** ⑤ *(open daily)* provide a short detour. In medieval times Chanonry was home to the canons of **St Machar's Cathedral** ⑥ – which is reached soon. The cathedral dates to the 13th century and has some fine stained-glass windows. Follow Chanonry past the cathedral to Don St, then turn right to rejoin the High St and pass King's College again. At the start of Spittal turn left down Orchard Rd, go right at the end and cross King St to turn left down Pittodrie Place. At its end turn right on Golf Rd – with golf links on the left and the football stadium on the right. Walk up the steps over a grassy hill to reach the seafront with a stretch of golden sand and **funfair** ⑦. To return to the city centre, continue south along the coast, then turn right at Beach Boulevard. Cross carefully at the roundabout to go down Justice St, past the Mercat Cross and back into Union Street.

Above View of Old Aberdeen seen from Union Street Bridge

EAT AND DRINK

AROUND BANCHORY

Cow Shed *moderate*
This restaurant in rural surroundings has great-value fixed-price lunches and splendid views. Try the butter-roasted monkfish and Inverurie pork belly. *Raemoir Road, AB31 5QB; 01330 820 813; www.cowshedrestaurantbanchory. co.uk; closed Sun dinner, Mon & Tue*

AROUND DUNNOTTAR CASTLE

The Creel Inn *inexpensive*
In Catterline, a few miles south of the castle off the A92, former fisherman's cottages have been turned into this popular inn. There's seafood on the menu, such as pan-seared scallops. *Catterline, Stonehaven, AB39 2UL; 01569 750 254; www.thecreelinn.co.uk*

ABERDEEN

Bistro Verde *inexpensive–moderate*
This popular bistro specializes in fish – try roasted sea bass, Basque-style monkfish, or sea bream in Parma ham. *59 The Green, AB11 6NY; 01224 586 180; closed Sun & Mon lunch*

The Marcliffe Hotel and Spa *moderate–expensive*
Enjoy the relaxing atmosphere at this popular hotel restaurant – and produce such as Scottish lobster and roe deer. There are also vegetarian options. *North Deeside Road, AB15 9YA; 01224 861 000; www.marcliffe.com*

Neo-Gothic Marischal College, Aberdeen

DAY TRIP OPTIONS

Children and adults will enjoy historic castles and stunning coastline.

War and Peace

From Inverness ❶ it's a short drive to Culloden ❷, where Bonnie Prince Charlie's campaign ended. Take a tour of Cawdor Castle ❸, then it's off to Nairn for a spell on the sandy beach.

Take B9006 from Inverness to Culloden, then B9091 and B9090 to Cawdor and on to Nairn. Return on the A96.

Speyside Delights

From Craigellachie, drive to the WCDS Wildlife Centre ❻ at Spey Bay to look for dolphins. Then head back to make a tour of Speyside Cooperage ❼, take a heritage railway trip at Dufftown ❽ and taste the whisky at the Glenfiddich Distillery, before dinner in a Dufftown restaurant.

Follow drive instructions in reverse to the WCDS Wildlife Centre, return on the same roads and take A941 to Dufftown.

Vintage Fun

From Aberdeen ⑬, visit the transport museum ⑩ at Alford, with tanks and vintage cars. Then head to Banchory ⑪, to watch salmon leaping up the falls and perhaps see Crathes Castle. Visit dramatic Dunnottar Castle ⑬ on the cliffs, before returning to Aberdeen and the beachside funfair.

From Aberdeen, take A944 to Alford, then A980 south Banchory. Then follow the drive instructions to Aberdeen.

Eat and Drink: inexpensive, under £25; moderate, £25–£50; expensive, over £50

General Index

Acknowledgments

Dorling Kindersley would like to thank the many people whose help and assistance contributed to the preparation of this book.

Main Contributors
Patricia Aithie lived and travelled in the Middle East for 25 years, writing extensively about travel, culture and faith there, before returning to her native Cardiff. She has written several books about Wales, including *Cardiff: Rebirth of a Capital* and *Cardiff and Beyond*.

Robert Andrews has been working on travel guides for 20 years, writing for DK, Rough Guides and Fodor's. He has authored, or co-authored, books on Devon and Cornwall, Sicily and Sardinia, and has written about all areas of Italy and southern England.

Rebecca Ford is an award-winning travel journalist who lives in London. She writes for national newspapers and magazines on everything from railway journeys to eco-travel, and has contributed to more than 30 guidebooks.

Nick Rider has a PhD on the history of Barcelona and has written travel books on Spain, Mexico and France. He has contributed to DK guides including those to France, Mexico, Great Britain and Poland. He is a regular reviewer for the *Time Out London Eating & Drinking* guide.

Rose Shepherd started her career as a freelance writer and editor at the *Good Food Guide*. Since then she has contributed regularly to newspapers and magazines including *Condé Nast Traveller*, the *Observer* and the *Sunday Times Magazine*. She is also a published novelist.

Gillian Thomas and **John Harrison**, who are married with three grown-up children, are both freelance travel writers who started their careers at the BBC. Members of the British Guild of Travel Writers, they have been visiting the West Country since their own childhood holidays. They are contributors to the *Good Holiday Cottage Guide*.

Roger Williams is a prolific writer who began his career in journalism. Formerly chief sub-editor on the *Sunday Times Magazine*, he is currently associate editor of *Cornucopia*. He has published several novels – the latest is *Burning Barcelona* – and non-fiction works, as well as contributing to countless travel guides.

Fact checker
Mary Villabona

Proofreader
Jane Ellis

Indexer
Hilary Bird

Editorial consultant
Donna Dailey

Revisions Team
Nick Bruno, Nina Bryant, Caroline Elliker, Scarlett O'Hara, John & Gillian Harrison, Kate Hughes, Sumita Khatwani, Jude Ledger, Darren Longley, Sonal Modha, Catherine Palmi, Sands Publishing Solutions, Claire Saunders, Ankita Sharma, Beverly Smart, Susana Smith, Ajay Verma.

Special Assistance
Julia Brownsword, Zara Camble, Clare Currie, Donna Dailey, Ian Gardiner at National Trust for Scotland, Jude Henderson at Visit Scotland, Martin Jackson, Stuart James, Sarah Lee, Anna Richards, John Richards, Rupert Small, Jocelyn Waterfall, Christian Williams

Photography
Charles and Pat Aithie, John Harrison, Alex Havret, Lynne McPeake, Robert Schweizer, Tony Souter, Linda Whitwam, Roger Williams

Additional Photography
Max Alexander, June Buck, Lucy Claxton, Joe Cornish, Andy Crawford, Bethany Dawn, Steve Gorton, John Heseltine, Rose Horridge, Bob Langrish, Gerald Lopez, Stephen Oliver, Rob Reichenfeld, Rough Guides/Chris Christoforo, Rough Guides/Tim Draper, Kim Sayer, Chris Stowers, Stephen Whitehorn, Paul Wilkinson

Maps
John Plumer, JP Map Graphics Ltd, www.jpmapgraphics.co.uk
Maps on pages 71, 80, 87, 93, 113, 123, 144, 180, 199, 210, 252 are derived from @ www.openstreetmap.org and contributiors, licensed under CC-BY-SA, see www.creativecommons.org for further details

Road Signs

SPEED LIMITS AND GENERAL DRIVING INDICATIONS

Give way

Compulsory stop

Roundabout

Crossroads

Congestion charge zone

Give way to oncoming traffic

No overtaking

No left turn

No access for vehicles over 4.4 m in height

Traffic enforcement cameras in use

Speed limit

National speed limits apply

Minimum speed limit

Entrance to 20 mph speed limit zone

End of 20 mph zone and start of 30 mph zone

WARNING SIGNS

Unspecified danger

Succession of bends

Slippery road

Risk of strong crosswinds

Risk of rockfalls

Speed bumps

Road narrows

Road narrows on the left

Level crossing with barrier

Level crossing with no barrier

Steep descent

Wild animals

Children crossing, or school

Pedestrian crossing

Road works

31901059287898